F=g∞

D0908358

SOUTHERN
BY THE
GRACE OF GOD

"The people of the Confederate States have made themselves famous. If the renown of brilliant courage, stern devotion to a cause, and military achievements almost without a parallel, can compensate men for the toil and privations of the hour, then the countrymen of Lee and Jackson may be consoled amid their sufferings. From all parts of Europe, from their enemies as well as their friends, from those who condemn their acts as well as those who sympathize with them, comes the tribute of admiration. When the history of this war is written, the admiration will doubtless become deeper and stronger, for the veil which has covered the South will be drawn away and disclose a picture of patriotism, of unanimous self-sacrifice, of wise and firm administration, which we can now only see indistinctly. The details of extraordinary national effort which has led to the repulse and almost to the destruction of an invading force of more than half a million men, will then become known to the world, and whatever may be the fate of the new nationality, or its subsequent claims to the respect of mankind, it will assuredly begin its career with a reputation for genius and valor which the most famous nations may envy."

—The London Times, 1862

SOUTHERN
BY THE
GRACE OF GOD

Michael Andrew Grissom

THE REBEL PRESS
P.O. BOX 158766
NASHVILLE, TENNESSEE 37215

TABLE OF CONTENTS

Preface

There is a popular slogan in the South today: AMERICAN BY BIRTH, SOUTHERN BY THE GRACE OF GOD. You'll see it on bumper stickers, car tags, T-shirts, baseball caps, and just about anything that lends itself to printing. It tells something about us — how we feel, how we think, how we perceive ourselves. Southerners, who enjoy a reputation for being among the most patriotic people in America, consider their southern status as something special, something above and beyond the good fortune of being American. It's the icing on the cake.

Yes, there *is* something about the South. Oh, yes, just say it: *The South*. The words hang heavy with dewdrops, honeysuckle, and magnolia blossoms. Steamboat 'round the bend. Fields of snowy white cotton. Southern belles. Smiling faces. Laughter on the levee. It's a storied land of romance and chivalry, fabled in legend and song and unlike anything known upon this continent. When you speak of the north, the east, or the west, you are speaking of a direction; but, when you speak of the South, you are speaking of a country, a time, a place. The Old

South. Margaret Mitchell told us it was "gone with the wind" and to "look for it only in books, for it is no more than a dream remembered."[1] But, we refused to let go of it, and today it lives not only in books, but in our souls as well.

Yet, at the same time, the Margaret Mitchell of 1936 may well prove to have been somewhat of a prophetess after all. I don't know whether our past glory lives on in fewer of us, or if it lives less well in all of us. One thing is for sure — we are edging ever more closely to the point of losing our southern heritage. If we become even a tiny bit more lethargic than we already are and fail to pass it on to our young, it truly will be found only in books. It can be lost in only one neglected generation. If we fail to perpetuate so glorious a legacy, then it truly may be spoken of us what Tacitus wrote of those who frivolously existed under the Roman Empire: "We cannot be said to have lived, but rather to have crawled in silence, the young towards the decrepitude of age and the old to dishonourable graves."[2]

North and South have never been alike, and never will be, as long as we remain free men and women. From earliest colonial days, the states north of Virginia followed divergent paths from those to the south. Two cultures developed, in opposite directions. About the only thing they shared in common was the same language, and even that they spoke with different dialects. Southerners developed a philosophy of complete independence and individual freedom and were relatively free from governmental restraint — a system which worked well in the thinly populated, though geographically large, South. It was, basically, a policy of non-interference; consequently, southerners cared little how northerners, or anyone else, carried on their day-to-day affairs. On the other hand, the populous north embraced the notion of a strong central government in which its citizens necessarily gave up a larger measure of individuality — a forerunner of the caretaker state. This ideology of universal governmental management was by its nature a policy of interference, whereby northerners operated upon the theory that if it was good for the North, then it ought to be good for the South, and correspondingly attempted to regulate both societies as one. (Sounds familiar, doesn't it?)

Considering the large expanse of land covered by the United States and the early polarization of North and South, it is a marvel that we long existed as one country. A more logical course might have been peaceful coexistence as two strong allies, similar to the relationship between the United States and Canada. Our strained attempts at holding together two cultures so diametrically opposed resulted in a disastrous war which proved only that it takes the form of government which relies on strong centralization to force us to cohabitate.

Conquered militarily, the South was expected to capitulate in doctrine as well. To a shocked world, we laid down our arms and picked up our pens. Unconquered in will, even after the oppression of Reconstruction, we exchanged our battle of bullets for a battle of the minds. Our love for independence and freedom from governmental supervision of our lives lived on, even under a system that was somewhat contrary to individual liberty. Today, the South is the conservative balance against that same old liberalism against which we defended and lost, and our dilemma is the struggle between our American patriotism and an America that moves further every year into the abyss of centralized rule.

Since Appomattox, or we might more precisely say, since Reconstruction ended in the 1870's, the battle to "harness" the stubborn southerner has moved from the bloody fields of Virginia to the halls of Congress across the Potomac. Between that political body and the Supreme Court, our traditions, laws, customs, and very mannerisms have been the objects of contention; nevertheless, we have had the fortitude to withstand each onslaught, perpetuating our heritage and handing it down from generation to generation. Indeed, we seemed to have won something of a reprieve in the early part of this century. We stood side by side with our northern counterparts in a World War, and those people seemed, suddenly, to have rediscovered the South, this time in a more desirable light. The war years and the 1920's were full of fascination with this land below the Mason-Dixon line. It seemed that nearly every other song was about Dixie, Swanee, or Mammy. Al Jolson ushered in an era of good feeling on the silver screen that reached its artistic apex in 1939 in *Gone With the Wind*. Right on into the fifties, movie-goers could pretty well count on a southern gentleman and his belle cast as the suffering hero and heroine, while Yankees represented the eternal invading villains of the halcyon land of cotton. At least the movies had it right, and southerners basked in the sunshine of cinematic vindication.

In writing a book, one has to answer as to why he undertook the project. He first has to answer to himself; then, he must justify his subject to his readers. There were various reasons leading to this particular endeavor, but I think the single most important motive was that it has become alarmingly apparent that the South's perception of itself has made a precipitous decline from the description in the preceding paragraph. Even though we do have this intuitive sense that we are *Southern, by the Grace of God*, we are less and less sure as to the reason, especially now that our old foes have entered among the flock and have made some converts among us who rise up and flail us as readily, or more so, than those from without. It is tragic enough to succumb to an outside attack, but it is a pity, indeed, to watch our heritage being dismantled year after year at the very hands of *southerners* themselves. It wasn't latter-day Yankees who banned the playing of *Dixie* at ballgames; it was spineless *southern* school boards and squeamish administrators. It wasn't Washington officials who retired our proud Confederate flags from our courthouses and city halls; it was timid, waffling *local* officials.

Southerners have become confused in recent years by the abundance of negative literature about the South. Literature, like clothing, is faddish, and it's unfortunate that poor, tasteless, pessimistic writing has been the fashion for some time now. Good material is relegated to the back shelf while the sensational witch hunters command the attention of the world with pejorative patter, resulting in a vacuum where truth and pride wither.

It occurred to me that southerners, no matter how stalwart or steeped in their heritage, could not withstand such a bombardment of demeaning criticism indefinitely. Then I remembered a scripture from my youth. In the book of *Hosea,* God says "My people are destroyed for lack of knowledge ." It was an eternal principle, and I saw at once the answer to the current situation. Knowledge.

But, where would one find that knowledge? Certainly not in the textbooks of our schools. It has been a continuing source of disappointment to see traditional heroes, values, and examples of valor culled every year from southern history texts. Today, virtually every school system in the South is equipped with American history books produced in the north by northern authors. Is there not a scholar in the South who can author an American history text designed to instill pride in southern youth? Maybe the question should be: Is there a state textbook committee or superintendent in the South who would adopt such a book if written? We definitely have a problem when children in the South are raised on the fables of *Honest Abe,* while they're taught that their own forebears were the villains of our country's history.

Today, I think it would be difficult to find a student of high school age who could name two Confederate generals or one important battle of that unfortunate war, which, for all its misery, welded the southern states into a solid community of people who share a common heritage unmatched among civilizations of the world. What student can recount one single story of courage and heroism from the pages of our history which are replete with examples of valor?

It's been said that an author writes the book he can't find on the library shelf. As I pondered the deteriorating situation, it was becoming clear to me that southerners — especially the deprived youth of today — need a short course in their own heritage. The next thing that became apparent was that there was no such book addressing the problem. There are volumes that deal with specific aspects of our heritage, but nothing that consolidates the phases of our heritage into a concise reference for southerners who need a general knowledge of their heritage without having to spend the rest of their lives sifting through library acquisitions in search of it.

Convinced of the need for such a book I set out to compile a volume which would do four things: (1) Provide the southerner with a general overview of his heritage; (2) instill in him a greater pride in being southern; (3) point him in the direction for further pursuit of the separate elements of his heritage; and (4) alert him to the fact that the distinguishing marks of our culture are fading away, in the hope that a conscious effort will be made to maintain our heritage for posterity.

Designed to be something of a *handbook for southerners*, this work attempts to familiarize the southerner with those elements of his heritage that are obvious as well as those which we take for granted. For instance, one chapter is devoted to a discussion of our delightful southern accent, which for all its pleasing delivery, is becoming a thing of the past as we sit like zombies in front of our TV sets, day in and day out, subconsciously mimicking its bland, robotic speech. Another chapter discusses the great tangible symbols of the South, our Confederate flag and *Dixie*, while one part of the book is devoted to a wide range of subjects, such as our religion, our music, and our food.

Much of the narrative is in the first person. I relied upon stories and illustrations from my own past that will, no doubt, be reflective of similar situations in the southern backgrounds of each reader. One chapter is full of tales told by southerners, who are, of course, the master storytellers. Most of the stories are previously unpublished but have stood the test of time, surviving in the vernacular of the common man, giving us an insight into the events which captured the imagination of the average man, as opposed to the professional writer of history. The famous *Bell Witch* of Tennessee claims her place in this section, which also includes a tale of dead reckoning in *The Hangin' at Ada.*

Genealogy is more important than ever nowadays, and in that respect I believe our heritage is alive and well. One chapter was planned with the beginning genealogist in mind, giving him or her a brief boost in getting started on that most fascinating of journeys into the past. For the reader interested in finding a Confederate ancestor in the family tree, I have included a comprehensive list of the major agencies across the South who hold Confederate records, along with mailing addresses for these repositories and hints on what to look for.

There are one hundred pages of old photographs, depicting family life, style of dress, modes of transportation, and architecture of yesteryear. Not only are the photographic plates entertaining, they are germane to the text — even more; they are essential to it. They present a picture of southern life from shortly before the War Between the States through the first World War. Except for photographs of well-known Confederate heroes, most of the pictures are previously unpublished images of the average southern citizen who, along with his neighbors, pulled himself up by his own bootstraps after the War and, by the proverbial sweat of his brow, raised the South back to prosperity. Collected from across the South over a period of years, the pictures come primarily from my own collection, with others borrowed from very kind friends and several state archives. The photographic section is designed to give us a look at real people who were typical ancestors of southerners like you and me. The photos give us a visual concept and help us put faces on the characters in the stories, underscoring the underlying theme of the whole book — pride in *our* southern heritage.

Of course, no book about the South would be complete without a look at the War, that paradoxical event which brought so much suffering yet called southern manhood to its finest hour. One chapter outlines that episode of southern history with an honest approach toward laying the blame for that bloody conflict squarely where it belongs. A section about southern heroes contains brief sketches of the lives of seven giants of the Confederacy, men who once graced the pages of our southern history books, inspiring the youth of the South to emulate their deeds. Then, there is a hard look at the era of Reconstruction, a period of time that is not as clear to modern southerners as it should be, owing partly to the efforts now underway to rewrite that disastrous political nightmare into a nice little novel about social progress.

As I travel across the South, I come in contact with hundreds of people who are weary of malcontents and politicians who feed off negative causes and continuously haul southerners before the court of public opinion hoping for a guilty verdict. Southerners have been worn down to the bone with the anti-South psychosis that has afflicted our critics for so many years. Even though some of our own were caught up in the stupor and still remain asleep in the dogma of self-destructive caviling, I believe there has been a recent turnaround. More and more southern citizens are willing to uncloset themselves and stand against the tide, and it's beginning to be fashionable to be southern once again. There are a lot of southerners who believe that the Confederate flag should still be flown, *proudly*; that the southern accent should still be spoken, *proudly*; that *Dixie* should still be played, *proudly*; and, that we should take great pride in knowing who we are — we of a splendid heritage. To those people this book is dedicated. Stand up and cheer!

Mike Grissom

Wynnewood, Oklahoma
January 1, 1988

I

SOUTHERN

Let me state my case, and state it certain: I love the South. No qualms. No apologies. No qualifiers. I love the South!

If you're looking for one of those trendy books in which the South is socially and politically dissected for the base purpose of defaming our fair region, you'd best pass this one up. This book reflects a genuine appreciation for the enchanted land of Dixie and the opportunity we southerners have of calling it home.

There's a curious phenomenon in the South today. It used to be that Yankees criticized everything we did, and we, with one voice, rose up in our own defense; but, a while back they slipped up on some of our slower folks and taught them to criticize themselves. Now the Yankees lie back and watch this new breed of loud southerners do their braying for them. This new bunch has decided to call themselves the *New South*. They like that. It helps them feel that they have risen above the rest of us; that they have shaken off the vestiges of the Old South of their ancestors which the Yankees have told us all along was

1

bad, bad, bad.

In their litany, they find nothing good south of the Mason-Dixon line. There is no joy to be had in being southern, and they pine for the day when South will be spelled with a little *s*. They also like to be called *revisionists*. That sounds real good. It makes them feel better when someone calls them aside and gently suggests that they are whipping themselves. They point with great pride to the exploits of Lincoln and Webster while holding their New South noses over the graves of Calhoun and Lee. How odd! Do northerners waste one moment berating themselves? Do westerners curse the memory of Wyatt Earp and relentlessly search for something sinister in the westward movement?

But, then, we've had to deal with other pests before, like boll weevils, fire ants, and mosquitoes; so, we can probably ride out the storm until they catch up with the 1980's and realize that being southern is fashionable now. And, even though our home-grown critics command the major attention of the pejorative press, I truly believe that they are in the loud *minority*. Most of us, and I might even add, most Americans in general, would have to admit that way down deep inside, where we do our secret thinking, we like having a place called Dixie. It's a place of the heart; it's a place of romance, legend, and song; it's a place called home.

Yet, there are those outside the South, who after having read so much of that hackneyed garbage of the past twenty-five years, are afraid that they just can't bring themselves to love the South altogether. Their apprehension, fueled by the New South columnists who find financial success in vitriol, is all too familiar, though somewhat understood, by long-suffering southerners; however, a simple cure-all is to be found in the form of a mere visit by these non-southerners to the embracing environs of the South. As they feel the warmth of the soothing southern breeze and come in contact with the friendly, accommodating natives, it pleases but doesn't surprise us to hear that universal answer to our hospitable question, "How y'all like it down here?" With a smile that might be found on the face of an Irish Sweepstakes winner, aforesaid visitors show immediate evidence of being cured on the spot with their vociferous testimony, "We love it!" And this usually in a *need you ask?* tone of voice.

Although some of our friends outside the South have been programmed to hold misgivings about Dixie, we southerners know better, don't we? This is the land of our fathers, the land of our birth and the land that we love. The special way we feel about our Southland has seldom been said so eloquently as by Edward Ward Carmack, former Congressman from Tennessee. Known as *Carmack's Pledge to the South*, these words, cast in bronze on the base of his statue in Nashville, were excerpted from a speech he delivered in the U.S. House of Representatives.

> The South is a land that has known sorrows; it is a land that has broken the ashen crust and moistened it with tears; a land scarred and riven by the plowshare of war and billowed with the graves of her dead; but a land of legend, a land of song, a land of hallowed and heroic memories.
>
> To that land every drop of my blood, every fiber of my being, every pulsation of my heart, is consecrated forever. I was born of her womb; I was nurtured at her·breast; and when my last hour shall come, I pray God that I may be pillowed upon her bosom and rocked to sleep within her tender and encircling arms.

Quite an apt description of our attachment to this country called the South. We're not always conscious of our deep devotion to it, but let some quarrelsome stranger undertake to criticize the South, and we rush to its defense as natural

3

as a reflex. Without hesitation, we take up for our country as decidedly as we would our own family, and it is then that the full realization of our devotion strikes us. It's there all right, completely intact. And, it's a good, confident feeling to be attached to something which we can so highly regard.

There's a sense of belonging here in the South. A sense of permanence. We belong to something lasting. A school-teaching acquaintance of mine once told me how much she envied the fact that I was able to teach my history classes from a partisan viewpoint. Having grown up in the bland, generic, *one-world* age of education, she was deprived of that sense of personal involvement in her southern heritage. She was teaching a course in Oklahoma history, frustrated by her inability to experience that great feeling of state pride and patriotic fervor for the South that she needed in order to transform historical facts into *heritage* for her deserving students. She knew something was missing. It was the feeling.

Those of us who have the feeling know that it's there. The question is: *Why* is it there? Why do we take such great pride in calling ourselves southern? Why, for instance, do people in Virginia feel a kinship to people in Texas, though separated by a distance of 1500 miles? And, what is this bond that holds the separate southern states together in a confederation of mutual affection? It doesn't seem to exist among other states — north, west, or east. Why do the governors of southern states, who attend the National Governors' Conference each year, hold their own supplemental gathering — the Southern Governors' Conference? Why this concept of *country within a country*, a concept inherent in southerners yet foreign to other Americans?

The most obvious and general answer is that the southern states share a common heritage, which is not to say that southern states do not have anything in common with other states of the Union. Naturally, all states hold several things in common under our compact called the United States of America, including our national day of independence, our English language, our republican form of government, our unity in two world wars, our mutual defense, and our national holidays, to mention but a few; however, despite the mutual aspects, there were, as early as colonial days, events and circumstances which led to fundamental differences between North and South. These occurrences — some discernible, some entirely intangible — continued to produce a people below the Mason-Dixon line who were similar to each other while polarizing them from those increasingly peculiar people north of it.

Most historians and philosophers agree that climate has a large impact upon the development of societies. Perhaps this factor alone became the foundation upon which our common heritage arose. Though there is a wide variance in temperature from the hills of Tennessee to the coasts of Florida, especially in the winter time, the entire South lies in a temperate or moderate zone. The southern summer is hot everywhere — and humid. The middle and upper South will see an occasional winter snow, but it is rare to have more than a flurry before mid-December, and nowhere in the South does snow stay on the ground for any appreciable length of time. Generally speaking, the South is warm, and when it does turn cold for more than a short period of time, people seem to think that something has gone wrong.

Climate virtually dictates the occupations of a country's inhabitants. It definitely affects an agrarian society, determining altogether the type of cash crop that planters may grow, if it allows the growing of a cash crop at all. The immigrant who settled from Virginia southward found that he could grow rice, tobacco, indigo, sugar cane, and eventually cotton, the crop that was to attain absolute supremacy.

Cotton has to have a long growing season, its harvest being accomplished any time from September through January. In the old days of picking by hand, a planter could get two or three pickings, beginning in September. Rural schools stayed in session through July and August, turning out in September and

5

October for the picking. Nowadays, mechanical pickers make one pass over the field rather late in the year, and it is not unusual to see fields of snowy white after Christmas. Not acclimated to the north, "King Cotton" has been grown in every southern state since its inception as a cash crop early in the 19th century. The dependence upon cotton dictated a life-style much different from that of the small farmer and the factory worker in the north. Growing cotton required the planter to acquire large parcels of land, and his home necessarily had to be in a rural setting close to his fields.

An agricultural society was developing in the South, with most of its citizens residing in the country. Southern towns were small. Even cities considered to be large were no match for the populous northern cities. New Orleans was, by far, the largest city in the South in 1860, though it numbered only 168,675. The next largest city was Charleston, South Carolina, with a mere 40,578. This rural society, based largely upon a cotton commerce, was insuring a common bond among the southern people. Across the South, farmers grew the cotton, and city dwellers, in one way or another, were connected with the operation, whether in marketing the planter's product or supplying his plantation needs. This is not to say that small independent farmers were to be found only in the north. The South abounded in small farms, some of which raised no cotton at all, especially in the hill country; but, the farmer, like the city dweller, was inextricably linked to a cotton economy.

Those who make a study of the effects of climate upon people tend to attribute many ordinary customs of a particular society to the climatic conditions of their country. Such elemental considerations as food, speech, dress, personality traits, and social customs are to some degree mandated by the weather, they say. For whatever reason, the South did give birth to many pleasing customs in this warm clime, many of which, thank goodness, we still enjoy today.

As the southern states multiplied toward the west to the

Republic of Texas and the Indian Territory, traditions and peculiarties from the southeast were spread into this new southwest territory, further solidifying our common heritage. One of the most inherent similarities among southerners, then and now, is the southern accent. Though there are regional differences, easily discernible among native southerners, all variations of the dialect are similar enough in comparison to the accents of other regions that all of these variations are usually addressed as one brogue. One can hear this soft, nearly musical speech of rather slow delivery spoken from Oklahoma to Florida. It falls easy on the ear, is highly-inflected, and is one of those easily recognizable dialects often imitated in the theater. Though it has been an unfortunate practice among schools of journalism and speech to try to eradicate this southern dialect, most people thoroughly enjoy an opportunity to hear southerners talk, and we should be thankful that it is one of those blessings that comes with the territory. It's just another one of those privileges of being southern.

It's amusing to hear others try to duplicate our accent. I enjoy hearing northerners trying to use our infinitely useful little word *you'all*. More than once I've heard national newscasters from their pinnacles of public enlightenment in New York trying to slip it in here and there amongst their carefully purified tones. It seems quite funny to hear *y'all* without a southern drawl either preceding it or following closely behind, but then we should give them plaudits for at least trying to improve their vocabulary, if not their dialect. I've always wondered how northerners talk to each other directly, especially when speaking to more than one person at a time, without using the word *you'all*. In the South, we would never be able to ask a group of people if they were ready to go somewhere, or tell our relatives to come back and see us if it weren't for that handy l'il old pronoun.

One southern lady, keenly aware and justly proud of her southerness, was sure that her hero, the Apostle Paul, was not

7

only the greatest of the Apostles, but was also a southerner. And, she could prove it, she said, as she turned in her Bible to Ephesians 4:6, where she read Paul's words: "One God and Father of all, who is above all, and through all, and in *you all.*" And it did absolutely no good to point out to her the fact that Paul could not have been southern at all because he was a citizen of Rome. "Why that proves it," she said with supreme confidence as her ally. "Rome is only fifty-two miles northwest of Atlanta!"

By 1860, southerners had endured, persevered, and survived. Eleven states, Indian Territory, and large portions of two other states (Kentucky and Missouri) were decidedly southern. Their culture was one, and it extended across a remarkably vast area, sometimes finding itself temporarily exported into areas as far north as Maryland and southern Kansas Territory, places which would, nevertheless, prove to be unfertile for southern culture. There was a feeling of southern nationalism across the South, and a common bond between southerners was already firmly established, but looming upon the horizon was a cataclysm which would, once and forever, seal those bonds of common cause. A savage war was about to burst upon these people in a fury that knew no bounds. The travail and horror of that trauma would weld them into that solid and singular entity sometimes referred to as the *southern race.*

The War itself could be likened to a family or clan feud. It was perceived in the South as a response to an attack upon the South's family honor. Literally speaking, though it is difficult for even southerners of today to comprehend the intertwining family/nation spirit that totally pervaded the Confederate South, we find that there was an actual blood kinship among the people of the southern states that bound them together as tightly as did pride of section. It would be an amazing study with surprising results that one could make of the familial relationships of the ante-bellum South. The passing references to kinship among Confederate generals alone in the southern biographies lead me to a sharper realization of the smallness and the resulting closeness of the southern population.

If we of the now heavily populated sun-belt could grasp the old cotton-belt idea of population, we might more fully appreciate the vast amount of territory which was populated and so admirably administered by a comparatively small number of people under the handicap of an oppressive war. With our gleaming southern metropolises of one and two million inhabitants each, it is hard to imagine the sparsity of the Confederate population. In 1860, there were only approximately five and a half million white people in the eleven states which would comprise the Confederacy. That number is equivalent to the present population of the single state of Georgia.

When we further consider the fact that families were large in those days, the perception of the brotherhood of the South comes better into focus. Small populations and large families don't leave much room for anyone but kinfolks! Not to be overlooked is the predominance of the Scotch-Irish and their centuries-old custom of living their life's existence within the realm of their own clan, which naturally necessitated inter-marriage between cousins of varying degrees. In *Gone With the Wind,* Scarlet O'Hara couldn't understand why Ashley Wilkes married Miss Melanie Hamilton instead of her. It was there, in the opening scenes of that classic, that Scarlet learned from her father about the importance of the clan. Mr. O'Hara gently explained to her that the Wilkes *always* married cousins.

This interrelated populace probably gave rise to the southern peculiarity of calling people *Aunt, Uncle, Cousin, Granny,* etc., who are actually not related at all. In most southern communities there are those who are known as Granny or Aunt somebody. Robert E. Lee was affectionately called *Marse Robert* (from the slave pronunciation of Master) and *Uncle Robert* by his men.

With an understanding of the clan South, which Andrew

Lytle has called a *republic of families,* one can see that when the blow of war fell, it fell upon a family. A common enemy was at the door, and southerners clung together in a desperate struggle for survival.

The calamity of that long war and the specter of ten abominable years of Reconstruction did more than any one thing to create a veritable nation out of several southern states, giving us a legacy of valor unsurpassed in the annals of history, and a roll call of heroes whose bravery has yet to be equalled and whose numbers have yet been told. Also born of the tragedy of that war were the symbols of our southern nationality: our proud Confederate flag, and *Dixie* — our southern "national anthem." It is interesting to note that no other section of the United States can lay claim to its own special flag or song, and that no other group of states ever existed together as a separate nation in the manner of the southern states during the four years that they were known as the Confederate States of America. Small wonder, then, that southerners possess this special bond that transcends state boundaries and gives full meaning to the term *sister states.*

When I was in high school and college, we laughed at a southern comedian called Brother Dave Gardner. In 1963, he made a sold-out appearance at the Municipal Auditorium in Oklahoma City, and I was there, along with a college buddy of mine. Brother Dave was strictly a southern comedian; he told jokes about the South that only southerners could appreciate and fully understand. He could imitate our southern drawl with hilarious perfection, and he made us laugh at ourselves with his witty satire and blatant comedy. He loved the South, and he had his own way of showing it.

On the night I attended, he took his text on the north, telling us that he didn't even believe in the north — that it was only a figment of our imagination. He said that he had never heard of anyone going north for a vacation. "Have you ever heard of anyone retiring to the north?", he yelled. "I think the only reason anyone lives up there is 'cause they got jobs there."

While the north was obviously getting the raw end of that deal, Brother Dave was making us proud that we lived in the South — even a South that was still feeling the negative economic impact of the twin disasters of War and Reconstruction nearly a century afterwards. Although poverty and lack of financial opportunity (our inheritance from the carpetbaggers) caused many of our bright young men and women to seek employment outside the South, we still possessed something that appealed to others, and Brother Dave was reminding us of it. People did take vacations in the beautiful South; people did retire to the warm regions of Dixie; they were finding something attractive here.

The South's strength lies in its people. It always has. Gerald O'Hara told Scarlet that land was all that mattered, that it's the only thing that lasts. He told her that she would always return to the land — to *Tara*. And, she did. But, the reason she did return and fight the elements and the carpetbaggers for her beloved land was that she had the tenacity and inward resolve to persevere. We southerners, of all people, are possessed of the land, our "native soil" as we like to call it; but, the strength of the *southern character* is what sustains us through perilous times, of which the South has seen more than its share. A Texas minister recently admonished his congregation, saying "Tough times don't last; tough people do."

Tradition. Anathema to the "throw away" society of the jet age world. But, southerners aren't afraid of tradition. We're not afraid of doing things the same way over and over. To the contrary, we enjoy saying, "This is the 40th Annual All-Night Singing at Overbrook." Never mind that it dwindled to nearly nothing in the 1970's, and only a handful of people showed up each year just to meet the annual requirements. At least is was held — to satisfy tradition. What we remember are the first fifteen years or so when thousands of people drove out

11

to this Indian campground, centered around the McAlester Baptist Church, to hear the biggest names in gospel music — The Happy Goodmans, The Dixie Echoes, The Blackwood Brothers. It took acres and acres of dusty pasture just to park the cars. The big old diesel buses were parked just behind the little open-air stage so that the gospel singers could step out of those traveling accommodations dressed in the finest business suits and tuxedos that you ever saw. The lady singers wore exquisite floor-length gowns that dazzled the eye as much as the music thrilled the ear.

All this on a hot, humid Saturday night south of Ardmore, Oklahoma, in a clearing surrounded by gnarled old oak trees and a roughly circular arrangement of wooden buildings used by the Chickasaw Indians for church, camp meetings, and upon this occasion, concessions, which included Indian pashofa along with hot dogs and cokes. You brought your lawn chairs or sat on the homemade wooden benches provided by the Indian church; and, you dressed in sharp contrast to the famous singers, the summer night dictating the light, cool clothing you needed in order to survive the heat. The music was turned as loud as it would go, so that it could be heard all across the yard above the sound of rhythmic hand clapping.

That's what we remember — the fun of it all. But, what matters is that the announcer can welcome us to the *40th annual* all-night singing. We have kept the tradition. And, why do we leave the air-conditioned comfort of our modern homes to sit in the heat and dust of an August night at an old-fashioned Indian assembly ground which hasn't changed in forty years (including the two outhouses which are difficult to visit after nine o'clock because there has never been electricity run out to them)? Why don't we just break down and hold this whole thing uptown inside a big air-conditioned church, complete with a modern his and hers, next year? Well, because it's always been done this way. It's traditional. Besides, I believe southerners have a healthy perspective when it comes to modern conveniences. We enjoy the results of modern technology as much as anyone, but we aren't enslaved to its products. Allen Tate once said that he much preferred an indoor commode to an outhouse if he didn't have to kneel down and worship the thing before he used it.

Southerners have such an affinity for tradition that we seem to get as much kick out of starting traditions as we do in keeping them. It's sometimes amusing to hear a community announce its *first annual* rodeo. How do they know it will be an annual event until next year, or the next? Well, never mind. It's going to be a tradition.

I suppose the most enjoyable tradition among southerners is the tradition of southern cooking. Until a person has sat down to a country dinner of fried potatoes, fried okra, cornbread, tomatoes, and blackeyed peas, he can't say he has fully sampled the culinary delights of the South. Yes, I know that people in the north call our blackeyed peas cowpeas, and I've heard that they actually feed them to the cows, but that's not the first mistake Yankees have made. Their first one was in landing at Plymouth Rock — by mistake. They were headed for the established colony of Virginia and got lost. At any rate, we eat our blackeyed peas, and somewhere along the line a tradition was born out of that lowly pea. If there is a southern home in the land that doesn't serve blackeyed peas on New Year's Day, we need to find it and make a tourist attraction out of it — a one-of-a-kind place. Just when and how the tradition found its way into our heritage is not known to me, but it is the custom to eat blackeyed peas on New Year's Day if you want to have good luck in the coming year. Some people (my mother, for one) consider blackeyed peas only half of the tradition, claiming you must also serve pork, be it ham, bacon, or hog jowl. And we have never, never, never missed our blackeyed peas and hog jowl on New Year's Day. You think we want bad luck?

That l'il old pea gained its place in history, too. In 1863, the citizens of Vicksburg, plus 29,000 Confederate soldiers, were surrounded and besieged by Yankee armies under the command of two of the meanest Yankee generals alive, whose names I can't bring myself to mention whilst speaking of something as pleasant as the blackeyed pea. (Let's just say that one of them was just plain lucky to have gotten his picture on a $50 bill, and the other has a skunk named after him at Stone Mountain, Georgia.) Those two Yankees actually thought that their combined force of nearly 70,000 could whip General Pemberton's 29,000 men who were surrounded by water and Yankee gun boats on one side and this huge bunch of Yankee foot soldiers on the other. When it became obvious that they were no match for us, the Yanks decided to wait until Vicksburg starved out. After a while, the food did run out; even the army mules were reportedly being eaten. Still, the citizens of Vicksburg, living in newly dug caves, continued to survive, along with their gallant army. The Yankees didn't know about that blackeyed pea, and that's what the people were eating. Even the bread had run out, so Vicksburg was making a sort of bread out of peas. It was a sticky, gooey mess, and it wouldn't keep in the humidity of a Vicksburg summer, but it did its part in keeping a huge Yankee army busy for forty-nine days, so that General Forrest could spend more time making hash out of the other Yankees wandering around in the middle South. No wonder we honor that humble little pea on the first day of the year! Even Robert E. Lee once said that the only unfailing friend the Confederacy ever had was the cornfield pea.

I think certain foods have become trademarks of the South, and, again, it illustrates the cohesiveness of the region to find many of those foods popular all across the South, a geographical area covering half the length and half the width of the entire nation. We're not talking about the fast-food items like pizza and fish, which have proliferated in chain stores across the South (and the rest of the nation) within the past twenty years. We're speaking of truly southern dishes which were developed in

14

southern kitchens years ago before any food was fast.

Without a doubt the absolute number one all-time southern favorite has got to be fried chicken. How could you have a church social or a picnic in the park without fried chicken? It's so intrinsically southern that other parts of the country have added it to their menus, calling it *southern-fried chicken*. I was in college before I had ever heard that term. We simply called it fried chicken, and I didn't know there was any other way to fry one. There must be, though. Celia Mae Bryant, my former piano instructor at the University of Oklahoma, was prominent in national music circles; consequently, this gracious and charming lady kept a busy schedule which sometimes took her to New York and other foreign countries. Once, in a fine New York restaurant, she ordered fried chicken. When it arrived, obviously cooked without having been near the flour bin, and extremely hard to identify, a discussion ensued which eventually brought out the master chef. Mrs. Bryant, always finding humor in every situation, offered to go into the kitchen and show the cook how to fry chicken; whereupon he readily accepted. She excused herself from her distinguished hosts for a while, rolled up her sleeves, and taught the master chef how to properly flour chicken and fry it to a golden brown. It was such a hit with the chef that the management promised that southern-fried chicken would henceforth be served at that establishment as a regular menu item.

Old-timers will tell you that nothing tastes as good as food cooked in a cast-iron skillet on a wood stove. Well, modern southern cooks are glad to be free from the wood-burning cook stove, but they hung on to those skillets. One lady in Ada, Oklahoma, said that she had used the same cast-iron skillet for thirty-five years. She had raised all of her children and part of her grandchildren out of that skillet, and when it broke, an era was gone. She bought another one, but of course it didn't seem the same.

The skillet is an integral part of southern cooking, for it

seems that most of the best-loved southern foods are those that are fried. Fried potatoes are a must on the southern table, especially if you want to please the kids. Coming in at second place, and sometimes first, with just about everybody, is fried okra. Not that battered, frozen, deep-fried type of nugget you get in cafeteria lines or fast-food restaurants. The real okra is fried in a mixture of flour and meal in a little bit of grease over a medium-hot fire. About the only places you can find it done up right anymore is at home and in small-town cafes. Okra can be boiled, but I've never seen a kid yet that would eat it.

Southerners fry squash also. Cut into thin slices, floured, and fried until somewhat crispy, it tastes similar to fried green tomatoes, which are prepared in the same way. And, in Tennessee they have to have their fried apples. Every meal in every restaurant is advertised with a helping of fried apples. Of course, the best-known fish entrée in the South is catfish. That, too, is fried. There are many catfish restaurants in the South, who generally serve side dishes of fried potatoes, brown beans, and hush puppies, but the most enjoyable way to eat catfish is at an old-fashioned outdoor catfish fry, held in the park, or more often, out in the country at some neighbor's house.

Almost as popular as fried chicken is that universal favorite, barbecue. Wherever one goes, he isn't far from the smell of some restaurant or back yard grill slowly cooking pork, beef, or chicken in a highly seasoned barbecue sauce. Many restaurants specialize in nothing but barbecue, evidence of the popularity of barbecued meat. There are so many commercial barbecue sauces for the home cook that no one sauce has claimed the number one spot among loyal enthusiasts. The only requirement is that the bottle's label show that the barbecue sauce, like hot sauce, is manufactured somewhere in the South; otherwise, true barbecue connoisseurs won't trust it.

The list of scrumptious southern foods is endless, and it is interesting to note how many different items are so indicative of the South. Just mention mashed potatoes, white gravy, cornbread, or poke salad, and someone thinks of Dixie. Even local areas within the South have come to be known by their food. Gumbo reminds us of Louisiana, and chili of Texas. If there were no other reason to live in the South, southern cookin' would be enough.

But, there are other reasons, not the least of which is our fundamental belief in the goodness of religion. We're not afraid of religion here in the South. Separation of church and state is important to us — after all, we wrote the Constitution — but we've always relied heavily upon our common sense down here, and it doesn't violate our collective conscience at all to have prayers in school or anywhere else we choose. I never attended a high school or college football game where a public prayer wasn't offered for the safety of the participants and the attitude of the spectators.

People in the South like to go to church. It may be the men who are in charge of the services, but I believe that the women are the real backbone of the church. Southern women are the ones who want their children raised and married in the church, and that is a formidable task these days. If they're not teaching a Sunday School class, they're busy making cool-aid and cookies for Vacation Bible School or making things to sell at the annual church bazaar. They're involved, all of their adult lives, in an endless string of revivals, Bible studies, visits to the old folks' home, church suppers, and youth activities. And, if someone in the hospital gets real bad off, they take turns sitting up with the sick person around the clock, relieving weary relatives to go home and get some sleep.

For, you see, religion in the South is that down-home, get-involved, deep-down kind of religion that sort of takes quiet precedence over the other activities of life. It's basic. This is the Bible Belt. We don't spend much time debating each other over the Holy Trinity, the Virgin Birth, and Divine Inspiration of the Scriptures. Those truths were accepted long ago and are quite taken for granted as basics in our religion. Nor would we be involved in the question of "to pray or not to pray" in our public schools if the Supreme Court could find something else to do for a while. The South, generally speaking, doesn't question its religion; instead, it tends to seek practical ways of employing its already fundamental belief in religion. Granted, you will find different levels of commitment. Some rarely ever attend a worship service; still, they believe. Others are the regular, three-times-a-week faithfuls who, without fanfare, march steadily along in their pathway of duty. Then, there are the truly colorful soldiers of the Faith, the evangelicals — those Christians who are very visible in their profession of belief. With a zeal for spreading the Gospel and converting lost souls, they're the ones called *dedicated* by their admirers and *fanatic* by the doubters. They're the ones Hollywood loves to ridicule. They're also the ones with the biggest churches.

A lot of the old ways have vanished. Before we had refrigerated air, church buildings were designed with real windows which actually opened. That wasn't too long ago. I can remember those hot summer revivals when the wind was still, and you were glad for any puff of air which might make its way through the open windows. The front door, usually a set of double doors, was always flung wide open to encourage some circulation. We lived in a small town and only a half block from the church house, so we always walked to church, followed all too often by two or three of our cats which we tried to scare into going back home. My mother was mortified when one of those cats would find its way in and start looking for one of us, especially when it would start that "meow" business. After a couple of episodes like that, she gave us strict orders to lock the cats in the garage before we left for church. Well, it was hard to find all of those cats at one time, and by the time we found most of them, the ones we had locked up first were smarter than the others and would jump out every time we opened the door to put another one in. The worst night I can remember was the time our old mama cat walked up on the stage and rubbed back and forth around the preacher's legs until it grew tired of that. Then, it jumped into the big pulpit chair just to his left, where it spent the rest of the sermon giving itself one of those cat baths. My mother tried to act like it wasn't ours, but everyone knew.

Cats weren't the only thing that came in. Bugs were attracted to the lights. We had all kinds of bugs. On Sunday mornings there were the wasps, but at night it was mostly millers and June bugs. Big old scary June bugs! The girls sat there in holy terror while the boys snickered and hoped one would land on them. One night, a June bug made an unexpected dive at me. Without thinking, I raised my songbook, which I just happened to be holding onto with both hands, and in one reflexive swat, batted the thing several rows back up towards the front. Unfortunately, like a bullet it went down the back of a lady's dress, and she kept the back two rows of us kids entertained for a good portion of the sermon by her desperate attempts to extract the beast without screaming or passing out from fright.

When it was hot, you could fan with one of those church fans. They were made of stiff cardboard, sometimes on a stick like the doctor uses when he wants you to say "Ah." Some were square and some were fan-shaped, and if they weren't on a stick, they had a hole at the bottom for your thumb to go through for a good grip. There was usually a picture of Jesus, walking on the water, on one side and an ad for a funeral parlor on the other side. The picture was nice, but I didn't much like the thought of dying and being buried by Spiller Funeral Home.

Funerals were another activity which involved the good people of the church. When a person died, he was usually laid out at home after being embalmed. The family would sit up with the body until the day of the funeral, which was held at the church. Nowadays, the body rests at the funeral parlor for the wake, though most funerals are still held at the church where the deceased worshipped. If churches did nothing more than what they do upon the death of someone in the community,

19

they would be worth their keep. No matter how back-slidden a person might be, when death comes, the family looks to the church for aid. The family needs comfort; they need a preacher; they need a funeral service; they need singers for the service; they need food for the relatives coming in from everywhere. The church provides all of these services and sends flowers. If the person isn't very well-known and it looks like the crowd might be thin, church members will attend the service to save the family the embarrassment of a small turnout. In rural communities, where churches are small, many times all of the churches will pitch in to help feed the incoming family members, which sometimes can number a hundred or more. As Phil Harris once said, "That's what I like about the South."

Cooperation between denominations of sometimes very different persuasions is a highly prized virtue among southern people. Shall we call it religious tolerance? Or is it merely practical application of the theory of southern hospitality? True enough, each religion, or church, is constantly vying for new converts in its community, with the occasionally awkward situation of contending for the same person. Regardless of the belief in each denomination that its own particular program, or its tenets of faith, is superior to the church down the road, religious rivalry takes a back seat to genuinely friendly relations among the churches of the typical southern community. When the Methodists throw their annual bazaar to raise money for redecorating the church parlor, everybody attends and makes a purchase — regardless of church affiliation. When the Baptists decide its time to conduct a religious survey of the community, the Pentecostals and Presbyterians pitch in, along with other denominations, and the survey is accomplished in record time.

Two of my favorite examples of interfaith relations in the South concern the Church of Christ, of which faith I have been a lifelong member. In the small Oklahoma town of Wynnewood, a small band of us desired to establish a new congregation but could find no building for our meetings. The Presbyterians, who

20

owned the oldest church building in town, had dwindled to only a few members and had been forced to abandon regular worship. When approached with a request from us to rent their building until we could find a permanent place, their remaining elders decided to loan us the building, rent-free. Their kindness went further. They continued to pay the insurance, while one couple sent regular contributions to our new congregation. That arrangement lasted for nearly five years, at which point, the little church was able to buy the building from the Presbyterians for a nominal sum. In a joint communion service, the Presbyterian Church was officially dissolved and the Church of Christ became new owners of the quaint old church house.

The second instance of another denomination coming to the rescue of the Church of Christ occurred in DeRidder, Louisiana. Not too many years ago, while doing one of my regular summer camps in the army reserves at Fort Polk, I drove, with my cousin, into that shady little town, which is the county seat of Beauregard Parish. It was Wednesday night, and we were headed for prayer meetin' — or Bible study. To our shock, all that greeted us were the charred remains of the former building. Neighbors informed us that the church house had burned during the midst of a recent revival, and they gave us directions to a building where the church was temporarily meeting. As it turned out, we found the congregation meeting in the Hall of the Knights of Columbus! It seems that the Catholic Church had salvaged the rest of the revival by immediately offering the Hall to the Church of Christ, with the additional understanding that it was at their disposal for as long as it was needed.

And then there's the town so small that the only Jewish lady sends her children to Vacation Bible School at the Methodist Church!

Society in the rural South is more informal than it is in the city, and church is no exception. About two years ago, on a warm Sunday evening, a wasp found its way into our little,

21

old-fashioned church building through the open doors at the front. It would circle for a while, bumping the lights every so often, and then suddenly burst into a kamikaze dive at some uneasy soul who was trying desperately to sit in the pew looking cool, calm, and collected, but who also knew that if the thing got on him he would have to come up fighting like the devil to keep from being stung. Tension mounted as the sermon wore on, every eye in the house on that wasp. The preacher had a habit of delivering his sermons from a position just in front of the mourner's bench (the first row). Behind him was the communion table which held the necessary items of communion as well as the collection plates. Unbeknownst to the preacher, the wasp lit on the table directly behind him. As he continued to hold forth in proclaiming the Word, a very lively lady, well into her seventies, stood up and dashed down the aisle. Thinking she must be leaving early, the young minister continued preaching. All of a sudden the lady, whose name was Delphia, made a sharp turn behind the preacher, raised her songbook over her head, and came crashing down on the resting wasp, the edge of her book catching the rim of the collection plate on the downswing, flipping it into the air. The preacher ducked, and coins from the airborne collection plate sailed through the air. As the congregation was reeling from the uproar and beginning to break into laughter, Delphia calmly replaced the collection plate and walked back to her seat. As things finally began to settle down, she offered her simple explanation. "Well, I didn't come to church to watch a wasp fly around; I came to hear a sermon."

Rural electrification of the South, as well as indoor plumbing and other modern conveniences, which didn't arrive in much of the rural South until the late 1940's and early 1950's, spelled the end of an old custom — the outdoor baptizin'. Indoor baptistries came to city churches much earlier than they did in the country, but at one time virtually all baptisms were held in a creek, river, or farm pond. Some churches would wait until

22

there were several souls desiring immersion before scheduling a baptism. Summertime, for obvious reasons, was the most desirable season. The entire congregation would assemble on the banks of the creek and watch as the preacher waded out to a spot where he could stand a little over waist deep, followed by a line of people waiting to be baptized one at a time, each person wading a little closer to the preacher as his time approached. If you happened to be of the persuasion that baptism was an immediate and integral part of your profession of Faith, your baptizin' might have to be accomplished in cold water. An old lady in the Church of Christ told me that she will never forget the day she was baptized. It was in November during a freak cold spell, and ice had to be chopped off the river so she could get into the water.

Church functions, even in small farm communities, were well-attended in the old days. Churches and schools were institutions about which the center of social life revolved. Not only were most people more visibly religious than they are today; the events provided even the less faithful with some place to go. It was a chance to meet someone — a chance to be around people. It was a refreshing break from the lonely farm chores and isolation of the rural environment. Some of the most popular religious activities centered around music and were held in both schools and churches. And, of course, you went. Everybody went.

Who hasn't heard of an *All-Day Singin' and Dinner on the Ground?* Though still found today, especially among rural churches, and usually only on church anniversaries or homecomings, this southern tradition was enjoyed often in the not-so-long-ago. People would arrive in wagons for the Sunday morning preaching, prepared to stay until the evening rays of the sun seemed to beckon them home.

As soon as the morning church service, which sometimes featured a few numbers by some of the special singers as a preview of what was to come, was over, the ladies began setting

23

out the food which had been brought. As anyone who has ever attended one of these feeds can bear witness, the victuals, which always featured an endless supply of fried chicken, were without equal anywhere this side of Heaven. After dinner (on the ground, of course), the singing would crank up back inside around the piano. All afternoon it would go on — congregational singing, as well as specials. There were good song leaders there, and anyone who had a favorite song could get it led. The favorite songs were those that took up two pages in the songbook and had lots of "repeats." The louder you could sing, the better. Finally, when everyone was about sung out, people would reluctantly begin leaving, already looking forward to the next one.

During the 1920's and 1930's the *singing convention* was at its peak. Each community would get up a chorus of singers, who would meet at night at the schoolhouse and practice for the monthly convention. They would pick the showiest and most difficult gospel song they thought they were capable of presenting and try to work it up to perfection, hoping to win the banner. My grandmother's group, representing the Pleasant Ridge community, had a blind piano player who was one of the best in the country. He could play anything they could sing. Each month, the singing convention would be held in a different schoolhouse around the area, and the crowds would be tremendous. Most southerners loved gospel music, and this was a chance to hear the very best of each community under one roof.

The very music they were singing was a tradition in itself, for gospel music, now known as *southern gospel,* is an original form of American music. Developed in the South, southern gospel probably had its beginnings in ante-bellum days, but the dark days of Reconstruction witnessed an increase in its popularity. With the advent of radio in the 1920's, it became a fully developed and recognized form of American music, especially popular in the South, and the singing conventions did more than anything

24

else to perpetuate it.

A company in Dallas, Texas, known as the Stamps-Baxter Company, became famous for its songbooks and *singing schools.* Each year, Stamps-Baxter would put out a brand new convention songbook containing the latest gospel songs, as well as the most popular old tunes. The songbook was printed in what were called "shape-notes," a system of notation whereby each note of the scale was assigned a particular shape (square, diamond, triangle, etc.). *Do* was always a triangle,*mi* was always a diamond, and *sol* was round. All seven of the syllables had a shape, and they were taught that way in what were known as singing schools, held at the local schoolhouse by a man who traveled around for that purpose. The community would get up enough money to hire a teacher for about a week, and he would have a singing school — another event widely attended in the rural South. And if you were especially gifted and could somehow find the money, you could attend the Stamps-Baxter Singing School in Dallas.

Though the singing schools and singing conventions have all but disappeared, southern gospel music itself endures at all-night singings, in concert halls, on radio and and television, and on recordings, as a distinctly southern tradition. Even the curious shape-note songbooks continue to be used by some present-day religious organizations in the South, mainly independent Baptists, Pentecostals, and the Church of Christ.

Probably the most nostalgic and popular event connected with the southern church, was the old brush arbor meeting, found generally throughout the rural South. As a custom it is gone now, although it is revived occasionally by a church looking for a change of pace from the normal springtime revival. Before air-conditioning changed the way we live, a church would often resort to going outside for a summer revival. For this occasion the men would build a brush arbor in the church yard. They cut small trees into poles eight or nine feet long and set them upright in the ground. A framework of limbs or boards was then nailed across the top to hold the brush, or small limbs, that were piled on top of the framework to make a roof.

Everyone went to the brush arbor meetin'. It didn't matter your denomination, you went to all of them — it was someplace to go. You sat under the arbor on the old home made benches and laid the babies down at your feet on pallets made of quilts. If there wasn't room there, you made a pallet on the ground just outside the arbor, or took the sleeping children to the wagon. Every so often, someone got home with the wrong children. In the darkness, wagons looked pretty much the same to a tired mother. The lanterns under the arbor were too weak to be of any aid as she laid the child in what she hoped was her wagon. Electric lights finally replaced lanterns before brush arbors were entirely a thing of the past, and the only one I can remember attending was strung with those yellow lights that we called bug lights because they were supposed to keep the bugs away.

Traveling evangelists of every denomination would come through the country holding revivals, usually in the local schoolhouse. Pentecostal revivals, whether under a brush arbor or in the schoolhouse, were the most popular, due to the demonstrable nature of that religion. One particular revival that my dad remembers drew record crowds, mainly, it seems, because of the two preachers — two young women who were extremely pleasant to look at, named Goldie and Vashti. One had black hair; the other was blond. Men who had been considered non-religious heretofore, were conspicuously more interested in religion during that particular revival. Some were even known to testify at that meeting who had never testified before nor have since.

The same war that divided the country north and south simultaneously divided most of the religions as well. The southern wing of the large Baptist denomination became known as the Southern Baptist Convention, and, developing along more conservative lines than the northern Baptists, it grew into what is today the nation's largest protestant denomination. The

26

Methodists, who were the largest group in the South at the time of the War, remained separated from their northern wing until recent years and were known after the War as the Methodist Espiscopal Church South. A friend of mine tells about her mother, a Methodist who was born in Mississippi and raised on tales of how they could hear the big guns while the Confederates were trying to keep the Yankees out of Corinth. Solidly southern, this elderly lady, when asked in later years to what denomination she belonged, straightened proudly and answered in a clear voice,"M.E. Church, SOUTH," with emphasis on the *South!*

They say that southerners are also characterized by a special affinity for home. Somehow, they tell us, we seem to be more vulnerable upon that point than are others. I guess we're just too close to it for objective analysis, but the observation does seem to have some merit. Those who deal with such things accuse us from our own work. Our literature, from Faulkner to folklore, is replete with reflections upon home, revealing the significance which southerners attach to the family circle. Even the land itself — the old home place — is sacred to our memory. Our music tells of home. I think Al Jolson captured a uniquely southern idea of home in his delightful *Mammy.*

> Mammy, Mammy —
> The sun shines east; the sun shines west.
> But I know where the sun shines best.
> Mammy, Mammy —
> My heart strings are tangled around Alabamy.
> I'm comin' — Sorry that I made you wait.
> I'm comin' — Hope that I'm not too late.
> Mammy, Mammy —
> I'd walk a million miles
> For one of those smiles,
> My Mammy.[1]

Country music is full of sentimental allusions to home.

27

Working in this idiom, southern songwriters consistently write about home, often drawing upon personal recollections for their material. Country music is southern in origin and is, consequently, a natural vehicle for expressing our strong home ties.

> Last night I went to sleep in Detroit city.
> I dreamed about those cotton fields back home.
> I dreamed about my mother,
> Dear old Papa, sister, and brother;
> I dreamed about that girl
> Who's been waiting for so long.
>
> I wanna go home — I wanna go home.
> Lord, how I wanna go home.[2]

Truly, home is the word that strikes the responsive chord with southerners. Tennessee invited us to *Homecoming '86*, and Mississippi beckoned us to visit there because *It's Like Coming Home*. Perhaps one of the reasons we reverence home so much is the fact that we southerners have had to make our stand in the literal doorways of our homes. We've had our homes violated, and we've watched as family heirlooms went up in the smoke of an invader's fire, and I think it makes a difference. A man fights a desperate battle when he stands upon his own ground. When the guns blazed in the frenzied struggle at Shiloh, General Pat Cleburne, from neighboring Arkansas, remarked, "The Tennesseans had more to fight for; the fight was for their homes and firesides."[3]

Southerners have a similar attachment to their native states for much the same reason. I used to enjoy seeing the southern states cast their votes at the televised national political conventions. "The *great* and *sovereign* state of Alabama, *heart of Dixie*, is *proud* to cast its twenty-six votes for . . ." None of that simple stuff, "Connecticut votes for . . ." No, Sir! There's state pride down here in Dixie. Anyone who doubts the fierce state pride in the South has never been here during football season. When Texas and Oklahoma do battle each year in the Cotton Bowl stadium at Dallas, it becomes more than a ball game. Like many classic rivalries across the South, state honor is at stake!

I had a professor at the University of Oklahoma who had moved down from New York. He was constantly frustrated by this unfamiliar state loyalty atmosphere in which we live. He didn't comprehend this extreme pride in being an Okie, or a Texan, or a Floridian. Didn't we take more pride in being Italian, or Irish, or German? Goodness, at that tender age, we didn't know that we were three-quarter Scotch-Irish and one-quarter English — we would learn that later. All we knew was that OU had better beat Texas or we'd never be able to show our face in Dallas again!

Another professor, this one from California, was also having some difficulty with our idea of state pride. He took it as a personal affront to his dignity as an educator that he was having to take a basic course in Oklahoma state history as a requirement for retaining his professorship. It was essentially the same course all of us had taken in high school. He was terribly insulted and angry about the situation, and we students heard about it more than once. California had no such law, and ours was archaic and absurd! Of course it did no good to tell him that most, if not all, southern states consider it important that you know something about the state in which you are instructing its students. What it finally boils down to is that old matter of state pride, and it's hard to explain that to someone who wasn't raised on it. It's another one of those intrinsically southern values that we seem to get from home.

State consciousness isn't new to the South. Phoebe Pember Yates alludes to it in her story of the Confederate military hospital in Richmond. She succeeded in obtaining permission to segregate Confederate Marylanders from Virginians, and it was found that a general division of rooms by state worked to keep down friction among the patients. Even Mary Boykin

Chestnut, whose keen insight during the War makes her diary the best to come out of the conflict, thought that little of great importance happened outside the scope of the eastern theater of the War — her immediate world.

That idea is still around. We grow up with the charmingly provincial notion that our particular state, somehow or another, played the key role in the defense of the Confederacy, and had it not been for such-and-such the victory might have been won. A natural but sometimes amusing outgrowth of that local pride is the feeling that "my state is the real South." When I began writing this book, I was living in Oklahoma. Later, I met a lady in Nashville who, upon discovering that I was writing a book about the South, looked at me in true astonishment and asked, "Well, do you think you can do that with the proper perspective — I mean, how can you write a book about the South if you've never lived here?" Only a few weeks later, I was visiting with another Nashville woman who had recently traveled to Charleston, South Carolina, where she toured several of those wonderful ante-bellum homes. At one house the hostess asked where she was from. When she proudly replied that she was from Nashville, the hostess asked, "Do you'all consider yourselves southern up there?" And, on it goes.

One thing is for certain. We're all claiming our southern heritage, and we won't be talked out of it very easily. It's a glorious heritage, and it's only natural that we tenaciously cling to it. Call it provincial. Call it sentimental. But, it's the way we are, and I'm glad. A recent country music song said it well.

> You ain't just whistlin' Dixie —
> You ain't just slappin' your knee.
> I'm a grandson of the Southland, Boys —
> An heir to the Confederacy.
> You ain't just whistlin' Dixie,
> 'Cause the cattle-call's callin' me home.
> So, put me down there where I wanna be;

Plant my feet with Robert E. Lee;
Bury my bones under a cypress tree;
And, never let me roam.[4]

Chivalry drew its last breath in the Old South. Descendants of gallant knights and ladies fair, southerners became the last society to embrace the remnants of the old European traditions of the Middle Ages, when a man's word was his sacred pledge, and the sanctity of womanhood was defended with near religious fervor. Its fate was sealed by the conquest of troglodyte invaders who instituted a new order, and the days of fair damsels and knights in shining armor were consigned to the pages of our memory.

Even so, the basic way we behave towards each other obviously has its roots in that old idealism of the past. Our common courtesy grew from those foundations, and traces of that chivalrous legacy are still to be found in simple examples of refinement, such as the gentleman who habitually opens the door for a lady, or the child who has been trained to say "Yes, Ma'am" and "No, Sir." One of the most respectful customs among us, one that must have sprung from our legacy of chivalric behavior, is the respect we show for the dead. When that dreary funeral procession winds its weary way toward the final resting place, I've seen bystanders cease their work and stand with heads uncovered in respect. In most southern states, it is customary to bring your vehicle to a halt until the procession has passed. I've seen traffic stop on busy interstate highways, an indication that southerners haven't lost their perpective. In fact, that practice is now law in some states, but the reassuring part comes in knowing that the custom gave birth to the law.

Southerners are true romantics in the classic style, with a passion for living and a zest for adventure; but, the high-strung, emotional side of our nature is prudently balanced by the restraint which comes from a code of conduct befitting a lady or a gentleman, even if it had to be reinforced with a switch.

31

during our adolescence. We still believe in part of that old idea of chivalry, whether we know it or not, and our adherence to a system of manners and decorous behavior should be a point of pride with us. That pride — not arrogant or boastful — should come from a gratitude for our past, a knowledge of who we are, and a confidence in knowing that we truly are *Southern, by the Grace of God.*

As Carmack so aptly said, the South is a "land of legend and song." Those among us who have come to a full realization of our rich heritage live with a deep satisfaction of being southern. And there are those friends of the South who, though not blessed by so rich an inheritance as ours, are, nevertheless, attracted to it. Noted historian, Burke Davis, alludes to these adherents — admirers who hold a kind of mystical longing to be able to claim a part of the legacy we so often take for granted. Noting a surprising amount of pro-southern correspondence from the north and midwest, Davis cited a letter from a sixteen-year-old boy in Pennsylvania: "Though I am a native of Gettysburg, I am a Johnny Reb in word, thought, and deed." And, a young man from Warren, Ohio, wrote: "My only regret is that I was not born a Southerner." [5]

Abram Joseph Ryan was a Catholic priest from Virginia who, as a young man, witnessed the destruction of his beloved South. He viewed with a heavy heart the ruins of a once-great civilization. But, as the famous "poet-priest of the Confederacy" pondered the effects of the catastrophe, he was struck by the solidarity of the people and the common trials through which they had suffered. He observed the inner strength born of war, and he reasoned that, after all, what good was a land without ruins? Out of the wreckage of the war-torn South came the inspiration for one of his great poems.

A Land Without Ruins

Yes, give me the land
    Where the ruins are spread,
And the living tread light
    On the heart of the dead;
Yes, give me the land
    That is blest by the dust,
And bright with the deeds,
    Of the down-trodden just.

Yes, give me the land
    Where the battle's red blast
Has flashed on the future
    The form of the past;
Yes, give me the land
    That hath legend and lays
That tell of the memories
    Of long-vanished days.

Yes, give me the land
    That hath story and song
To tell of the strife
    Of the right with the wrong;
Yes, give me the land
    With a grave in each spot
And names in the graves
    That shall not be forgot.

Yes, give me the land
    Of the wreck and the tomb;
There's grandeur in graves —
    There's glory in gloom.

33

For out of the gloom
    Future brightness is born;
As, after the night
    Looms the sunrise of morn.

And the graves of the dead
    With the grass overgrown,
May yet form the footstool
    Of Liberty's throne;
And each simple wreck
    In the way-path of might
Shall yet be a rock
    In the temple of Right.[6]

II

THE SOUTHERN ACCENT

One of the defining characteristics of any culture is its language. From the unique words and phrases of the region to the inflection with which they are employed, a society is somewhat reflected in the speech of its people. Those who study linguistics have among them scholars who believe that the hot southern climate has had a languid effect upon the South's inhabitants, slowing down not only their actions but their speech as well; thus, we hear a more slowly delivered conversation, indicative of a slower life style.

If you've ever lived outside of the South or had to be away long enough to begin noticing that something was missing, do you remember how nice it was to hear that first hint of a southern accent as you crossed back into Dixie? It's kind of pleasant and reassuring just to hear the waitress say, "How y'all doin' today? Would you like some nice cold iced tea, Honey?" I'll never forget the first southern accent we heard coming home from a trip out west. We'd been to California for about two weeks and had begun to grow accustomed to the plain sound of the natives, while they, in turn, had almost quit asking us to amuse them with our dialect. All across Arizona and New Mexico we heard not a word that sounded familiar, but, as soon as we crossed the Texas state line, we heard it. At a little cafe in the Texas panhandle, our waitress smiled and said, "Darlin', I'll be right with y'all in just a minute." As she sailed over to take an order at another table, my friend smiled, leaned over towards me, and whispered, "Southern." We had hundreds of miles to go, but we felt like we were almost home.

The South has been uniquely blessed with one of the most recognizable and agreeable dialects of the English language. There is no mistaking a southern accent. It matters not which local variation of the accent is being spoken, any non-southerner can readily indentify the speech as southern. And, there are, most assuredly, variations within the South. Take the east coast, for instance. There, the word "about" comes out sounding like "aboot," especially in tidewater Virginia, probably due to the old English influence. In Texas, the long "i" is about as flat and straight as a human can pronounce it, while people of the interior South, especially Georgians, would make a Yankee think they were testing his hearing by their frequent, repetitious use of "Ya hear?"

Most of the characteristics of the dialect are, however, common to the whole region of the South, making it easy to identify. Most southerners speak rather softly, and in a rhythm that is smooth, at times even musical. It is a highly inflected dialect, reflecting the expressive nature of southerners. The "r" consonant is never heavy, frequently sounding like no more than "ah," and the language is one of constant diphthongs. A simple one-syllable word such as "there" comes out in a diphthongal "they-ur" sound. The southern accent is one of those rare gems of culture that make life on this planet a little more interesting.

Now, granted, most southerners are not aware of the intricacies of their brogue. They grow up with it, and it's second nature to them, just like walking. We certainly wouldn't expect a modern teenager to bother with a topic of such trivial proportions, would we? Well, not until his girl friend, whom he cherishes more than anything else, turns up minus her southern-belle accent! Just a few months ago, a sixteen-year old boy from Hermitage, Tennessee, was recounting for me how that his girl friend had moved up north for a while but later had the opportunity of moving back to Tennessee. Like me, he is amazed at how fast a southerner can lose the accent, and such was the case with his lady love. "She came home talking like a Yankee," he lamented. "Have you ever heard Yankees talk? They whine! And they talk through their noses — and too fast!" He went on, "I don't like to hear it. When she starts that stuff around me, I tell her to knock it off!" (And who said teenagers aren't aware of their heritage?!)

It would probably surprise us to find out just how many non-southerners secretly admire the southern accent. Last summer, two nicely dressed and very mannerly young men were seen walking down my street in Nashville. Probably two Mormons, I thought. Sure enough, they turned out to be a couple of those fine young men who give two years of their lives evangelizing for their church. Both of them were only nineteen years old, though one of them had been in the field four months longer than the other. From their lingo, it was obvious that they were definitely not from Tennessee. When asked how they liked the South, the enthusiastic answer came almost before the question was finished. "We love it!" The old-timer of the group asked, "Could you tell that I'm not from the South by the way I talk?" Of course there was not a hint of southern in his voice, and I answered in the affirmative. With a genuine look of disappointment on his face, he said, "I've already been here six months, and I was hoping that I was picking up some of it."

Notwithstanding all the beauty, grace, and charm of the southern accent, this silver lining is not without its cloud. A few years ago, a well-known news commentator from the north made a plea on his nation-wide radio broadcast. "Attention, Southerners! Do posterity a favor. Get a tape recorder and record your older friends and relatives while they're still living, for the southern accent is vanishing from the American scene."

And, so it is. With every generation, more of it is lost. Just listen to an older person sometime; then, compare his melodic southern brogue with that of our modern youth. The absence of a regional accent in the latter will illustrate how quickly it is going out of our speech. But what is causing this apparent bleaching of our dialect, and why do we see it at such an accelerated pace nowadays? The answer is manifold, but the major culprit responsible for the rapidity with which it is leaving us is none other than the modern god of *Television*. A dialect is traditionally passed from parent to child, for it is in the home that the child learns his first words, and it is there where he will ultimately copy phrases and inflections from his mother and father. Local association with friends and teachers who speak the same dialect provides reinforcement, and the peculiarities of the language are thus perpetuated for generations. But, enter television, and the game plan changes. Recent surveys have concluded that the average child spends more than eight hours a day in front of the TV. That's more time than he spends in school, or talking to mom and dad, or being with friends. And, without exception, you will not hear southern dialect on TV in any measurable degree — even in the South.

That ought to tell us something, as we hustle about our furiously-paced modern lives, leaving our children to learn their language from *Sesame Street* and similar syndicated broadcasts originating up north. I've seen a huge pair of thick lips, enlarged about thirty times and completely covering the television screen, urge the children of America to "Repeat after me." The number "10" is repeated over and over. "Tan, tan, tan."

What is this? We don't say "tan" here in the South! We say "ten" and pronounce it as if it were "tin." At least, those of us who pre-date television do!

Then, there is the *conscious* effort on the part of media executives who demand that southerners renounce their southern accents before gaining employment in the field of communications. The theory holds that the southern accent is equivalent to ignorance, and should you be caught using it on the air, your background would become suspect and listeners would lose respect for both you and your almighty employing station. That's an arrogant presumption if I ever heard one. There is a difference between poor grammar (whether it be from hillbillies or Bostonians) and correct English spoken with a pleasing southern drawl; but, so far, media moguls have not drawn that distinction. The southern accent is taboo in their world.

This narrow view is quite pervasive, affecting even the beauty pageants. I once had a piano student from Elmore City, Oklahoma, who, at the age of fifteen, had won quite a few beauty pageants across the country. Soon, the Oklahoma City promoters moved in and were priming her for a future run at the Miss Oklahoma Pageant, and, eventually, the Miss America Pageant. One of the first things she was encouraged to do was to change her southern accent. Though she was an excellent student and spoke perfect English, her accent was unacceptable to them. They reasoned that her accent would portray the fact that she was from a small southern Oklahoma town of only 1,500 people — in other words, a rural girl. She must portray an enlightened city girl of mid-America in order to win. After all, she had nearly three years to change her cultural blemish so that she could fool the judges. (I wonder how Miss Mississippi used to win so many times before they changed the accent!)

There are a lot of things vanishing from our language. One of the customs that I miss the most is the way ladies used to be addressed by their first names, preceded by *Miss* — like Miss Mary. As I remember, it was usually, though not exclusively, applied to unmarried ladies (especially older ones) whom we might refer to as spinsters or old maids, except for the fact that I never did think either one of those terms sounded very kind. In my daddy's day, it was much more common to address someone in this way. I have heard him speak many times of a favorite school teacher, Miss Leanna. And, during the depression, my parents traded at a country store run by a Miss Lula. When a person "traded out" enough groceries, as my mother called it, they would get a free bowl — one of those milk-colored bowls, kind of thick like ovenware and decorated around the rim with a little band of flowers and a thin gold stripe. Mother got several bowls of different sizes, and she still refers to those dishes as "Miss Lula bowls."

I can remember two elderly, unmarried ladies in my home town whom we called Miss Irene and Miss Clifford. Miss Irene was a small woman, very thin and just a little bit stooped at the shoulders — not much. She taught piano lessons and wore lots of black, but she always looked neat. Her white hair was always fixed — cut short and curled — and she always wore some kind of dressy shoes, usually black patent. She carried a big patent leather purse because she walked everywhere and needed her pencils, gummed stars, and a few music books with her at all times. She taught wherever she could, mostly at the schoolhouse or the Methodist Church, and she was there in good weather or bad. Miss Irene was a very quiet, unassuming lady, who had been born before the turn of the century in Indian Territory. Her parents sent her to the conservatory in Ohio to study music, and by the time I knew her, she was back in her home town imparting that knowledge to her students. It never entered my mind that Miss Irene had a last name.

I always thought we were calling Miss Clifford by her last name because I had never heard of a girl named Clifford. When I was in my twenties, she passed away, and I heard a niece refer to her as Aunt Clifford. It was then that I finally asked and learned that her first name was, indeed, Clifford. It had been given to her by parents who were wanting a boy. Miss

Clifford was the Avon lady in my home town. I remember how we liked her. She drove an old 1952 Chevrolet and made regular calls on my mother. She was alert and interesting, and we always enjoyed her visits. When most older women wore their hair long and rolled up in a little bun, Miss Clifford kept hers cropped short in sort of a carefree manner. I remember her as a tall thin lady who wore black high heels and took little quick steps, but what intrigued me the most was the way she wore her silk stockings rolled all the way down to her ankles in a neat little roll. I had never seen anyone do that.

In addition, I remember people older than me speaking very nostalgically of two school teachers who were sisters, Miss Sallie and Miss Pearl. But, those two ladies had retired long before I entered school.

When I was in school, we called all of our teachers by their last names, although we still pronounced *Mrs.* as *Miss* (or *Miz*). Even though we knew they were married, it was *Miss* Schafer, *Miss* Holland, and *Miss* Williams. I think it's still much that way in the South today. It's just too much of an effort to say *Missis*, and, besides, it sounds a little pretentious. I can remember a few occasions when one of our classmates would come up saying *Missis* all of a sudden, as if she knew something that the rest of us didn't. It usually didn't last too long. Maybe someone told her how it sounded. I don't know. About the only time I can ever remember *Mrs.* being pronounced in its "proper" manner is when someone was being announced from a rostrum.

I also recollect hearing people speak of an unmarried seamstress named Miss Gertrude; and, I can remember hearing of a Miss Debbie, though Miss Debbie was a widow. And then there was Miss Jane, who always brought the Sunday School lesson on television every Sunday morning.

It seems too bad to let such a nice southern peculiarity go. A few years ago, it was encouraging to hear an older gentleman at the county courthouse in Hernando, Mississippi, address one of his younger employees as Miss Debbie, and it made me wish every place was like that courthouse.

Another peculiarity of the southern language is the old practice of naming children, especially girls, after states and southern cities. Savannah is one of the most popular names that comes to mind. I used to go to church with a lady named Savannah. Texas has supplied us with a couple of popular names — Dallas and Houston. I've known several men named Houston, and I can remember both men and women who went by the name of Dallas. Florida has contributed the name of Miami, popular among girls in the South, and I even knew a lady by the name of Cherokee, who was undoubtedly named after the southern Indian tribe of the mid-South and Southwest.

The South abounds in beautiful place names, and it is quite natural to take advantage of them, keeping in mind, of course, that most southerners will allow themselves to stray only so far from the old custom of using family names over and over. Thus, if the first name happens to be Richmond, after the Virginia capital, then the middle name is apt to be Lee, James, Howard, or something quite normal, after father, grandfather, or Uncle James.

Among states, I suppose Virginia gets passed around more than any other, and well it should. It is a beautiful name, for a state or a girl, and has been cherished among southern families for generations. I have a cousin named Sharon Virginia Burkes, who was named for her aunt, Virginia Holland. Sharon has passed the name to her daughter, Virginia Ruth, perpetuating a tradition born out of the lovely name of an old southern state.

In Oklahoma, there are several people, now in their eighties, who were born on or near November 16, 1907. That was statehood day, and several of them were christened with the new state's name. A rather celebrated set of twins were named Okla and Homa. Of course, North and South Carolina have been the inspiration for numerous Carolines and Carolinas through the years. And, what southern family doesn't have its Georgia?

SOUTHERN BY THE GRACE OF GOD

The aunt of a friend of mine goes by the name of Aunt Sippi, which is short for her real name, Mississippi. My great-grandmother was born in Mississippi, but there were kinfolks in Texas, so she was named Texas Adaline Wyatt. And, who can forget the famous playwright, Tennessee Williams? Or, how about the lady at our church named Florida? And then there's that universal southern name that heads everybody's list — Dixie. I've known dozens of people who go by the name of Dixie.

The abundance of state pride in the southern states surely gets some of the credit for this quaint practice, as well as the underlying notion that the state is, in the abstract, merely an extension of the southern family. But, more than that, I think that southerners seek beauty in life, and it is my opinion that there is a natural proclivity towards utilizing the beautiful state names, with a realization that state pride, or southern affection, plays a basic role in the choice. The names of all of the southern states fall with a pleasing lilt upon the ear, most of them flowing in a near musical cadence of four syllables. Somehow, I just can't imagine a girl named Connecticut or New Jersey.

It's a pleasant custom among us, an inherently southern tradition that sets us apart from other cultures; but, like our dialect, it seems to be much less prevalent than before, and, like a vapor, it soon may vanish into the mist of our forgotten heritage.

For several years we've been living in a one-world warp that promotes the strange notion that regional and provincial differences are somehow inherently evil, or at best, *not cool*. Southerners, who have always been so steeped in cultural tradition, are the first to suffer when societies are required to give up their identifying marks, and our dialect is an easy target. It's getting tough nowadays to know the players without a scorecard. Miss Louisiana sounds like Miss California, and Miss Florida sounds like Miss Ohio. Charles Kerault, who claims a southern background, sounds like Walter Cronkite. And what has happened to our Congressmen? There isn't the slightest trace of a southern accent in the voice of Tennessee's Albert Gore or Virginia's Paul Tribble.

I don't know if it's possible to stop the deterioration of our pleasant regional dialect or not, but I do believe that it will take a conscious effort by each individual if it stands a chance at all; and that's something we've never had to do, because our accent has always been such an involuntary process.

We can take heart, though, in knowing that some southerners who have to spend great periods of time outside the South still take great pride in being and speaking southern. The enormously popular country-rock group, *Alabama*, introduced themselves to the world with a song entitled *My Home's in Alabama*, in which they proclaimed their southern accent.

> I'll speak my southern English
> Just as natural as I please;
> I'm in the Heart of Dixie —
> Dixie's in the heart of me.[1]

If we were grading accents in Congress, I belive an "A+" would have to go to Senator Thurmond of South Carolina, Senator Heflin of Alabama, and Senator Nunn of Georgia. They evidently believe that it is still advantageous to bear certain marks that identify them as southern gentlemen.

Recently, I read some remarks made by one of the South's most successful business women, Dolly Parton, in a new southern magazine. She spends more time in the hills of Hollywood nowadays than she does in the hills of Tennessee, but unlike so many entertainers who hail from the South, she refuses to play down her southern attributes. "I have a lot of southern pride. . . . I've never changed my accent. I've never tried to. I've always been proud of the South. It's a pity when people are ashamed of who they are and where they're from."[2]

Another magazine, *Southern Partisan*, is obviously in

44

agreement with Miss Parton, and even optimistically envisions a turn of events in our favor. Commenting recently on Ted Turner's amazingly successful Cable News Network, which, believe it or not, is based in Atlanta, the magazine wittily remarked, "After watching CNN we can lean back, close our eyes, and dream of a day when we will finally have stolen all the people, all the money, and all the technology from the Northeast. At that point, people in Boston and New York will be huddled around their television sets every night — eyes wide, mouths closed — listening to the anchor men on all three networks begin the evening news by saying: 'Evenin'. How y'all doin'?"[3]

While we wait for the dawn of that day, tenaciously holding onto what's left of our southern accent and hoping that most of our youth will ultimately decide that they really don't want to sound like Arthur Lymon (Congress's legal counsel in the Iran-Contra Hearings) after all, we can take some solace in knowing that one of our southern attributes is alive and well — the ability to laugh at ourselves. Southerners have always had an abiding sense of humor, even when we are on the receiving end of our own jokes. We've been able to laugh through the hard times as well as the good times. Had we not possessed this sustaining quality, we might not have been so successful in withstanding the nightmare called Reconstruction when there was little in our world to laugh at except ourselves.

Having survived as we did, however, and realizing that Yankees still flock south to spend their money (which vastly enhances our ability to laugh), we good-naturedly offer the following guide to understanding us, just in case a Yankee gets hold of this book. We even include some hillbilly terms for those who always seem to get lost in east Tennessee or southeastern Oklahoma.

SOUTHERN DICTIONARY

abode: a flat piece of wood.

addle: to bother or annoy. (Let that snake alone, now! Don't *addle* it, or we'll both get bit.); also, nervous confusion. (Sister Smith talked so loud and so long, I was about half *addled* when she left!)

ah: the 18th letter of the alphabet.

aigs: A chicken lays 'em. If he dropped 'em, they'd break.

ain't: a little critter that lives in an *ain't* bed and carries a powerful sting; also used to address the wives of your uncles, as in Uncle Case and *Ain't* Lyde.

all: what you put in your car that has to be changed every now and then. (My car is low on *all*.)

awf: opposite of on. (Cut *awf* the stove.)

bad awf: sick, or financially distressed. (He's real *bad awf*.)

bawl: what they hit with a bat when they play the World Series.

bone: the way you arrive in this world, regardless of what the stork says. (He was *bone* yesterday.)

bud: a little animal that flies. (humming*bud*, mocking*bud*.)

caw: an automobile.

cheer: a thing you sit in.

chitlins: Don't eat 'em!

Clock: The first name of the movie star who played Rhett Butler.

cut off: to turn off. (*Cut off* the lights.)

dawg: the correct pronunciation of dog.

declare: what you have to say every so often if you live in the South. (Well, I *declare*!)

Dixie: the national anthem.

dock: opposite of light. (I'm afraid of the *dock*.)

doll: the way you operate a telephone. (You look up the number, and I'll *doll* it.)

dollin': a term of endearment. (What's the matter now, *Dollin'*?)

dreckly: in a little while. (We'll be along *dreckly*.)

faints: a bunch of boards set up end-ways and runnin' around the yard to keep out the dogs.

far: the biggest one of these happened in Atlanta.

foe: comes after three and before five.

Fode: They make a real good Model T.

fussed: what you win if you're the very best; better than second place.

General Sherman: a pet skunk at Stone Mountain.

hot: the part of your anatomy that better not stop beating; sometimes shaped like a valentine.

Jefferson Davis: the best President we ever had.

jist about: nearly; almost. (We're, *jist about* done.)

leaven: the number after ten and before twelve.

line: telling an untruth. (He's *line* like a dog, Ma!)

mall: a measurement of distance. (We live about a *mall* down the road.)

mayan: the male human being. (Leave my *mayan* alone!)

mock: what you make with a crayola or pencil; also the name of the writer of the second gospel. (Matthew, *Mock*, Luke, and John.)

moonshine: This has nothing to do with the night sky.

mow: opposite of less. (I want some *mow* grits, please.)

naw: another way to say no.

own: opposite of off.

paint: to breathe like a dog. (Listen to that old dog *paint*.)

po: down and out; also, the first word of *Po* white trash.

poplar: a person with lots of friends. (A real *poplar* boy.)

rainch: a tool used for tightening. (Hand me that *rainch* and I'll tighten this here bolt.)

rassle: what two men do when they throw one another down. (Betcha ten dollars Junior here can out-*rassle* old big boy.)

rat cheer: opposite of over there. (Pull up a chair and sit *rat cheer* beside me.)

Robert E. Lee: the finest gentleman who ever drew breath.[4]

rot: opposite of left.

47

rotten pepper: stationery. (Give me a pencil and some *rotten pepper*.)

Santy Claws: the fat man who wears red and white.

sebm: the number after six and before eight.

see it: to take a seat; used especially when exasperated. (*See it* down, right now!)

Shivalay: a shiny car that lots of people drive instead of a Ford.

show nuff: positively authentic; real. (She is one of the last *show nuff* Daughters of the Confederacy.)

sofa: (*Sofa* the last time, would you please quit asking me that question?!)

sprang: the time of year when flowers bloom and birds sing.

Star-Spangled Banner: a song we sing at ball games when Yankees are watchin' us on TV.

stoke: a large bird with long, skinny legs, who has the responsibility for blessed events.

stow: a place of business. (Let's go to the grocery *stow*.)

tail: to relate a story. (Uncle Remus, please *tail* me a story.)

tar: what your car rolls on. Sometimes they go flat, but usually only on the bottom.

tar out: to become fatigued. (He sure does *tar out* fast.)

thank: to use your head.

that there: a double indicator meaning a particular thing. (*That there* dog looks awful poor.) Southerners would never use one word when two will do.

this here: meaning a particular item right at hand. (How do you like *this here* rain we're having?)

thud: after second and before fourth.

tin: the number after nine and before eleven.

wail: opposite of sick. (I hope he gets *wail* soon.)

waller: to roll around in the mud, as in a hog *waller*. (Sometimes, people *waller* around like a pig.)

whad jawl: a question. (*Whad jawl* do with that old coon you caught?)

whiz: a question you ask when you're looking for something. (*Whiz the phone book?*)

win: fast air. (My, that *win* sure has been blowing strong today!)

y'all: the handiest l'il old pronoun in the South; used when addressing more than one person.

yo: another l'il old pronoun. (That's none of *yo* business!)

MY MAMMY
THE SUN SHINES EAST — THE SUN SHINES WEST.
STANDARD EDITION

By AL JOLSON
In Sinbad

Music by
WALTER DONALDSON

MY SUNNY TENNESSEE

By
BERT KALMAR,
HARRY RUBY &
HERMAN RUBY

When Dixie Stars Are Playing Peek-a-Boo

By
AL. BERNARD and
"JO" HENNING

III

SYMBOLS OF THE SOUTH

Oddly enough, the idea of secession was not born in the South. As a practical solution to a problem of antithetical interests, it was first considered in December, 1814, by a group of New England states who were disgruntled by the War of 1812 and taxes, and who held a general anti-southern sentiment against President Madison, a native Virginian. Ironically, it was a large group of southern states who, forty-nine years later, translated the theory into resolute action, withdrawing from the old union of states and joining together under a new compact called the Confederate States of America.

Even under the guns of a relentless war, the Confederacy endured for four courageous years. When the sound of battle died, and with it, the experiment in independence, the South was left with a memory and many symbols of its fleeting existence. Some of those symbols have endured through the years, growing more significant with time.

Two southern cities have taken on symbolic significance as a result of that war — Montgomery and Richmond. Both served as capitals of the Confederacy, and today people make pilgrimages to those cities in order to savor their unique history and pay homage to the Confederate government that existed there. Within those two cities are the executive mansions used by President Jefferson Davis, miraculous survivors of an incendiary war. The Confederate White Houses have become shrines to a great man and a noble southern experiment in liberty.

Many homes across the South are an important part of the Confederate legacy, due to their connection with the great leaders of the struggle. Birthplaces of virtually every hero are marked, and their graves are veritable shrines. The green lawns of southern courthouses are picturesque showcases of the permanent symbols of the South, the granite and marble monuments that tell the story of our past glory.

One obvious and most interesting emblem of the new nation was a practical item — the Confederate money. Most of it was in currency, as opposed to coin. This new and immediate token of the Confederacy touched everyone's life and was destined to become a lasting memento of a nation born of necessity under a rising cloud of northern pressure.

The physical appearance of the currency was striking. It was quite handsomely designed, carrying elaborate works from earlier U.S. issues and local bank notes. There were pastoral scenes of slaves picking cotton and idyllic scenes of American Indians. Railroad images appeared on some issues, while one bill carried the picture of an artillery unit from the Mexican War. Subjects from classic mythology were utilized, and many public buildings of Greek Revival architecture in the ante-bellum South appeared as centerpieces, set amidst flowing script which set forth the denomination, terms of the note, and other pertinent details. The first bills were printed in New York and smuggled south, but most of the Confederate currency was eventually printed in Richmond, Columbia, and Augusta. As production moved south, the money began to feature portraits of early southern heroes such as Calhoun, Washington, and Jackson, with subsequent printings honoring contemporary Confederate heroes, including Jefferson Davis and Stonewall Jackson. One interesting note carried the likeness of Lucy Holcomb Pickens, wife of South Carolina's Governor Pickens. Variously known as the "Sweetheart of the Confederacy" and the "Queen of the Confederacy," she was considered to be very beautiful. Mrs. Pickens has the distinction of being the only woman to have her image appear on American currency.

Confederate currency was strong at the beginning, but towards the end it had shrunk in value to nearly nothing. It took 1,200 Confederate dollars to equal one Yankee dollar in the closing days of the War. I grew up hearing exaggerated stories about people who papered their houses with the worthless bills, and of the man who supposedly said, "I used to go to the store with my money in my hand and come home with a bushel basket of bread; now, I go to the store with a bushel of money and come home with a loaf of bread in my hand."

Such thoughts, among others, must have been on the melancholy mind of Major S.A. Jones, one of Gen. Stephen D. Lee's staff officers. The army had surrendered, and he was making arrangements to return to Mississippi when he penned these words, appropriately enough, on the unprinted back of a $500 Confederate note.

Lines on a Confederate Note

Representing nothing on God's earth now,
And naught in the waters below it,
As the pledge of a nation that's dead and gone,
Keep it, dear friend, and show it.

53

SOUTHERN BY THE GRACE OF GOD

Show it to those who will lend an ear
    To the tale that this trifle can tell
Of Liberty born of the patriot's dream,
    Of a storm-cradled nation that fell.

Too poor to possess the precious ores,
    And too much of a stranger to borrow,
We issued to-day our promise to pay,
    And hoped to redeem on the morrow.

The days rolled by and weeks became years,
    But our coffers were empty still;
Coin was so rare that the treasury'd quake
    If a dollar should drop in the till.

But the faith that was in us was strong, indeed,
    And our poverty well we discerned,
And this little check represented the pay
    That our suffering veterans earned.

We knew it had hardly a value in gold,
    Yet as gold each soldier received it;
It gazed in our eyes with a promise to pay,
    And each Southern patriot believed it.

But our boys thought little of price or of pay,
    Or of bills that were overdue;
We knew if it brought us our bread to-day,
    'Twas the best our poor country could do.

Keep it, it tells all our history o'er,
    From the birth of our dream to its last;
Modest, and born of the Angel Hope,
    Like our hope of success, it passed.

SOUTHERN BY THE GRACE OF GOD

"Save your Confederate money, Boys! The South shall rise again!" I've heard that expression all of my life, and I've always sort of hoped that it would someday come true; however, I was a sixteen-year old boy before I ever even saw a real Confederate bill and realized that people were actually saving them. Good reason. They're worth more than Yankee money nowadays. They're handled by coin dealers in the South, and even though they're thin and fragile, I've bought a few, just in case. . . .

Without a doubt, the two most enduring symbols of the Confederacy are the Confederate flag and the song, *Dixie*. Both of them have grown from the popular emblems of the Confederacy into hallmarks of the South of today. Unlike Confederate money, they are still in use today and have become the trademark of our southern heritage — our physical link to our intangible past. They represent our vigor, our zest, our patriotic fervor. They symbolize our fierce loyalty, our love for independence, and our reckless courage in demanding it. Without them we have no fire, no electricity, no enthusiasm for who we are and where we've been.

Non-southerners find it difficult to understand our attachment to emblems of a defeated nation, finding in it too much of a paradox in that we simultaneously hold dear the symbols of the United States. Is it contradictory that we should respect our past loyalties and hold as steadfastly to them as we do our present ones? Perhaps an average perspective would, indeed, allow for some incongruity; but then, that's just part of being southern, and we don't expect anyone else to completely understand it. I'm reminded of one of William Faulkner's characters who, in answer to a similarly perplexing question from his northern roommate at college, told him that no one could really explain the South to him — that he would just have to have been born there.

The familiar red flag with its blue bars and white stars, universally recognized as the flag of the South, is known by various names, including the *Confederate Flag,* the *Battle Flag,* and the *Southern Cross.* It is suprising to many that this popular flag was never officially prescribed for use by the Confederate government, though it was carried on the field of battle as the ensign of the Confederacy and is today regarded as the bona fide Confederate flag.

There were three *official* flags adopted by the Confederate Congress, even though the battle flag was not one of them. The very first flag was known as the *Stars and Bars,* and it featured two broad red stripes (or bars) with a broad white stripe between them, plus a blue union in the upper left hand corner carrying seven white stars in a circle. When you hear Aunt Semantha exclaim, "Oh my Stars and Bars!", this is the flag about which she is exclaiming (though she probably doesn't know it). This flag was official. It was first raised at Montgomery on March 4, 1861, by Miss Letitia Tyler, granddaughter of former President John Tyler. A fine flag it was, and southerners were as proud of it as they were of their brand new republic; however, it soon proved to be fatally flawed. Through the smoke and haze at the Battle of Manassas, it was mistaken for the U.S. flag more than once, creating much confusion. It was decided, largely by the military, that a different flag would have to be devised.

Enter the Confederate Battle Flag. Gen. P.G.T. Beauregard, then commanding part of the Confederate forces in northern Virginia, proposed a new flag, consisting of a blue St. Andrew's Cross emblazoned with thirteen white stars, resting on a red background. The flag was entirely symmetrical, perfectly square, and bordered by a narrow band of white. Due to its magnificent appearance and, partially, to the popularity of General Beauregard, it was immediately accepted for use in the field by the armies and the navy. The first actual flags were made by three of Richmond's leading belles, the Misses Cary — Constance, Hettie, and Jennie — and formally accepted by Generals Beauregard, Johnston, and Van Dorn in ceremonies before massed troops at Centreville, Virginia. The date was

October, 1861.

The Battle Flag became very popular, and by 1862, General Beauregard had introduced it into the western armies. The Army of Tennessee used both square and rectangular versions, as did many outfits outside of northern Virginia. Still, the official flag of the government was the Stars and Bars. It flew over the capitol and other government buildings throughout the Confederacy, and at times was still to be found among some military units in the field.

Popular acceptance of the Battle Flag contributed to the adoption of a second official flag for the Confederacy, this time a solid white flag with a small Battle Flag design appearing in the top left-hand corner. It was a handsome flag called the *Stainless Banner*, but when carried onto the field and hanging limp from the flagpole, it resembled a white flag of truce; consequently, the Battle Flag retained its preeminence upon the battlefield.

The Stainless Banner was official from May 1, 1863, until Congress corrected its "flag of truce" appearance on March 4, 1865, by adding a broad red bar across the end of it. The action came a little too late to be of practical use. On April 9, 1865, General Lee began the first of many surrenders which culminated in the capitulation of Gen. Stand Watie and most of the Indian Territory, some 1500 miles to the southwest, on June 23, 1865. The official flag of the Confederacy never made it onto the battlefield; consequently, the flag that was surrendered over and over in scenes of wretched despair across a defeated Southland was the same flag under which brave soldiers had marched for four arduous years — the unofficial, never-adopted Confederate Battle Flag.

A dream was dying; a nation was dying; and nothing remained but a tattered symbol of immense significance. Thousands of brave souls who had spilled their lifeblood under its banner were absent from the hallowed ranks who now had the solemn duty of retiring the proud emblem from the field.

Many strong hearts in war-weakened, undernourished bodies wept over the final furling of the banner they had so gallantly defended. Soldiers gazed upon it and strove to touch it for the last time, bitter tears streaming down their furrowed faces as the scenes were reenacted time and again across the late land of cotton.

How it must have hurt to give that flag into hands that hated it — to see it carried off by men who had cursed it, reviled it, spat upon it! Reduced to the status of cheap souvenir in the hands of Yankees, many a wartorn Confederate flag was carried off by the conquerors, only to end up in a northern courthouse, state capitol, or museum.

In 1887, President Cleveland, himself a northern Democrat, proposed to return the numerous surrendered Confederate regimental flags, which were lying in the attic of the War Department, to the southern states as a gesture of reconciliation. He was bitterly assailed by the still vengeful Republicans and veterans of the Union army, and was defeated in the next election. It would be forty years after the War before northern attitudes softened enough to allow President Roosevelt, a Republican, to return the flags in 1905. Over the years, other flags have been returned, although some still remain far away from Dixie's fair clime.

A young man in gray sat down soon after Robert E. Lee's surrender and penned what is often called "the requiem of the Lost Cause." Only twenty-seven years old, Abram Joseph Ryan expressed the finality of the last furling of the flag, verbalizing the thoughts of a grief-stricken people.

The Conquered Banner

Furl that Banner, for 'tis weary;
Round its staff 'tis drooping dreary;
    Furl it, fold it, it is best;
For there's not a man to wave it,
And there's not a sword to save it,
And there's not one left to lave it
In the blood which heroes gave it;
And its foes now scorn and brave it;
    Furl it, hide it — let it rest!

Take that banner down! 'tis tattered;
Broken is its staff and shattered;
And the valiant hosts are scattered;
    Over whom it floated high.
Oh! 'tis hard for us to fold it;
Hard to think there's none to hold it;
Hard that those who once unrolled it
    Now must furl it with a sigh.

Furl that Banner! furl it sadly!
Once ten thousands hailed it gladly,
and ten thousands wildly, madly,
    Swore it should forever wave;
Swore that foeman's sword should never
Hearts like theirs entwined dissever,
Till that flag should float forever
    O'er their freedom or their grave!

Furl it! for the hands that grasped it,
And the hearts that fondly clasped it,
  Cold and dead are lying low;
And that Banner — it is trailing!
While around it sounds the wailing
  Of its people in their woe.

For, though conquered, they adore it!
Love the cold, dead hands that bore it!
Weep for those who fell before it!
Pardon those who trailed and tore it!
  But, oh! wildly they deplored it!
  Now who furl and fold it so.

Furl that Banner! True, 'tis gory,
Yet, 'tis wreathed around with glory,
And 'twill live in song and story,
  Though its folds are in the dust:
For its fame on brightest pages,
Penned by poets and by sages,
Shall go sounding down the ages —
  Furl its folds though now we must.

Furl that Banner, softly, slowly!
Treat it gently — it is holy —
  For it droops above the dead.
Touch it not — unfold it never,
Let it droop there, furled forever,
  For its people's hopes are dead!

SOUTHERN BY THE GRACE OF GOD

Noble sentiments, to be sure, and fairly universal in the South, but just as time works its merciful duty of healing the heart after the death of a loved one, so did it slowly soften the shock of defeat into a nostalgic desire to see that flag wave once again over the conquered land. It was an Englishman, Sir Henry Houghton, who advised southerners to rise above their grief and unfurl their gloried banner. His own England, though much in sympathy with the Confederacy, never officially recognized her, and he alludes to his regret in a few lines of his poem.

A Reply To The Conquered Banner

Gallant nation, foiled by numbers!
   Say not that your hopes are fled;
Keep that glorious flag which slumbers,
   One day to avenge your dead.
Keep it widowed, sonless mothers!
Keep it, sisters, mourning brothers!
Furl it now but keep it still —
   Think not that its work is done.
Keep it till your children take it,
Once again to hall and make it,
All their sires have bled and fought for;
All their noble hearts have sought for —
   Bled and fought for all alone.
All alone! ay, shame the story!
   Millions here deplore the stain;
Shame, alas! for England's glory,
Freedom called, and called in vain!
Furl that banner sadly, slowly,
Treat it gently, for 'tis holy;
Till that day — yes, furl it sadly;
Then once more unfurl it gladly —
   Conquered banner! keep it still!

We haven't always enjoyed the freedom to fly the Confederate flag. Soon after the War's tragic end, the dark days of Reconstruction fell upon the South like a vulture upon its prey — a period of persecution which lasted three times as long as the War in many parts of the South. As the hated Yankee flag continued to shelter the carpetbag governments shackling the South, the furled banner became even more dear to southerners. As a vindictive measure, the Reconstruction despots forbade postwar display of the Confederate flag.

In 1877, when the South finally succeeded in overthrowing the carpetbag regimes, the veterans of the Confederate army began to emerge with a new enthusiasm for their heroic past. The famous reunions were initiated as soldiers began to hold mass gatherings on county, state, and national levels, always displaying their now unfurled banner.

As time thinned the ranks of the old soldiers, a grateful South resolved to honor the memory of the old Confederacy by erecting monuments and protecting the flag. Remembering the relative ease with which the flag was once arbitrarily banned, the state of Mississippi cleverly ensured its perpetuity by incorporating the Confederate flag into the design of a new state flag in 1894. The Confederate Battle Flag became the main feature of the new flag, appearing in the upper left hand corner of the state banner.

Two other states gave similar honor to the Confederate flag by using the flag's principle feature, the St. Andrew's Cross, in their official state ensigns — Alabama in 1895, and Florida in 1899. And, as late as 1956, the admirable state of Georgia hoisted a proud new state banner, one-third of which contains the state seal while the other two-thirds depicts the Confederate Battle Flag. In this age of forgotten values when southerners regrettably fail to fly the Confederate flag, it is most inspiring and pleasurable to travel across Georgia and see their extremely significant state flag playing in the southern breeze. The Battle Flag portion of the Georgia flag is the prominent part and is at once reminiscent of by-gone days when the Confederate flag flew in all its glory atop schools, courthouses, and city halls.

Up until about twenty-five years ago, the South was awash in Confederate flags. Hardly a hamlet could be found without its flag catching the wind. Not only were the flags a monument to the Confederacy, they were symbolic of the tenacity with which the South holds onto its fundamental belief in government at the local level, independence, state's rights, and a right to rebel against wrong.

How things can change in such a short time! Today it is possible, even likely, to drive across the entire breadth of the South without seeing a single Confederate flag against the southern sky. It has fallen victim to malicious attacks by emotional, misguided, and uneducated people who are looking for something sinister in our affection for the flag of our fore-fathers. Our accomodating southern nature has caused us to compromise our convictions and haul down the flag, when standing tall would have eventually restored respect and truth to the blameless flag. Acquiescence to falsehood casts a cloud of suspicion upon the innocent and lends credibility to the liar. The way to refute lies about the Confederate flag is for responsible southern citizens to fly the flag *more* — not less.

It's probably a blessing that the old veterans who followed that flag through the din of battle in quest of our independence are not around to see the vacant flagpoles. It would, no doubt, remind them of the Reconstruction ban. There is, however, a ray of hope shining through the darkness of the present distress, and as usual, it comes not from officialdom but rather from the spontaneity of the same class of people who gave it birth on the battlefield, the common southerner. Notwithstanding constant diatribes and scathing denunciations of the Confed-erate flag from the fanatic liberals who now have a strangle hold on most of the editorial functions of our southern newspapers, the general southern populace continues to resist being brain-washed. In a recent poll (April, 1988) conducted by one of the most powerful of these arch liberal enemies of the flag, it was found that 88% of the southern citizenry highly regard the Confederate flag and approve of its official display. It is not the fault of the average southerner that official exhibition of the flag is scarce nowadays; that dubious honor can be accorded the malcontents of the media and public officials who see themselves as our overseers rather than our dedicated public servants.

Though absent from official display in near totality, the flag goes forth on the highways and byways of the nation, thanks to truckers and teen-agers, bless 'em! That's where you'll see the flag. Antenna flags, bumper-stickers, mud-flaps, decals, radiator shields, car tags, T-shirts, ball caps, key chains. I wish there were as many flags flying from homes and businesses as are to be found on the bedroom walls of our southern teen-agers. The flag companies would have to put on an extra shift! And, how about those amusement parks — Opryland, Six Flags, Disneyworld? You'll find flags there, for sure. Then there are the football games. Go to a game at Alabama, Ole Miss, or Auburn, and you'll see what the whole South used to look like!

So it is that the flag may have to be carried by the *real* southerners until our leaders recover from their amnesia. Perhaps residential streets ablaze with Confederate flags would give our timid public officials new courage. We can fly the flag from our homes in the same manner that we fly the U.S. flag. Flying the U.S. flag sends one clear message: *I'm American and proud of it.* Flying the Confederate flag sends an additional message: *I'm southern and proud of it.*

Confederate flags are available in nearly every conceivable size, the most common size for outdoor use being the popular 3' by 5' version. Both cotton and nylon flags are suitable for outdoor display, and can be found at most retail flag stores in the South. For mail orders, the following list of flag suppliers is offered.

Arkansas Flag and Banner
1619 Main Street
North Little Rock, Arkansas 72114

Telephone:
800-445-0653

The Flag Shop
8946 Interline Avenue
Baton Rouge, Louisiana 70809

Telephone:
800-821-5626

National Capital Flag Co., Inc.
3256 Colvin Street
Alexandria, Virginia 22314

Telephone:
800-368-3524

The Floding Company
684 Spring Street, NW
Atlanta, Georgia 30308

Telephone:
404-881-8000

United Daughters of the Confederacy
328 North Boulevard
Richmond, Virginia 23220

Telephone:
804-355-1636

If there is another single element in the South capable of eliciting the same kind of emotion produced by the Confederate flag, it would have to be the wild, throbbing strains of *Dixie.* — the unofficial "national anthem of the South."

It has been said that America has no martial music like the countries of Europe, but that if this country has one song which can excite the people, it would have to be *Dixie.* Why does this one song inspire southerners so? How is it that this modest tune with its simple words can create absolute pandemonium in two short bars? How does it yank us up out of our seats and force us to shriek and yell as if we had suddenly reverted to an aboriginal state? As it is with many aspects of the South, the *how* and *why* are lost somewhere in our heritage. We can only demonstrate the fact and leave the reason to philosophers.

Having been a pianist by trade, I am frequently called upon to provide that rather smooth, dull type of repertoire we call dinner music, while people sit and talk to one another rather than listen to the music. I always work *Dixie* in at least once, whether it be banquet, party, or reception, and the result is always the same. The conversation stops; all eyes are on the piano; and, if it is not inappropriate to the event, the crowd gathers around the piano as quickly as summer storm clouds, singing and clapping their hands in time to the music. And then, as regular as rain, the last note of the song brings on a chorus of Rebel yells.

A typical scene depicting the marvelous chaos generated by the playing of *Dixie* is played out each year at the annual convention of the Sons of Confederate Veterans. The three-day affair culminates in the Cotillion Ball, a delightful vignette of the Old South. Ladies with their hair done up in ringlets are attired in hoop skirted ball gowns, while the gentlemen stride around in brilliant Confederate uniforms and dazzling tuxedoes. After presentation of the debutantes, who lead the cotillion in the opening dance, the orchestra plays traditional dance music for the elegantly garbed southerners. Decorum is preserved, quite naturally, until the orchestra strikes up *Dixie*. Then, notwithstanding hoop skirts, tuxedoes, and aristocratic pageantry, pandemonium breaks loose in war-like fury! It is extremely difficult to hear an orchestra — or a freight train — over the Rebel yells and clapping of hands. And to think that all of this wonderful hysteria was brought on by one l'il old plantation walkaround!

There is no real agreement as to the origin of the word itself, though *Dixie* has been used since long before the War to designate the Southland. Some think it may be a derivative of the Mason-Dixon Line, while others believe it came from a French ten-dollar bill called a "Dix," the French word for ten. The latter theory is interesting and plausible. In Louisiana, where the French language was common, bank notes carried the word

"Dix" in each corner, and people referred to their money as their "Dixies." Eventually, the entire lower South became known as the land of Dixies, or Dixieland.

The song has been credited to Daniel Decatur Emmett, though there is also uncertainty as to its full origin. The melody, according to Emmett, was inspired by part of a tune his mother had sung to him as a child, while others think that a similar tune had been sung around plantations and the big river for several generations. What we do know is that the song of the sunny South was written in New York on a cold, rainy day in 1859. Emmett, composer of *Old Dan Tucker*, was asked to write a "plantation walkaround" for Bryant's Minstrels, and *Dixieland* was the result. Over the years, the title was shortened by general usage to *Dixie*. Confusion also surrounds Emmett's feelings about the adoption of the song as the southern anthem. Some have reported that this Ohio native was pro-southern; others say that he was sorry he had written the song, for in his mind it had become a symbol of treason.

Whatever the origin of *Dixie*, it didn't seem to matter to southerners. In 1860, it was heard in New Orleans amidst approaching fears that the North was goading the South into war, and the song electrified its southern audience upon the spot. For southerners it was love at first sight — or sound, as the case may be. It immediately became the rallying cry of the South, and only a few months later this brand new song was given the official nod when it was used in the inauguration of President Davis on February 18, 1861. A Montgomery music teacher became the first person to orchestrate the number for band, and thus it was played all day and into the night by bands gathered for the occasion. The president's escort, soldiers of the First Alabama Infantry, became the first men to march to the sound of *Dixie*.

As a gesture of respect for the South, it has always been our custom to stand whenever *Dixie* is played. Besides, who can sit still while that magnificent tune is blaring? Even so, the same spectre that haunts our flag now haunts our music as well; consequently, our youth, especially, are deprived of the opportunity to experience the excitement of *Dixie* by mere fiat of short-sighted school administrators all across the South who have banned its playing, even though the lyrics are so innocuous as not to offend even the most hard-bitten Yankee or any other peculiar group of people. As a result, we're raising generations of young southerners who never feel the exhilaration or learn the protocol.

A humorous, though pertinent, illustration comes to mind. A few years ago we had a particularly obnoxious governor in Oklahoma who was literally swept back into office on a rock-hard pledge of "No New Taxes!" Then, in an apparent abrogation of all principle, the man besieged the legislature, in his second week in office, with the most startling list of tax proposals since statehood. From his first term as governor, we were already saddled with the most massive hike in the property tax in state history. The heavy tax burden culminated in a state-wide tax revolt at about the time the governor was taking office for his second term.

A friend of mine became the co-chairman of the tax revolt, and as such, had occasion to receive insults from the governor's machine. She is a Jewish lady, formerly of Shreveport, Louisiana, and she is married to a doctor in my hometown. Shortly after the tax revolt had run its course, Marilyn was attending a doctor's convention near Tulsa, an annual event which gives her a chance each year to visit with a long-time girl friend whose husband is also a doctor. As luck would have it, the selfsame governor was there for the evening gala, and upon being introduced, received the customary standing ovation from everyone — except Marilyn. Her friend, quite obviously embarrassed, looked down and said "Marilyn, what are you doing sitting down?", to which Marilyn replied, "He is not a man deserving of an ovation, and it would be hypocritical of me to accord him one, especially after the way he has treated us." Later in the program, after the audience was once again comfortably seated, the band played *Dixie*, and to Marilyn's dismay, not a single soul was standing — except Marilyn. Her friend, further embarrassed, looked up and said, "Marilyn, what are you doing standing up?" As straight as a soldier, Marilyn looked down at her and calmly answered, "They're playing *Dixie*. What are you doing sitting down?"

Failure to train and educate the present generation in regard to the significance of our traditional symbols is one problem. Compounding that are the deliberate attempts to discredit our embattled emblems and force their removal from public use. Until recently, most of the latter efforts have been localized attacks, although quite successful in many cases. In early 1987, a frightening new phase emerged in the form of a *national* effort to ban the Confederate flag from official display anywhere in the country. Its radical design hints of a cultural revolution, a kind of purge of the southern heritage in which the flag will become only its first fruits, followed by a general campaign to redefine the symbols of the Old South and erase our former glory. Already, streets formerly named for Confederate generals have been changed, and pressure is being applied to dismantle Confederate holidays.

In the recognition that we have been too long resting on our laurels instead of contending for our heritage, a respected group of southern citizens met in April, 1987, and launched a counter-offensive. The founders included several noted authors, members of SCV and UDC, the publisher of a national magazine, and other community leaders.

Spokesman for the press conference, held in Columbia, South Carolina, was Richard Hines, a senior executive consultant to President Reagan and assistant editor of the *Southern Partisan*. "We are launching the Southern Heritage Association to be an organized effort to educate the public as well as the politicians who represent us on the true meaning of the southern heritage, including the symbols of the South. We are educational because those who are now attempting to pull down the Confederate battle flag are badly in need of accurate information. . . . The War Between the States was a great and complex event in American history. Since the end of that conflict, there has been an unfortunate effort in some quarters to rewrite the history of that period into a simplistic morality play, a neat contest between good and evil. We must take it upon ourselves to defend the true meaning of our symbols, our tradition, and southern history. We must not allow radical elements on either side to dominate this debate."

Seeking to become the South's pressure group, a kind of southern anti-defamation league, the Southern Heritage Association not only intends to educate through the mass media, it is already lobbying, passing petitions, raising funds, and voicing its positions through the press. Its success — our success — depends upon the degree to which we involve ourselves. The Association needs all of the volunteers and funds it can find. Our heritage hangs in the balance.

The Southern Heritage Association
Post Office Box 11719
Columbia, South Carolina 29211

CONFEDERATE HOLIDAYS

Our Confederate state holidays stand as a yearly reminder of the uniqueness of our southern culture, and yet these most obvious symbols of the South were almost neglected in the preparation of this work. It's often difficult to focus on things closest to you, and these living tributes to our Confederate progenitors might have, through the habitual nature of their observance, gone unnoticed had I not been quite puzzled by reading a strange statement concerning Abraham Lincoln.

In a recent essay about the South, there appeared an odd observation that southerners truly believe Lincoln to be one of the greatest presidents ever. The author of that statement, a well-known figure in America who was purportedly speaking for the South, claims a southern background by virtue of having spent his childhood here, although, to my knowledge he has lived his adult life in the north. He went on to opine that Robert E. Lee was no longer perceived as a hero in the South, and, in a bold assertion that smacked of New South propaganda, he mused that this new rejection of Lee was probably good.

My first impression was that the new author was out of touch. I knew he wasn't in touch with the southerners I know, because Lee is synonymous with heroism in the South and unquestionably the most popular hero of the War. As to Lincoln's popularity, the errant writer does have on his side the common misperceptions about Lincoln that cause misinformed individuals to accept the carefully contrived notions of his fatherly, harmless, kind, deeply religious, ever-suffering image. Southern ministers are notorious for accepting these myths at face value, quoting Lincoln with wild abandon while unsuspecting of his irreverent character. It is not my desire nor purpose, however, to fault ministers of the gospel for studying their Bibles rather than their history books, but rather to encourage those of us who seek truth to insist upon accuracy in histories.

However slanted those histories may be, it is still a stretch of the imagination to pretend that Honest Abe has become the consummate *southern* hero. Granting even the concession that southerners are now educated by northern writings, there are enough contemporary accounts of the character of Mr. Lincoln to prohibit an embracing faith in him among the people of the South. Mary Boykin Chestnut repeats a comment by Mrs. Scott, describing Lincoln as "the kind who are always at corner stores sitting on boxes, whittling sticks, and telling stories as funny as they are vulgar."[1]

Lincoln's proclivity for vulgar stories was commonly known during his lifetime. Mrs. Chestnut tells of the report from Mrs. Gibson, formerly a Miss Ayer of Philadelphia who had married south and, though she was residing in Richmond, did not believe in the Confederacy. "Oh yes, his best friends say the Yankee President is just the ugliest, the most uncouth, the nastiest joker, etc."[2] Mrs. Chestnut herself responded to someone who had tried to quote one of Lincoln's better statements. "I was very glad to hear it, to hear something from the President of the United States which was not merely a vulgar joke, and usually a joke so vulgar that you are ashamed to laugh — funny as it is!"[3]

Several years ago, I read a description of Lincoln that stayed with me. Written by the editor of a Richmond newspaper, shortly after Lincoln's election, it depicted him as a candidate of "scanty political record — a Western lawyer, with the characteristics of that profession — acuteness, slang, and a large stock of jokes — and who had peculiar claims to vulgar and demagogical popularity, in the circumstances that he was once a captain of volunteers in one of the Indian wars, and, at some anterior period of his life, had been employed, as report differently said, in splitting rails, or in rowing a flat-boat."[4]

Has the rail-splitter from Illinois eclipsed General Lee in the admiration of southerners over the past one hundred and twenty-five years? I determined that I should make a survey of the southern states in regard to their holidays, reasoning that a fairly accurate gauge of public opinion could be thus ascertained. I knew that Oklahoma had no holiday in honor of Honest Abe, and I was not surprised to find that ten of the eleven former Confederate states also disregarded his birthday as worthy of special note. The real surprise came from Florida, the southernmost state of the South, where the birthday of Lincoln is a state holiday! As to how this aberration occurred, I can only offer conjecture that perhaps Florida has become the retirement haven of several million more displaced Yankees

72

than Floridians had bargained for. Concerning the thesis that Robert E. Lee was no longer a hero, the results showed a resounding *not so*! Lee's birthday is an official holiday in nine of the eleven Confederate states. In addition, the border state of Kentucky, obliged to honor Lincoln because of his birth in that state, more than compensates by having a state holiday on the day of General Lee's birth and another state holiday, called *Confederate Memorial Day*, on June 3, birthday of Jefferson Davis.

It was due to this entire incident that the resulting survey was made, a survey which awakened in me a greater appreciation for the fundamental premise upon which southerners bestow honor. Southerners have always resisted the *might makes right* psychosis which causes otherwise intelligent people to foresake principle and just "go with the winner." How easy it would have been to forget the defeated soldiers of the Lost Cause and accept the heroes of the victorious power in Washington. The Southland could have been strewn with monuments of Lincoln, Grant, and Sherman, paid for, most likely, with federal funds. The poverty-stricken women of the South, with homes ruined, could have dispensed with their bake sales, ice cream suppers, little home-talent plays, and bazaars, with which they laboriously gathered in their nickles and dimes that would one day build the magnificent monuments to men who had lost a war.

But, the easy road wasn't taken, and we who are their posterity are all the richer in heritage for it. The conquered boys in gray came home to a hero's welcome, while the women of the South looked upon the magnificent northern memorials and resolved that there would be ample memorials throughout Dixie which might even rival the appearance of those to the north and would, without a doubt, surpass them in sentiment. In the same vein came the official holidays honoring the heroes of the Confederacy.

As true symbols of the South, the official holidays in honor of our Confederate heritage are listed herein, according to state. It was disappointing to find no such honor given in Tennessee, the state who gave so many volunteers to the Confederacy; in Oklahoma, the last stronghold of the Confederacy; in Missouri, for whom one of the stars was placed upon the Confederate flag; and in Louisiana, who suffered so much at the hands of the invader during the War and in Reconstruction. To the other nine states of the old Confederacy go the praise of a grateful people.

ALABAMA	Birthday of Robert E. Lee (third Monday in January) Confederate Memorial Day (fourth Monday in April) Birthday of Jefferson Davis (first Monday in June)
ARKANSAS	Birthday of Robert E. Lee (third Monday in January)
FLORIDA	Birthday of Robert E. Lee (January 19) Confederate Memorial day (April 26) Birthday of Jefferson Davis (June 3)
GEORGIA	Birthday of Robert E. Lee (January 19) Confederate Memorial Day (April 26) Birthday of Jefferson Davis (June 3)
MISSISSIPPI	Birthday of Robert E. Lee (third Monday in January) Confederate Memorial day (last Monday in April) Birthday of Jefferson Davis (last Monday in May)

NORTH CAROLINA	Birthday of Robert E. Lee (January 19) Confederate Memorial Day (May 10)
SOUTH CAROLINA	Birthday of Robert E. Lee (January 19) Confederate Memorial Day (May 10) Birthday of Jefferson Davis (June 3)
TEXAS	Confederate Heroes Day (January 19)
VIRGINIA	Birthdays of Robert E. Lee and Stonewall Jackson (third Monday in January)

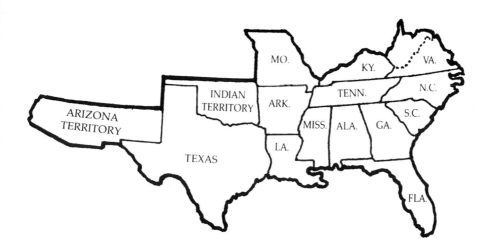

THE CONFEDERACY IN 1861

In its first year, the Confederacy included the southern half of the two future states of New Mexico and Arizona, and the entire state of Virginia, whose western counties would become the Union state of West Virginia in 1863. Although the secession governments of Kentucky and Missouri were quickly overrun by Union hordes, some form of Confederate government continued to operate in both states throughout the War. The five Indian nations in Indian Territory became the only official allies the Confederacy ever had.

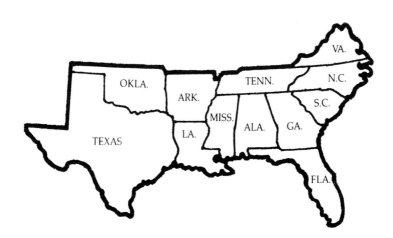

THE SOUTH TODAY

Most current political maps do not include Kentucky and Missouri, although there are many loyal southerners in both states who, due to their history more than their geography, consider themselves southern.

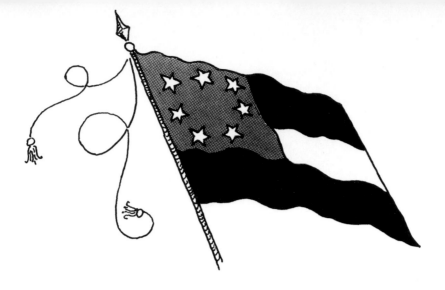

THE STARS AND BARS

This was the first Confederate flag adopted by the Confederate Congress. It was raised on March 4, 1861, at Montgomery, Alabama. The seven stars represented the seven states which had seceded at that time.

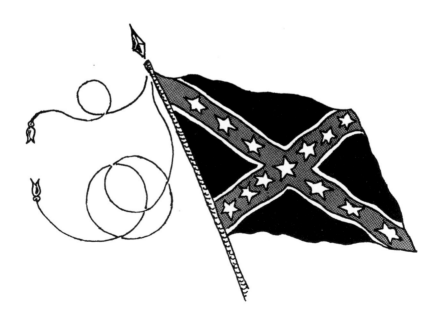

THE BATTLE FLAG

General Beauregard introduced this flag for use upon the battlefield in October, 1861, after the Stars and Bars became mistaken for the U.S. flag at the Battle of Manassas in July. The original flags were square, although the navy jack and the flags in the Army of Tennessee were rectangular, as shown here. This flag was never officially adopted but, through general usage, has become the favorite and is generally known today as *The Confederate Flag.*

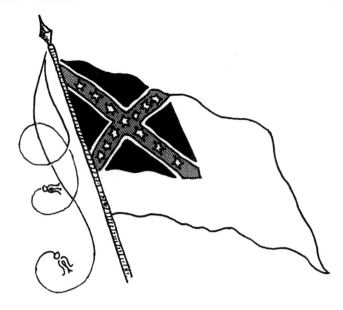

THE STAINLESS BANNER

A magnificent flag, this one was officially adopted on May 1, 1863, by Congress. Its main feature was a smaller version of the increasingly popular Battle Flag, resting upon a large field of pure white. Its drawback upon the battlefield was that, when hanging limp from a pole, it resembled a white flag of truce; consequently, the Battle Flag continued to be the favorite in the field.

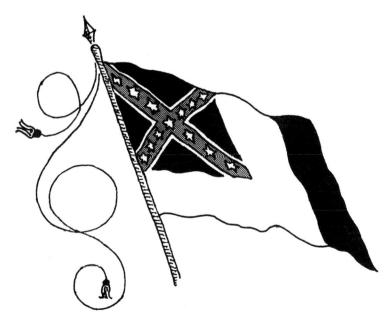

THE LAST OFFICIAL CONFEDERATE FLAG

By adding a red bar across the end of the Stainless Banner, Congress hoped to remedy the "flag of truce" problem, but it came too late to be of practical use. This flag was adopted on March 4, 1865, only thirty-seven days before Lee was forced to surrender at Appamattox.

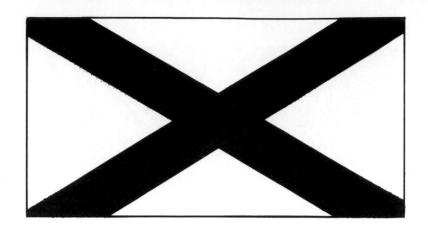

ALABAMA   (Adopted in 1895)

FLORIDA   (Adopted in 1899)

Four noble southern states have honored the Confederate flag by incorporating its entire design or its principal feature, the St. Andrew's Cross, into their individual state banners.

GEORGIA   (Adopted in 1956)

MISSISSIPPI   (Adopted in 1894)

SALUTE TO THE CONFEDERATE FLAG

"I salute the Confederate flag with affection, love, and undying remembrance."

This salute is used by the United Daughters of the Confederacy. Another version, used by the Sons of Confederate Veterans, is:

"I salute the Confederate flag with affection, reverence, and undying devotion to the Cause for which it stands."

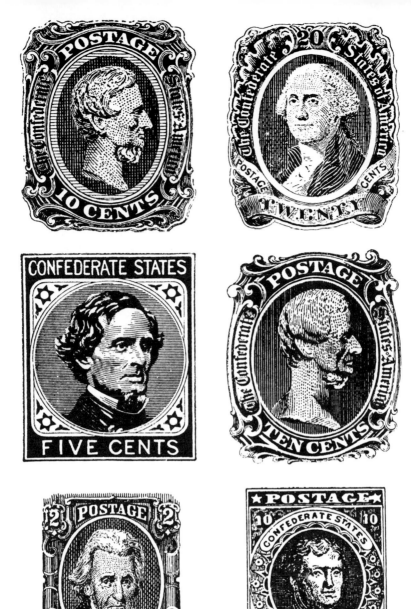

CONFEDERATE POSTAGE STAMPS

These ornately decorated stamps, bearing the likenesses of George Washington, Jefferson Davis, Andrew Jackson, and Thomas Jefferson, are shown here approximately 275% larger than the actual stamps. Postmaster-General John H. Reagan established the Confederate postal system under the most trying circumstances of war and a blockaded coast, but, to the amazement of the South and other watchful eyes, he soon had it operating so efficiently that not only did it break even, it showed a modest profit as well.

Examples of Confederate currency, shown here at 70% of original size.

Examples of Confederate currency, shown here at 70% of original size.

This Confederate Monument at Palmyra, Missouri, was dedicated in 1907 to the memory of ten innocent men executed by the Yankees in 1862. It still stands on the courthouse lawn, and is surrounded by the same fence, which features four short fence posts topped by authentic cannon balls from the War. This photograph is from an old post card made about 1910. *See story in Chapter VIII.*

86

**THE GREAT SEAL
OF THE
CONFEDERACY**

**THE
SOUTHERN CROSS
OF HONOR**

    The southern soldier came home to desolation, wreck, ruin, and the grave. There were no Federal pensions or medals for soldiers who wore the gray. Southern states, laboring under severe financial burdens, still managed to provide small pensions for destitute veterans, and in 1900, the UDC began presenting a medal of valor for Confederate veterans who had served honorably during the War. The bestowals were to end in 1913, but in 1912, after 78,761 medals had been awarded, the UDC voted to extend the bestowals indefinitely. Each and every cross has been numbered and recorded in Richmond.

Was Gen. John Hunt Morgan really killed in 1864, or did he assume the name of Dr. John Hunt Cole and live until 1899? The photo at left is of Dr. Cole at about the age of 65 or 70. The other picture is a photograph-portrait of Morgan when he was about 37 years old. Could these two men be one and the same? *See story in Chapter VIII.*

The annual Reunion of Confederate Veterans was cause for great celebration in the South. The host city was transformed into a wonderland of festivities. In 1901, Little Rock was the scene of the UCV Reunion, and this piece of music was written especially for the event. (Courtesy Devereaux D. Cannon, Jr.)

The birthplace of Jefferson Davis is marked by this towering monument at Fairview, Kentucky. It is the tallest concrete-cast obelisk in the world and the fourth tallest monument in the United States. It was constructed between 1917 and 1924 with funds raised by the old Confederate veterans and the UDC.

DIXIE

D. D. E.

DAN D. EMMETT

1. I wish I was in de land ob cot - ton,
2. Dar's buck - wheat cakes an'___ In - jen bat - ter,

Old times dar am not for-got-ten, Look a - way! Look a - way! Look a - way! Dix-ie
Makes you fat, or a lit - tle fat - ter, Look a - way! Look a - way! Look a - way! Dix-ie

Land. In Dix - ie Land whar I was born in, Ear - ly on one
Land. Den hoe it down an' scratch your grab-ble, To Dix - ie Land I'm

frost - y morn - in', Look a - way! Look a - way! Look a - way! Dix-ie Land!
bound to trab - ble, Look a - way! Look a - way! Look a - way! Dix-ie Land!

CHORUS

Den I wish I was in Dix-ie, Hoo-ray! (hoo-ray) Hoo-ray! (hoo-ray) In Dix-ie Land I'll

take my stand to lib and die in Dix - ie; A - way, a - way, a -

A - way, a - way,

way down south in Dix - ie, A - way, a - way, a - way down south in Dix - ie.

A - way, a - way,

An old copy of *Dixie,* the "National Anthem of the South." Though generally attributed to Daniel Decatur Emmett, a northerner, the tune was sung by steamboat workers long before Emmett wrote it down in 1859. There is also the belief that the original words were written by a southerner named William Shakespeare Hays. The report of its having been taught to music students at La Grange, Tennessee, in 1858, further clouds its origin. Several versions have been sung through the years, but the words appearing here are the most popular throughout the South.

The original Ku Klux Klan (1866-1877) played a vital role in ridding the post-war South of brutal carpetbag rule. This 1921 poster advertises the classic silent movie, *The Birth of a Nation*, based upon Thomas Dixon's novel about the KKK, entitled *The Clansman. See Chapter V.*

IV

THE WAR

Granny, in a delightful episode of TV's *Beverly Hillbillies*, was trying to educate somebody — probably Jethro — about the War Between the States. In only one sentence, she explained the War. "It was when the North invaded America!"

That's the best description I've ever heard. And it's just about the way southerners feel about it. The real spirit of America — independence, individual liberty, a readiness to defend America's honor — seems to spring from southern soil. The conservative South has always been the bulwark against liberalism and socialism when it seemed that northern ideas were allowing the country to drift in that direction, and southerners are the ones who can be counted on to dig in and say "No" to radical change. After all, we've always felt a bit motherly toward the Constitution and the principles connected with that great document and the early days of this republic. We're usually the last to be convinced, if at all, that change is needed in that noble charter, and we are not in the habit of questioning the intent or the wisdom of those statesmen

93

of two hundred years ago who produced it and gave us our first taste of liberty.

Not to diminish the heroic efforts of northern colonists, such as Benjamin Franklin, Samuel Adams, Nathan Hale, and Paul Revere, southerners, nevertheless, have always regarded the institution of self-rule in this country as a fundamentally southern enterprise, and with good reason. Names like George Washington, Patrick Henry, George Mason, James Madison, Thomas Jefferson, James Monroe, the Lees, and the Randolphs, all belong to Virginia. Jefferson wrote the Declaration of Independence, Henry initiated the call to arms, Washington commanded the armies, Randolph presided over the Constitutional Convention, and Madison became the "Father of the Constitution." Nine of our first twelve presidents were southern-born, six of them from Virginia alone.

In light of the nation's early history, it's not too difficult to understand Granny's estimation of the conflict, and one can but imagine the shock and outrage at the thought of northern troops invading the virtual footstool of liberty. Southerners, who had no intention of invading anybody, were aghast as northern plans became more evident. Robert E. Lee was the most notable of many southern military men who were asked by an upstart president named Lincoln to take up arms and invade their native states, an invasion that meant Lee would have to attack Virginia, the home of his father, Revolutionary hero Light Horse Harry Lee. Such propositions would have been thought ludicrous had they not been urged with such diabolical solemnity.

It was a collision of two different worlds, and perhaps the course had been set for some time. Southerners were, no doubt, expecting confrontation of some kind. After all, there had been strife between gentlemen in the halls of Congress for years, but an *armed invasion* was not expected by the populace in general. Southerners considered secession a peaceful solution, and notwithstanding exhortations to military preparedness by some of their farsighted leaders, they were caught terribly unprepared for a prolonged defense of their borders when the invasion materialized.

More than 125,000 volumes have been written about the War, and there seems to be no final chapter that satisfies the thirst of those who study the conflict. This lone chapter, or even this one book, can but whet the appetite for further information about that cataclysmic event; consequently, a suggested reading list is furnished in the last chapter of this text for those who wish to delve into the wealth of material existing in libraries and bookstores. The recommended works are primarily those written from a southern viewpoint, on the assumption that southerners write from something akin to a first-hand account, owing largely to the fact that the War happened to us in our own "backyards." Indeed, in the case of many of the suggested volumes, the accounts are written by actual survivors who give vivid details of the calamity of that war. The emphasis upon reading southern literature is guided by the same reasoning that prompts us to look to the Jews for the most credible records concerning their persecutions in the Holocaust, rather than to the voice of Naziism for its feeble defense and glorification of those heinous crimes.

If most readers are like me, they will make only a small dent in the tons of information available to us today. To expedite the acquisition of a fundamental grasp of the War, the following three works are recommended as a must, especially for interested readers who consider themselves beginners in a study of the most fascinating war in the annals of history. Edward A. Pollard's *Southern History of the War* was written as the War happened, year by year, though it is not in the form of a diary. Pollard was the editor of the *Richmond Examiner*, and as such, had a forum in which he could — and did — vent his wrath against Jefferson Davis, blaming him with many of the government's problems. Mary Boykin Chestnut's *Diary From Dixie* is precisely what the title indicates, a diary. It covers every topic under the sun from 1861 through 1865 and is considered the best-kept diary of the War, becoming a history best-seller in 1981. Incidentally, Mrs. Chestnut provides a happy balance against Pollard's anti-Davis stance with her unflagging support for the man through his trials as president of a vanishing nation. The third book, entitled *Gray Fox*, is enjoying a new popularity in the 1981 reprint of Burke Davis's splendid work about Robert E. Lee. Not only does it bring Lee to life for the reader, it contains a wealth of information about the fighting in Virginia, a major theater of the War.

There have been many names given to that conflict of 125 years ago, including *The War for Southern Independence*, *The War of the Rebellion*, *The War Against Northern Aggression*, and a few facetious names, among them *The Late Unpleasantness*. Over one hundred designations have been assigned to that war, the two most frequently heard, of course, being *The Civil War* (used chiefly by northerners and those southerners who are unaware of its offensive nature) and *The War Between the States* (used almost exclusively by southerners and those who are pro-South in their convictions).

The term *Civil War* has always been opposed by southerners on the grounds that it was not, as Lincoln tried for four years to imagine, an internal war among the citizens of the same country. In true ostrich-like fashion, he pretended that the Confederate States of America did not exist upon the planet Earth. For all of his buffoonery, though, Lincoln, surprisingly enough, was a master of intricate political manipulation, and in this case his objective was to convince the world that there were simply a few uprisings in several of the states of his protectorate, thereby giving him some perceived moral right to military invasion of those states. Southerners, on the other hand, cited the Constitution and the rights of sovereign states to disengage themselves from each other as readily as they had chosen to engage in the first place. The new nation formed by the withdrawing states necessarily precluded the use of the term *civil war*, and southerners viewed it as a war between a nation of southern states and a nation of northern states, hence the term *War Between the States.*

Today, the average person uses the term, *Civil War,* without making a distinction between the two labels, not in a conscious effort to defend Lincoln's academic position, but because he is more familiar with the concise expression, *Civil War.* One event that paved the way for southerners to include *Civil War* in their vocabulary occurred in 1961, the beginning of the centennial of the War. Every state that was involved in the conflict, north and south, was to create a centennial commission which would cooperate with the National Civil War Centennial Commission, for the purpose of coordinating commemorative events throughout the four-year observance. After some resistance, the southern states were prevailed upon to use the term *Civil War* for the sake of uniformity. Even so, southerners who understand the War's ramifications usually defer to the wisdom of the past and continue to speak of *The War Between the States.*

Generally speaking, a specific label isn't even required, for southerners simply talk about *The War,* as if there had never been another armed conflict since '65. Everything in the South is dated by the War. "That was before the War" . . . "My folks were ruint by the War" . . . "I reckon it happened about fifty years after the War." That War, that catastrophe of monumental proportions, was enough to cause anything since to pale in comparison. Coupled with the black years of persecution called Reconstruction, the War did become a milestone, or should we say *the* milestone of southern history. An entire civilization was completely turned upside down and dared by ruthless watchdogs, who wielded bayonets over a disarmed southern citizenry, to pick itself up. Not just any civilization. Not by any means. This society was among the most highly-developed in the world. It was a nation of people endowed by nature and in love with the arts. A highly refined agricultural class of people, tillers of nature's soil, the southern culture reflected a people at peace with nature and one another. The war that demolished that system is, then, truly the South's point of reference, for the halcyon world that existed before is no more than a fond memory.

Time heals all wounds, so they say, and today North and South are much more tolerant of the differences which exist between them, differences which will always be there to some degree, but which are becoming remarkably less all the time. That feeling of good will is much to be desired, although the very unity that promotes the harmonious relations has a way of demanding its toll, in this case the exaction being our individuality and recognition as a distinct section of the country. The quaint, provincial charm that once was ours has given way to the rule of Wall Street, and the same fast-food strips that feed our northern neighbors have blighted every one of our once-alluring southern cities. Atlanta's skyline could be Detroit's, or Pittsburgh's. In the prosperous South of the 1980's, we are stampeding toward anonymity and boring conformity to a way of life which is only a carbon copy of another culture. That's the price we pay. If we could achieve the better relations and at the same time retain the uniqueness of our heritage, it would be the course of wisdom.

Each year, as we move further away from the scenes of the War, the very years themselves diminish the bitterness, the acute feelings, and the personal involvement with the issues of the conflict. We laugh at our North-South jokes and cooperate in sports, music, and leisure-time activities in an overall spirit of congeniality, quite unlike the days preceding and immediately following the War. But, do we really want to reduce our grasp of the War Between the States to a Blue-Gray football game in Montgomery? I think not.

There is virtue in remembering. Not all memories are pleasant ones by any means; some are quite odious. The survivors of Hitler's concentration camps know this better than anyone. If, however, we refuse to remember, we fall victim to our own carelessness, and fulfill the old saying, "Those who

ignore the mistakes of the past are doomed to repeat them."
The Jews must never forget the Holocaust, and southerners must
not forget the War.

The invasion of the South was so senseless, so unnecessary.
The burning of homes, destruction of entire communities,
pillaging, looting, killing, violation of southern women, torture,
summary executions. All of it was so uncalled for. Gentlemen
should have been able to bid each other farewell and part
company without firing a shot. To the credit of the leadership
of the South, let it be said that this course of action was pursued
vigorously, and to the credit of many in the North, it was equally
acceptable. At first, even the influential Horace Greely, in his
New York Tribune, proclaimed, "Wayward Sisters, Depart in Peace!"
Unfortunately, the constant drumbeat of Abe Lincoln and the
fanatic abolitionists who had raised him to sudden power
drowned out the voices of reason, and once the War was
enjoined, converted many of the former peacemakers.

In her diary, Mrs. Chestnut noted the war hysteria sweeping
the North.

> The New York Tribune is so unfair. It began
> howling to get rid of us. We were so wicked. Now
> that we are so willing to leave them to their over-
> righteous self-consciousness, they cry "crush our
> enemy or they will subjugate us." The idea, that we
> want to invade or to subjugate! We would only be
> too grateful to be let alone. Only let us alone. We ask
> no more, of Gods or men.[1]

Such absolute perfidy reigned throughout the Lincoln
regime that any early hopes of peace were dashed to pieces
by pure deceit. Lincoln needed a war. His political back was
against the wall, and war seemed the only way out. For his
relentless manipulation of events which precipitated the awful
conflict, he earned the dubious distinction of creating one of

the most widely used contemporary terms for the calamity: *Mr. Lincoln's War.*

Lincoln was the tragic figure of the War, if, indeed, anyone can be more tragic than war's victims. A rough-cut, backwoods character who claimed he had educated himself, he was always running for some kind of public office and, just as often, losing. A tall, gangling, awkward fellow with crude manners, he literally stumbled into the presidency by a quirk of fate. His only base of support was the abolitionist Republican party, the fanatic element of the day, whose leaders kept them worked into a frenzy. His campaign remarks had inflamed and frightened seven states so badly that they seceded upon the mere news of his election, and his presidency became the first sectional administration of the Union. He lost a son during the War; his wife became mentally unbalanced; and, he was nearly defeated in the election of 1864 due to the unpopularity of his war. He was inexperienced and virtually unqualified to guide the nation in its moment of crisis but ended up with the job that would send over 360,000 northern boys to an early death. And, then somebody shot him.

Mr. Lincoln was keenly aware that his chances for the unlikely goal of president rested solely with the Abolitionist Republicans' extremely sectional appeal to northerners. They had no delusions of support in the South; in fact, most southern states didn't even put Lincoln's name on the ballot. By promising the North every plum of victory, including that one item that lay at the bottom of the eternal division, a high tariff on imported goods which would force the South to buy manufactured items from the North at inflated prices, Honest Abe had served warning to the South as to what his election held in store for it. The Democrats split into factions, and four men ran for the presidency, virtually assuring the election of the partisan Lincoln.

In December, 1860, when the results were known, South Carolina called for a state convention which first met at the

Baptist Church in Columbia, then, due to a small-pox epidemic, removed itself to Charleston, where, on December 20, the state voted unanimously to sever its ties with the United States. Years of fighting those same issues that Lincoln now championed had come to a head, and southerners who had very deliberately considered their options for several years, met in state conventions throughout the lower South and systematically voted to secede from the Union. Forty-three days after South Carolina's brave lead, all seven states of the Deep South were out of the clutches of the new administration.

Meeting in Montgomery, Alabama, in February, 1861, the seven seceded states formed the Confederate States of America and selected Jefferson Davis as the provisional president. They immediately set about organizing a government similar to the one their ancestors had fashioned for the United States, adopting the same Constitution with minor changes that clarified states' rights once and for all. Limited military preparations were begun as a precaution, though there were many voices, North and South, advocating compromise and peaceful coexistence. Wishing to avoid what might be a ruinous war, an event which would hinder the already complicated and precarious task of instituting a complex new government, to say nothing of the prospective loss of life that such a war would visit upon the people, the Confederacy sent a peace commission to Washington for the purpose of securing peace with the United States, negotiating removal of Federal troops from Fort Sumter, and settling all claims of public property.

The embassy, composed of Martin J. Crawford of Georgia, Alfred B. Roman of Louisiana, and John Forsyth of Alabama, traveled to Washington and requested a meeting with Lincoln's Secretary of State, William H. Seward, on March 12, exactly one month to the day before the Battle of Fort Sumter would launch the two nations into actual war. Tension was in the air, a tension heightened by the puzzling tenacity with which Mr. Lincoln doggedly held on to two military bases in the Confederacy while the U.S. government had abandoned scores of others without a great deal of obvious reluctance.

From the beginning, there was an air of mystery and lack of protocol surrounding the treatment of the peace commissioners in Washington. The president never officially recognized them, and Secretary of State Seward would communicate with them only through Supreme Court Justice John A. Campbell. President Davis, in Montgomery, was baffled over the lack of information received from the peace embassy, who in turn were puzzled by the stalling efforts on the part of Mr. Lincoln.

The Confederacy was asking that Federal troops be removed from Fort Pickens, Florida, and Fort Sumter, which lies in the harbor at Charleston, South Carolina. The underlying question: What was Mr. Lincoln's purpose for forcing two garrisons of northern soldiers to remain in disputed territory? His cabinet, even though made up of rabid abolitionists, advised him to evacuate Fort Sumter, as did his General of the Army, Winfield Scott. All kinds of peace proposals were flying throughout the North, and southern peace commissioners were on the steps of the Washington capitol. Still, Mr. Lincoln refused even to convene Congress in this crisis until as late as July, 1861, long after the guns of war had decided the issue. James David Altman, historical analyst from Charleston, South Carolina, recently wrote, "Faced with a delicate situation of such national importance as he was in the spring and summer of that year, it seems odd that Lincoln did not desire the aid of Congress to search for a peaceful solution during those turbulent months."[2]

Fort Sumter is an island fortress, whose Federal troops had exhausted their food supplies soon after South Carolina seceded from the Union. Since January 20, the governor of the state had been supplying food daily to the garrison, which consisted of about 130 military personnel, while patiently awaiting their hoped-for removal. While the month of March dragged on, Justice Campbell could get little out of Lincoln or Seward as to the future of the men stranded at Fort Sumter. Occasionally, he reported to the peace ambassadors from Dixie that Seward had assured him of the president's intention to evacuate the fort, but the commissioners were noticing an extremely increased military activity in Washington. The capitol was taking on the look of a fortified city, and soldiers were arriving in droves. The Mediterranean squadron was ordered home, as were other forces, and several ships were being outfitted in New York for a journey somewhere.

Altman writes, "Was it Lincoln's intention for war to begin at Fort Sumter? Historical evidence seems to point to that conclusion. There were many people in the North who were opposed to coercing the southern states back into the Union. Certainly there was little groundswell support for an overly aggressive policy on the part of the United States. Lincoln knew this, and yet he also was aware that should it appear that it was the Southern Confederacy that began hostilities, the Northern people would feel themselves symbolically injured and would rally to the flag."[3]

Rose O'Neal Greenhow, the Confederate spy who moved in the best of Washington's society circles, confronted Oregon's Senator Edward D. Baker, a close advisor of Lincoln's, on the issue of Fort Sumter. His reply was revealing. "It is true, a great many lives may be lost, and we may not succeed in reinforcing Fort Sumter. But the President was elected by a Northern majority, and they are now becoming dissatisfied; and the President owes it to them to strike some blow by which he will make a unified Northern party."[4]

During March, while both countries waited for some kind of solution, Lincoln sent two of his political cronies on separate surreptitious visits to Charleston to determine the attitude of the people of Charleston toward the Union and the secession movement. Of course, he found that Charlestonians were solidly opposed to the old Union and would look upon an effort to send military provisions to the Yankees at Fort Sumter as an act of war. As a cover for the subterfuge, his second agent, Ward Lamon, paid a visit to Governor Pickens, declaring he was there for the purpose of arranging the removal of the garrison. Even the fort's commander, Major Anderson, having already advised the president that it was too late to provision the fort, was of the opinion that he and all of his troops would soon be sent home.

Thus it was of tremendous shock, when suddenly, on April 8, the Lincoln government rebuffed the Confederate peace ambassadors and announced to Governor Pickens that twelve vessels with an aggregate force of 285 guns and 2,400 men had already sailed for Fort Sumter! Confusion reigned supreme. Major Anderson, inside the fort, wrote to Washington, "I ought to have been informed that this expedition was to come. Colonel Lamon's remarks convinced me that the idea, merely hinted at to me by Captain Fox, would not be carried out. We shall strive to do our duty, though I frankly say that my heart is not in the war which I see is thus to be commenced. That God will still avert it, and cause us to resort to pacific measures to maintain our rights, is my ardent prayer."[5]

In Montgomery, President Davis and his cabinet tried to come to some kind of decision before the heavily armed Yankee fleet reached Charleston. Their dilemma: If the Confederacy demanded surrender (which would surely be rejected by Major Anderson) and had to take the fort by force, then history would record that the South had fired the first shot in a terrible war; on the other hand, if no action were taken until the fort was strengthened by a massive fleet, countless lives would be lost in an extensive battle. Lincoln's debating days, in which he had mastered the technique of placing his opponent in a dilemma, were serving him well in this situation, even though the interest of peace was ill-served by his political *savoir faire*.

Weighing the matter heavily, President Davis opted for the plan which might avoid the effusion of blood, and correspondingly ordered General Beauregard to take the fort as soon as possible. Beauregard responded in a letter of April 11 to the commander of the fort.

> SIR: The Government of the Confederate States has hitherto forborne from any hostile demonstration against Fort Sumter, in the hope that the Government of the United States, with a view to the amicable adjustment of all questions between the two Governments, and to avert the calamities of war, would voluntarily evacuate it.
>
> There was reason at one time to believe that such would be the course pursued by the Government of the United States, and under that impression my Government has refrained from making any demand for the surrender of the fort. But the Confederate States can no longer delay assuming actual possession of a fortification commanding the entrance of one of their harbors, and necessary to its defense and security.
>
> I am ordered by the Government of the Confederate States to demand the evacuation of Fort Sumter. My aides, Colonel Chestnut and Captain Lee, are authorized to make such demand of you. All proper facilities will be afforded for the removal of yourself and command, together with company arms and property, to any post in the United States which you may select. The flag which you have upheld so long and with so much fortitude, under the most trying circumstances, may be saluted by you on taking it down.
>
> I am, sir, very respectfully, your obedient servant,
> G.T. BEAUREGARD,
> Brigadier General, Commanding

Major Anderson replied that he could not surrender; whereupon, General Beauregard sent word that he would open fire in one hour. As luck would have it, the Confederates, racing to reduce the fortress before reinforcements arrived, were aided by a storm at sea and a mixup in orders which resulted in delay of the expected entry into Charleston Harbor of the expedition fleet. The battle erupted with the simultaneous appearance of some of the ships who had reached their rendezvous point in the offing of the harbor. Though the battle raged from 4:20 a.m., April 12, until 1:30 p.m., April 13, the fleet made not one move from its observation position, even when the fort caught on fire at two separate times. General Beauregard sent an offer to help in extinguishing the second conflagration; whereupon, Major Anderson took advantage of the opportunity afforded by the temporary truce and made the surrender he had rejected nearly two days earlier.

There had been no casualties, and General Beauregard's terms were lenient. He allowed Major Anderson to keep his surrendered sword and lower his flag with ceremony, guaranteeing him safe passage out of the harbor. During the gun salute to the flag, an accidental explosion killed one man and mortally wounded another, the only casualties of the entire affair. As the troops were being ferried out of Charleston Harbor, bound for New York on the steamer *Isabel*, they passed by the Confederate batteries on Cummings Point, where the southern soldiers stood in silence with uncovered heads, paying tribute to the reluctant warriors who had so gallantly defended themselves.

The first major battle was now history. What had begun as a gentlemen's war would end exactly four years later as a holocaust, punctuated by deeds of savagery against the inhabitants of the invaded South. Infamous reputations would follow Generals Sheridan, Wilson, "Beast" Butler, Sherman, and a host of others, in their safari-like expeditions through the fabled land of cotton. Brevet Major George W. Nichols, staff officer of General Sherman, chronicled his experiences on the abominable "march to the sea" in a diary.

The solemn truth is, that the Southern people have never had any conception of the National Idea. They do not know what it is to be an American. . . .

. . . Our work has been the next thing to annihilation. . . .

. . . and then he (Sherman) added, "There is a class of people at the South who must be exterminated before there can be peace in the land." . . .

. . . Nearly all these places are deserted, although here and there we find children, whom it is difficult to persuade that they are not at once to be murdered. . . .

. . . it may be for the good of future generations that this Rebel horde should be swept from the earth. . . .

In the record of great wars we read of vast armies marching through an enemy's country, carrying death and destruction in their path; of villages burned, cities pillaged, a tribe or a nation swept out of existence. . . . History, however, will be searched in vain for a parallel to the scathing and destructive effect of the Invasion of the Carolinas.[6]

History is replete with wars, and it is too often true that war, in all its ghastly horror, is inaugurated for political advantage rather than to right some moral wrong. For the 20th century student of American history, it has always been difficult to ascertain the truth pertaining to the War's commencement because assassination tends to deify a character, as it certainly did in the case of Lincoln . True to form, the assassin's bullet worked its mysterious magic and seemed for almost a century to have absolved Lincoln of even the capability of ulterior motive. In the better light of the hindsight of 125 years, emotional analysis has given way to factual study, and modern historians are not so timid in accusing Mr. Lincoln of a political plot to prevent

107

peaceable relations between the Confederacy and the United States.

The scheme seems to have been primarily the handiwork of Secretary of State Seward, President Lincoln, and a political crony named Gustavus V. Fox, all Republicians. Lincoln's election was the first victory for the new Republican party, and already seven states had bolted the Union — a disastrous beginning for a new administration. The northern Democrats were furious, calling for peace, not war. One can but imagine the scenarios conjured up by the Republicans as they surveyed the dismal situation: possible impeachment of the new president; likely defeat in the Congressional elections of 1862; a reputation as the party that split the nation. Out of such desperate minds the plot was hatched. If the South could only be made to fire upon the flag, public opinion in the North would most likely crystallize in favor of the new president.

An observant English editor wrote of Lincoln, "He has thought that a political object was to be obtained by putting the Southerners in the wrong, if they could be maneuvered into firing the first shot."[7] His Secretary of the Navy, Gideon Welles, wrote, "It was very important that the Rebels strike the first blow in the conflict."[8] Lincoln's confidant, G.V. Fox, outlined the plan: "I simply propose three tugs convoyed by light-draft men-of-war. . . The first tug to lead in empty, to open their fire."[9]

Not waiting for Mr. Fox's grand scheme, of course, the Confederacy fired upon Fort Sumter, playing directly into the hands of the waiting Lincoln. The helplessness felt by southern diplomats was noted by E.A. Pollard. "Nothing was left but to accept the distinct challenge of the Lincoln government to arms."[10]

On May 1, 1861, after the commencement of war was a *fait accompli*, Lincoln explained to Fox, who was disappointed that the ships had arrived too late to have participated in the action of his own planning, "I sincerely regret that the failure of the attempt to provision Fort Sumter should be the source of annoyance to you. . . . You and I both anticipated that the cause of the country would be advanced by making the attempt to provision Fort Sumter, even if it should fail; and it is no small consolation now to feel that our anticipation is justified by the result."[11]

The action at Fort Sumter had the predicted effect. There arose an outcry in the North, and Lincoln called for 75,000 volunteers to "put down the rebellion." The seven states of the Confederacy — Alabama, Florida, Georgia, Louisiana, Mississippi, South Carolina, and Texas — were soon joined by four more southern states. Virginia was immediate in her action, seceding four days after Fort Sumter. By June 8, Arkansas, North Carolina, and Tenneesee had joined their southern neighbors. In the Indian Territory, each of the Five Civilized Tribes (Cherokee, Chickasaw, Choctaw, Creek, and Seminole) seceded in separate actions and, joining the Confederacy, became its only official allies.

Though Maryland was populated to a large extent by southerners, the reigns of government were quickly seized by the Lincoln government, preventing secession of that small state which encircles Washington, D.C. Many of Maryland's sons went south and joined regiments from other states, while some managed to organize a few Maryland units to fight for the South. Missouri and Kentucky had similar situations, though the southern sympathizers were numerous enough there to contribute large numbers of soldiers and sums of money to the Confederacy. In gratitude, the South determined that the two extra stars in the Confederate Battle Flag should stand for Kentucky and Missouri.

In the west, Arizona Territory was claimed by the Confederacy, and the southern half was reinforced by Confederate military units. The territory comprised the two present-day states of Arizona and New Mexico, and stayed in Confederate hands for about a year. Then, in the Battle of Glorieta Pass on March 28, 1862, the Confederates, after winning a victory there, had to fall back to Sante Fe because of the loss of their supply wagons, resulting in a gradual withdrawal from the entire west.

Today, the term *South* is both geographical and political, and generally refers to the eleven states of the old Confederacy, plus Oklahoma (formerly Indian Territory), although a large per cent of the populace in Missouri and Kentucky — perhaps a majority in Kentucky — lays claim, and rightly so, to the privilege of being called southern. Some overly enthusiastic cartographers include even West Virginia, Delaware, and Maryland, especially when commissioned by a commercial firm seeking to push some "southern" product. It's amusing to watch the borders of the South expand when a southern publication is looking for subscribers.

There were certainly peculiarities dividing North and South long before the War, but it was the collision of the two cultures that provided close encounters with each other, further defining and sharpening those differences. Each side viewed the other with corresponding contempt. An amusing, though earnest, illustration comes from Lee's march into Yankee territory just before the Battle of Gettysburg. As the Confederates entered Chambersburg, Pennsylvania, Mr. Hoke, an observant merchant in that city, believed that the Confederates were awe-struck with "the rich and beautiful country," and bragged that "the evident superiority of the country north of the Potomac to that south of it . . . excercised a discouraging effect upon the soldiers."[12]

They were stricken all right, but it wasn't with awe. Writing from the same city at the same time, a Confederate soldier, Captain Blackford, wrote to his wife in Virginia. "We are now in the Cumberland Valley, and a fine country it is — that is, as yankees count fineness — small farms divided into fields no larger than our garden, and barns much larger than the houses in which live their owners, their families and laborers. The land is rich and highly cultivated, much more highly than the men who own it. . . . While I note physical comfort, I see no signs of social refinement. All seem to be on a dead level, like a lot of fat cattle in a clover field. . . . You never saw a country so densely populated. . . . Never in my life have I seen as many ugly women since coming to this place."[13]

Captain Blackford would not long have to look at ugly women, however, for this was the last of only two times that General Lee took his troops north. Outside of a few cavalry dashes into the lower North by Gen. Jubal Early, Gen. John Hunt Morgan, Col. John S. Mosby, and other daring cavaliers, the War was fought exclusively in the South.

The armies were as different as night and day in nearly every conceivable aspect. One look at them, and the difference was apparent. Northern armies were always dressed according to regulation in an endless supply of new uniforms. As they progressed into the South, they stretched long supply lines behind them to various northern bases, assuring themselves of abundant food, medicine, toiletries, and items necessary to a comfortable life in the military. Yankee soldiers could crawl into tents at night and listen to the bands play their favorite tunes. None had to go barefooted, and there were ample overcoats and blankets during the cold winters.

Ammunition was no problem to the Federal army. The great northern factories turned out armaments of war faster than the Yankees could use them, and eventually, the introduction of the repeating Spencer rifle gave them an advantage that was tantamount to victory. While Confederate soldiers had to drop back and load their old muskets after every single round, Yankees could fire in rapid succession, decimating ranks of re-loading southerners.

The ever-increasing cavalry units rode on the finest horses, outfitted with the finest saddles to be found anywhere in the world. There were adequate numbers of doctors and nurses attending the Union army, with an ample number of ambulance wagons to transport the wounded behind the lines for treatment.

In all, it was a well-heeled army and a well-oiled operation.

The North had the factories and the population, as well as the money, to back such an effort. There were approximately 22,000,000 people in the northern states at the outbreak of war. Replenishment of their army was never in doubt. From their masses, the army steadily increased throughout the four years of conflict until southern soldiers were outnumbered by three to one.

It was a different story in the South. The Confederate soldier has been called the "Eighth Wonder of the World." How a southern army stayed in the field for four years under the conditions with which it was faced has not yet been fully answered. As Burke Davis said, "No one had ever seen such an army."[14]

When uniforms were available, many of the men would resemble one another in their Confederate gray, but often it was a mixture of homespun outfits that merely tried to give the appearance of anything but the Yankee blue. The most common homemade uniform consisted of a pair of pants and a shirt or coat dyed with the hulls of the butternut, or walnut tree. After several months, uniforms could be more truthfully described as rags, with little hope of replacing them at frequent intervals.

The shoe supply was a matter more serious. In 1862, the First South Carolina reported 100 of its 300 men barefooted in northern Virginia, where General Alexander said, "The lack of shoes is deplorable, and barefooted men with bleeding feet were no uncommon sight. . . . For rations, we were indebted mostly to the fields of roasting ears, and to the apple orchards."[15] On November 15, 1862, General Longstreet's men started on a long march to Fredericksburg, about 3,500 of them without shoes. Lack of shoes was a continual problem, made worse for the soldiers of Stonewall Jackson, who took his acclaimed infantry on so many of those famous rapid flanking marches that they were referred to as Jackson's "foot cavalry." It was said that

Jackson's scantily shod forces were easily tracked in the snow by the blood from their feet.

Food was meager at best. Meat was scarce, and sometimes a biscuit would be one day's rations. Just before the end, General Wise complained to General Lee that his men had not had a bite for more than a week; whereupon, General Lee searched until he found a small portion of food to divide among them. His own breakfast that very day had been a cup of tea from the kindness of a nearby home. It was often that men would go two or three days without a meal, and many times that meal came from whatever was growing along the road. A few kernels of corn could be carried in the pocket until the army stopped long enough for it to be parched. General Lee once said that he had lost more men from lack of proper food than to enemy bullets.

Many of these soldiers were men from plantations, sons of wealthy and educated figures in southern society, now living in trenches with not a tent over their heads, suffering from scurvy, dysentery, and lice. Starvation was their lot; yet, when a shipment of bacon made it through the blockade from Nassau and was offered to Lee's troops, some regiments voluntarily turned over food to the poor in Richmond who were as destitute as the lowly soldier.

In late June, 1863, as Lee's men passed through Chambersburg, Pennsylvania, a citizen of that northern community described them. "The Confederate infantry . . . presented a solid front. They came in close marching order . . . their dress consisted of every imaginable color and style, the butternut predominating. . . . Hats, or the skeletons of what once had been hats, surmounted their partly covered heads. Many were ragged, shoeless, and filthy . . ." though "well armed and under perfect discipline. They seemed to move as one vast machine."[16]

There were few factories in the South to manufacture the needs of war. The 4,000 miles of coastline had been blockaded by U.S. ships, and the northern borders of the Confederacy were lined with Yankee troops. The South was virtually an island, unprepared to sustain itself apart from world commerce. Lacking an effective navy, it lay isolated from Europe's supplies.

At the end of four toilsome years, General Gordon, surrounded by his affectionate men just after Lee's surrender, looked over his beleaguered boys in gray and shouted to them, "Soldiers of the Second Army Corps! No mathematician can compute the odds against which you have contended!"[17] These odds included having to scramble around the battlefield after a fight, picking up bullets left by Yankees, so there would be ammunition enough for the next scrap.

The fundamental perception of war, itself, contrasted the two nations as lucidly as the physical condition of their armies. The wreckage strewn across the Southland from border to border was not merely that of military significance. The infamous northern general, W.T. Sherman, unabashedly declared war on the civilian population of the South, proclaiming that women and children must be made to feel the war as heavily as the soldier in the field. In her diary, Mrs. Chestnut called him a nightmare, a ghoul, and a hyena. He needlessly burned virtually everything in his meandering path from Atlanta to the sea, a distance of approximately 300 miles. His army, spread out over a width of sixty miles, destroyed homes, schools, churches, and entire communities. The heart of Georgia was cut out. Then, he turned northward and destroyed the center of the fine old state of South Carolina, home of many Revolutionary War heroes.

On March 5, 1865, writing from a refuge in Lincolnton, North Carolina (a town not named for Honest Abe!), Mrs. Chestnut had gotten word of the destruction in Columbia from a Catholic priest.

> Sherman's men had burned the convent. Mrs. Munroe had pinned her faith to Sherman, because he was a Catholic, and now! Father O'Connell saw the fire. The nuns and girls marched to the old Hampton

house and so saved it. They walked between files of soldiers. Men were rolling tar barrels and lighting torches to fling over the house when the nuns came. Columbia is but dust and ashes, burned to the ground. Men, women, and children are left there, houseless, homeless, without a particle of food. They are picking up the corn left by Sherman's horses in their picket ground and parching it to stay their hunger.[18]

There were, of course, men in U.S. uniform who were participating in the invasion of the South out of some vague sense of duty or who had been drafted against their will, and were repulsed at the wanton attacks against southern civilization. It is unfortunate, though, to have to believe that men of principle were the minor part of this alien force. The incursion of the South, which bore the novelty and sensation now associated with the excessive buffalo hunts of the western plains, was executed with a "soldier of fortune" abandon fostered by a widely held conviction in the North that southerners were the dregs of humanity and, therefore, legitimate prey. The imagined heathenism of the South seemed to assuage the guilt of violating the southern home and basic human decency.

Mrs. L.S. Hall, wife of a state legislator from Wetzel County, in the western part of Virginia, was forced to walk the streets of New Martinsville, her clothes tied in a bundle over her head. After being submitted to a terrible outrage, her home was burned by the Yankees.

William Gilmore Simms, the noted author, wrote about the scores of negro women who were molested by regiments of Yankees in sucessive relays. He told of a negro woman who was viciously assaulted in Columbia by northern soldiers, who then drowned her in a mud puddle. White women, likewise, were left to the mercy of unbridled Yankee soldiers, while their husbands and fathers were dying upon the war front. Yankees imprisoned women for the mere infraction of waving their handkerchiefs at passing southern prisoners, and subjected them

115

to indignities in their incarceration.

In the mountains of Virginia where partisan rangers, or guerillas, were sometimes the only effective resistance to the looting and burning, a ranger shot one fleeing bluecoat in the head and stopped to search his body. From a burning home, he had stolen women's clothing, wine, two bolts of cloth, sheets, curtains, and lace — all tied to his saddle. In his pockets were found jewelry and a letter from a northern girl who begged him to send her stolen things from some of the "Rebel" homes he passed.

The beautiful Shenandoah Valley was blackened from one end to the other by command of various officers, the most notorious being Gen. Phil Sheridan, a heartless individual who seemed to have a proclivity for playing with fire. At times he burned people out for simply having a gun in the house. Sometimes, he entertained himself by burning every fifth home. Upon occasion, he selected his target by accusing the occupants of sending a message by lantern to the Confederate guerillas on the hill, when in reality it had been only a grieving mother and father who had lit a lamp in the dark to read a message of death from the front. Sheridan decreed that any person who aided a partisan ranger in any way would be burned out immediately, the mere suspicion of which caused numberless burnings.

The Union officers, from Grant on down, were as guilty as those who committed the acts, for in their hands rested the power to prevent the atrocities; but, rather than forestall, they sent forth orders to wreak havoc. General Grant, in particular, was responsible for goading Sheridan toward his barbarity in the Shenandoah Valley, one of the richest and most beautiful sections of Virginia. As columns of smoke swirled skyward day after day, Sheridan was acquiring one of the vilest reputations of the war. With great alacrity he received Grant's brutal orders to hang any of Colonel Mosby's men they could find, *without trial,* and to abduct all of the families of Mosby's Rangers, taking them to Fort McHenry as hostages. In August of 1864, Sheridan rather boastfully sent a message back to Grant. "Mosby has annoyed me and captured a few wagons. We hung one and shot six of his men yesterday. I have burned all wheat and hay, and have brought off all stock, sheep, cattle, horses, etc. south of Winchester."[19]

Much of the blame for this overkill rests squarely at the top. Mr. Lincoln was constantly criticized for what had become a lengthy war with no end in sight. The election of 1864 was at hand, and the Democrats had chosen their candiate — George B. McClellan, a general whom Lincoln had removed from command in 1862. Even Lincoln's closest friends confided that he had no chance of being reelected. Always the politican, Lincoln increased his already relentless pressure upon his generals for more victories at any cost and a harsh prosecution of the war in general. Sherman's obliging devestation of Georgia delighted the president and, most importantly, provided the ten per cent margin by which he was soon reelected, a political victory bought with blood.

An officer attached to Sherman's command wrote of his disgust in a letter. "I tell you the truth when I say we are about as mean a mob as ever walked the face of the earth. It is perfectly frightful. If I lived in this country, I never would lay down my arms while a 'Yankee' remained on the soil. I do not blame Southerners for being secessionists now. I could relate many things that would be laughable if they were not so horribly disgraceful."[20]

Athens, Alabama, was invaded in 1862 by one of Lincoln's arsonist generals, Russian-born John B. Turchin, who told his troops that he would shut his eyes for an hour while they "stopped" in this town. After a while he noticed that all was relatively peaceful, so he inquired of his adjutant as to the expected torching of the city. No arson was reported. The general then said to inform the men that he would close his eyes for an hour and a half this time. Finally, the soldiers took the hint and fell to work looting, plundering, and burning Athens. In a rare show of discipline and conscience, his superiors had General Turchin court-martialed and dismissed from the service; however, when Lincoln got wind of it, he rewarded the Russian beast by restoring his command and handing him a promotion!

Nothing was sacred. On their way into Virginia, prior to the first large land battle of the war, Yankees had entered Bethel Church where they scrawled on holy walls, "Death to the traitors!" and "Down with the Rebels!"[21] Even though battle had not yet occurred on Virginia soil, Col. Daniel Hill had to send out a company to rout a bunch of Federal soldiers who were already plundering a house. William Gilmore Simms reported incidents of Yankees digging up fresh graves in search of jewerly buried with the dead.

Civilians seemed equally as determined to give no quarter. On the retreat from Gettysburg, a rapid flight to avoid being overtaken by the victorious Federal army, terribly wounded and dying soldiers had to be jostled along rough, rocky roads, all the while screaming in their death agony for help. General Imboden's cavalry rode ahead of the cumbersome, slow-moving wagons carrying the pitifully maimed men, most of whom hadn't eaten in thirty-six hours. At Greencastle, Pennsylvania, after the vanguard had passed through the town, leaving the wagons unprotected for a long stretch, about fifty citizens of the community rushed from the houses, and, wielding great axes, hacked the wheels of the wagons, collapsing them in the road. General Imboden furiously raced back to the town, rounded up all the guilty citizens he could find, and held them as prisoners of war. Several wagons had to be abandoned.

Without a doubt, the most senseless acts were those involving the torture of helpless prisoners in northern prisons. Only one instance of such contemptible behavior is sufficient to illustrate the horror. Taken from *Southern History of the War*, it is best told in Pollard's own poignant narrative.

This statement was taken from the lips of Captain

118

Calvin C. Morgan, a brother of the famous General Morgan.

Captain Morgan was among those of his brother's expedition who, in last July, were incarcerated in the penitentiary of Ohio. On entering this infamous abode, Captain Morgan and his companions were stripped in a reception room and their naked bodies examined there. They were again stripped in the interior of the prison, and washed in tubs by negro convicts; their hair cut close to the scalp, the brutal warden, who was standing by, exhorting the negro barber to "cut off every lock of their rebel hair." After these ceremonies, the officers were locked up in cells, the dimensions of which were thirty-eight inches in width, six and a-half feet in length, and about the same in height. In these narrow abodes our brave soldiers were left to pine, branded as felons, goaded by "convict-drivers," and insulted by speeches which constantly reminded them of the weak and cruel neglect of that government, on whose behalf, after imperilling their lives, they were now suffering a fate worse than death. But even these sufferings were nothing to what was reserved for them in another invention of cruelty without a parallel, unless in the secrets of the infernal.

It appears that, after General Morgan's escape, suspicion alighted on the warden, a certain Captain Merion, who, it was thought, might have been corrupted. To alleviate the suspicion (for which there were really no grounds whatever), the brute commenced a system of devilish persecution of the unfortunate Confederate prisoners who remained in his hands. One part of this system was solitary confinement in dungeons. These dungeons were close cells, a false door being drawn over the grating, so as to exclude light and air. The food allowed the occupants of these dark and noisome places, was three ounces of bread and half a pint of water per day. The four walls were bare of every thing but a water-bucket, for the necessities of nature, which was left for days to poison the air the prisoner breathed. He was denied a blanket; deprived of his overcoat, if he had one, and left standing or stretched with four dark, cold walls around him, with not room enough to walk in to keep up the circulation of his blood, stagnated with the cold, and the silent and unutterable horrors of his abode.

Confinement in these dungeons was the warden's sentence for the most trivial offences. On one occasion one of our prisoners was thus immured because he refused to tell Merion which one of his companions had *whistled contrary to the prison rules.* But the most terrible visitation of this demon's displeasure remains to be told.

Some knives had been discovered in the prisoners' cells, and Merion accused the occupants of meditating their escape. Seven of them, all officers, were taken to the west end of the building and put in the dark cells there. They were not allowed a blanket or overcoat, and *the thermometer was below zero.* There was no room to pace. Each prisoner had to struggle for life, as the cold benumbed him, by stamping his feet, beating the walls, now catching a few minutes of horrible sleep on the cold floor, and then starting up to continue, in the dark, his wrestle for life.

"I had been suffering from heart disease," says Captain Morgan, speaking of his own solitary confinement on another occasion. "It was terribly aggravated by the cold and horror of the dungeon in which I was placed. I had a wet towel, one end of which I pressed to my side; the other would freeze, and I had to put its frozen folds on my naked skin.

120

I stood this way all night, pressing the frozen towel to my side and keeping my feet going up and down. I felt I was struggling for my life."

Captain Morgan endured this confinement for eighteen hours, and was taken out barely alive. The other prisoners endured it for *sixteen days and nights.* In this time they were visited at different periods by the physician of the penitentiary — Dr. Loring — who felt their pulses, and examined their condition, to ascertain how long life might hold out under the exacting torture. It was awful, this ceremony of torture, this medical examination of the victims. The tramp of the prisoners' feet, up and down (there was no room to walk), as they thus worked for life, was incessantly going on. This black tread-mill of the dungeon could be heard all through the cold and dreary hours of the night. Dr. Loring, who was comparatively a humane person, besought Merion to release the unhappy men; said they had already been taxed to the point of death. The wretch replied, "They did not talk right yet." He wished them to humble themselves to him. He went into the cell of one of them, Major Webber, to taunt him. "Sir," said the officer, "I defy you. You can kill me, but you can add nothing to the sufferings you have already inflicted. Proceed to kill me; it makes not the slightest difference."

At the expiration of sixteen days the men were released from the dungeons. Merion said "he would take them out this time alive, but next time they offended, they would be taken out feet foremost." Their appearance was frightful; they could no longer be recognized by their companions. With their bodies swollen and discolored, with their minds bordering on childishness, tottering, some of them talking foolishly, these wretched men seemed to agree but in one thing — a ravenous desire for food.

"I had known Captain Coles," says Captain Morgan, "as well as my brother. When he came out of his dungeon, I swear to you I did not know him. His face had swollen to two or three times its ordinary size, and he tottered so that I had to catch him from falling. Captain Barton was in an awful state. His face was swollen and the blood was bursting from the skin. All of them had to be watched, so as to check them in eating, as they had been starved so long."

We had had in this war many examples of Yankee cruelty. But the statement given above, may be said to take precedence of all that had ever yet been narrated of the atrocities of the enemy; and it is so remarkable, both on account of its matter and the credit that must naturally attach to its authorship that we doubt whether the so-called civilized world of this generation has produced anywhere any well-authenticated story of equal horror.[22]

War, in all its ghastly array, is horrible enough without barbaric deeds and crimes against humanity, but it was precisely this excessive wickedness that generated the bitterness, hatred and mistrust toward the northern people that lasted so long. The very term *Yankee* is, to this day, one of the most offensive words in the southern vocabulary, although it is a shorter word nowadays than it used to be.

Reflecting the fundamental antithesis of North and South, southern society had difficulty comprehending such inhumanity. Chivalry was a system still in practice, and the southern code didn't allow for the depravity of hanging a teenager whose only fault lay in having written down the locations of Federal positions within his own hometown of Little Rock, Arkansas, which was then under Yankee occupation. Accused of being a spy, David Dodd was intimidated and hanged, and in a scene parallelling that of the young Sam Davis in Tennessee, he would not implicate another human being, saying "I will not betray a friend." His youthful body, frail and lean, was not heavy enough to choke him, so the officer ordered two privates to jump up and hang on to his legs until he died. All this, while an unarmed Little Rock citizenry looked on in horror, voicing an outcry that went mercilessly unheeded.

General Lee's prosecution of the War depicted the southern idea of what's fair in war and what isn't, procedures which were essentially embodied in the later Geneva Convention, an agreement between nations to insure humane treatment of prisoners of war, the sick, and the wounded. In addition, Lee's chivalric code forbade injustices against civilians and set the standard for Confederate military officers. His orders were published and read to his troops: "It must be remembered that we make war only upon armed men, and that we cannot take vengeance for the wrongs our people have suffered without lowering ourselves in the eyes of all whose abhorrence has been excited by the atrocities of our enemies . . ." and "offending against Him to whom vengeance belongeth."[23]

Lee took 75,000 men into Pennsylvania, clashing with the Federal army at the little village of Gettysburg. Behind them, their own homes lay in ashes, yet, according to renowned historian, Clifford Dowdey, they did not burn a single house in the enemy's land. Strict orders were issued against plundering, and foraging was to be done under supervision of officers. A British observer made note of the good behavior of the southern troops, writing that he saw none of the inhabitants disturbed or annoyed by the soldiers.

General Ewell had been the first to pass through the country, requisitioning provisions for his troops. When General Lee came upon the fertile Pennsylvania farmlands, a lady of the area visited him with the story that some citizens were starving because of General Ewell's recent visit. Lee replied, "We requisitioned to provide food for our troops, so that the men could be kept from coming into your houses themselves. God help you if I permitted them to enter your houses."[24] Always magnanimous, though, he told her to send a miller to the commissary officers, and he would see that they were provided with adequate flour.

There were southerners, true enough, who, out of sheer anger and desperation, would have retaliated against Yankee civilian property, although they remained in the minority while most southerners chose the high road taken by General Lee. Edward Pollard was a voice of the minority opinion which held that retaliatory destruction of northern civilian property might serve to shorten the War, which, incidentally, was an excuse used by the Yankee government to justify their depredations, and he often criticized Confederate reluctance to retaliate.

The fertile acres of the Pennsylvania valley were untouched by violent hands; all requisitions for supplies were paid for in Confederate money; and a protection was given to the private property of the enemy, which had never been afforded even to that of our own citizens. So far as the orders of Gen. Lee on these subjects restrained pillage and private outrage, they were sustained by public sentiment in the South, which, in fact, never desired that we should retaliate upon the Yankees by a precise imitation of their enormities and crimes. . . . Such a return for the outrages which the South had suffered from invading hordes of the Yankees, would in fact have been short of justice . . . But Gen. Lee was resolved on more excessive magnanimity; and at the time the Yankee armies, particularly in the Southwestern portion of the Confederacy, were enacting outrages which recalled the darkest days of medieval warfare, our forces in the Pennsylvania valley were protecting the private property of Yankees, composing their alarm, and making a display of stilted chivalry."[25]

Whether stilted or not, it was definitely chivalry. The officers of the Confederate Army, to a large degree, had come directly off the plantation, where an honor code was an integral part of the system. General Zollicoffer, upon entering Kentucky, announced that every citizen of that state, regardless of political allegiance, was to receive protection from the men of his command, an exact duplicate of General Lee's offer to the people of Maryland when he penetrated into that northern state. Out in Missouri, Gen. Sterling Price received the sword of the defeated Yankee, Colonel Mulligan, then promptly returned it to him, making Mulligan and his wife guests at his own headquarters while the colonel awaited exchange. General Price put his personal carriage at their disposal and offered them every courtesy.

These men were cavaliers. They were dashing, daring, and debonair. They captured the fancy of many women, North and South. These captivating courtiers, the last of the world's knightly warriors, were given to tipping their hats, serenading their ladies, and forever bowing. One impetuous Confederate officer — in all his glory — dashed into a Yankee town, trying to catch up with Lee's troops headed for Gettysburg. Having ridden through the familiar, friendly country of North Carolina and Virginia, he didn't realize how conspicuous his gray uniform had become as he crossed into enemy territory. When he rode straight into the village of Greencastle, Pennsylvania, hostile townspeople made him suddenly aware of the danger, at which point he covered his mortal fear by lifting his hat and bowing profusely to the startled villagers until he had literally bowed out of town.

A Yankee colonel gave a long account of the "soft-mannered Rebels" when he encountered Jeb Stuart's troops at Chambersburg. This was newsworthy stuff, as it wasn't often that northerners felt the presence of Rebels upon their own turf. He described their "politeness" and how they thanked him for his candor when informing them that he was a Republican.

He further related that these southerners "politely" asked him for food, and he commented as to how one private soldier bowed to him and asked for a few coals to light a fire.

Not to be forgotten, however, was the terrible fire with which Jeb Stuart could strike. And strike he did! The raid of October 9 and 10, 1862, wasn't all bowing and manners. He wrecked military stores, telegraph lines, and railroads used for carrying Yankee soldiers south; but, true to his chivalric instincts, he left private property unmolested.

A disparity developed from the very beginning concerning treatment of prisoners of war. In too many cases, southern soldiers in northern prisons were deprived of food, warmth, and medical attention, not because of any lack of supplies, but rather for punitive purposes. When emaciated northern prisoners were found in the southern prison camp at Andersonville, Georgia, near the end of the War, the universal belief in the North was that southerners had imitated the cruel punishment inflicted in northern prisons. A kangaroo court hastily convicted Capt. Henry Wirz, commander of the Confederate prison camp, and hanged him.

The North, while resting on full bellies, had continuously destroyed the South's food supply until Lee's troops were starving at Appomattox; yet, they naïvely tried to believe that the swollen population of Andersonville Prison, which numbered 35,000 (more men than were present for duty in many Confederate armies), were somehow to be fed like princes. In fact, the Confederate Congress had enacted a law allowing prisoners the same rations as soldiers in the field, the problem being that there was little food for either.

Hoping to rectify this appalling situation, President Davis and the Confederate Congress tried, throughout the War, to exchange prisoners with the Lincoln government, but met with little success. In the early phases of the War, there were exchanges, but it became an elemental part of Lincoln's war plans to keep all of the southern soldiers, thereby preventing them from returning to the desperately thin ranks of their armies. Upon occasion he would publicly voice regret at the callousness of his chosen method, but with some common little fable he would attempt to mollify the mothers who cried for release of their captive sons.

These northern mothers provided a large proportion of the opposition in the North to Mr. Lincoln's War. By late 1862, the War had dragged on for nearly two years with little success on the battlefield. Support for it was flagging. Searching for a way to infuse it with new vigor, Lincoln embraced the idea, advocated by the fanatic abolitionists, of freeing the slaves. It was a slick political move, in that it would rally to his side those radical one-issue demagogues who had provided the margin of his presidential victory but who had increasingly become disenchanted with him for his silence about slavery. Many of these extremists, their passions aflame, were bordering on lunacy. One of their leaders in particular, William Lloyd Garrison, celebrated the 4th of July by publicly burning a copy of the U. S. Constitution, calling it an "agreement with Hell." Still, Lincoln needed their support, and the Emancipation Proclamation did the trick, even though the document was purely academic, for it did not free one slave in those states still in the Union, yet somehow sought to order the freeing of slaves in the Confederacy, which was not within the purview of Honest Abe.

After the interjection of the slave issue, confusion abounded as to the purpose of the War, with many soldiers under the impression that they were now fighting to free the slaves from something, while others contended they were opposing the southern theory of states' rights. Still others were merely serving out the tedious terms of their drafts. The *Richmond Daily Dispatch* published a letter found on the battlefield of Murfreesboro. It was from a northern girl to her brother in the Federal army.

But poor boy, you are not out of this horrid war yet. If you had married and settled down, instead of going to war, it would have been better for you. Look at the slaughtering that has been done, and the negro is still not free yet. There have been enough white men killed to have paid for the infernal negro fifty times over, and you will never conquer the South until you have killed the last man of them — There is too much grit there. They have been wronged, and they know it, and will die rather than give up.[26]

There was a rudimentary misconception among northerners about slavery and the negro in general. Fiercely believing that slaves, who in the mild form of slavery practiced in the South would more fittingly have been called servants, were an unhappy lot just waiting for a chance to escape, northern abolitionists promoted the idea of slave uprisings and rebellions. Underground newsletters circulated, and secret agents were sent south to foment rebellion. One of their few successes, if murder can be called a success, occurred in 1831 when former slave Nat Turner led several slaves on a brutal killing spree in the dead of night. Before he was caught, over sixty white people had been viciously murdered by decapitation and other abhorrent means, including amputation of arms and legs by a meat cleaver while family members were forced to look upon the hideous handiwork of slaves incited by Garrison's abolitionists.

Old John Brown, an abolitionist who roamed the country, revelled in such gory activity. In May, 1856, he led a similar raid near Osawatomi, Kansas, massacring five settlers in the night. He next appeared in the public eye when, in 1859, he started south with a band of abolitionists intent upon instigating a large scale servile revolt. Heavily armed, his band entered Harper's Ferry, Virginia, where they seized the Federal arsenal and captured a locomotive roundhouse. They killed the town's mayor and took forty citizens as hostage, but the first victim of the madman was a free negro named Heyward Shepherd, whom John Brown killed in a rage when the negro refused to join the insurrection. On October 10, 1931, the United Daughters of the Confederacy dedicated a monument to all of the faithful slaves of the South, placing it at Harper's Ferry in memory of Heyward Shepherd.

During the War, as Yankees plundered their way southward, they were dismayed at finding no interest among the slave population for an insurrection against their masters. Indeed, notwithstanding the many tales of the "underground railroad," whose glories and numbers continue to grow with each new textbook, Yankees found a surprisingly universal loyalty. One Yankee soldier, perplexed at not being able to persuade a slave in Columbia to leave his master, remarked, "If you want to stay so bad, he must have been good to you."[27]

Mrs. Chestnut included in her diary a vignette which illustrates the harmony between slave and owner. Dr. Gibbes had been visiting a particular country home in Virginia when a Yankee soldier who had lost his way came in and asked for brandy. When the lady of the house brought it, he declined it, saying that he thought it might be poisoned. Mrs. Chestnut writes:

> She, naturally, was enraged. "Sir, I am a Virginia woman. Do you think I could be as base as that? Here Tom! Bill! Disarm this man! He is our prisoner." The negroes came running in, and the man surrendered without more ado. Another Federal was drinking at the well. A negro girl said: "You go in and see Missus." The man went in, and she followed crying triumphantly: "Look here, Missus, I got a prisoner too!". . .
>
> . . . Now if slavery is as disagreeable as we think it, why don't they all march over the border where they would be received with open arms?[28]

Federal troops soon tired of the negroes, especially those who were left homeless by the burning of their plantations, for they followed the armies begging for food and the proverbial promise of "forty acres and a mule." Those who could be persuaded to go into the Yankee army were organized into colored regiments, but they were unaware of the real intent of their recruitment. In the basest fashion, they were placed in the front charge when a particularly murderous fire was expected. Sometimes a colored company was sent in to "test the fire of the other side." If it resulted in heavy casualties, the regular troops would make other plans.

At the end of the War, there was little semblance of law and order in the South under the occupying Federal forces. A story came out of Richmond about the fat, rather dirty, negro barber who was one of those who thought he was glad to see the dawning of Yankee rule. Apparently too affectionate, he threw his arms around a Yankee officer who freed himself from the negro, drew his pistol, and shot him dead on the sidewalk, declaring that it was time to stop that kind of nonsense.

In this unusual war, it was common for officers and men of wealth on both sides to have body servants attending them. Northerners had the strange notion that the body servants of southern men were eagerly awaiting an opportunity to flee. "George Wills, the North Carolina preacher's son, had one of these personal servants, who acted as chef, valet, and forager. This Wash was one of the negroes whom well-intentioned Pennsylvania housewives tried to induce to steal away from their masters. One woman, trying to get at Wash's loyalties, asked him if he were treated well. 'I live as I wish,' he replied politely, 'and if I did not, I think I couldn't better myself by stopping here. This is a beautiful country, but it doesn't come up to home in my eyes.' "[29]

Today, the northern view of slavery is about as foggy as ever, due primarily to a constant input of false information. Rather than delve into historical narrative on the subject, it is much easier and more entertaining to derive a notion from the prurient, profane world of TV. The disconcerting thing is that more and more *southerners* are falling victim to the TV dogma of *Roots, North & South,* and other fictional works. In a day and age of imagination run wild, we southerners would do well to consult the works of scholars like Ulrich Phillips, the foremost authority on slavery who wrote the classic treatise, *Life and Labor in the Old South.*

Had it not been for the political considerations leading to the Lincoln administration's issuance of the Emancipation Proclamation, slavery would undoubtedly have been relegated to its rightful place as a peripheral issue of the conflict. It still amazes some to discover that, out of six million southerners, less than 400,000 owned a slave. In other words, only seven per cent of the southern population were slaveholders in even the strictest sense of the word. The number of practical slaveholders, those holding large numbers of slaves, varies from 2,200 to 10,000, depending upon the researcher, the study, and the criteria, but at any rate, it is in the neighborhood of only one-tenth of one per cent. Another statistic that surprises modern readers is that 250,000 of the three million slaves were owned by other blacks, part of the 3,000 free negroes in the South.

Among the relatively small number of large slaveholders, one could find those who did not like the "peculiar institution," but considered it a problem with no immediate solution. Mary Boykin Chestnut was one of them. From a family of large slaveholders, she surmised that she was probably the biggest abolitionist of them all, stating flatly, "I hate slavery."[30] She was a woman who would gladly have given up her house servants for the privacy which she said the northern women enjoyed.

The average southern soldier was not fighting for slavery — he had no direct connection with it. In simple terms, he fought because honor called, and called, and called. There was a crying need for soldiers at the front as the men in gray fell by the hundreds, or thousands, in each battle. The small southern population couldn't replenish the ranks, even when it had to turn to young boys of thirteen and old men of seventy-three. Upon rare occasion were Confederate forces equal to the number of Yankees opposing them. Most of the time they were outnumbered by at least a third. The last two years of the war would find southern forces outnumbered by two to one and three to one in nearly every major military action. Pursued by well over 200,000 men, General Lee surrendered his effective force of only 8,000 — a loyal group of patriots among whom not one man was found who favored surrender, but rather would have fought on, with rifle butts and doubled fists, if need be.

Those overwhelming numbers have always been a source of regret to southerners, causing us to have to make up in quality what we lacked in quantity. While growing up, I frequently heard the old brag that "Any Rebel can whip five Yankees." Sometimes the number was as high as ten, depending upon the virility of the spokesman.

And the saintly Robert E. Lee, for whom untold numbers of southern boys would be named over the next hundred years, was not to be held accountable for having to succumb to such engulfing odds. No, Sir. Southern women would see to that. Ten years ago, I was invited to dinner at the home of Laura Youngblood, a charming octagenarian who lives in what is known around Davis, Oklahoma, as the Youngblood Mansion. Situated at the end of a winding gravel road in the country just west of Davis, the home is a three-story structure in the Victorian style, looking much as it did when built by Laura's father, Dr. Thomas Howell, in 1899. The Howells were from Mississippi, and as I remember, were related to Jefferson Davis's second wife, Varina Howell, of Natchez, Mississippi.

There were about eight of us, including a Georgia cousin named Madeline Howell, a very colorful lady, also in her eighties, who was dressed that evening quite elegantly in a light green floor-length evening gown. Seated around the Victorian dining table under a crystal chandalier, we were a motley crew of young and old, representing various interests, and were therefore engaged in nothing more than light, frivolous conversation. When a lull came in the discourse, the silence was broken by the elderly Madeline who, in her heavy Georgian drawl that had not changed in over seventy years of living in Oklahoma, turned to me as if there were no ears but mine within the distance of her voice, and announced in a proud and serious tone of voice, "Do you know what General Grant said to General Lee?"

Now I know quite a bit of what Grant said to Lee, but Madeline asked it as if it had happened within the week, so I sat dumbfounded, and replied, "No." Not even half-way cognizant that all eyes and ears were on her, awaiting this profound answer, she looked straight at me as if she hadn't yet surrendered and stated, "He said, 'General Lee, I have not out-generaled you; I have just out-numbered you.' "

To be honest, I had never heard that remark, but every southerner subscribes to the message in Madeline's defense of General Lee. No one has ever "out-generaled" Robert E. Lee, and likely never will. There has never been a more capable assembly of generals in recorded history than those of the Confederacy. Even Mr. Lincoln once remarked that the problem was that all of the good generals were on the other side.

Much fun has been poked at the inept, blundering amateurs out of which Lincoln had to make generals. To oppose Lee in Virginia, he went through seven generals in four years, one of whom was John Pope, a pompous, bombastic individual who was replacing the timid General McClellan, an officer who cautiously dug in and set up elaborate headquarters, awaiting the most opportune circumstances before engaging Lee in battle. General Pope, upon assuming command, announced to his troops that he had come from the Western theater where he followed his enemy, attacking him where found, and that the policy of taking strong positions and holding them was over. His headquarters were to be in the field and his troops on the move. In theory he was right, but his pomposity gave amusement to Lee's magnificent Army of Northern Virginia, and the story that made the rounds was that Pope had shouted, "My headquarters are in the saddle!" Lee's army laughed over Stonewall's purported retort, "I can whip any man who doesn't know his headquarters from his hindquarters."[31] Before General Pope could differentiate between the two, Stonewall Jackson's boys had indeed whipped him. Two months after Pope's blustering, Jackson and Lee rolled him up at the Second Battle of Manassas, and he was through.

There were many victories on the battlefield for the boys who wore the gray. The First Battle of Manassas and the Second Battle of Manassas were Confederate victories on the same field of battle only thirteen months apart. At the Second Battle, Lee's 48,500 Confederate troops faced 75,000 Yankees, yet won an astounding victory. At the Seven Days Battles around Richmond, in June, 1862, his army of 80,000 drove 115,000 enemy soldiers back upon the James River. On a cold December day of the same year, 78,000 Rebels routed 110,000 Yankees in a stunning victory at Fredericksburg, Virginia. In May of the following year, they once again defeated the Yankees at the same Fredericksburg.

The Second Battle of Fredericksburg was a one-day event, part of the four-day Battle of Chancellorsville, in which Lee delivered what was probably his most marvelous tactical defeat of the enemy. With only 57,000 men, Lee and Jackson divided the army and attacked a Federal army of 134,000 men, scattering them like seed across the countryside and back towards the Rappahannock River. Lee spent the fifth day planning for an attack which would have annihilated the huge Federal army, but as he cautiously felt his way toward them, he found that they had slipped across the river on pontoons during the night and were in retreat.

The fact that Lee's tactics at Chancellorsville have been studied the world over is a monument to his military genius, but the battle was too dearly won, for the South was plunged into its deepest mourning by the death of Lee's right-hand man. The beloved Stonewall had been accidentally shot by his own men during the second evening of the battle and died eight days later. It was a tragic personal loss for Lee and a strategic loss for the military. There is a popular school of thought among historians that, had Stonewall Jackson lived, the South would likely have won the war.

In 1864, as the Confederate army continued to shrink with each battle, Union numbers swelled. At the Wilderness, 63,000 Confederates successfully resisted 141,000 of the enemy, but Grant could now afford to divide his army, forcing Lee to send troops he actually couldn't spare to counter the separate moves of the Federal masses. Still, Lee's embattled Confederates thwarted every attempt Grant made to invade Richmond, soundly thrashing him at Cold Harbor on June 1, 2, and 3, with a force of only 60,000 men. Grant, who had 117,000 present for duty that day, later regretted having even attempted the charge at Cold Harbor. He lost 7,000 men in one hour alone. Total losses for the three days were 12,000 men for the Federals and about 1,500 for the Confederates.

Out in the west, General Albert Sidney Johnston's Army of the Mississippi had won a tremendous victory at Shiloh in April, 1862, but Johnston was killed. General Beauregard assumed command and was preparing to push the Yankees into the Tennessee River when he learned that General Earl Van Dorn's Army of the Trans-Mississippi could not arrive in time to offset the 20,000 additional Federal troops who had arrived during the night. The Confederate army withdrew to Corinth. Two major victories occurred in 1863, when General Bragg's Army of Tennessee defeated the Yankees at the Battle of Murfreesboro, concluded on January 2, and the Battle of Chickamauga on September 19 and 20.

Of all the battles of the War, victories and defeats, the Battle of Manassas, later termed the Battle of First Manassas due to the occurrence of another battle there, has always intrigued me the most. For one thing, it was the first major land battle of the War. The troops on both sides were untested, and the first battle could be expected to give indication of things to come. The atmosphere in Richmond was indicative of the mood of the South — wary and apprehensive. The Confederate capitol had been moved to Richmond, and Congress was scheduled to begin its first session on July 20. For about a month prior, northern papers, led by the shrieking *New York Tribune*, had excited public emotions with their incessant cries of "Forward to Richmond! Forward to Richmond!", declaring that the "Rebel Congress" should not be allowed to convene on July 20. For the new Confederacy, it was victory on the battlefield or death in Richmond. The Confederate capitol, primary target of the invasion, lay only 100 miles south of Washington, D. C., and a cautious Confederate army was setting up a line of defense in northern Virginia.

Admist the hysteria of howling politicians and the constant drumbeat of the northern press, newly assembled Union troops, reflecting the cocksure attitude of the North, pranced out of Washington on July 16, crossing the Potomac onto Virginia soil, gayly outfitted in the newest of dark blue uniforms complete with brass buttons and trappings that fairly sparkled in the summer sun. The big battle loomed just five days ahead and would take place only twenty miles from Washington, D.C., but the troops were feeling their way along, somewhat uncertain as to just where they would run upon those "Rebels." By the time they reached the battlefield where the Confederates were waiting at Manassas, they had already run afoul of some of them on July 18 at a crossing of the Bull Run. A Federal detachment on reconnaissance met some of General Longstreet's Confederates who repulsed them, capturing twenty prisoners, 175 stands of arms, and a large number of blankets and accoutrements. Sixty-four bodies were found and buried by the Confederates.

An amusing incident occurred which further reduced the

esteem in which this Yankee army held itself. If spit and polish were to win the War, it surely didn't show when a group of Union soldiers became divided by a thick growth of tall shrubs as they marched ever onward to crush the "foolish Rebels." It's not clear as to just who first noticed those glistening rifles of the "enemy," but there they were, bobbing up and down, as the Rebels apparently and unknowingly marched alongside their foes. Someone gave the order to fire, and a barrage of lead was unleashed upon the tall hedgerow. On the other side, having been suddenly attacked, the supposed Rebels, who were in reality only a separated line of the same Federal outfit, dropped down and fired back, thinking they had been caught by Rebel fire. How the shooting stopped is not known, but someone evidently discovered the mistake, and these troops arrived upon the battlefield rather nonplussed, having already fought among themselves.

The active Confederate spy in Washington, D.C., Mrs. Greenhow, had sent word to General Beauregard that the Yankees were advancing for an attack upon his position, which lay along the south side of Bull Run for a distance of about eight miles. In Washington, you would have thought it was Mardi Gras for all the festivities and excitement in the air. Carriages were actually being loaded with picnic lunches, and overly confident politicians were ticketing their luggage for Richmond.

The grand army of Lincoln was facing the untried army of the South across Bull Run. Union generals had their orders to advance on Sunday, July 21. "The movement was generally known in Washington; Congress had adjourned for the purpose of affording its members an opportunity to attend the battlefield, and as the crowds of camp followers and spectators, consisting of politicians, fashionable women, idlers, sensation-hunters, editors, etc., hurried in carriages, omnibuses, gigs, and every conceivable style of vehicle across the Potomac in the direction of the army, the constant and unfailing jest was, that they were going on a visit to Richmond."[32]

It had all the trappings of a collegiate football game. "The idea of the defeat of the Grand Army . . . seems never to have crossed the minds of the politicians who went prepared with carriage-loads of champagne for festal celebration of the victory that was to be won, or of the fair dames who were equipped with opera glasses to entertain themselves with the novel scenes of a battle and the inevitable rout of 'rebels' ". . . Such was the "revolting spectacle of the indecent and bedizened rabble that watched from a hill in the rear of the army the dim outline of the battle and enjoyed the nervous emotions of the thunders of its artillery."[33]

The two armies faced each other and lay in parallel lines like two toothpicks, separated by Bull Run, a stream which had several fords and a strong bridge. The battle plan for the Confederates was to swing their right flank against the Federal left. Meanwhile, the Federal commander, General McDowell, had decided to swing his right flank against the Confederate left. A simultaneous charge could have resulted in both armies going in a circle, but the Yankees opened their attack first, having sent 13,000 men south and west around the extreme left end of the Confederate line during the night. Early on the morning of July 21, the Union artillery opened fire in front of the line while waiting for the column that had swung around the Confederate left to attack. Delayed by several things, they lost the element of surprise, and the boys in gray were waiting for them, though in greatly reduced numbers resulting from the long thin line.

In the meantime, General Beauregard's planned attack on the Federal left had not happened yet, and, from the sound of battle, he began to suspect that his left was in trouble. And, indeed, it was. The overwhelming Yankee force was pushing Gen. Barnard Bee's left flank back upon the Confederate center, and his inferiority in number had resulted in losing some high ground to the oncoming foe. His men were trying to retreat and at the same time cover themselves from a devestating fire of enemy bullets, when five regiments under Gen. Thomas J. Jackson arrived in the nick of time. It was General Bee who rallied his troops and simultaneously gave General Jackson his sobriquet by a calling out: "See, there is Jackson standing like a stone wall; Rally on the Virginians!"[34] It was an effective rally. The southerners turned upon the Yankees, gradually pushing them back, but General Bee was soon to be mortally wounded. It was the habit of southern officers to be near the van of the charge, leading their men into battle, but it cost the South many, many able leaders.

The Yankees, numbering about 37,000 men, had pushed across to the south side of Bull Run, where they were facing down upon the readjusting lines of Confederates. They had extended their right flank very widely around the Confederate left, when in the distance there could be seen more troops headed towards the Confederate left. As it happily turned out, the troops were those of Gen. E. Kirby Smith who had just arrived on the Manassas Gap Railroad from the Army of the Shenandoah. General Johnston, senior commander of the southern forces, ordered Smith's 1,700 infantry and Beckham's battery to fall upon the Federal right. General Beauregard seized the opportunity of having fresh reinforcements on his left and attacked the Federal center.

With a combined force of about 35,000 now, the southerners dismantled the Grand Army of the United States. Up and down the line, southern soldiers began to yell, thrilled beyond their wildest expectations at seeing the backs of the much-heralded army of the invincible North. It probably began as an instinctive response, but it soon swept throughout the entire line in wave after wave, having such a demoralizing effect upon the fleeing warriors that the famous "Rebel Yell," born here in a spontaneous instant, would be used purposely in many a future battle. Firing directly into the Union lines, yelling and running at the mass of confusion before them, the formerly untested southern army had before them the grandest spectacle of chaos and horror that would be seen during the whole war. Throwing off every item that would slow their feet, the Yankee soldiers left behind them miles of litter, including guns, canteens, jackets, hats, horses, artillery pieces, knapsacks, and a host of every item necessary to war.

"The retreat, the panic, the heedless, headlong confusion was soon beyond a hope. Officers with leaves and eagles on their shoulder straps, majors and colonels who had deserted their comrades, passed, galloping as if for dear life. Not a field officer seemed to have remembered his duty. The flying teams and wagons confused and dismembered every corps. . . . Army wagons, sutler's teams, and private carriages choked the passage, tumbling against each other amid clouds of dust, and sickening sights and sounds. Hacks containing unlucky spectators of the late affray were smashed like glass, and the occupants were lost sight of in the debris. Horses, flying wildly from the battlefield, many of them in death agony, galloped at random forward, joining in the stampede. Those on foot who could catch them rode them bareback, as much to save themselves from being run over as to make quick time."[35]

At the outset of the rout, a shell from the Confederate artillery blew up a wagon on the Cub Run Bridge on the main retreat route through the little town of Centreville, so it was sheer pandemonium upon that road, with men getting across that stream as best they could, leaving artillery and other weapons in the hands of exultant, screaming Rebels who turned the artillery around and further added to the panic by firing over the terrorized, unorganized mass of fleeing humanity. It must have been a thrilling sight, indeed, to view the backsides of Yankees who, only hours before had bragged that they would whip those Rebels in one day and with little effort!

The frightened, running swirl of civilians, soldiers, and ladies in full society regalia didn't stop at Centreville, in spite of the reserve that had earlier been posted there. Straight into

Washington they fled with no looking back, for it was generally feared that the Confederates were right on their coattails and would soon be in Washington to capture the capital city. Nor were many content to stop in Washington. People were evacuating by every road out of the city, and a guard had to be placed at the depot to keep the panic-stricken soldiers from getting aboard the outbound trains. The army was disorganized, and the city quaked for days, expecting the terrible fighting force of the Confederacy to descend upon it forthwith. What a remarkable difference a day had made!

Why that follow-up was not made has been debated since that fateful day. President Davis had arrived upon the battlefield in time to witness the victory, and in the evening met with Generals Johnston and Beauregard concerning an advance upon Washington. Many historians have believed that if the tired southern troops would have gone on into the Yankee capital and captured it, the War would have come to a decisive end then and there, resulting in a treaty of peace between two American nations, thereby precluding four hard years of anguish and death.

But we have to deal with what was, not what could have been. Mr. Lincoln, having been spared the humiliation of an occupied capital, though evidently singed by embarrassment, tried for four years to humble the Confederate president in the same fashion. Disastrously unsuccessful and visibly flustered, he once asked General Winfield Scott the question: "Why is it that you were once able to take the City of Mexico in three months with five thousand men, and we have been unable to take Richmond with one hundred thousand men?" "I will tell you, Sir," said General Scott, "The men who took us into the City of Mexico then are the same men who are keeping us out of Richmond now."[36] Finally, though, the end came, and Richmond was simply evacuated. It had withstood every malicious design against it, for its protectors were Robert E. Lee and his marvelous men in gray.

141

Lee's remaining army of only 35,000 was no larger than the first band of patriots who had marched out to do battle with the enemy at Manassas almost four years earlier. They were now stretched out for thirty-six miles, from north of Richmond to Dinwiddie Court House, southwest of Petersburg, in a very vulnerable, thin line of defense. The Yankee hordes were multiplying like flies and swarming like bees, as they tried to break Lee's defensive line of a border he had guarded for nine long months in the same position.

Cut off from food and ammunition supplies on all sides except to the west, General Lee and President Davis had discussed the nearly foregone conclusion that Richmond would have to be given up soon. On April 2, General Lee notified President Davis that he was abandoning the Petersburg line and that Richmond should be evacuated immediately. Lee headed west toward Amelia Court House where food and supplies were supposedly awaiting him, hoping that he might make a successful stand or link up with General Johnston's army to the south. Nothing was there, so he headed out across the hills toward Lynchburg, all the time being raided and slashed by the Yankee cavalry who burned his wagon train and captured General Ewell and his troops.

With only 28,000 men left, of whom only 8,000 were now armed, General Lee was virtually surrounded by 200,000 men under Ulysses Grant. It seemed uncanny that the whole Federal army had at last divined Lee's plan of retreat and had so effortlessly countered his escape where they had failed in four years to anticipate his moves. In truth, what had happened was an unfortunate blunder upon the part of the fleeing Richmond government. Confederate officials there had required General Lee to advise them in writing of his plan of withdrawal in the event that Richmond had to be evacuated. In their haste to escape with their lives, the departing officials had left details of Lee's proposed route in the abandoned city, and Grant had but to follow a map!

Against the wishes of his proud veterans, General Lee assumed the entire dishonor which he feared would fall upon this army if it surrendered, and entered into negotiations with General Grant. He reasoned that his little band of starving patriots could not save the South at any cost and that any further spilling of blood would be futile. It was all over.

Gen. Joshua Chamberlain, a Union general from Maine, who would later become governor of that state, recorded what he saw of the sad surrender. He was most impressed by the men's devotion to the Confederate flags they were giving up. He didn't know it, but many of those flags disappeared from their staffs before the surrender, hidden inside the shirts of disillusioned, heartbroken soldiers of the Lost Cause.

And now they move. The dusky swarms forge forward into gray column of march. On they come, with the old swinging route step and swaying battle flags. In the van, the proud Confederate ensign, the great field of white with a canton of star-strewn cross of blue on a field of red, the regimental battle flags . . . following on . . . the whole column seemed crowned with red.

Before us in proud humiliation stood . . . men whom neither toils and sufferings, nor the fact of death, nor disaster could bend from their resolve; standing before us now, thin, worn and famished, but erect, and with eyes looking level into ours. . . .

On our part not a sound . . . but an awed stillness . . . as if it were the passing of the dead.

As each . . . division halts, the men face inward towards us across the road, twelve feet away; then carefully dress their line . . . worn and half-starved as they were . . . they fix bayonets, stack arms; then, hesitatingly remove cartridge boxes and lay them down. Lastly — reluctantly, with agony of expression

— they tenderly fold the flags, battle-worn and torn, blood-stained, heart-holding colors, and lay them down: some frenziedly rushing from the ranks, kneeling over them, clinging to them, pressing them to their lips with burning tears."[37]

The War was over; but what awaited the defenseless Southland now that it had lost its noble experiment in freedom? As both armies lay poised at each other in the hours before the famous meeting between Lee and Grant, some of the officers in Lee's presence began to wonder aloud what the world would think of surrendering such an army as this? Would it not be better to die?

With a remark foreboding gruesome days that perhaps few but Lee foresaw, he sadly answered, "How easily I could be rid of this, and be at rest! I have only to ride along the line and all will be over. But, it is our duty to live. What will become of the women and children of the South if we are not here to protect them?"[38]

THE SAD SURRENDER

By RICHARD BROOK

"This was our hour of intense humiliation. So long as we carried our guns we felt something of the dignity of soldiers; but when we tramped away leaving these behind, we felt like a lot of hoboes stranded upon an alien shore."

—A.C. JONES, 3RD ARKANSAS REGIMENT, CSA

A CARPETBAG LEGISLATURE

"The reek of vile cigars and stale whiskey . . . was overwhelming. . . .
The space behind the seats of the members was strewn with corks, broken
glass, stale crusts, greasy pieces of paper, and picked bones. . . . Each member
had his name painted in enormous gold letters on his desk, and had placed
beside it a sixty-dollar French spittoon. . . . The uproar was deafening. From
four to six negroes were trying to speak at the same time. . . . The most of
them were munching peanuts, and the crush of hulls under heavy feet added
a subnote to the confusion. . . . the speaker was drowned in a storm of
contending yells."

—THOMAS DIXON, 1904

146

V

RECONSTRUCTION — NIGHTMARE OF THE SOUTH

"Their felonious fingers were made long enough to reach into the pockets of posterity. They coined the industry of future generations into cash and snatched the inheritance from children whose fathers are unborn. A conflagration, sweeping over the state from one end to the other, and destroying every building and every article of personal property, would have been a visitation of mercy in comparison to the curse of such a government."[1]

The dark days of Reconstruction encompass a period of ten wicked years, from 1867 to 1877. The War had ended in 1865, and southerners who had been driven from their homes all over the invaded land, returned, along with newly paroled soldiers, to scenes of destruction and desolation unknown before or since on the North American continent. They didn't cross bridges, for the bridges had been primary targets of war. They didn't ride horses, for horses went first to the Confederate army, and if any were left, the Yankees stole what they wanted and killed the rest. And, rarely did they ride in a wagon. When they did, it was a dilapidated remnant of war pulled by a bone spavined old mule unfit for war duty. Railroads were nothing more than a fond remembrance, so in the end, war-weary feet carried war-ravaged bodies slowly across the trails and dirt byways of the South, each turning off to his former home along the way.

From 1865 until 1867, when Reconstruction got under way in dreadful earnest, the southerner was occupied with physically rebuilding the South, with little time to entertain political thoughts. Confederate generals plowed fields with broken down old plows in the same way as their neighbor who might have been the lowly private. Men of former means sat in the midst of demolished cities, cleaning mortar off bricks which would be used to construct a new building, if and when the money could be found to erect a new structure. There were virtually no fences left, the rails having been burned for firewood. Even if there had been fences, cattle had long ago been driven off and eaten by invading Yankees. Where once had been miles of lovely homes, neatly framed by well-kept yards and gardens, only tall, blackened chimneys now stood. Alabama, Mississippi, Georgia, South Carolina, and North Carolina had been thoroughly sacked and burned, and hardly a cotton gin stood anywhere in Dixie. Homes that weren't burned to the ground were systematically looted with the passing of every Yankee army. When Reconstruction visited its venemous presence upon the South, the southerner, beset with seemingly insurmountable physical tasks, had no interest in an academic debate as to the right or wrong of military rule, by the name of Reconstruction or any other name. He innately knew it was wrong and was interested only in stopping it. That, in itself, though, would take nearly ten long years, for there was no longer a southern army facing the foe. It was now a matter of an unarmed, southern populace pitted against the largest army ever assembled on the continent.

The story of Reconstruction is not a pleasant epoch, and it isn't easy to tell. It is not only politically complicated, as would be almost any given ten-year period of U.S. history, but it is almost inconceivable to most modern southerners — and northerners, for that matter — that situations could deteriorate in the United States to such a degree as to permit such degradation as occurred in that fateful decade. It has been rather difficult to find volumes which want to deal with the subject in its shocking truth, many authors having written from the peripheral viewpoint of their northern background, a handicap which causes them to try — though vainly — to put a pretty face upon that era. Their works, in too many cases, attempt to find redemption among the hideous political crimes of the times, and at the same time, ignore the sufferings sustained by the actual southern citizen who bore the indignities. It has been my experience that the most significant gleanings are to be found in the many community and county libraries across the Southland, where locally written collections give vivid first-hand accounts of that period. One work which did attain wide acceptance and is oft quoted by honest historians is Myrta Lockett Avary's *Dixie After the War*, published in 1906. In addition, there is the newly discovered autobiography of Thomas Dixon, a work entitled *Southern Horizons*.

Admittedly a complicated and unpleasant era, Reconstruction is, nevertheless, considered here because it shows the true mettle of our southern ancestors in their patient endurance and eventual triumph over outrageous persecution, and I would be remiss if I withheld its saga in a text on southern heritage.

Some background is in order. First, it must be understood that the present day Republican and Democrat parties are not mirror reflections of their 1870's counterparts, of whom we will be compelled to speak often in the following pages. To the contrary, the two political parties have, over the past one hundred years, almost wholly changed roles, so that the *national Republicans* of today stand for practically the same ideas that the Democrats of the Reconstruction era upheld, while the *national Democrats* of today would find themselves closely akin to the Republicans of the 1870's. The negro vote of the 1870's, of which one hundred percent belonged to the Republicans, now belongs nearly in its entirety to the Democrats. Notwithstanding the apparent about-face within the two parties, this author would be the first to admit that white southerners have been loath to disconnect from the Democratic Party due to the hatred of Republican Reconstruction, and, indeed, to recognize that a majority of southerners still call themselves Democrats, refusing to concede to a label change to match their convictions.

Secondly, we need to make a brief survey of the political condition of the North for a better understanding as to how Reconstruction could have happened at the hands of a society calling itself civilized. Their cities were gleaming, untouched by the cruel hand of war, and their factory output was at unprecedented levels as the war machine ground on at full speed. But, sometimes those who wage war suffer from their own hands as surely as their victims were made to suffer.

A war of aggression tends to brutalize — to bring out the worst in the aggressor. Incessant railings by northern abolitionists took their toll upon the better part of the northern character. A representative denunciation of the time was found in an abolition pamphlet of 1863, entitled *Interesting Debate*. It contained part of a speech made in the Pennsylvania State Senate:

> I said that I would arm the negro — that I would place him in the front of battle — and that I would invite his rebel master with his stolen arms to shoot his stolen ammunition into his stolen property at the rate of a thousand dollars a shot. I said further, that

were I commander-in-chief, by virtue of the war power and in obedience to the customs of civilized nations, and in accordance with the laws of civilized nations, I would confiscate every rebel's property, whether upon two legs or four, and that I would give to the slave who would bring me his master's disloyal scalp one hundred and sixty acres of his master's plantation; nor would I be at all exacting as to where the scalp was taken off, so that it was at some point between the bottom of the ears and the top of the loins.[2]

This type of diatribe fostered abhorrent actions by the northern military forces who so often went unchecked in their foul deeds. Personal hatred for the planter ran deep among northern civilians and soldiers. One of their favorite indignities was to subject the white populace to insults from former slaves whenever they could manage to arrange it. An example, among thousands, is drawn from the activities of General Wild, a Yankee whose disposition matched his name.

In North Carolina, burned plantations had resulted in roaming bands of negro bandits. In the northeastern part of that state, the crimes perpetrated by these hoodlums were particularly atrocious. They raided the unprotected countryside, burning houses and looting with near impunity. They entered the homes of defenseless ladies, forced them to entertain at the piano, cursed them, robbed them, stripped them of their clothing, and subjected them to indignities better left unprinted.

This kind of activity fit perfectly into the scheme of General Wild, who commanded a force of "free" negroes. When his army invaded northeastern North Carolina, he found only local militia volunteers trying to protect the country. Calling these citizens "guerillas", he urged the negro bandits and white scoundrels traversing the area to step up their depredations against the population. The governor had granted a Daniel Bright permission to raise a small unit for local defense, but Bright failed and retired to his farm. General Wild's soldiers hunted him down, hung him at the side of the public road near his farm, and hung a placard upon his body.

With virtually none to repulse them, Wild's soldiers plundered ceaselessly. Upon one occasion, though, two of his negroes were captured; whereupon, the infuriated general arrested two "hostages" in retaliation. They were two of the most respectable married ladies in the area, Mrs. Phoebe Munden, wife of Lt. W.J. Munden, and Mrs. Elizabeth Weeks, wife of Pvt. Pender Weeks. Both husbands were away in the service of the Confederate army, and Mrs. Munden was at home with her three young children.

It was a cold December, and Mrs. Munden seemed to have fallen victim to the larger portion of General Wild's wrath. Arrested by his soldiers, the lady watched her home laid in ashes. In delicate health, she was allowed to save nothing except what she wore. Taken to Elizabeth City, she was bound hand and foot and confined in a room with several male prisoners, having no fire, bed, or bedding. The next day Mrs. Weeks was thrown into the same room. Neither of the women were allowed to leave the room except for the most necessary duty, and then only under the constant guard of an armed negro soldier. After several days, they were removed to Norfolk, Virginia, with General Wild permitting a negro to hold the rope by which Mrs. Munden was bound so tightly that her wrists were bleeding, thus leading her into Norfolk.

Wild's despicable, cowardly deeds were matched throughout the invaded land of Dixie by countless other Yankees in uniform. These were the soldiers who, hardened by war and accustomed to brutality, would go home at war's end to vote, influence public opinion, hold public office, and elect to office those who would promulgate a vindictive, vengeful Reconstruction upon a prostrate South.

Did the perverted prosecution of this war breed corruption among the northern politicians at home, or was it the degenerate condition at home that fueled the depravity at the war front? Whatever the answer, the situation began feeding upon itself, and the North did not escape the backfire of its own rage.

Unlike the South which had unity of purpose, mainly to protect its firesides from ruthless marauders, the North was a mixing bowl of confusion and internal turmoil. There were many factions, most of whom opposed the War or some aspect of it; in fact, the abolitionists and the increasingly fanatical Republicans were about the only ones in favor of a war that fed their sons into a sausage grinder of conflict, and even they opposed what was perceived to be a hesitation upon the part of the president to turn the War into a fight to free the slaves. About the only point of agreement — and even this was disputed in the southermost parts of Illinois, Ohio, and Indiana, as well as the border states which stayed in the Union — was the unmitigated hatred of the people of the South.

The president had bullheadedly dragged the nation into a war that soon lost its novelty and patriotic passion. To preserve the war effort, he assumed the duties of a dictator and operated as if the entire North were under martial law, in an attempt to squelch his opposition. Newspapers were suppressed, editors were arrested, and unreasonable searches and seizures were made in direct violation of Constitutional rights. In Kentucky's elections of 1863, the Democrats had offered a ticket of candidates who ran on a platform calling for an end to the War and restoration of the Union. Mr. Lincoln's government arrested the candidates for Congress in two congressional districts and one candidate for the state legislature from Lyon and Livingston counties. On July 31, General Burnside declared martial law in Kentucky.

The government had instituted in every city and town in the state a Board of Trade which regulated shipments of goods into the interior of the state. To receive a permit for his business, an individual was required to demonstrate his loyalty, each board having the right to make its own loyalty test. Usually, this test took the form of requiring a "loyal" vote in an election, thus the 1863 electorate was blackmailed into retaining the Lincoln Republicans in office. Historian James Ramage points out the shift in allegiance towards the end of the War. Kentucky had stayed within the Union, but the Lincoln government there was so oppressive that Kentuckians became pro-South and, most likely, would have gone with the Confederacy if it were to do over. Ramage noted the people's requests for historical markers when Kentucky began its program of marking significant sites and events in that state — birthplace of Lincoln. The overwhelming majority of requests came for events and places connected with Confederate General John Hunt Morgan, leaving Honest Abe and even Daniel Boone to a distant second and third places.

Lincoln's obsession was subjugation of the South, Constitutional or not. On September 24, 1862, he suspended the most basic of democratic rights, that of *habeas corpus*, the right of an individual to be brought before a judge or court upon restraint of his liberty. Borrowed from England, it is intended to protect a person from illegal imprisonment. In its place, the North was under martial law, with military tribunals making arbitrary arrests and handing out summary punishments in lieu of civil courts of law.

General Burnside, after his defeats upon the battlefield, had assumed command of the military district of Ohio, Indiana, and Illinois. Issuing orders that he would not tolerate free speech when it meant declaring sympathy with the South, he arrested former U.S. Representative Clement L. Vallandigham, of Ohio, who had expressed his dismay at the loss of civil liberties in the United States under Honest Abe. Denied access to civil courts, he was tried and convicted by a panel of eight army officers, then sentenced to imprisonment in Massachusetts. Fearful that political repercussions would follow his confinement, Lincoln had him banished to the Confederacy.

Lincoln was witnessing near revolt in the midwest. Burnside

had even sent troops to occupy the offices of the Chicago *Times* to prevent its publication; whereupon, the president adroitly rescinded the occupation after 20,000 angry northerners demonstrated.

The Supreme Court closed its eyes during the dark days of the War, adding to the growing despotism of the administration. Vallandigham's arrest in 1863 had resulted in a challenge by him to the suspension of *habeas corpus* in the U.S. Working its way through the courts, it reached the Supreme Court in 1864, only to find that the court would decline to assert jurisdiction over Lincoln's military tribunals.

In 1862, the Democrats had gained control of the Indiana and Illinois state legislatures. Governor Morton, of Indiana, blocked the assembling of the legislature by persuading the Republican minority to boycott the sessions, thereby preventing a quorum. Illinois Governor Yates seized upon a technicality and adjourned the legislature in his state for two years, a tyrannical action which resulted in a mass rally by 40,000 angry Democrats at Lincoln's hometown of Springfield.

In early 1863, more newspapers were suppressed in Pennsylvania, Ohio, and Iowa. The lights of freedom were going out all over the United States, who now had not the moderating conservative influence of the states' rights advocates of the South to temper the traditional recklessness with which northern politicians were prone to trample civil liberties under foot. Just how close America's experiment in democracy came to failure under Lincoln and the Republicans of the 1860's and 1870's would shock modern Americans were it fully known. Lincoln's Secretary of War was a malevolent enemy of the common man. "In a chilling preview of twentieth-century totalitarianism, Stanton once told a visitor to his office, when pointing out an object on his desk, 'If I tap that little bell, I can send you to a place where you will never hear the dogs bark.' "[3] His military tribunals were responsible for the arrest and imprisonment of approximately 38,000 citizens during the War Between the States.

With elections held at the point of the bayonet and liberties of the press, speech, and public meetings curtailed, it was only natural that parallels were drawn between Russia and the United States. In New York Harbor, at a lavish banquet given to a Russian fleet, northern orators proclaimed that the day had come for the twin civilizations to unite in dominating the world as partners in the manifest destiny of the nineteenth century. While the United States tried to reshape the Confederacy into its own image, Russia was subjugating the Poles. " 'Russia and the United States', said a French writer of the time, 'proclaim the liberty of the serf and the emancipation of the slave, but in return both seek to reduce to slavery all who defend liberty and independence.' "[4]

Lincoln's attempts at replacing the old republic to which northerners had grown accustomed with one of despotic rule had caused frequent public outrage, which took its most violent form when directed at the draft. Instituted in 1863, it was an abomination to many northerners, and extreme opposition occurred throughout the North. Particularly offensive was the provision that allowed the rich to escape military duty by either paying a substitute to go to war or by simply paying $300 to the government. Approximately 203,000 men avoided the draft by virtue of the provision.

The most violent reaction erupted in New York City on July 13, when a riot broke out and raged for three days in what historian Burke Davis called "the nearest approach to revolution" during the entire war. Mobs surged through the streets, burned buildings, and destroyed the drum from which the names of 1,200 New Yorkers had been drawn for military service. There were no soldiers to check the violence, due to the concentration of all available troops at Gettysburg, so policemen and militia units had to face the rioters alone.

The angry mob burned fine homes, business buildings, the draft office, a Methodist church, a negro orphanage, and sundry other buildings. A negro was hung, then burned as people danced around the burning body. More than thirty negroes were killed — shot, hung, or trampled to death.

The mobs grew to an estimated strength of between 50,000 and 70,000. For three days they swarmed through the streets, setting up barricades on First, Second, and Eighth Avenues, where sometimes a force of only 300 policemen would have to face 10,000 attackers at a time. Some troops filtered into the town, and the crowds took to alleys and rooftops where they killed soldiers with bricks and guns. The gangs caught the colonel of a militia unit, stomping and beating him to death. After dragging him to his home, men, women, and children demonically danced around his body.

Eventually, enough troops arrived to put an end to the rioting. Casualties were heavy — nearly 2,000 people were dead from the melee. An embarrassed government tried to affix blame upon certain political foes, including New York's Governor Seymour, a Democrat, and Fernando Wood, former mayor of the city. Still, nothing swayed Mr. Lincoln from his grim determination to pursue the War to its bitter end.

Chaotic conditions in the North were in sharp contrast to those in the beleaguered Southland where one might have expected that the exigencies of war would necessitate curtailment of basic privileges, yet never was the *writ of habeas corpus* suspended during the lifetime of the Confederacy.

Aghast at the despotic rule of the Lincoln government, northern Democrats met at their national convention in Chicago on August 29, 1864, to lay plans for dismantling the Republican administration, though chances were slim that the minority Democratic party could do so. Calling the convention to order, August Belmont intoned, "Four years of misrule by a sectional, fanatical, and corrupt party has brought our country to the verge of ruin."[5]

The temporary chairman, former Pennsylvania Governor Bigler, said, "The termination of democratic rule in this country was the end of the peaceful relations between the States and the people. The men now in authority, through a feud which they have long maintained with violent and unwise men at the South, . . . are utterly incapable of adopting the proper means to rescue our country from its present lamentable conditions."[6]

So desperate was the situation of the country that the permanent chairman of the Democratic National Convention, Gov. Horatio Seymour, of New York, was willing to adopt a conciliatory demeanor toward the South. Inveighing acridly against Lincoln and the Republicans, he said, "They were animated by intolerance and fanaticism, and blinded by an ignorance of the spirit of our institutions, the character of our people, and the condition of our land. . . they will not have the Union restored unless upon conditions unknown to the Constitution. They will not let the shedding of blood cease, even for a little time, to see if Christian charity, or the wisdom of statesmanship, may not work out a method to save our country. . .This administration cannot save the Union. We can. We demand no conditions for the restoration of the Union. We are shackled with no hates, no prejudices, no passions. We wish for fraternal relations with the people of the South. We demand for them what we demand for ourselves, the full recognition of the rights of the States."[7]

What a pity the Democrats were denied victory on November 8, 1864. With it might have come the end of the War and no ensuing Reconstruction nightmare, but Lincoln's oft-used and well-timed victories upon the battlefield secured for him the presidency that November. July had brought victory at Gettysburg and the fall of Vicksburg, followed a little more than a month before the election by Sherman's capture of Atlanta — that action taken after much prodding by the embattled president.

Against this background, which gives only a slight indication of the political and social turmoil in the North, the black night of Reconstruction fell upon the South.

Lincoln had succeeded in holding enough captured territory

in Arkansas and Louisiana to set up *de facto* governments in both states in 1864, claiming that ten percent of the population had taken an oath of loyalty to the United States. That was his requirement for bringing the "wayward sisters" back into the fold — that, plus a demand that each state agree to emancipation. Though the vast majority in Arkansas and Louisiana remained true to the Confederacy, the Lincoln governments in both states promptly elected members to the U.S. Congress; but Congress, in its first clash with the president over the procedure for "reconstructing" a state, refused to seat the new members.

The contention was that the South must be punished, not merely readmitted to full fellowship and good will without a little bloodletting. It was also of supreme importance to Republicans that they maintain their voting majority in Congress. The War had propelled this comparatively new political party into a position of control for the first time, and they jealously contended for preservation of that power. If Lincoln allowed the southern states to rejoin the Union with so little requisite corrective action, how could Republicans prevent the return to power of the southern Democrats who would be taking their old seats in Congress again? Therein lay the challenge.

Whether Lincoln would have succeeded in his relatively lenient plan for reunification will never be known, for he was assassinated on April 14, 1865, only five days after the surrender of Robert E. Lee. Vice-President Andrew Johnson, a Democrat who had been chosen to siphon off Democratic votes in the 1864 presidential election, ascended to a presidency that would collide head-on with the increasingly vicious Republican Congress.

Like Lincoln, Andrew Johnson assumed that it was the duty of the president — not Congress — to reconstruct the Confederate states. He also held the same pollyanish notion as Lincoln that the southern states had never really left the

159

Union after all, insisting, therefore, that only a simple, quick formula of his invention would suffice.

In May, 1865, he recognized the governments of Arkansas, Louisiana, Virginia, and Tennessee, as legitimately reconstituted under Lincoln's plan, and he granted amnesty to Confederate citizens who took a loyalty oath, providing that they did not own taxable property worth more than $20,000. As to the other seven Confederate states, he outlined his plan of four steps: (1) abolish slavery, (2) repudiate the Confederate debt, (3) rescind the ordinances of secession, and (4) ratify the Thirteenth Amendment, which Congress had passed in January, 1865. The Thirteenth Amendment abolished slavery. It became the first of only three amendments to the venerable Constitution which were ratified under pressure tantamount to political blackmail.

By December, 1865, all of the southern states, except Texas, had fulfilled President Johnson's requirements. Texas did so in April, 1866, and all of the southern states elected members to Congress.

Congress was full of radicals, but two men particularly stood out as leaders of the mob: Thaddeus Stevens, in the House of Representatives, and Charles Sumner, in the Senate. Stevens represented a Pennsylvania district, and was a hotheaded politician who drove Republicans with an iron hand. Bald since his youth, he wore a wig which sometimes rearranged itself when he was railing vigorously against southerners in his House speeches. He was extremely caustic — a perfect ally for Senator Sumner, who had been a senator from Massachusetts for several years. Sumner was dogmatic and uncompromising and held a special hatred for southerners in general, an attitude made more vicious by an incident in 1856 in the Senate. During a Senate speech, he had launched a personal attack upon southerners, and more specifically upon the aged Senator Butler from South Carolina. Two days later, Senator Butler's nephew, Preston Brooks, who himself was a Congressman, caught Sumner alone in the Senate chamber and avenged his uncle by beating Sumner mercilessly with his cane, leaving the senator an invalid for three years.

The consuming hatred of the twin Republicans, Stevens and Sumner, was a precursor of radical Reconstruction. The Republicans who followed their lead were soon referred to as *Radical Republicans,* or *Black Republicans.* As early as 1865, Thaddeus Stevens had left no doubt as to his plans for the South in a speech delivered before the House of Representatives:

> The whole fabric of southern society *must* be changed and never can it be done if this opportunity is lost. Without this, this Government can never be, as it has never been, a true republic. Heretofore, it had more the features of aristocracy than of democracy. The Southern States have been despotisms, not governments of the people. It is impossible that any practical equality of rights can exist where a few thousand men monopolize the whole landed property. The larger the number of small proprietors the more safe and stable the government. If the South is ever to be made a safe republic let her lands be cultivated by the toil of the owners or the free labor of intelligent citizens. This must be done though it drive her nobility into exile. If they go, all the better.[8]

The first item of business was to deny southerners their seats in Congress, giving Republicans time to bolster their strength in the fall elections of 1866. In the meantime, they created a congressional committee to investigate and report on "southern representation" in Congress. They had already established the Freedmen's Bureau in 1865 to aid negroes in the South, but in 1866 Congress gave it new powers, including authority to hold military trials for people suspected of denying rights to negroes, as well as the authority to intervene in any dispute concerning labor contracts between white land owners and the negroes hired by them.

After the War, freedmen aimlessly roamed the countryside with little purpose or direction. The North had freed them, Republicans promising to take the white man's land away, divide it up, and give each freedman the proverbial "forty acres and a mule." Freedom, in reality, brought poverty, hunger, and homelessness. Many former slaves either tried to stay on their plantations or tried to return after a brief experience with their elusive freedom, and just as many former slave owners tried to hold their plantation families together, but the North had done away with the system and destroyed the land. Many former planters were in a shape similar to former Confederate Major General M.C. Butler. At home in South Carolina, he was twenty-nine years old, had lost a leg in the War, had a debt of $15,000, three children and a wife to support, seventy freed slaves, and only one dollar and seventy-five cents in cash.

It was generally suspected by those who had owned slaves that the freedmen would not work under wage arrangements unless they were compelled to. Their suspicions were confirmed to a large degree by the large congregations of freedmen around army camps, near towns, and in their own shantytowns along the highways where they existed on handouts from the Freedmen's Bureau and sympathetic whites. To get them back into the fields and give them supervision once again, southern legislatures enacted Black Codes, which primarily set forth the terms of labor contracts between freedmen and land owners. It was stipulated that freedmen would have to take proper care of their employer's tools, animals, and property; and, to insure against wandering off the job, the codes required the freedman to honor his yearly contract for the full year or forfeit all of his wages earned up to the time of abandonment.

In the absence of any definition from Washington, the Black Codes attempted to define the status of the freedman, who was neither a slave nor a citizen. Though they varied from state to state, the codes conferred upon the negro certain rights to own property, make contracts, sue in court, and enter into legal marriage. Restrictions were placed upon him in certain areas, especially those pertaining to social convention and bearing of arms.

The freedmen payed little attention to the work contracts, as is graphically depicted in a diary kept by Mrs. Mary E. Rives. Widowed by war, she and her three children tried to proceed with business on their plantation a few miles from Shreveport, Louisiana. On June 26, 1865, she made the first of several entries concerning her effort to work her former slaves by contract:

> Some are willing to stay and work a little and be fed, clothed and doctored as I have always done, but all are unsettled in their minds and hardly know what to do. . .
>
> 4th of July, 1865. Well, this Day of Independence is celebrated in grand style by the Yankees. . . I fear even the next 4th will not be so gay. . .
>
> 4th August. . . All the freedmen's work lost this week. . . there is neither profit nor pleasure living with them now. They will not work. They do not average five hours a day work. They do not feel free when they are at work. . .
>
> August 22 — The freedmen are idling away nearly all their time. They have been threshing wheat and have not done as much in four days as they should have done in one. . .
>
> Sept. 9 — I am getting very anxious to leave my home. There is no pleasure living where no one is willing to do their part. My horses are not fed and watered as they used to be. The corn is pulled and left on the ground for four or five days. . . My fine mare was stolen last night by a Freedman.[9]

On November 9, Mrs. Rives moved into Shreveport where

she lived with Mr. & Mrs. M.H. Estner.

Northerners viewed the Black Codes as an effort by southerners to retain the use of negro labor and, in a sense, ignore the abolition of slavery. They were also incensed by the sight of ex-Confederate statesmen, elected to Congress and waiting to take their seats in the new session. Georgia had elected former Vice-President of the Confederacy, Alexander H. Stephens, to the United States Senate, an action that both vexed and confounded the general northern citizenry.

The northern mind has never understood the southern heart, and this was a prime example of the great gulf existing then and now between the two peoples. Deluded by way of the old adage that "might makes right", northerners thought that southerners would somehow turn against principle and reject Confederate leaders simply because of military defeat. Many good causes fail, but failure doesn't define the rightness or wrongness of the cause. Southerners did not feel that they had done wrong in their pursuit of independence, nor do they feel guilt today. It was a brave attempt at securing states' rights that failed, and fate's decree was accepted; but to dishonor southern heroes — never.

Major R.E. Wilson, formerly of the 1st North Carolina Battalion of Sharpshooters, spoke the southern mind when he said, "If I ever disown, repudiate, or apologize for the cause for which Lee fought and Jackson died, let the lightnings of Heaven rend me, and the scorn of all good men and true women be my portion. Sun, moon, stars, all fall on me when I cease to love the Confederacy. 'Tis the cause, not the fate of the cause, that is glorious!"[10]

Unable to grasp the mood of the South, northerners saw Reconstruction as a Heaven-sent opportunity to remake the South in the image of the North. A recent college history text states, "Reconstruction represents the most extreme example in our history of an attempt by the majority to impose a social concept upon a minority that did not wish to be changed."[11]

While southern Congressmen, denied their seats in Congress, waited for the next move, Congress lost precious little time in designing a plan to disfranchise southern whites and give the negro the right to vote. There were nearly 4,000,000 negroes in Dixie, most of whom could neither read nor write. Most of them had no comprehension of matters beyond the boundary of the plantation, this ignorance of affairs presenting a golden opportunity to the Republicans who could instruct them how to vote. Forbid white people to vote, and negroes could be manipulated into sending Republicans to Congress from every southern state.

First, the negro had to be given citizenship. Congress passed a Civil Rights Act in April, 1866, bestowing citizenship upon everyone except Indians. The legislation was so bad that even some Radical Republicans doubted its constitutionality, causing them to press Congress to incorporate its provisions into an amendment to the Constitution in order to protect it from action by the courts. The Fourteenth Amendment also prevented most prominent southerners from holding office, thereby eliminating most of the Congressmen from the South who were awaiting their congressional seats.

President Johnson opposed the amendment, and battle lines were drawn. The mid-term elections of 1866 were upon the country, and both sides vied for support of the people. President Johnson went across the country urging the election of Democrats to defeat the Radicals' harsh programs, including the Fourteenth Amendment. The Radicals concealed their bizarre plan to force negro suffrage upon the South; instead, they diverted attention to emotional issues, storming across the North, reminding voters of the horrible war and the soldiers who had been killed at the hands of southern armies, all the time equating southerners with Democrats. This particular phenomenon was called, "waving the bloody shirt", and Radical Republicans became quite adept at it. They would use it in many elections to come.

Having many agents in the South operating behind the facade of the Freedman's Bureau, the Radicals possessed the machinery for instigating race riots at opportune times. With a little prodding, the illiterate negro masses could be worked into a frenzy at most any time. It seemed more than coincidence that several riots among the negroes broke out before the election in several southern cities. In Memphis and New Orleans, large riots occurred, in which many negroes were killed, the events playing directly into the hands of the Radicals who screamed for more troops, more money, and more discipline of the white population in the South.

A third element that worked to the advantage of the Radical Republicans in the election was the political recalcitrance of Andrew Johnson. He was a stubborn Democrat faced with a Republican Congress, and he opposed nearly everything the Radicals tried to ram through. Like Lincoln, he had the rough, vulgar langauge of the back country from which he sprang, and when heckled at his speeches throughout the midwest, he lost support for those for whom he spoke by evidencing his uncouth expression and intemperance. Johnson was a political outcast; he was neither southern nor northern. Southern by residence only, he denounced Tennessee when she seceded, remaining in his congressional capacity as U.S. Senator from that state, even though she was absent from the Union. He had never really liked the planters of the South, but he didn't care for the majority of northern liberals either. As a reward for being the most prominent southerner to desert the South, he was appointed military governor of Tennessee during the War, an appointment that displeased the people of that state. By a quirk of fate, this tailor from Tennessee had been projected into the highest office in the land and was now in the political battle of his life.

The Radicals won an overwhelming victory. The makeup of the new Senate would be 42 Republicans and 11 Democrats, while the new House would pit 143 Republicans against only

49 Democrats. Thus mandated, their machine rolled on, over the constant veto of President Johnson. In March, 1867, the first Reconstruction Act was passed, dividing the ten unreconstructed states into five military districts. Each district was under command of an army general, and thousands of troops were spread throughout southern towns and villages to do his bidding. Tennessee was spared military occupation since it had been the only southern state to ratify the Fourteenth Amendment, the other ten having refused to do so.

Declaring their contention that the states had indeed left the Union, the Radicals announced that they would treat them as conquered provinces. The very sons and daughters of those who framed the revered old Constitution that the Radicals were effacing with their meddlesome amendments, were now to be treated as barefooted aborigines of a banana republic.

Every southern state was required to rewrite its constitution in a constitutional convention of delegates chosen in a state wide election of *all* adult males, *except those with disqualifications.* This meant that many ex-Confederates could not vote, and it meant that negroes, even though they were not citizens, could vote. To insure that enough whites were disbarred so that the convention would be composed of a manageable group of pro-Republican delegates, the Radicals established registrars armed with enormous powers. Each voter had to step before the registrar and swear a complicated loyalty oath which was offensive to native southerners; however, even if a southern white man could bring himself to make an oath of allegiance to such a despotic government, the registrar was empowered to reject the oath if he deemed it made in bad faith. In this way, the registrars in every community could reject enough southern votes to guarantee a safe Republican majority. As a result, they registered 703,000 negroes and only 627,000 white men in the South.

At the end of the War, the South had begun to be overrun by the worst element among the Yankee people — the *carpetbagger*, so called because he came South carrying all of his belongings in one small suitcase made, in the fashion of the day, of a piece of floral, carpet-like material. It said two things of him: Firstly, that he was either a man of no means — a financial failure — and could, therefore, carry all of his belongings in such a bag, or that he was so seized of greed that his haste necessitated packing so lightly; and, secondly, that he intended to prey upon a disconsolate people. His southern counterpart, the *scalawag* (pronounced "scallywag"), was baser yet. A southern white man, turned traitor for betterment of his financial lot, he forsook the plight of his own people and welcomed the carpetbagger with open arms. Together with the benighted negro, they comprised the triumvirate that would wield a reign of terror over the broken South for more than ten years.

State constitutions, framed by noble sires and men of letters, would thus be relegated to the trash in favor of cheap pamphlets produced by inferior minds, pretending to be duly elected delegates to these so-called "constitutional conventions." Typical of the self-serving arrangements incorporated into the new constitutions was Article 99 of the Louisiana Constitution of 1868, which embodied the *Recantation Oath*, a provision which effectively disfranchised white voters. A man had to swear that he had never, of his own free will, served the Confederacy in a military or civil capacity, voted for secession, or, "acting in advocacy of treason, wrote or published newspaper articles or preached sermons."[12] Few honorable men could bring themselves to declare such a falsehood, and the records of Caddo parish are indicative of the disastrous effects the oath had upon the entire state. In 1868, no white men in the parish took the recantation oath. The 3,586 registered voters in Caddo parish were mostly negroes who voted the Republican ticket, just as the Radicals had planned.

With Andrew Johnson's plan completely scrapped and the Radicals' hand greatly strengthened by the 1866 elections, Congress laid out the rest of its Reconstruction plan. In addition to writing a new constitution, each state had to guarantee negroes the right to vote, and ratify the Fourteenth Amendment. (By requiring *conquered provinces*, or states who were out of the Union, to ratify a constitutional amendment, this haphazard Congress cast a constitutional cloud upon an already cumbersome amendment — a flaw still unresolved by Constitutional scholars of today.) If the requirements were met, Congress reserved the right to scrutinize the constitution of each province, and, if it met the qualifications of their diabolical scheme, to readmit the province to the Union as a state and to consider removing Federal troops from the state. In other words, Congress would be glad to have the state back in the Union if it was apparent that Radical Republicans were in control.

Congress kept all bases covered. Subsequent reconstruction acts increased its power over southern politics. One especially dictatorial act was extremely useful to the Radicals. It empowered the military commanders to remove elected state officials who displeased the regime and appoint officials more to their liking.

Constitutional law and order had taken a holiday, and Congress was determined that nothing should stop their radical idea of centralized government. President Johnson was next on their hit list. His opposition to them was a source of irritation, and the Radicals had been plotting to impeach him at the very slightest provocation. Two pieces of legislation had been "cooked up" to both trap him and diminish the power of the presidency. The first act required him to issue all military orders through General Grant, a Radical Republican. The second act prohibited him from removing any of his Senate-confirmed officials without permission of the Senate.

Their golden opportunity arrived when Johnson deliberately removed Secretary of War Stanton from his cabinet without the consent of the Senate. The House of Representatives promptly passed articles of impeachment against him, and on March 13, 1868, the Senate began the only impeachment trial of a United States President. It was a shameful episode in U.S. history, and perhaps the disgrace of the event evoked the slightest tinge of conscience among seven Republicans who voted against removing Johnson from office, thereby saving him from conviction by one lone vote.

In the same infamous year, Congress attempted to silence the Supreme Court. In this black endeavor, they were more successful. The Supreme Court had already posed a problem to them. In 1866, in the case of *Ex parte Milligan*, it had ruled that Lincoln had been acting unconstitutionally when he did away with civil courts, replacing them with military tribunals. In 1868, the Supreme Court agreed to hear the case of *Ex parte McCardle,*, a challenge to the constitutionality of the first Reconstruction Act. Before the court could hear the case, Congress passed an act withdrawing appellate jurisdiction of the Supreme Court in cases of this type. In addition, it sought to essentially do away with the court by stipulating that if a justice died or resigned he was not to be replaced. Under this decree, the Supreme Court dwindled to only six members.

The attacks upon the executive and judicial branches were evidence that Congress was creating an imbalance in the American system. They intended to make the legislative branch supreme. Suffering from an anti-South psychosis, the Radical Congress saw itself as a revolutionary body — architects of a new order that would replace the cherished idea of checks and balances with a totalitarian regime committed to a new social order in the South.

The year of 1868 also brought a long-awaited presidential election. The unmanageable Andrew Johnson was dumped by the Democrats in favor of nominee Horatio Seymour, while the Radicals gleefully nominated the popular, cigar-chomping, General of the Army, Ulysses S. Grant. The general has been perceived by most historians not so much as a vicious Radical like his colleagues in the Congress, but as a weak official who, given to much drink, was easily pulled along by a strong

Congress. Influenced by more persuasive men and dominated by that Congress, Grant acquired the distinction of having the most corrupt administration of any U.S. President.

His election was secured by the carpetbag governments in the South who gave military protection to thousands of negroes and instructed them to vote Republican. Realizing more fully the importance of the negro vote to the perpetuation of the Radical Republican movement, Congress lost little time in drawing up another of its "pressure amendments." This one, the Fifteenth Amendment, made sure that the negro right to vote was protected everywhere, even in the North, where Ohio, Michigan, Kansas, and Minnesota had balked at incorporating negro suffrage in their state constitutions. To offset possible rejection of the amendment by some northern states, Congress once again made ratification of an amendment a requirement for readmission of the states still out of the Union — Texas, Mississippi, Georgia, and Virginia.

By 1870, all of the southern states were back in the Union, but carpetbag rule continued until Grant left office in 1876. Carpetbaggers had swarmed the South at war's end in 1865. Like vultures, they swooped down from the North to pick the carcass of the dead Confederacy. It was a swindler's dream. Southerners owned the land and could, therefore, be taxed to support a corrupt government in which they were not allowed to participate. Scalawags, carpetbaggers, and negroes were elected by each other to the state houses of every southern state, where their proceedings were a travesty of justice.

In South Carolina, out of 155 state legislators, 144 were Radical Republicans. Of those, 98 were negroes, of whom only 22 could read and write. The State Treasurer and Secretary of State were negroes, and the Governor was a carpetbagger. Voting unto themselves gold watches, horses, carriages, champagne, and other outlandish things, they quickly bankrupted South Carolina, the state debt rising from $7,000,000 to $29,000,000 in a very brief period of time. South Carolina would go well into the 20th century before overcoming the effects of carpetbag plunder.

The negroes were interested in social services to be paid for by the southern taxpayer. Coached by the wily carpetbagger, who made sure he received his share of the revenue, the negro in the legislature was responsible for raising the Louisiana tax rate by 400% in four years. Throughout the South, carpetbag tax assessors took delight in humbling land owners by demanding higher taxes in scenes reminiscent of *Gone With the Wind's* white trash Jonas Wilkerson, who, elevated to status of tax collector, demanded that Miss Scarlet fork over $200 or lose *Tara*.

In the *March of Democracy*, James Truslow Adams wrote, "The political trash, white and black, grew rich selling franchises, public property, and political favors for any price they could to get money for themselves. One carpet-bag governor cleaned up a half million dollars in his term."[13] That governor was H.C. Warmoth, of Louisiana, who built his private fortune from public money. He smugly insisted that corruption was the fashion.

A sketch of Reconstruction in Louisiana indicates the situation that existed throughout the South, and though we can chronicle the most significant events of the era, it is impossible for those of us living in this age to grasp the horror that almost daily stalked our ancestors for nearly twelve years.

The events in northwestern Louisiana are especially illustrative, owing partly to the fact that Shreveport was the wartime state capital after Federal forces occupied southern Louisiana, making it a seat of political activity. In addition, the *Shreveport Times*, newly organized in 1871, became the leading spokesman for Louisianans during Reconstruction.

When the Confederate government was dismantled, Governor Allen, in his farewell letter, said, "I would advise that you form yourselves into companies and squads for the purpose of protecting your families from outrage and insults and your property from spoilation. . . . Within a short while the United

States authorities will no doubt send you an armed force to any part of the State where you may require it for your protection."[14] He had no way of knowing that the United States would send a huge force of negro troops to garrison Shreveport for two years. The troops were undisciplined, arrogant, and resentful of the white people of Louisiana. The people of Shreveport were unwilling hosts to these former slaves who reveled in their new role of master over white men. They humiliated the citizens with every kind of insult imaginable, while their Radical political leaders, black and white, systematically looted the state.

The governor of the occupied section of the state, J. Madison Wells, called for an election to be held in November, 1865. The Democrats, who at this time could still vote, nominated him for governor, and he won the election. In April, 1867, fearing Radical reprisals, the people of Caddo parish submitted resolutions of cooperation with the Union to the military commander of the state, who was the notorious Phil Sheridan. Notwithstanding expressions of accommodation from state citizens, General Sheridan, who had violently destroyed the Shenandoah Valley of Virginia, removed Governor Wells from office and appointed a man more in tune with the Radicals.

With enough Radical Republicans in the legislature, Louisiana constructed a constitution containing the infamous Recantation Oath, and in 1868, the white loyal southerners were disfranchised. Henry Clay Warmoth, the corrupt Republican, and Oscar Dunn, a Republican negro, were elected as governor and lieutenant governor, respectively. Warmoth presided over a legislature composed of scalawags, carpetbaggers, and newly-freed negroes, who spent the state into ruin.

With a negro police force in Shreveport who cared little for the safety of white citizens, the white men organized the Knights of the White Camellia. The Knights in Caddo parish declared "a white man's government or no government" and made night rides, breaking up political meetings in which scalawags and carpetbaggers were instructing and inflaming the gullible freedmen.

In 1868, two race riots broke out in Bossier parish, resulting in the death of 150 negroes. A negro leader from Arkansas was reportedly the instigator, but further evidence involving previous uprisings pointed to the Freedman's Bureau and its incendiary friends.

By 1870, the Knights of the White Camellia had been so successful in Caddo parish that Governor Warmoth threatened to send the state militia there to protect the negroes in the fall elections. But, this was the same year that saw the elimination of the hated Recantation Oath from the state constitution. The southerners were once again among the voting population of their homeland, and the Knights disbanded.

In late 1871, these downtrodden souls acquired the public voice of their resistance in the form of the *Shreveport Times*, a brand new daily newspaper which set the state ablaze with its brave criticisms of the Reconstruction hoodlums. On June 1, 1872, it defiantly called for an end to carpetbag rule in Louisiana, and a mysterious organization soon appeared.

The organization was preceded by a continuing series of disturbing events. John McEnery was the Democratic candidate for governor in 1872, and Shreveport businessmen solidly pledged that they would not advance money or supplies for the coming year to any planter who rented land or gave employment to any laborer who voted the Republican ticket in the forthcoming election. Though the election was rife with fraud, McEnery was the winner at the ballot box; however, the Radical Returning Board declared Republican William Pitt Kellog the winner. He was inaugurated on January 14, 1873, ushering in a reign of constant lawlessness and political turmoil, as yet unmatched in the state.

Virtually controlled by negroes who were goaded by carpet-baggers, the state government had organized the Metropolitan Brigade, a military organization composed generally of negroes and commanded by former Confederate General Longstreet. A brooding man throughout the War, he had forsaken the South in its despairing days of Reconstruction, consigning himself to a place of low esteem among southerners, who were especially incensed by his actions in New Orleans. There, during an emotional confrontation with a group of white citizens, including among them some Confederate veterans, he ordered his negroes to fire into the crowd. His Metropolitan Brigade was complete with a gunboat, fashioned from the steamboat *Ozark*, in which he could land his troops at any port desired.

By the spring of 1873, the stage was set for the organization of the White League. Colonel James Hollingsworth, of Shreveport, called a meeting of several like-minded individuals, to whom he explained the plan. A White League would be set up in every parish and would consist primarily of a political club, but with an auxiliary rifle club which would be composed entirely of ex-Confederate soldiers. Hollingsworth further explained that the political club would be open to every white man who would join, and that it would serve as a camouflage for the inner workings of the association. The men sitting before him were asked to be the secret inner circle. They were each to find eight loyal men to aid them, and the membership of this executive committee would not be increased so as to keep Radicals from infiltrating the group.

The purpose of the rifle club was to oppose the Metropolitan Brigade, but the inner circle was commissioned with a broader goal. Rallying the entire White League membership behind its efforts, the executive committee was to try to stop the killing of negroes when the carpetbaggers instigated a race riot. Hollingsworth pointed out that the negroes of Louisiana were ordinarily a harmless people who committed outrages only when stirred up by the carpetbaggers, and that the death of a negro was fuel for the fire of the corrupt government. Instead, Hollingsworth proposed that no carpetbagger be allowed to escape alive from any future race riot. The *Shreveport Times*

175

immediately concurred, when in 1873, it declared, "Their career is ended; we are determined to tolerate them no longer, if they care for their infamous necks, they had better stop their work right now, and look for a safer field of rascality. If a single battle gun is fired between the whites and blacks, every carpetbagger and scalawag that can be caught will in twelve hours be hanging from a limb."[15]

Just as the White League was forming itself, the Radicals incited a bloody riot in Colfax, where about 300 negroes were killed. The riot probably helped swell the membership of the League in those parts, for the *Minden Democrat* estimated that northwestern Louisiana had 10,000 who were ready to ride.

In response to the White League, the Radicals further incited the negroes, forming them into Union Leagues. In June and July, large shipments of arms arrived from New Orleans and were delivered to negroes along the rivers between Natchitoches and Shreveport. Fearing more uprisings and massacres, the parishes of Caddo, DeSoto, and Bossier petitioned the state of Texas for annexation. Resolutions of sympathy were made by the people of Texas, but the proposition was repressed by the Radical government in Louisiana.

The *Shreveport Times*, always in the vanguard, called for a convention of the white people to assemble at Alexandria on September 1, 1874; however, the Democrats, convinced that the time was ripe, assumed charge and scheduled a meeting in Baton Rouge on August 24.

In the midst of this encouraging political activity, a Radical and two of his negro henchmen threw the state into turmoil by killing two white pickets who were posted on the road leading into Coushatta, on August 28. The town of Coushatta immediately called for help, and men began assembling in Shreveport the next day. Dispatches arrived from the Texas cities of Marshall, Longview, and Jefferson, promising help if needed.

Before the Shreveport contingent could move south, word came that a Coushatta posse had captured several white Radicals and some negroes who were responsbile for the crime; therefore, the men from Caddo parish stayed home. Unaware of the arrests, though, were about a thousand men from other parishes and Texas. Their presence in Coushatta frightened the daylights out of the white prisoners who, accordingly, offered to resign their carpetbag offices and leave the state. Their offer was gladly accepted, and they were started, under guard, toward Shreveport, which is about forty-five miles north of Coushatta. Seventeen miles south of Shreveport, the party encountered a group of men who murdered the prisoners.

On September 2, Governor Kellog, alarmed at the resistance to his carpetbag government, wired President Grant for military intervention, a request which, surprisingly enough, Grant denied. The next day Governor Kellog declared martial law in Louisiana. Two days later, Grant changed his mind and ordered massive bodies of troops into the state. The old carpetbag trick had worked again. Once more Louisiana was under military occupation, and carpetbaggers seemed to breathe more easily.

But this was 1874, and the people of Louisiana were growing tired and bolder. In August, Natchitoches parish had succeeded in running off its tax collector, judge, district judge, and police jury. Two weeks after the riot at Coushatta, there was a bloody upheaval in New Orleans, where the White League overthrew Governor Kellog's administration and installed the Democratic officials who were the rightful winners of the 1872 election. Several parishes in northwestern Louisiana followed suit and set up their own *de facto* governments after forcing the Radicals to flee.

Grant, ever accommodating to his scurrilous carpetbag friends, ordered the *de facto* governments to disperse within five days. Additional troops and warships were sent to the state, and by September 19, Kellog had forced his way back into the governor's chair. A few days later, the *Shreveport Times* declared, "The President's soldiers may reinstate there the officials of fraud, but the moment the troops retire Mr. Kellog will be expelled or killed."[16]

Going on, it commented about the expected demise of the *de facto* governments in other parishes. "If the federal government again strikes them down, then let the infamy of the deed rest upon the shameless Northern people, beneath whose withering influence no sentiment of liberty can survive; under whose policy of meanness, cowardice, and hate, every community that does not worship it must be trampled in the dust and every civilization that does not pay tribute to it blasted by its curse."

On October 16, a Federal posse began a march through four northwestern Louisiana parishes, arresting large groups of men without warrants and on charges of conspiracy and intimidation in the murder of the white prisoners south of Shreveport. In DeSoto parish, the men of the White League escaped to the woods, but in Caddo parish, about seventy-five men were arrested, including the organizer of the White League, Colonel Hollingsworth.

A virtual state of war existed in Louisiana for the next two years, and various atrocities occurred throughout the entire period. In 1876, the White League supported a Confederate war hero, Francis Nicholls, for governor, while the Radicals put up Stephen Packard as their candidate. True to form, the Radical Returning Board threw out enough ballots to declare Packard the winner. The votes in eight parishes were completely thrown out as punishment for the Colfax and Coushatta affairs of 1874.

Like most southern states, Louisiana had about decided that the words of Patrick Henry were as true as they had been a hundred years earlier. Life was not so dear, nor was peace so sweet, "as to be purchased at the price of chains and slavery." As the carpetbagger Packard was inaugurated, the southern men of the state defiantly swore Nicholls in as governor and helped him to establish a legislature made up of men elected by the white citizens. Parish and city governments across the state rebuffed the Packard government and recognized the authority of Nicholls. A new Supreme Court was appointed by Nicholls, and the state taxes were deposited into the treasury of his government.

On March 24, 1877, Nicholls boldly announced that his government was complete and invited the newly-elected President Rutherford B. Hayes to inspect the situation. On April 20, President Hayes ordered all troops out of the State House, and Governor Nicholls moved in. Louisiana's nightmare was over, and southerners could once more walk in the sun in their lovely old Deep South state of majestic oaks and Spanish moss. Paradise regained.

Not only had the people of Louisiana resolved to do or die, President Hayes was making good on a promise he had made in securing his election. In 1873, a severe financial panic had hit the United States, giving the Democrats an issue in the 1874 congressional elections. The corruption of Grant's presidency, coupled with the panic, had swept the Democrats to victory, making them the majority party in the House of Representatives for the first time since 1858. This new power was to play a significant role in the disputed presidential election of 1876.

The Democrats chose Samuel Tilden as their candidate and preached reform, while the Republicans chose Hayes and "waved the bloody shirt" once again. The returns were in dispute in Oregon and the three southern states still occupied by troops — Louisiana, Florida, and South Carolina. An electoral commission, consisting of eight Republicans and seven Democrats, was created by Congress for the purpose of recommending a winner. Voting along party lines, the commission selected Hayes. The Democrats, who held a vast majority in the House, agreed to the decision with the stipulation that *all troops still protecting the carpetbag governments in the South be withdrawn*. Though the other eight states had, in one way or another, regained home rule, a Republican machine still existed in each state, creating a precarious balance that could be upset as long as the Republicans in Washington had the authority to send troops back into the South. Without a doubt, it was the most important compromise ever to affect the South, for with the departure of the last troop went everything that makes life unbearable to a civilized society.

The withdrawal of the troops put an immediate end to the carpetbag governments. Radical Republican rule had made a two-party system in the South impossible for more than a hundred years to come. Not a phase of southern life escaped their vindictive eye. Even the old gray woolen jackets worn home from the War were called a uniform and summarily forbidden to be worn. Many who had nothing else to break the winter cold, sewed gray bits of cloth over the brass buttons in an effort to declassify the old garments lest a guard find him plowing the field in a "criminal's coat."

There were three requisite conditions for Republican power in the South: the negro vote, Republican control of the national government, and federal troops. Should any one of these supports be weakened or removed, Republican rule would collapse. The southerner had little control over troops or national politics, having himself been barred from voting, so he turned his efforts to the local scene, where the secret societies began to spring up in an effort to stop negro voting and run the carpetbaggers out of the South. The romance of the period, with its night rides, daring plots of retribution, and scenes of southern women sewing costumes by day that southern men would wear by night, has best been captured in the works of Thomas Dixon. For a true sampling of the tenor of the times, it is highly recommended that the reader obtain a copy of Dixon's 1905 classic, *The Clansman*, which inspired D.W. Griffith's motion picture epic, *The Birth of a Nation*. The movie, which portrays the classic struggle between the carpetbag regime and the Ku Klux Klan, was so controversial that Dixon and Griffith enlisted the aid of United States Chief Justice Edward Douglas White in overcoming would-be censors. It has passed into our literature as a masterpiece of American drama, described by President

Woodrow Wilson, who held a White House screening of the silent movie, as "history written with lightning."[17]

The clandestine organizations which proliferated across Dixie were called by different names, including the Knights of the White Camellia, the Red Shirts, the White League, and the White Brotherhood; but, the association which attracted the most attention was the Ku Klux Klan. Not to be confused with the Ku Klux Klan of the present day, the original Klan was organized for the same reason as the White League of Louisiana — to rid the land of the curse of carpetbag tyranny. Formed in Pulaski, Tennessee, in 1866, the Ku Klux Klan quickly spread across the South. The members wore robes and hoods of symbolic, mysterious designs, while frightening negroes and whipping scalawags and carpetbaggers. An alarmed Radical Congress passed two acts in 1870 and 1871 aimed at suppressing the Klan, and by 1877, there was no more need for secret societies; therefore, the last units of the Klan were disbanded.

Without the secret societies and rifle clubs, it is doubtful that home rule would have returned before the end of the century. Violence in Hamburg, South Carolina, on July 4, 1876, gave birth to the Red Shirts, who rode through hill and dale with the same fervor of Paul Revere who had ridden a century earlier for the sake of freedom. Brutal insults were the daily fare from the foul mouths of freedmen, and womanhood was imperiled in the state. Former Confederate Generals M.C. Butler and M.W. Gary advocated the "straight-out" system, declaring that nothing but a straight-out fight could now succeed in overthrowing the corrupt government. In response to an order forbidding him to interfere in the election of 1876 in his native state, he responded, "You could put a soldier in front of every cottage in the State and could not prevent the return of South Carolina to her own people."[18] Adopting as their uniform the red flannel shirt, in derision of the cheap sensational Radical practice of "waving the bloody shirt," they moved as swiftly as the minutemen of old in ridding the state of the unwanted thugs who had become leaches upon southern society.

In Indian Territory, military troops occupied the entire area, where the Five Civilized Tribes were being punished for their allegiance to the Confederacy by wild Republican threats in Congress to colonize former slaves from the entire South on lands to be taken from the Indians. Although this didn't come to pass, the idea of "forty acres and a mule" was so seriously and widely projected, it had the effect of enticing ex-slaves from Texas, Arkansas, and Missouri to pour into the territory, where they squatted on Indian lands and raided the corn cribs and smokehouses of Indian citizens. To make matters worse, the Radicals proposed to give the former slaves of the Indians all of the rights held by Indians, plus an equal share in tribal annuities, lands, and other benefits — some of which came to pass in the resulting harsh Reconstruction treaties forced upon the tribes. Eventually, the government would take away one-half of Indian Territory and give it to the wild plains Indians who attacked the Five Civilized Tribes with frequency — the price exacted for southern loyalty.

Conditions in Indian Territory were the worst in the old Confederacy. A full twenty-five percent of the population was dead from the effects of the War, and virtually every home and village was destroyed from the constant raiding. Today, hardly an ante-bellum structure is to be found within the state of Oklahoma, mute testimony to the near total destruction of the War.

The grinding poverty was worsened by the freedmen who stole chickens, hogs, horses, and cattle. The federal armies of occupation were there to protect the negro, not the Indian, so the Five Civilized Tribes resorted to vigilante committees to restore order and check the thievery of the freedmen. The Choctaws and Chickasaws were the first to form their mounted patrols. They met secretly, devising signals and determining punishment for violators of the vigilante code. They maintained secret communication channels and made night rides to intimidate freedmen, who usually congregated together in their shanty towns. If, after having been warned, a negro was found outside his community, he would be whipped by these Indian patrols. If, when caught, he was in possession of a hog, cow, or horse, the freedman was executed on the spot. The success of the Choctaw and Chickasaw vigilante committees led to the formation of similar groups among the Creeks, Seminoles, and Cherokees, and some semblance of order returned.

Reconstruction was a nightmare to the South, and its effects left deep scars. Thomas Dixon spent his childhood in an occupied North Carolina, consequently devoting his life to writing the horrors of it all. The world authority on slavery, Ulrich B. Phillips, was born in Georgia during the last year of Reconstruction. In 1889, at the age of twelve, he persuaded his parents to rename him Ulrich. At birth, he had been christened Ulysses, but he had seen enough to know that he did not want to share the name of anyone who had played such a role in defeating and humiliating his homeland. Former Confederate Secretary of War, Robert Toombs, another Georgian who remembered, was said to have gloated over the great Chicago fire of 1871. Even today, Reconstruction's memories evoke indignation among southerners. In 1987, a Tennessee state senator succeeded in having a huge portrait of "Parson" Brownlow removed from the state capitol. The oil painting, depicting the unpopular Reconstruction governor ostentatiously pointing towards the U.S. flag, was placed in the basement museum across the street where, as one Nashville attorney told me, it is hanging at eye level so that one can see the tobacco juice stains made by the spitting of ex-Confederates upon the image of the governor who denied them the right to vote.

The *Southern Partisan* recently wrote, "Many Americans today, in this age of historical amnesia, would disbelieve that one part of their country was once put under military occupation by another part, that heinous crimes went unpunished, that summary arrests and summary executions were common, that courts were subverted, legislatures corrupted, and the majority of the electorate disfranchised — all at the instance of the federal government."[19]

Indeed, some wish to cover it up — or worse, to rewrite it into a distortion. Even the Board of Education in the state of South Carolina decided, in 1985, to rewrite the textbooks in such a fashion that Reconstruction would be characterized as a *milestone in social progress*. Even a carpetbagger knows the folly of such an absurd idea. Albion W. Tourgee, an Ohio-born carpetbagger who descended upon North Carolina, knew it for what it was. It wasn't social progress, and, writing of its abject failure in his novel of 1879, entitled *A Fool's Errand*, he admitted, "We tried to superimpose the civilization, the idea of the North, upon the South at a moment's warning. We presumed, that, by the suppression of rebellion, the Southern white man had become identical with the Caucasian of the North in thought and sentiment; and that the slave, by emancipation, had become a saint and a Solomon at once. So we tried to build up communities there which should be identical in thought, sentiment, growth, and development, with those of the North. It was *A Fool's Errand*."[20]

Corporal Sam R. Watkins, of Columbia, Tennessee, was living proof that Reconstruction had failed to diminish devotion to the Lost Cause. Writing in 1881, he said, "Secession may have been wrong in the abstract, and has been tried and settled by the arbitrament of the sword and bayonet, but I am as firm in my convictions today of the right of secession as I was in 1861. The South is our country, the North is the country of those who live there. We are an agricultural people; they are a manufacturing people. They are the descendants of the good old Puritan Plymouth Rock stock, and we of the South from the proud and aristocratic stock of Cavaliers. We believe in the doctrine of State rights, they in the doctrine of centralization.

"John C. Calhoun, Patrick Henry, and Randolph, of Roanoke, saw the venom under their wings, and warned the North of the consequences, but they laughed at them. We only fought for our State rights, they for Union and power. The South fell battling under the banner of State rights, but yet grand and glorious even in death."[21]

Let none among us disparage our southern ancestors. Let us only hope that even a trickle of the revolutionary blood that flowed in their veins has remained in ours. It is ironic that the very code of honor, which the Yankees thought four years of cruel war had eradicated, was the same standard that silently sustained us through Reconstruction. It's that inner faith and stamina, particularly southern in nature, that makes us what we are — Southern, by the grace of God.

VI

A PORTRAIT
OF DIXIE

They say a picture's worth a thousand words. The photographs in the following pages tell many more stories than the short captions beneath them. One of my favorites is the one I found in an antique store in Thomasville, Georgia. The back of the picture carried only the words: *Aunt Lucy Ann.* On the front, there is a woman — obviously Aunt Lucy Ann — with her family, posed in front of three hand-lettered cards and a picture of a lady, which together spell out the year of the photograph — 1910. The large picture frame serves as the "0" of the date. From the smile of satisfaction on the face of the little boy kneeling behind the cards, one might guess that dating the picture was his handiwork.

With the exception of a few Confederate Veterans' Reunions of the 1920's, all of the photographs date backward from the World War I era and are intended to depict southern life in that period as only the photographer could capture it. Most of the images have never been published before and are not of presidents, generals, first ladies, and men of great fame, but

187

rather of the average citizen of the South who might have been an ancestor of yours and mine.

There are photographs from all twelve southern states and the border states of Kentucky and Missouri. The large majority of them are from my own collection, augmented by loans from friends and several archival agencies.

Much of my collection comes from purchases at antique stores and flea markets. In acquiring pictures from these sources, I have found that old southern photographs are scarce in comparison to those from the north. When found, they are usually inferior in quality — faded, worn, damaged, and printed on poorer stock. It occurs to me that the poor condition and scarcity of southern photographs is a consequence of the War and Reconstruction and the general economic depression of the South following those years of turmoil.

MONTGOMERY, ALABAMA, ca. 1890. B.F. Goolsby, "The Pretty Boy"; George Preiss, "The Gentleman"; George McAdam, "The Good Thing"; James Hawkins, "The Irish Sport"; J.D. Carney, "Too Young."

OLD PHOTOGRAPHS FADE WHEN EXPOSED TO THE LIGHT. KEEP THEM IN A BOX OR DRAWER. NEVER FRAME AND HANG THEM ON THE WALL. IF YOU WANT TO DISPLAY AN OLD PHOTOGRAPH, HAVE IT COPIED, AND FRAME THE COPY. STORE THE ORIGINAL IN A DARK PLACE.

NASHVILLE, TENNESSEE,
ca. 1880.

WACO, TEXAS, 1909. Minnie Willis. (Courtesy Leona Holland)

MINERAL WELLS, TEXAS, 1890. A camp meeting in this north Texas community. Camp meetings were popular in the Old South. People would come and stay for about a week or so, camping out under the stars. Each day would be filled with preaching, studying the Bible, and singing. (Courtesy William F. King)

MEMPHIS, TENNESSEE, ca. 1917. A proud southern mama and her four boys, two of whom are in the military

WYNNEWOOD, INDIAN TERRITORY, November, 1896. Cotton market in Wynnewood. Bales of cotton being inspected by cotton buyers on South Commercial Street.

SOMEWHERE IN THE SOUTH, PROBABLY SOUTH GEORGIA, 1910. A hard-working rural family of the South, probably dressed in their Sunday best. A most unusual photograph, it shows the year 1910 spelled out by three hand-lettered cards and a large, framed family picture which serves as the "0". The smile on the little boy's face may be an indication that dating the picture was his handiwork. The back of this photo carried only three words: *Aunt Lucy Ann.*

194

JONESTOWN, MISSISSIPPI,
ca. 1905. C.P. Shelby.

YEAGER, OKLAHOMA, 1908. Carlos Grissom and
his grandmother, Laura McFarland Linn.

MAMMOTH CAVE, KENTUCKY, Aug. 12, 1908. A group of tourists and their guide.

MURFREESBORO, TENNESSEE,
1878. Two southern boys.

CHATTANOOGA, TENNESSEE, December, 1895. The same southern girl, now a pretty young lady of sixteen or seventeen.

VICKSBURG, MISSISSIPPI, ca. 1890. Miss Lizzie W. Small, twelve years old.

WHITESBORO, TEXAS, ca. 1899. Ida Irene McFarland, about twelve years old, in her first store-bought dress, which cost 15¢.

WACO, TEXAS, 1910. William Cyburn Crawford Willis. (Courtesy Leona Holland)

MURFREESBORO, TENNESSEE,
1878. R.B. Furguson.

FRANKLIN, TENNESSEE, 1864. Capt. Tod Carter joined the Army of Tennessee in 1861 and was captured at Chattanooga in November, 1863. The young soldier escaped in late 1864, rejoining his command only a few days before the Battle of Franklin, which swirled about his family's home. He was wounded only 200 yards from the house, where his family huddled in the basement for protection. Brought home after the battle, he died within forty-eight hours.

WYNNEWOOD, INDIAN TERRITORY, ca. 1903. A brave lady holds a six-foot snake by its tail.

TEXAS, 1911. Three happy children in a new 1911 Ford Model T. (Courtesy William F. King)

MONTREAL, CANADA, 1867. The children of Jefferson Davis. Only one child, Margaret, would live a full lifetime. From left to right: Jefferson Davis, Jr., age 10, died of yellow fever in 1878 at age 21; Margaret, age 12; William Howell, age 6, died of diphtheria in 1872 at age 11; Varina Anne "Winnie", *the Daughter of the Confederacy*, age 3, died of complications of a cold in New York, in 1898, at the age of 34. Little five-year-old Joe Davis, not pictured here, had died in 1864 when he fell from the balcony of the White House in Richmond.

EASTMAN, GEORGIA, ca. 1907. Mary Edward.

BIRMINGHAM, ALABAMA, ca. 1905.

Two Southern Belles in
their winter fashions.

202

WYNNEWOOD, OKLAHOMA, ca. 1907. Bessie Roberts in her graduation cap.

TENNESSEE, ca. 1880's. A west Tennessee family.

McMINNVILLE, TENNESSEE, ca. 1900. This young girl is posing as a gypsy in the studio of W.S. Lively. Known as "Dad" to those who knew him, Lively established the famous Southern School of Photography in 1904. He constructed the world's largest camera, which measured 11' by 6' by 5'. Some of his 30" x 60" prints were considered masterpieces, and today they hang in the Smithsonian Institution in Washington, D.C. The subject in this picture is identified on the back of this photo as *Gillie Thurman, Mrs. Ada Terrell's sister.*

ARLINGTON, VIRGINIA, ca. 1915. The Custis-Lee Mansion, home of General & Mrs. Robert E. Lee before the War. The Yankees seized it at the outset of the War and, by burying northern soldiers all around the yard and next to the house, made sure that the Lees would never return to live there. Today, the home sits in the middle of Arlington National Cemetery.

KENTUCKY, ca. 1910. A doctor and his fine rig, ready to make calls.

BOWLING GREEN, KENTUCKY, November 20, 1884. A handsome Kentucky boy, Leonard Phebus, at the age of seventeen.

MURFREESBORO, TENNESSEE, 1878.

WYNNEWOOD, INDIAN TERRITORY, ca. 1900. Interior of First National Bank. At the window are J.D. Daugherty and ... left to right are Ira Mitchell, A.L. Goff and M.H. Deal.

SULPHUR, INDIAN TERRITORY, ca. 1898. Wynnewood residents camping out at a favorite spot which would soon become Platt National Park. From left to right across front of picture: Mattie Winbray, A.D. Patterson, Dora Boone, Dan Liddell, Mamie Liddell, Mrs. Wirt Randolph, George Bradfield, Walter Martin, Miss Ida Lewis, Miss Patterson of Gainesville (?), Walter Cravens. Those behind front row, left to right: Mrs. Ira Mitchell, Ira Mitchell, Edith Riggan, Mrs. Hoover, Garland Strange, Tom Jarrett, Mrs. Geer, Miss Fannie Hodgkiss, Miss Nealy Winbray (or Sallie Lawrence ?), Sam Long, Edna Lawrence. Unidentified boy behind Edna Lawrence.

HUBBARD, TEXAS, ca. 1890's. The Faulkners. A well-to-do, prosperous family, if the fashionable clothes are any indication.

c Spring. Eureka Springs. Ark.

EUREKA SPRINGS, ARKANSAS, ca. 1910. Lover's Leap and Mystic Springs, two popular attractions at the Arkansas resort.

Lover's Leap, Harding Spring, and the House Upon the Rock, Eureka Springs.

MONTGOMERY, ALABAMA, May 29, 1893. President Davis's body, lying in state in the rotunda of the state capitol. His remains were being moved to Richmond from New Orleans by special train which made stops at Montgomery and Atlanta. The body had been temporarily interred at Metairie Cemetery in New Orleans on December 11, 1889, until it could be permanently laid to rest in Hollywood Cemetery at Richmond.

BIRMINGHAM, ALABAMA, ca. 1916.
Flower girl at a wedding.

NEW ORLEANS, LOUISIANA, 1876.
"For Charlie if he wishes it — Mama,
34 yrs. old."

BONHAM, TEXAS, August, 1905. Aubrey L. McRae, who sometimes rode his horse across the Red River into the Choctaw and Chickasaw Nations. Two riders, a man and a woman, stopped him on a road through the woods one day. The woman said, "That's a fine horse you're riding." At the next crossroads, McRae described them to the storekeeper, who told him that the woman was Belle Starr.

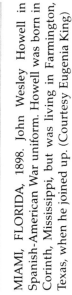

MIAMI, FLORIDA, 1898. John Wesley Howell in Spanish-American War uniform. Howell was born in Corinth, Mississippi, but was living in Farmington, Texas, when he joined up. (Courtesy Eugenia King)

CHATTANOOGA, TENNESSEE, ca. 1890's.

FORT WORTH, TEXAS, ca. 1900.

PAULS VALLEY, OKLAHOMA, ca. 1913. Nora Jane Grant, a beautiful Chickasaw Indian, outfitted in an exquisite winter ensemble. Her father, C.J. Grant, was one of the founders of the First National Bank of Pauls Valley in 1895, and her grandfather, Tom Grant, was one of the leading citizens of the Chickasaw Nation.

216

ARDMORE, INDIAN TERRITORY, ca. 1900. The Grissom brothers: Sam, Joseph Columbus, Abraham Jackson, Stephen A. Douglas, Albert Hamilton, and George Ernest. They were gathered for the funeral of their only sister, Nancy Jeffries, near Wilson, I.T. Sam, Abe, and J.C. had come from the Creek Nation, Albert from Alabama, and Douglas from Texas. George lived near Wilson. It was the last time they would ever be together, so, before boarding their separate trains, they went to a studio in Ardmore and had this picture taken.

TENNESSEE, ca. 1910. A west Tennessee man with his tools for shoeing horses.

217

TAMPA, FLORIDA, Aug. 28, 1898. On the Hillsborough River, this is the full rigged brig, *Ampala*, of Barcelona, Spain. Captured by a U.S. war ship off the coast of Key West, Florida, while trying to run the blockade, she was carrying 74 Spanish refugees from Havana, Cuba, to Tampico, Mexico, during the Spanish-American War.

During the War Between the States, many women and children were forced to flee their homes — more than once. The roads were full of refugees trying to stay ahead of the invading Yankees.

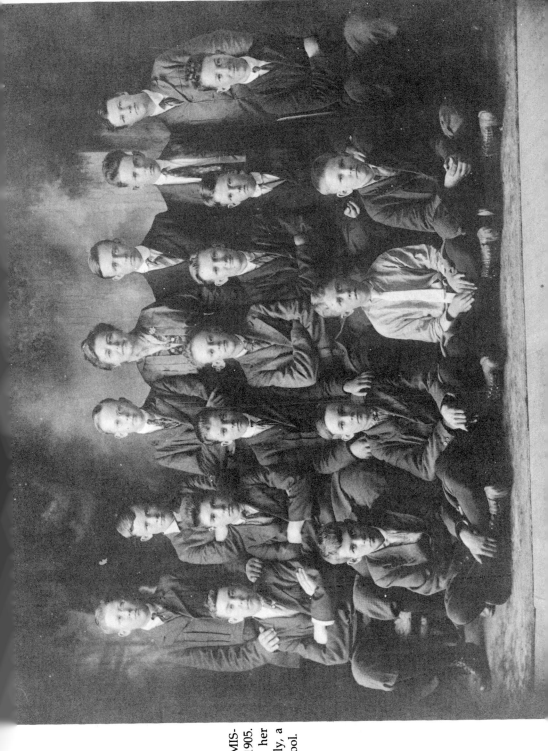

GULFPORT, MIS-
SISSIPPI, ca. 1905.
A lady and her
boys. Probably, a
boarding school.

NEW ORLEANS, LOUISIANA, Dec. 11, 1889. The solemn funeral procession winds its way down the narrow New Orleans streets toward Metairie Cemetery. An astonished north looked upon the South in disbelief as more than 200,000 mourning southerners made their way into the Crescent City for the largest funeral ever held in Dixie. Jefferson Davis, the most important link to the old Confederacy, was bade an affectionate farewell.

FRANKLIN, TENNESSEE, ca. 1915. *Carnton*, where Mrs. McGavock brought 200 wounded soldiers into the shelter of her home on the cold night of Nov. 30, 1864, after the bloody Battle of Franklin. The next morning, the bodies of four generals were laid out on this porch, awaiting burial. *See story in Chapter VIII.*

WOODFORD, OKLAHOMA, 1910. The Baptist Church, holding an outdoor baptizin' in a nearby creek. The preacher, John Perkins, has baptized twenty-four people while the congregation looks on from the hillside. A buggy with two horses waits in the right background. (Courtesy Joyce Duncan Jordan)

GREENSBORO, ALABAMA, May 19, 1900. Confederate Veterans of Hale County, Alabama, at Hobson's Grove.

GAINESVILLE, GEORGIA, ca. 1908. John Orr, student at Riverside Military Academy.

HANNIBAL, MISSOURI, ca. 1870.

RICHMOND, VIRGINIA, ca. 1868.
Rosa Jackson.

LEXINGTON, KENTUCKY, ca. 1890. The trotting track at the Fayette County Fairgrounds.

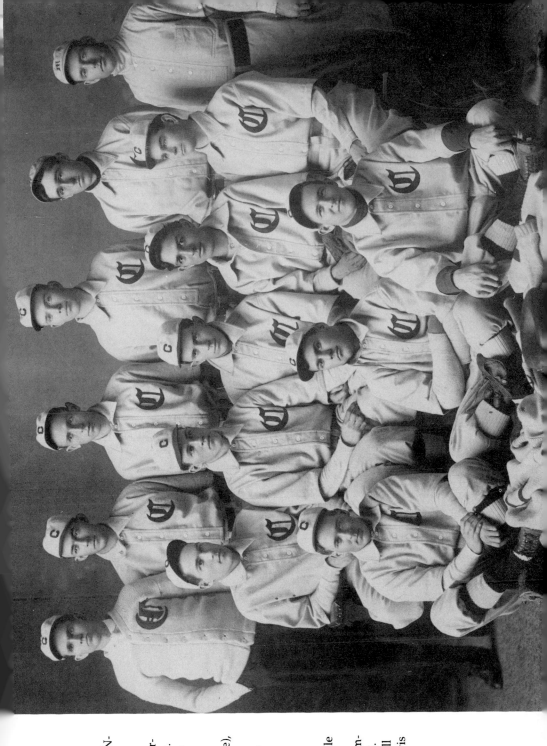

LEBANON, TENNESSEE, 1909. The baseball team at Cumberland University. Back row: Hudson (mgr.), Barbee (pitcher), Allison (1st base), Ball (pitcher), Miller (pitcher), Clark (coach). Second row: Crump (3rd base), Luna (catcher), Carlisle (left field), Frye (short stop), Templeton (pitcher). Front row: Small (2nd base), Lewis (center field), Gipson (right field).

OUR LEGACY FROM THE YANKEES

The South is the only section of the country ever to have been invaded by another section. The invasion and its thorough devastation of the southern countryside was so unnecessary. Scenes like this were universal throughout the once peaceful land of cotton. The photo above shows a warehouse in Richmond in April, 1865. Below is the once magnificent Phillips house after the Battle of Fredericksburg, Virginia.

South Carolina was especially hated by the Yankees. As Sherman's vultures marched northward out of Georgia in February, 1865, they began to make good on their boasts that they would make South Carolina pay dearly for having been the first state to dare to leave the oppressive Union. Everything was put to the Yankee torch. Nothing was sacred. The top photo shows a church in Columbia in 1865. The bottom photo shows all that is left of a railroad depot in Charleston in 1865.

Sue Lipscomb, of Franklin.
ca. 1875.

ca. 1875

TWO FASHIONABLE YOUNG LADIES OF KENTUCKY.

LOUISIANA, date unknown. Mailman in the Cajun country of south Louisiana.

ADA, INDIAN TERRITORY, summer,
1904. Building the Citizen's National Bank
and adjacent buildings on West Main.

VICKSBURG, MISSISSIPPI, ca. 1882. Charles.

TROY, TENNESSEE, ca. 1890's.
Ed and Jack.

230

WYNNEWOOD, INDIAN TERRITORY, ca. 1900. Exterior and interior views of Indianola College, showing a penmanship class in progress. The college was bought by the Presbyterians and moved to Muskogee, where it became Henry Kendall College. Before long, it was moved to Tulsa and has been known as Tulsa University ever since. The main academic building in Wynnewood was converted into the town's first high school.

TENNESSEE, ca. 1920. A group of Confederate veterans standing in front of a Confederate monument. Most of the aged men are holding canes, although one old gentleman holds his sword high in the air. What a pity those stalwart defenders of the Old South are all gone now! Walter Williams, the South's last soldier, died in 1959 at the age of 117, and is buried at Franklin, Texas.

232

WYNNEWOOD, OKLAHOMA, 1910. The main building of Indianola College, shown here in flames, had been purchased in 1909 by the city for use as a high school. When fire broke out in a tall building back in those days, about all anyone could do is stand by and watch it burn.

WILMINGTON, NORTH CARO-LINA, date unknown. The South is known for its stately homes which feature large front entries framed by graceful white columns. This old photo shows the typically southern entrance to the Bellamy House near Wilmington. It was built in 1859 by the Bellamy family.

233

JACKSON COUNTY, OKLAHOMA TERRITORY, ca. 1900. The family of William H. & Mary A. Portwood, of Warren. Jackson County, named after Stonewall Jackson, was originally part of old Greer County, Texas. In 1896, the Supreme Court awarded Greer County to Oklahoma, who created the counties of Harmon, Jackson, and Greer from it. (Courtesy Joann Schnorrenberg)

WEATHERFORD, TEXAS, ca. 1887. William David Lee McJunkin, seated at left, and four of his friends. The *Lee* was added, for good reason, after the War. (Courtesy William F. King)

LEBANON, TENNESSEE. The administration building at Castle Heights School burned in 1915 and again in 1916. From this hull, it was built back after both fires. In 1987, the beautiful building is exact in every detail, and one would never guess it had ever burned. Castle Heights was a military preparatory school for boys, established in 1902. Unfortunately, its stately campus with fine old Victorian buildings closed its doors in 1986, and will, without doubt, soon be transformed into the usual eyesore of parking lots, shopping malls, and drive-in banks that blight our southern cities.

CLEBURNE, TEXAS, ca. 1916. A mother and her daughter. Ruby Douglass and Garland.

STAUNTON, VIRGINIA, ca. 1902. An attractive Virginia family. Southerners are a handsome race of people with classic, refined features, the result of nearly 300 years of a delicate blending of Europe's old world nationalities. The most commonly found bloodlines among southerners are French, German, Dutch, English, and Scotch-Irish, with an occasional trace of American Indian.

CORSICANA TEXAS ca 1890's

JONESBORO ARKANSAS ca 1890's

ANTA, GEORGIA, 1898. A magnificent photograph of six Confederate veterans. These old
diers, some of them maimed by war, served as Miss Winnie Davis's last escort at the Confederate
nion in Atlanta in 1898. The *Daughter of the Confederacy* died later that year at the age of
From the United Confederate Veterans Camp #435, they are W.M. Dunbar, W.I. Delph, F.E.
, W.A. Gibbes, W.J. Steed, and George P. Bush.

May, 1864. This poor lad was found near a farm house at Spotsylvania, Virginia. He had bandaged his own leg with an old shirt, but probably bled to death from a bullet hole in his shoulder.

July 3, 1863. Pvt. Andrew J. Hoge, of the 4th Virginia Infantry, killed at Gettysburg. He was only 18 years old. The Confederacy had no uniforms for these boys. They wore what they could find and gave dignity to rags.

THEY SOUTHERN BOYS WHO GAVE THEIR ALL AND DID THEIR BEST TO STOP THE INVASION. THEY FOUGHT

CAMDEN, TENNESSEE, ca. 1900

Children from Benton County, Tennessee.

HOLLADAY, TENNESSEE, June, 1911.

DENTON, TEXAS, ca. 1905. Smoot's Drug Store.

NEW ORLEANS, LOUISIANA, ca. 1885. The *Natchez,* fabled steamboat which raced the *Robert E. Lee,* taking on a load at a Mississippi River dock in New Orleans.

NATCHEZ, MISSISSIPPI, ca. 1919. An old photo of the imposing Natchez mansion, *Dunleith.*

ADA, OKLAHOMA, April 19, 1909. The lynching of four suspects in the death of A. A. Bobbitt, local rancher. From left to right: Jim Miller, Joe Allen, B. B. Burwell, Jesse West. Miller was a notorious killer, with over 30 murders to his credit, including Sherrif Pat Garrett, the law officer who had killed Billy the Kid. Ada citizens were determined to bring these outlaws to justice and hung them before some clever lawyer had a chance to get them off the hook. (Courtesy Ada Chamber of Commerce) *See story in Chapter VIII.*

DENTON, TEXAS, ca. 1901. Homer Curtis.

GEORGETOWN, TEXAS, ca. 1909. Finis Crutchfield, well-known Methodist preacher. Message on back of picture: *Our Finis Stewart was named for him. Clint Stewart, Sr. was converted while he preached at Ben Arnold, Texas, in 1907.*

BROKEN ARROW, INDIAN TERRITORY, 1906. From left: Clara Brady and baby, Hope Burkes, Gladys Burkes, Clyde Burkes, Eulalie Burkes, Norma Burkes (in buggy), Andrew Jackson Burkes, and Doc Brady. Our ancestors lived in homes like this, yet never demonstrated in the streets for public housing and government give-away programs. They preferred that government leave them alone. They worked hard, raised large families, kept themselves clean, dressed their children in the best they could afford, and made their homes in places like this one until they could get ahead — by their own honest work. They would not recognize today's society of cry babies. *See diary in Chapter VIII.*

BROKEN ARROW, INDIAN TERRITORY, 1906. A grocery store, operated by the Thompsons, kinfolks of the people in top photo.

MURPHY'S BLUFF, ALABAMA, ca. 1890. The *Mary S. Blees* on the Tombigbee River. (Courtesy University of Alabama)

PENSACOLA, FLORIDA, 1861. A Confederate camp at the Warrington Navy Yard. Bands of southerners like these, with no uniforms and very little equipment kept a huge Yankee army at bay for four years. Little wonder that they became known as the "Eighth Wonder of the World." (Courtesy The Bettman Archive)

WYNNEWOOD, INDIAN TERRITORY, 1905. Miss Beatrice Wilson, who became Mrs. George Bradfield in 1906. For seventy years, she was one of the most dedicated and tireless workers in the Oklahoma Division of the United Daughters of the Confederacy. (Courtesy Leta Ferguson and Elizabeth Baker).

LIGHTNING RIDGE, OKLAHOMA, 1916. When the traveling photographer pays a visit, everybody gets into the act — including the horses and mules. Why not? From left to right: George Preston Willis, Havel Willis, Jeanette Willis, Lena Alma Rogers Willis, Leona Mae Willis, Azalea Willis, and William Cyburn Crawford Willis. (Courtesy Leona Holland)

WHITESBORO, TEXAS, ca. 1919. Ready for the parade, an old car is upholstered in festive material, representing the firm of McMahan-Foster. (Courtesy William F. King)

OKLAHOMA CITY, OKLAHOMA, ca. 1912. St. Luke's M.E. Church South. After the War, the Methodist Church was known in the South as the Methodist Episcopal Church South. It was reunited only a couple of decades ago with the northern wing. Most all churches ceased affiliation with the north during the War, and it has been only recently that many of them have rejoined. The Presbyterians reunited in the 1980's, while the Baptists have not done so yet.

VAN BUREN, ARKANSAS, ca. 1870's.

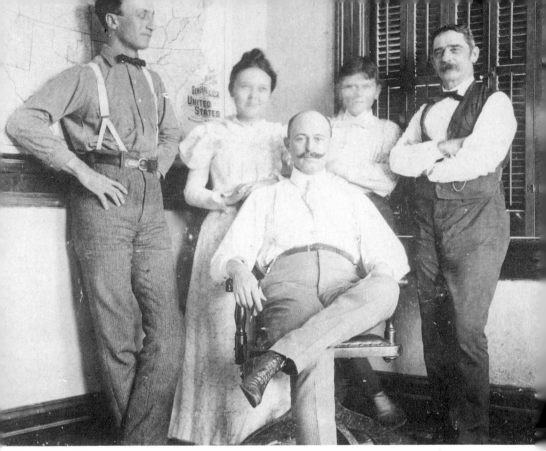

TAMPA, FLORIDA, Aug. 20, 1898. The Depot Quartermaster's Office during the Spanish-American War. H.E. Burks, of San Antonio, Texas, seated in picture, is the Chief Clerk.

SEABREEZE, FLORIDA, 1900.
Known today as Daytona Beach.

DENTON, TEXAS, ca. 1900. "My pet, the little Boren boy."

IDABEL, OKLAHOMA, ca. 1919. J.C. Elliott, of Pauls Valley/Wynnewood area, posing wi
a deer shot in southeastern Oklahoma.

LEBANON, TENNESSEE, 1909. The girls' basketball team at Cumberland University. Mr. Thad Orrh, Coach, Miss Dovie Martin, Miss Vaughan, Miss Mary Franc Coile, Miss Jessie Culbertson, Miss Mae Gwin, Miss Mary Sue Davis, Miss Korrie Rice, and Miss Mildred Bone, Manager.

BANKS, ALABAMA, 1910. The Brantley Hotel.

FANNIN COUNTY, TEXAS, ca. 1898. A group of kinfolks who, in 1902, would move with their parents to Broken Arrow, Indian Territory, by wagon train. They are thought to be Oscar Thompson, Hilliard Burkes, Eva Thompson, Edna McRae Burkes, Robert Burkes, Joe Thompson, and Hattie Thompson. *See diary in Chapter VIII.*

NASHVILLE, TENNSSEE, ca. 1861.
A Confederate soldier, Lt. Tom
Bransford, of the Nelson
Artillery.

NASHVILLE, TENNESSEE.
ca. 1861. A Confederate
soldier, Lt. Daniel Dwyer
Philips, of the 1st
Tennessee Artillery.

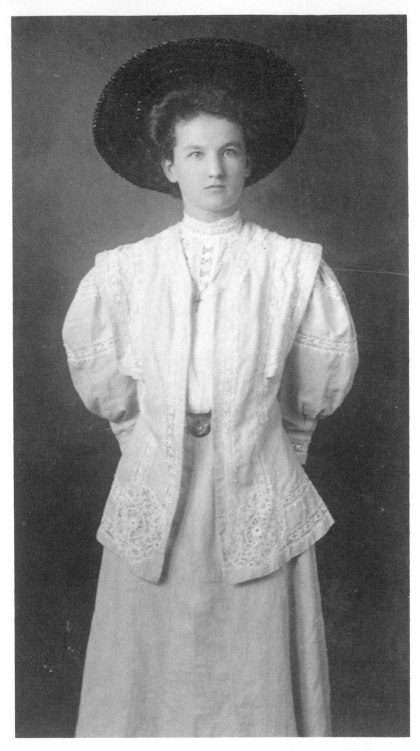

FREDERICK, OKLAHOMA, ca. 1908. Miss Bess Crump. Although this photo was made in the southwestern Oklahoma town of Frederick, Miss Crump was a resident of Wynnewood.

WYNNEWOOD, INDIAN TERRITORY, ca. 1893. A typical town of the Old Southwest. In 1893, the town was only six years old, yet it could boast many wooden business buildings and five made of brick. The town was established in 1887 when the Santa Fe Railroad went through the Chickasaw Nation and has, to this day, maintained a consistent population of 2500.

Those wonderful new Kodaks! They were so popular in the early 1900's. In the top photo, a young man named George tries to sell a "No. 2 Flexo Kodak" to a man in a store thought to be in Texas.

The photograph below shows several new owners trying out their Kodaks. The Spanish moss and live oak trees indicate a location in the lower South.

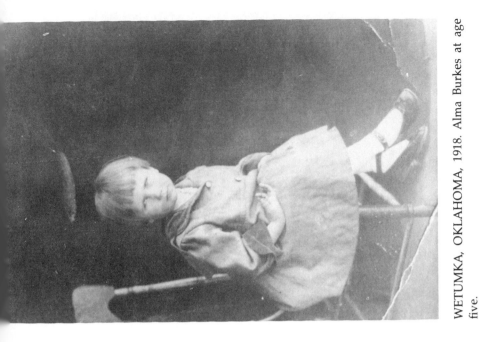

WETUMKA, OKLAHOMA, 1918. Alma Burkes at age five.

CAMERON, TEXAS, ca. 1880's. "To Uncle Hugh from Little Hugh."

EASTERN KENTUCKY, ca. 1900. The most famous mountain feud was the one that broke out between the Hatfields and the McCoys along the Kentucky/West Virginia border. Here, the Hatfields pose with some of their "artillery."

BROKEN ARROW, INDIAN TERRITORY, ca. 1902. This faded photograph has been passed down in the family that made the wagon trip from north Texas in 1902. These cotton pickers are thought to be members of that family. *See diary in Chapter VIII.*

WYNNEWOOD, INDIAN TERRITORY, 1900. *McRae*, named in the 1960's in honor of the McRae family and Confederate cavalry officer Hugh James McRae of Fannin County, Texas. Originally the home of William F. Moore, a native of Arkansas, the house is shown here upon completion. From 1917 until 1936, it was the home of Dr. W. E. Settle, well-known doctor in Indian Territory and Oklahoma.

HENRIETTA, TEXAS, ca. 1911.

NASHVILLE, TENNESSEE, ca. 1919. An old photo of *Clover Bottom Mansion,* built in 1858. One of the most beautiful mansions in Tennessee, today it is in a disastrous state of neglect. Owned by the state of Tennessee, which stubbornly and curiously rejects all efforts and offers of restoration.

PURCELL, INDIAN TERRITORY, ca. 1897. Seated are Melinda Catherine Crabtree and her husband, George Washington Crabtree, who was a Confederate soldier with Co. A, 32nd Regiment, Texas Cavalry. Behind them is their son, Cecil Redman Crabtree. His wife, Livy Ann, holds their baby, Mary Alice Crabtree, while their son, Gilbert, leans on his grandfather's knee. (Courtesy Sandy Mott)

TWO OLD TINTYPES.

Photography began in 1839 in Paris, France. It was brought to America by Samuel F. B. Morse, developer of the Morse Code.

The first images were on pieces of glass and were called daguerreotypes. By 1852, a similar type of image on glass was being produced and called an ambrotype.

Paper soon became the most popular medium, but there were many photographs developed on pieces of tin from the 1860's through the 1890's. They were called tintypes and were cut in many irregular shapes. The images are usually rather dim and gray-looking without sharp contrasts.

ELWOOD, TEXAS, ca. 1880. Hugh James McRae, former Confederate soldier who served as a lieutenant in Co. C, 31st Regiment, Texas Cavalry.

ELWOOD, TEXAS, ca. 1880. Mary A. McRae, oldest daughter of Hugh James McRae.

266

YEAGER, INDIAN TERRITORY, ca. 1906. The home of Dr. J. Woodie Grissom, first doctor in Yeager. From left to right: Clarence R. Lollis, Mrs. Tealie Grissom Lollis, Gertrude Lollis, Preston Caswell Grissom, Nancy Ann Ferguson Grissom, Mrs. Willingham, Mrs. Cleo Willingham Grissom, and Dr. J. Woodie Grissom.

LEBANON, TENNESSEE, 1908. A beautiful southern girl, Mary Sue Davis, at graduation.

COURTIN' IN THE OLD DAYS

Top Photo: Wynnewood, Indian Territory, ca. 1903.

Middle Photo: Climbing the hills at Turner Falls, in the Arbuckle Mountains near Davis, Indian Territory, ca. 1904.

Bottom Photo: Dixie, Texas, ca. 1892. Laura Hester Reast and a friend, at Flowing Wells, a popular park that was inundated by the waters of Lake Texoma in 1944. (Courtesy William F. King)

SAN ANTONIO, TEXAS, summer, 1885. H. E. Burks.

270

FRANKLIN, TENNESSEE, January 15, 1921. Surviving members of Co. B, 1st Tennessee Regiment, United Confederate Veterans, in front of the Pension Office at Franklin. The United States, in dividing up tax money, paid huge monthly pensions to Union veterans, while refusing these old men a penny because, sixty years earlier, they had fought on the "wrong side." Small wonder that Yankees have been called *sore winners*. The women of the South never tired in finding support for these old veterans. They raised money and convinced every single southern state legislature to provide Confederate pensions to fill the gap left by a vindictive Federal government. (Courtesy Carter House & Museum)

271

MARIETTA, INDIAN TERRITORY,
ca. 1905. Zuleka Wolfenbarger.

MACON, GEORGIA, ca. 1900
Smith Thomaston.

272

DENTON, TEXAS, ca. 1900. "Ed Smoot's little boy."

LAREDO, TEXAS, 1918. William G. Burks.

WYNNEWOOD, OKLAHOMA, October 25, 1918. The funeral of W. Wilkie Crump, a 23-year-old boy who was called for military service on September 3, 1918, in the last draft before the armistice was signed on November 11. Crump caught the flu in the terrible epidemic that swept the country, and died on October 21 at Fort Worth, Texas. He was the first soldier buried in Oaklawn Cemetery with a military funeral.

WYNNEWOOD, OKLAHOMA, 1918.
W.B. Crump, Jr., brother of
Wilkie Crump.

FORT WORTH, TEXAS ca. 1903. Abraham Jackson Grissom, the first doctor in Wetumka, Indian Territory. Grissom received his medical training first at Memphis, Tennessee. This photograph was made while he was doing further study in Fort Worth. *See reminiscence in Chapter VIII.*

BROWNSVILLE, TEXAS, ca. 1864.
"Grandmother's cousin."
(Courtesy William F. King)

RICHMOND, VIRGINIA, ca. 1865.

277

SHAWNEE, OKLAHOMA, ca. 1908.
A southern belle.

MURFREESBORO, TENNESSEE, 1878.

278

CHICKASHA, OKLAHOMA, July 10, 11, 12, 1917.

CHICKASHA, OKLAHOMA, July 1, 2, 3, 4, 1924.

Confederate veterans held a large reunion each year on the state level, as well as an annual gathering at the national level. Two Oklahoma reunions are pictured here. The reunions were well attended and supported by the ladies of the UDC. The photographer had to use those long, narrow photographs — some measuring three feet — to get everyone in the picture.

NASHVILLE, TENNESSEE, date unknown. An old photo of the entry hall at *The Hermitage,* home of Andrew Jackson.

WYNNEWOOD, INDIAN TERRITORY, ca. 1906. A band of gypsies, photographed near Wynnewood. Gypsies passed through the country frequently, camping on the outskirts of a community.

STEPHENVILLE, TEXAS, ca. 1908.

TWO
BRIGHT-EYED
BABIES

WETUMKA, OKLAHOMA, 1913.
Elba R. Grissom.

ELWOOD, TEXAS, ca. 1898. Andrew Jackson Burkes and Eulalie McRae Burkes. *See diary in Chapter VIII.*

PARIS, TENNESSEE, ca. 1898. A west Tennessee family.

GARVIN COUNTY, OKLAHOMA, ca. 1915. J. C. Elliott, butchering hogs at Peachland Farm, near Pauls Valley and Wynnewood.

RICHMOND, VIRGINIA, 1869. A proud Virginia soldier poses before the camera in a Richmond studio four years after the end of the War. The Federal government did away with civil authority and appointed a provost marshal, backed by troops, to enforce various rules, one of which was a prohibition against the wearing of a Confederate uniform. Henry Kyd Douglas, former staff officer to Stonewall Jackson, had his picture made, and in his haste to get back home, wore his uniform out on the street. He was arrested, convicted by a military tribunal, and thrown into prison.

284

LIGHTNING RIDGE, OKLAHOMA, ca. 1913. George Preston Willis, former Confederate soldier of Co. F, 26th Mississippi Infantry, shown here wearing his Southern Cross of Honor, awarded by the United Daughters of the Confederacy. (Courtesy Leona Holland)

CHEROKEE NATION, INDIAN TERRITORY, ca. 1865. Elias C. Boudinot, a close friend and confidant of General Stand Watie. Boudinot served as a major in General Watie's First Cherokee Mounted Rifles, made up mostly of Cherokee mixed-bloods. After the War, Boudinot became one of the Southwest's most successful railroad attorneys. During the War, the Indian Territory was allowed three non-voting delegates to the Confederate Congress. Boudinot served as a delegate from the Cherokee Nation.

285

VICKSBURG, MISSISSIPPI,
December, 1897. Mrs.
C. E. Wright at age 55.

PADUCAH, KENTUKCY,
ca. 1895.

286

PAULS VALLEY, OKLAHOMA, ca. 1915. Miss Stella Grant.

YEAGER, INDIAN TERRITORY, ca. 1904.
The Yeager schoolhouse.

ROGERS, ARKANSAS,
ca. 1898.

ELWOOD, TEXAS, ca. 1890
Eva Bishop

ATLANTA, GEORGIA,
ca. 1885.

BONHAM, TEXAS, ca. 1890's. The old courthouses of the South are examples of some of finest architecture in each respective state. The Texas courthouses are monumental, as evidenced by this magnificent specimen in Fannin County. Most of the Texas courthouses have survived into the 20th Century, although this one did not.

The steamboat, *Pat Cleburne,* named after the famous general, carrying the mail somewhere in the South, ca. 1880's.

FANNIN COUNTY, TEXAS, ca. 1895. Andrew Jackson Burkes, who lived in the Elwood/Telephone area near the Red River.

LOOKOUT MOUNTAIN, TENNESSEE, ca. 1910. Leander Columbus Thompson, known as "Uncle Dump", shown here at Umbrella Rock. The Battle of Wauhatchie was fought here on Oct. 28, 1863, and perhaps Uncle Dump was a southern participant in that battle.

Home of Jefferson Davis, Montgomery, Ala.

SOUTHERN SHRINES

No other American president has been so honored by the preservation of his home and personal effects as has been Jefferson Davis, President of the Confederacy. His birthplace and residences have become virtual shrines to southerners. In Fairview, Kentucky, reproduction of his birthplace has been constructed. His boyhood home, near Woodville, Mississippi, has been restored as a working plantation. The photo, *above,* is from an old postcard, showing the first White House of the Confederacy, in 1919, when it was located at the corner of Lee and Bibb Streets, in Montgomery, Alabama. In 1920, it was moved near the capitol (a distance of 10 blocks) and restored. President Davis, his wife, and children occupied the house from mid-April until late May, 1861. The capital was moved to Richmond, and Mr. Davis was there by May 29, while Mrs. Davis stayed behind to pack and move. The photo, *below,* made about 1905, shows the White House in Richmond, which today is restored and part of the massive Confederate Museum.

BILOXI, MISSISSIPPI, date unknown. *Beauvoir*, the last home of Jefferson Davis, where he wrote *The Rise and Fall of the Confederate Government*, is located on the beach at Biloxi, overlooking the warm waters of the Gulf of Mexico. After his death, it became a home for Confederate veterans, their wives, and widows of veterans. Today, it is fully restored, and is considered to be the most important shrine of the Confederacy. To the rear of the property is a Confederate cemetery, holding the mortal remains of over 700 soldiers. It is here that the Tomb of the Unknown Soldier of the Confederate States of America is located.

MONTGOMERY, ALABAMA, ca. 1905. The Alabama state capitol. It was here that the Confederate Congress first met in 1861. Jefferson Davis took the oath of office on the front portico on February 18. The exact spot is marked with a bronze star.

KENTUCKY, ca. 1910.

TEXAS, ca. 1905. Aunt Shug (Frances Smith), and her mother, Elizabeth Willis. (Courtesy Leona Holland)

294

BIRMINGHAM, ALABAMA, ca. 1903. Bride and groom.

BIRMINGHAM, ALABAMA, ca. 1902. A pretty southern belle
in her fashionable dress of tucked linen and straw hat with
roses.

NASHVILLE, TENNESSEE, ca. 1880. A handsomely-dressed young southern gentleman.

297

LEBANON, TENNESSEE, April 19, 1906. Baseball Team, Castle Heights School. Small (Mgr.), Padleford (S.S.), Crump (L.F.), Cowen (C.F.), Noell (2nd B.), Anderson (3d B.), Foreman (P.), Ellis (S-), Shelby (R.F.), Terry (P.), Jeffreys (C.), Johnson (S-), Wilson (S-), Professor Smith (Coach).

All of these men are brothers. From left to right, George, Samuel, Jesse, Andrew, and Francis Marion Settle. Their father had fought in the Revolution under Francis Marion, South Carolina's famous "Swamp Fox," naming one of his sons after the hero. In 1862, this son joined the 13th Texas Volunteers. The other brothers probably served the Confederacy also. This photo was probably made in Texas about 1920.

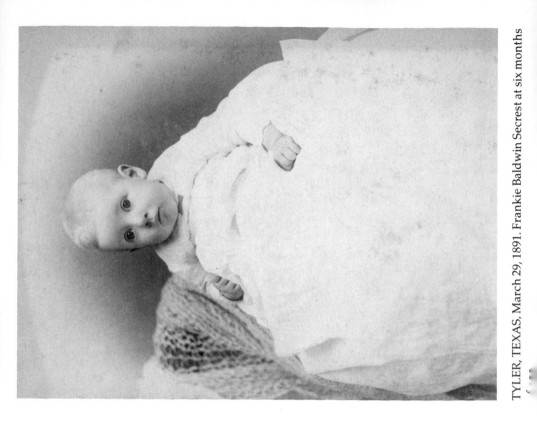

TYLER, TEXAS, March 29, 1891. Frankie Baldwin Secrest at six months

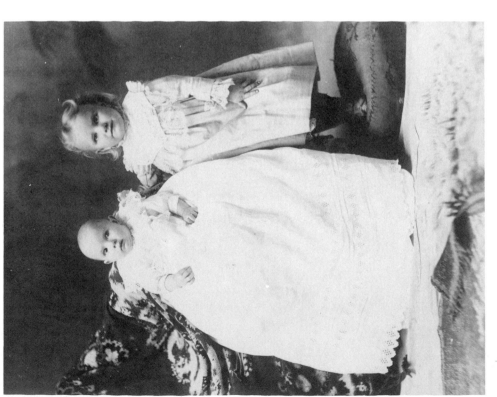

DUBLIN, TEXAS, ca. 1890.

VII

CONFEDERATE HEROES

C.S.A.

Do we weep for the heroes who died for us,
Who living were true and tried for us,
And dying sleep side by side for us;
    The Martyr-band
    That hallowed our land
With the blood they shed in a tide for us?

Ah! fearless on many a day for us,
They stood in front of the fray for us,
And held the foeman at bay for us;
    And tears should fall
    Fore'er o'er all
Who fell while wearing the Gray for us.

How many a glorious name for us,
How many a story of fame for us
They left: Would it not be a blame for us

301

SOUTHERN BY THE GRACE OF GOD

If their memories part
From our land and heart,
And a wrong to them, and shame for us?

No, no, no, they were brave for us,
And bright were the lives they gave for us;
The land they struggled to save for us
    Will not forget
    Its warriors yet
Who sleep in so many a grave for us.

On many and many a plain for us
Their blood poured down all in vain for us,
Red, rich, and pure, like a rain for us;
    They bleed — we weep,
    We live — they sleep,
"All lost," the only refrain for us.

But their memories e'er shall remain for us,
And their names, bright names, without
    stain for us;
The glory they won shall not wane for us,
    In legend and lay
    Our heroes in Gray
Shall forever live over again for us.

—Abram Joseph Ryan
(1838-1886)

The South is a land of heroes, strewn from border to border
with countless thousands of monuments to those who put duty
above self and left in their wake a fabulous southern legacy.
Their deeds, permanently recorded in granite, marble, and

bronze, shine as a beacon to the youth of every generation. Hardly is there a community in the South without its graven memorial to valor, from the simple block of stone in a rural Arkansas community to Richmond's magnificent "Monument Row" with its overwhelming statues of Lee, Davis, Jackson, and Stuart.

The panorama of southern history, from the earliest days of the Lost Colony of Roanoke and Jamestown, is resplendent with individuals of courage and resolve. Who can match the roll call of southern statesmen during the American Revolution and the first fifty years under the newly acquired republic? Patrick Henry, John Randolph, James Madison, George Washington, Thomas Jefferson, James Monroe, Lighthorse Harry Lee, Daniel Boone, Davy Crockett, Andrew Jackson, John C. Calhoun, Zachary Taylor, James K. Polk, John Tyler — to name but a few. These men are truly national figures, for we share them with a nation who proudly concurs in their achievements.

But, it is to the heroes of the Lost Cause that southerners give more attention — not from any lack of patriotism, as has been our criticism, but rather from a fuller measure of patriotism. Southerners are raised to be hero worshippers. It's a part of our heritage. We're taught from childhood to emulate the deeds of great men and to reverence their memory. Whether the cause succeeds or fails is not the point; if it is right in precept, we accord the honor.

While compiling this book, I visited many commemorative sites in the South, finding one of the most inspiring attractions in Chattanooga, Tennessee. It was there that I encountered a young man who, probably on a vacation trip through the South, had run head-on into the southern emphasis upon paying homage to our Confederate defenders and was obviously quite aggravated by it all when I ran afoul of him. The place was *Confederama*, a wonderful diorama of the battles around Chattanooga, expertly produced with lights, taped music, and a taped narrative that leaves no doubt as to which side should have won the War.

As several were milling around the souvenirs in the lobby, I couldn't help but notice the man, who looked to be near thirty, purchasing his ticket for the next narration. The elderly hostess, who was as gracious as she could be, smiled and welcomed him as she handed him the ticket and made change for him. To everything she said, he grunted an impatient sound, then began pacing the floor nervously awaiting the doors to open. Soon, the hostess announced that we could go on in, as she turned up the music. The sounds of *Dixie* had already raised the hair on my arms, and I followed the man through the auditorium door, feeling about a foot taller since the music started.

About three feet ahead of me, he abruptly stopped, glanced at the diorama and the displays around the wall, and said to me in a curt, sneering tone, "These people down here take this stuff seriously, don't they?"

I was caught completely off guard, and at first said nothing. *Dixie* was blaring away in the background, and I was mentally unprepared to deal with a man who had paid three dollars for the privilege of scorning a popular patriotic attraction. Recognizing the contempt in his voice, I finally responded, "Well, yes sir, they do, and I'm one of them!"

"Well, I'm not", he said in his clipped brogue. "I'm from Hawaii (though he was not one of the dark-skinned, congenial natives), and I don't know why you people fought all those wars and why you keep fighting them!"

"We were invaded by the North. We picked up our guns and shot back. That's why we fought. And, I dare say that you would have fought, too, had you been invaded."

"We were invaded," he snapped.

"Not by Yankees, you weren't."

"By the Japanese, in World War II."

"And, did you fight back?"

Here I could see *his* pride showing through. Elevating his

chest as would befit a naval midshipman in dress parade, he fairly bristled as he blustered, "Yes, we fought back, and we whipped them, too."

"And, did you build monuments to the memory of your military dead there in Pearl Harbor?"

"Of course, we did," he answered, as if I were the one asking foolish questions now.

"Well, sir, now you know why we fought all those wars, as you call them, and why we remember." That was what I said. I hope it was a little bit of southern breeding that kept me from saying what I wanted to say. I would like to have told him that, when his funds for the U.S.S. Arizona Memorial in Pearl Harbor were running low, it was a *southern* boy, by the name of Elvis Presley, who came to the rescue!

Because we give so much glory to our Confederate heroes, we are so often accused of "still fighting the War," as if we enjoyed the carnage, the destruction, the famine of that holocaust. No, we're not still fighting the War; we're still giving the glory. There is something intangible about a lost cause that specially marks its heroes, and I suppose that only a southerner — or one who has gone down with a lost cause — can comprehend the peculiar devotion it generates towards its champions. Henry Timrod captured its essence when, in 1867, he wrote an ode to be sung at the decoration of Confederate graves in Charleston's Magnolia Cemetery. Called the most perfect ode ever written, here is the last stanza:

> Stoop angels, hither from the skies,
> There is no holier spot of ground
> Than where defeated valor lies,
> By mourning beauty crowned!

A hero — or heroine — is usually someone who risks life and limb, and certainly a protracted war provides the clime of danger from which heroes are beckoned. The War Between the States ground on for four long years in the literal yards of our homes, requiring the utmost of every man, woman, and child, who, except for the exigencies of a prolonged home front war, would have remained uncalled to heroic deeds.

In a sense, everyone became a hero by merely opposing the onslaught. Certainly, the aged man of seventy who marched away to bolster the thinning ranks of gray and face the Yankee soldier of twenty would have to be counted a hero, as well as the teenage boy — not much more than a child — who fell in the front line, ripped by torturous fire from a thousand enemy guns. Poor George Lamkin, of Winona, Mississippi, was only eleven years old when wounded at the bloody Battle of Shiloh. Every man who shouldered a gun in defense of his home deserves a hero's tribute. Honor, also, to the faithful slave who outwitted the Yankee soldier and saved his master's home from the torch. And, the noble woman of the South! Who could have cried more tears, sewed more socks, read more casualty lists, prayed more prayers, buried more sons? Who could have endured more — and complained less — than the southern woman? Yet, never did she raise her voice to claim her rightful station as heroine of the Lost Cause, but was content, rather, to enshrine the warriors of the battlefield in the temple of a country's praise.

Heroes every one of them — and yet, convention dictates that some must rise above others to become the objects of our gratitude. Even so, the roll of honor is awesome, and it was exceedingly difficult for this author to have to arbitrarily select from it only a minute number for inclusion in this small volume. Left unheralded here are the feats of the flamboyant *Cavalier of Dixie*, Jeb Stuart, who, with his twelve hundred cavalrymen, rode completely around the Federal army of 115,000 before Richmond; the fearless spy, Belle Boyd, who dashed wildly through an open field in front of the Federal army, waving her bonnet to the Confederates as a sign to advance; the elusive *Gray Ghost*, John S. Mosby, who entered enemy lines one night with six men, capturing a Yankee general asleep in his bedroom; the courageous George Pickett, and his 15,000 men, who had to make the dreadful assault upon Cemetery Ridge; the daring young John Pelham, *the gallant Pelham*, whose two small artillery guns held the entire enemy at bay in Fredericksburg; the enormously brave scout, DeWitt Smith Jobe, who, like Sam Davis, refused to divulge his information, and was consequently tortured by his Yankee captors who put out his eyes, pulled out his tongue, and strangled him to death with a piece of leather; the intrepid southern spy, Rose O'Neal Greenhow, who was carrying gold and important dispatches from England when she drowned off the North Carolina coast, weighted down by coins sewn into her clothes for secrecy; the 247 young cadets from VMI who aided General Breckinridge in defeating the Yankees at New Market, Virginia; and a host of others equally as valiant.

> Can the victors give a reason
> Why the men who wore the gray
> From our hearts should march away
> And should pass from us forever
> Like the dreamings of the night?

> —Abram Joseph Ryan

JEFFERSON DAVIS

A biographical sketch cannot begin to do justice to the memory of a man who was probably the most qualified and distinguished statesman in America by the time of the demise of the three political giants, Calhoun, Clay, and Webster, in the early 1850's. Had it not been for the War that intervened, he might well have been President of the United States, and, if his prior accomplishments were a presage to his abilities as a possible president, no doubt he would have ranked with Washington, Jefferson, and Jackson as the best-known representatives of that office. His name had, in fact, been placed in nomination at the Democratic National Convention in 1860, but he did not seek the position, preferring instead to work for the nomination of John C. Breckinridge.

Such was the pattern of his life. He was not instinctively imbued with political ambition. His biographer, Hudson Strode, observed that history pursued Davis. In nearly every instance of his life, his candidacy or appointment was pressed upon him by his friends, and out of a deep sense of duty, he served in public office; but, his most contented hours were spent at his plantation on the Mississippi River and, later, in the balmy, serene environment of *Beauvoir*, on the Gulf Coast.

Jefferson Finis Davis was the tenth child of Samuel Davis and Jane Cook. His father was a Georgian of Welsh descent, who had fought in the Revolutionary War. His mother was a South Carolinian of Scotch ancestry. After the birth of five children, the Davises moved to Kentucky, where Jefferson was born on June 3, 1808, in a rural area now known as the village of Fairview. During his infancy, the family moved to Wilkinson County, Mississippi, where young Jefferson grew to manhood in the low country of the Deep South.

In November, 1889, only a month before his death, he dictated a brief autobiography for *Belford's Magazine*. Concerning his education, he said, "After passing through the county academy I entered Transylvania College, Kentucky, and was advanced as far as the senior class when, at the age of 16, I was appointed to the United States Military Academy at West Point, which I entered in September, 1824. I graduated in 1828, and then, in accordance with the custom of cadets, entered active service with the rank of lieutenant."[1]

At Transylvania, he developed a lifelong friendship with George W. Jones, a boy from Iowa who would later become a U.S. General and Senator. He described Davis at college as, "always gay and brimful of buoyant spirits, but without the smallest tendency toward vice or immorality. He had that innate refinement and gentleness that distinguished him through life. He was always a gentleman in the highest sense of the word."[2]

Judge Peters of Mount Sterling, Kentucky, remembered him as a good student who was, "always prepared with his lessons, very respectful and polite to the president and professors. I never heard him reprimanded for neglecting his studies or for misconduct of any sort . . . He was amiable, prudent and kind to all with whom he was associated, and beloved by teachers and students."[3]

At West Point, a fellow-cadet described him. "Jefferson Davis was distinguished in the corps for his manly bearing, his high-toned and lofty character. His figure was very soldier-like and rather robust; his step springy, resembling the tread of an Indian 'brave' on the war path."[4] Davis saw routine duty on the frontier and distinguished himself when, in 1832, his detachment cut off the retreat of Black Hawk, thus ending the Black Hawk War.

It was also in 1832 that Davis evinced his firm belief in the doctrine of states' rights. South Carolina had drawn the wrath of President Jackson over the nullification issue, and it looked for a time as if the regiment to which Davis belonged would be sent into South Carolina. "By education, by association, and by preference, I was a soldier, then regarding that profession as my vocation for life. Yet, looking the issue squarely in the face, I chose the alternative of abandoning my profession rather than be employed in the subjugation of, or coercion of, a State of the Union, and had fully determined and was prepared to resign my commission immediately."[5] Fortunately, the confrontation never occurred.

In June, 1835, Davis resigned his commission, married Sarah Knox Taylor (daughter of Col. Zachary Taylor, future president), and settled into the life of planter at his Brierfield Plantation on the Mississippi River, near Vicksburg. Tragedy struck with the force of swift lightning — Sarah died of malaria only two months after their wedding. Davis lived in "great seclusion", as he put it, for seven years "on the plantation in the swamps of the Mississippi."[6]

On February 26, 1845, he married Varina Anne Howell, of Natchez, Mississippi. In November he was elected to the U.S. House of Representatives, where he served until June, 1846. At that time, a regiment of Mississippi volunteers was organized at Vicksburg for duty in the Mexican War, and it would have none other than Jefferson Davis as its colonel. Resigning his seat in Congress, Davis and the Mississippians proceeded to Mexico, where he further distinguished himself by bravery and ingenuity at Monterey and Buena Vista, returning to the United States as a hero of the Mexican War. At Monterey, he was one of three commissioners appointed by General Taylor to receive the surrender and carry on negotiations for the capitulation. President Polk attempted to reward Davis for his meretorious war service, but once again, principle and a firm belief in states' rights took precedence. Polk had offered him a commission as brigadier-general of volunteers, but Davis refused it on the grounds that only states had the right to appoint officers in the militia.

History continued its pursuit of Jefferson Davis. As soon as he arrived home, the Mississippi legislature appointed him to the unexpired term of U.S. Senator Speight, who had died. After serving Senator Speight's term, Davis was elected for his own six-year term in 1850. The *Macon Telegraph and Messenger* wrote, "The historian, Prescott, pronounced him the most accomplished man in that body when it was full of giants."[7] His plaudits did not go unnoticed, and when the Democratic candidate for governor in Mississippi retired from the race in mid-stream, a call went forth for Davis to replace him in the governor's race. Oddly enough, Davis was not elected to the only state office for which he would ever run, but his candidacy had required him to resign the U.S. Senate seat; consequently, he retired to his plantation in 1852, though it would prove to be only a brief period of political inactivity. The newly-elected President Franklin Pierce was not content to let talent as that which Davis possessed lie idle on a remote plantation. Though he had to persuade Davis to accept the position, Pierce finally succeeded and appointed him Secretary of War, in 1853.

As Secretary of War, Davis was able to complete some of his proposals as Senator. Recognized by most historians as the ablest Secretary of War ever, his accomplishments are far too numerous to enumerate here, though a few will be mentioned. The Smithsonian Institution was established under his authority; he instituted the civil service system; he began the movement to construct a canal across Panama, designating the exact spot where construction began fifty years later; he had three routes surveyed for a transcontinental railroad; he introduced the rifled musket, the Minié ball, and the light infantry; and, he introduced a humanities program at West Point.

When his tenure as Secretary of War was up in 1857, he rejoined the Senate, having been reelected by his home state. By this time, North and South were in a shouting war, and the U.S. Senate was consumed — as was the House — with the constant elements of that controversy.

Northern historians have always delighted in promulgating the idea that Davis was a hot-headed secessionist — "secessionist" being a bad word in their view of centralized government. The myth is perpetuated in textbooks today in an effort to discredit Davis, and in a larger sense, to discredit all who claimed state sovereignty and the right of secession. Nothwithstanding their accusations, "Mr. Davis was active and earnest in his efforts to effect a compromise and reach a basis which would permit the Southern States to remain in the Union. He was a member of the committee of the Senate to whom was referred the famous 'Crittendon compromise,' and avowed himself willing to accept that or any other plan that the opposing factions could agree upon, and that promised any reasonable hope of success. But the 'Republican' members of the committee rejected absolutely everything that the Northern and Southern Democrats and Whigs agreed on, and seemed determined not to consent to anything that promised a settlement."[8]

His reticence concerning secession caused his fellow-members of the Mississippi Congressional Delegation to suspect that he might be opposed to secession altogether; however, upon hearing that his state had seceded, he resigned from the Senate and made his farewell speech to his colleagues. In an emotional goodbye, he asserted Mississippi's right to secede, tempering it with an advocacy of peace and friendship between North and South. His illustrious career in Washington, D.C., came to an end as he walked out of the Senate chamber on January 21, 1861. That night, Mrs. Davis overheard him praying for peace.

The Davises went back to Brierfield, and Mr. Davis accepted a commission as Major General and was appointed as Commander-in-Chief of all Mississippi Volunteers. Though advocating peace, Davis was a prudent man. He recommended immediate military preparations "to meet the war which he believed the Republicans of the North would force upon the South."[9] While thus engaged in Mississippi, he was not present at the meeting of the Provisional Congress of the Confederate States in Montgomery, Alabama. On February 9, the delegates unanimously chose Davis as Provisional President of the Confederacy, and a telegram was dispatched to Vicksburg immediately.

Jefferson Davis was helping Varina prune rose bushes at Brierfield on Sunday afternoon, February 10, when a courier arrived from Vicksburg with the telegram. History, in its relentless pursuit, was calling him to his greatest role — a role which he was inwardly reluctant to accept. Though quite humbled to be the recipient of such an offer, Davis had always enjoyed military pursuits and was expecting to aid his new country in that capacity; however, in his characteristic way, he answered the call of his people and made plans to leave for Montgomery.

Without a doubt, he was the man for the job. In an interview with the *Baltimore Sun* on the day Davis died, John H. Reagan, U.S. Senator from Texas and former Postmaster-General of the Confederacy, voiced that sentiment. "Mr. Davis was one of the few men who measured the full force of the war. He from the first contended that it was likely to last a number of years instead of a few months, as many persons predicted. It was at first proposed to enlist an army . . . for six months. Mr. Davis promptly disposed of that suggestion by declaring that it would take at least a year to organize an efficient army, as soldiers could not be made in a few days."[10] Ironically, it was Davis who, after the complete rout of the Yankees in the first battle of the War, foresaw a chance to end the War at once by a vigorous pursuit of the fleeing enemy into Washington, only to find that he could not persuade his generals to advance.

Davis had no delusions about an easy beginning for the new republic. His first letter to his wife after reaching Montgomery reveals his keen awareness.

> I was inaugurated on Monday, having reached here on Saturday night. The audience was large and brilliant. Upon my weary heart was showered smiles, plaudits, and flowers; but, beyond them, I saw troubles and thorns innumerable.
>
> We are without machinery, without means, and threatened by a powerful opposition; but I do not despond, and will not shrink from the task imposed upon me.[11]

What a monumental task was before him. Within ninety days, he had to form a government. He had to create a navy, an army, a currency, and a postal system. The South had only one rolling mill and one powder mill, and its ports were blockaded. Under his direction, the new Confederacy brought forth a fighting unit that held the North at bay for four long years, and victory was close at hand upon several occasions.

The victory at Manassas proved the value of his preparations. "At this period his popularity with his people knew no bounds. It was only after disaster came that grumblers arose to criticise and condemn his conduct of affairs; but he always had with him the hearts of an overwhelming majority of the soldiers and the people."[12] Critics can always be found when reverses occur, and Davis had a very vocal one in the person of Edward Pollard, editor of the *Richmond Examiner*. Corporal Watkins, on the other hand, probably spoke for the average man in the trench, when he wrote, in 1881:

> Hon. Jefferson Davis perhaps made blunders and mistakes, but I honestly believe that he ever did what he thought best for the good of his country. And there never lived on this earth from the days of Hampden to George Washington, a purer patriot or a nobler man than Jefferson Davis; and, like Marius, grand even in ruins.[13]

Recognizing the magnitude of the task before President Davis, and commending him for his efforts, the editor of the *Raleigh News and Observer* wrote, sometime after the War:

> It is profitless to discuss how far any measure of the Confederate government was right or wrong, but as for Mr. Davis, he had the responsibility; he had full knowledge of all the circumstances; he had the general plan of the whole war from Texas to the Potomac to subserve and watch and to carry out. It is to our glory that there was no Fort Lafayette at the South. It is to the honor of the Confederate

government that no Confederate secretary ever could touch a bell and send a citizen to prison.[14]

Asked what he thought was Davis's principal motive behind his participation in the conflict, Senator Reagan, in 1889, said, "To secure a government that should be friendly to the people. He was an intense believer in the doctrine that the States should control absolutely their domestic affairs . . ."[15]

On April 2, 1865, Richmond was evacuated. President Davis and his cabinet started south. On April 9, Robert E. Lee surrendered, followed by the surrender of Joseph E. Johnston on April 26. Davis and some of his cabinet members were threading their way through the occupied parts of Georgia, hoping to slip undetected across the Mississippi and into the Trans-Mississippi South where resistance was strong, when they were surrounded at Irwinville, Georgia, at a camp in the woods.

Lincoln had been assassinated on April 14, and a wild and crazed North demanded Davis's head. He was already tried and convicted in the northern mind, and posters were out for his reward — a ridiculous display of mob psychology. The President of the Confederacy was captured on May 10, transported to Fortress Monroe, Virginia, and chained in a damp cell. For two years he was tortured and denied many of the most humane rights. He had absolutely no privacy, being placed in an open casemate where guards and the curious were allowed to watch him like a caged lion. A light was kept burning twenty-four hours a day, giving him virtually no rest, until after many months his wife was allowed to make him a mask for his eyes. The full account of his suffering can be read in the *Prison Life of Jefferson Davis*, written by a northern physician, Dr. Craven, who was assigned to Davis, and who became very attached to his notable patient.

The frenzied North trumped up charges of complicity in the assassination, cruelty to prisoners during the War, and treason. Even the "packed" jury couldn't find a trace of evidence on the first two counts, but they vindictively charged Davis and Robert E. Lee with treason. General Grant had Lee's indictment removed, but Davis waited two years to go to trial, eager to defend himself of the pernicious charge. As time passed, his imprisonment became an embarrassment to the North, and his accusers were without any grounds. The result was his release on May 11, 1867. In Richmond, thousands were wild with exultation, and soon there was rejoicing throughout Dixie. The hero of the Lost Cause had suffered for them, and the vindication of Davis was the vindication of the South.

Two years of prison had seriously impaired his health, and in an effort to regain a measure of it, Davis spent the next few years travelling — sometimes abroad. Eventually, he went to Memphis as president of an insurance firm, then on to his final residence on the beautiful Gulf Coast. There, at Biloxi, Mrs. Sarah Dorsey offered him her home, *Beauvoir*, and encouraged him to do nothing more than write his history of the War. It was a peaceful place, and he began making payments on it. Mrs. Dorsey became ill and passed away, leaving the home to him. In 1881, Davis published his *Rise and Fall of the Confederate Government*, accomplishing the monumental work he had envisioned for years.

Though Davis did not often appear in public, he occasionally spoke at various Confederate monument dedications across the South, where he received the adoration of a grateful people.

At 81, he went to Brierfield on some business, and became ill. Starting back home, he made it to the home of Judge Fenner, a long time friend. On December 6, 1889, he passed away under the anxious eye of the South. Upon hearing of his illness, many friends, including Senator Jones, the intimate comrade from Iowa, made their way towards New Orleans, though most of them arrived too late to see him alive.

As he lay in state in the New Orleans City Hall, which, like every business building in the city, was draped in black, a spontaneous movement was underway for a funeral befitting a king. Ten thousand people passed his casket on the first day, December 7. By December 11, viewing hours had been lengthened to 10 p.m. each night. Dignitaries had arrived, plain folks had come, and thousands of dispatches were received from every Confederate state and the Indian Territory.

At noon, December 11, the casket was removed to the porch where the funeral was preached to a sea of people filling every standing space as far as the eye could see. The funeral procession consisted of every organization conceivable, numbering probably 10,000 participants, including the governors of eight southern states. The crowd was the largest ever assembled in the South for a funeral, numbering over 200,000 people. A shocked North reeled in astonishment, finally convinced that the hearts of southerners would ever belong to Jeff Davis and the Confederacy, notwithstanding every attempt to discredit the philosophy and disparage the leaders of the glorious Lost Cause.

Even the *New York Herald* showed a bit of envious longing to be able to claim the legacy of Jefferson Davis. "In the essential element of statesmanship, Davis will be judged as the rival and parallel of Lincoln. When the two men came face to face, as leaders of two mighty forces, bitter was Northern sorrow that Providence had given the South so ripe and rare a leader and the North an uncouth advocate from the woods."[16]

The *New Orleans Times-Democrat* related a special incident which bears repeating. It is illustrative of the gentle character of the man who had to be tough enough to withstand a War, imprisonment, ill health, and three decades of slander for carrying the cross of the South.

As a result of his gracious dignity, Mr. Davis never came in contact with a menial but that at once they grew devotedly attached to him. More than once have family and friends quizzed him regarding the absorbing love of the porters, servants, and slaves that accident threw in his way. Never was a man more loved by those who served him, and this was peculiarly noticeable among the negroes he owned before the war. One of the most affecting incidents connected with the death, was the arrival and grief of this old negro, a former slave of Mr. Davis' brother, the late Joe Davis.

For a number of years Miles Cooper, a decrepit colored man has sent from his present home in Florida, little tokens in the way of fruits raised by his own hands for the hospitable Beauvoir table. Through the local press, Miles heard of Mr. Davis's extreme illness, and, putting every personal interest and comfort aside, hastened to see the master he loved. Unused to travelling, aged and uncertain in his movements the unselfish servant again and again missed connection in the short trip, was delayed, left behind, and put to every possible annoyance and inconvenience. Finally he arrived, and full of pleasant anticipations, hurried up to look once more in those kindly eyes and feel the cordial grasp of that genial hand. Reaching the residence, all stilled as it was surrounded by an atmosphere of death, the servant learned of Mr. Davis's death the night previous. It was more than he could bear and breaking down with an outburst of deep grief, Miles sat crushed and hopeless, only asking the one favor to be admitted to the presence of his master. Every one, save the family, had been denied entrance, but Mr. Farrar, at Mrs. Davis's request, led the way, and soon the ex-slave stood face to face with the noble dead. It was pitiful to hear the sobs and wails of the old man. He mourned with unaffected grief for the "Mars Jeff" of his youth, and prayed earnestly for the welfare of those he left behind.[17]

While the choir sang *Rock of Ages*, President Davis was temporarily entombed in the Army of Northern Virginia Monument at Metairie Cemetery in New Orleans. On May 31, 1893, he was finally laid to rest at Hollywood Cemetery in Richmond. "Thus was broken another cord that bound the living, throbbing heart of the South to the dead, but loved and unforgotten past."[18]

PAT CLEBURNE

A life-size figure of a Confederate general proudly watches over throngs of sight-seers in a most unlikely place — New York Harbor. There, in the American Museum of Immigration, located in the basement of the Statue of Liberty, stands the only statue of a general, an inspiration to all immigrants who come to America to better their lot. It is the statue of Patrick Ronayne Cleburne, an Irish immigrant who volunteered for Confederate service as a private, then rose in less than two years to the rank of Major General.

Pat Cleburne, whose name is pronounced as if it were spelled Clayburn (except in Texas, where the city named for him is pronounced exactly as it is spelled), was the third child born to Mary Anne Ronayne and Joseph Cleburne of County Cork, Ireland. Named for Patrick Ronayne, his maternal grandfather, little Pat was born March 16, 1828, only one day before St. Patrick's Day, a coincidence that may have served as a good omen for the development of an extraordinary young Irishman.

He was called Ronayne in his Irish youth, though he would come to be admired and loved by the people of the South as General Pat Cleburne. His early education came at the hands of private tutors. At twelve, he was enrolled in an expensive private school for boys, where the discipline was strict and served him well for the role he was to play in commanding a division of Confederate soldiers. After three years at Spedding School, he was forced to withdraw due to the death of his father, who had been a successful physician, and who had intended that Pat become a doctor as well.

For three years, Pat was apprenticed to Dr. Thomas H. Justice of Mallow, some twenty miles north of the Cleburne home place. In 1846, he traveled 165 miles to Dublin to take an entrance examination at the medical school there, only to fail the exam. Pat was a very sensitive boy. He was nearly eighteen years old, and having failed the test, he thought he had disgraced his family name. As a result, he decided to lose himself for a while in the military. He joined the British 41st Regiment of Foot, where he would stay for three years and seven months, rising only to the rank of corporal, that rank coming after more than three years of steady service in the British unit which never left its patrol duty in Ireland. Pat would be heard to remark many years later that he rejoiced more over his long-awaited promotion to the lowly rank of corporal than his attainment of the rank of Major General.

Heavy taxes — the scourge of civilized societies — brought hardships to the Emerald Isle, sending the Cleburne estate into a precipitous decline. Pat's mother had died when he was an infant, his father when he was fifteen. His stepmother, of whom he was very fond, reluctantly made the decision that the four oldest children, all of whom were over the age of nineteen, should immigrate to the United States.

Pat was twenty-one years old, and having received a small legacy from his real mother's family, he purchased his discharge from the British army on September 22, 1849, for a sum of twenty pounds. With his sister, brother, and stepbrother, he boarded the *Bridgetown*, which set sail from the Port of Cork on November 5, 1849, bound for New Orleans, Louisiana, where it arrived on Christmas Day. A letter of introduction accompanied the young voyagers, but Pat boarded a steamboat for Cincinnati, leaving his brothers and sister to present the letter to Mr. Duncan in New Orleans. Two days later the relatives followed him up the Mississippi, and they were reunited in Cincinnati. Within six months, Patrick Cleburne would leave Cincinnati forever, bound for Dixie and his destiny.

Cleburne had made a good hand in a Cincinnati drug store and was recommended for an open position at a drug store in Helena, Arkansas, a town of about 600 people on the west bank of the Mississippi River. In June, 1850, he arrived in Helena and accepted the position of manager, a move which resulted in the lifelong friendship of Dr. Nash, one of the owners. For the next eleven years, Cleburne would spend his time among the friendly inhabitants of Helena, the citizens of which accepted the affable young man into its best society.

His physical appearance was described as a man of 150 pounds, five feet nine inches tall, having large, gray eyes, thick brown hair, and a muscular build. He possessed great strength and stood erect with a military bearing. In 1856, his health was permanently impaired by a shooting involving a friend named T.C. Hindman, who was to become one of five Confederate generals hailing from Helena. As Hindman and Cleburne walked down a street, some political enemies of Hindman shot them both. Before collapsing, Cleburne shot and mortally wounded his assailant. The bullet which felled Cleburne entered his lower back, and he hovered between life and death for a week, while Dr. Nash tried desperately to pull him through. Cleburne had studied law, and he later complained of the pain which afflicted him during long court room debate and hours of bending over law books in his library. Oddly enough, the military career he would later pursue seemed to improve his condition.

Pat Cleburne was a deeply religious person, having been baptized an Episcopalian at St. Mary's Church in Ireland. In 1852, he became a Mason and also joined the Sons of Temperance, a group of men who advocated abstinence of liquor. He was a regular visitor at the Presbyterian Church, but the outdoor camp meetings in the woods impressed him more than anything else, and he wrote about them to his stepmother in Ireland. He refused to listen to smut, and his dislike of vulgarity was well-known. Dr. Nash, who later became his biographer, said that he had never heard Cleburne swear an oath in his life.

Cleburne's interaction with the warm people of Helena, in addition to his study of constitutional law, brought him into perfect alignment with the southern idea. He was as southern as the most native-born, and his patriotism was evident from the beginning. On June 24, 1853, Cleburne gave a public address at a large Masonic celebration in Helena; whereupon, the *Southern Shield*, Helena's newspaper, found this to say in its account of the following day: ". . . Mr. C. we believe hails from over the water, but he is thoroughly Americanized. The eloquent bursts of patriotism that fell from his lips on yesterday stamps him as a patriot in the broadest sense of the term. . ."[19]

He was thrilled with ante-bellum life in Helena, which had more than doubled its population since 1850. By 1860, he had made several major purchases of land and, like all southerners, was alarmed at northern threats and fulminations. When the Yell Rifles were formed in the summer of 1860 to protect Phillips County in the event of hostilities, Cleburne volunteered as a private. In January, 1861, he wrote to his half brother, Robert, saying:

> As to my own position I hope to see the Union preserved by granting to the South the full measure of her constitutional rights. If this cannot be done I hope to see all the Southern States united in a new confederation and that we can effect a peaceable separation. If both of these are denied us I am with Arkansas in weal or in woe. I have been elected and hold the Commission of the State as captain of the volunteer Rifle Company of this place and I can say for my company that if the stars and stripes become the standard of a tiranical majority, the ensign of a violated league, it will no longer command our love or respect but will command our best efforts to drive it from the State.[20]

On April 27, the Yell Rifles departed for Camp Rector, just north of Memphis. Assembling at the courthouse Sunday morning, they marched one block to the Methodist Church for worship. The yard was full of people who could not get inside, including many of the young ladies of Helena who had presented Captain Cleburne with the Stars and Bars. A Bible was presented to the company, and they marched to the landing, where hundreds of cheering, crying people bade them farewell.

On May 7, 1861, one day after Arkansas seceded by a vote of sixty-nine to one, Cleburne wrote again to Robert:

> I am with the South in life or in death, in victory or defeat. I never owned a Negro and care nothing for them, but these people have been my friends and have stood up to me on all occasions. In addition to this, I believe the North is about to wage a brutal and unholy war on a people who have done them

no wrong, in violation of the constitution and the fundamental principals of the government. They no longer acknowledge that all government derives its validity from the consent of the governed. They are about to invade our peaceful homes, destroy our property, and inaugurate a servile insurrection, murder our men and dishonor our women. We propose no invasion of the North, no attack on them, and only ask to be let alone.[21]

On May 14, Cleburne was elected colonel of the 1st Arkansas Regiment, which, on July 23, put itself under the authority of the Confederate Army, joining General Hardee's command. Cleburne's previous training with the British Army and his natural proclivity for military discipline played a role in winning him command of a regiment on October 28. He instilled pride and discipline in his men who, in return, gave him undying devotion and loyalty. His troops were known, far and wide, as the best-drilled brigade in the army. Pat Cleburne's remarkable qualities were unmistakable, and by March 4, 1862, the Irish immigrant had risen from private volunteer to Brigadier General.

The first battle for Cleburne's men came at Shiloh on April 6 and 7, 1862, where they led the advance of the army and fought in the front line both days, and as Cleburne said in his official report, "were never rested or relieved for a moment."[22] The first day of the battle was witness to General Cleburne's routing of General Sherman's entire division from their camp. In concert with other units, Cleburne's brigade finally pushed the Yankees from their stronghold at the "Hornet's Nest", and by evening, the entire Union army was huddled with its back to the Tennessee River.

On December 13, 1862, Cleburne was promoted to the rank of Major General, continuing to distinguish himself throughout the succeeding days of the War. At Chickamauga, Cleburne pushed his division upon the Federal line and drove the enemy back a mile and a half, all the time riding back and forth from brigade to brigade in a fury of effort and speed, cheering them on and directing their attacks upon the reeling Yankees. It was here, on September 19, 1863, at Chickamauga, that Cleburne earned his sobriquet, "The Stonewall Jackson of the West."

The fighting around Chattanooga, Tennessee, included the Battle of Missionary Ridge, fought on November 25, 1863, a day General Sherman wouldn't soon forget, for he suffered defeat again at the hands of Pat Cleburne. The Confederate Army was posted along the top of Missionary Ridge in a long, thin line — a line so thin in the center that it would give way during the battle, causing the Confederates to have to retreat towards Dalton, Georgia. Cleburne's division formed the Confederate right on the north end of the Ridge where a railroad tunnel runs through the hill. Sherman attacked straight up the precipitous hill, but was repulsed by the determined Confederates who couldn't even get their artillery guns trained down on the bluecoats because of the sharp slope of the ridge. To compensate, the resourceful Rebels rolled boulders down upon the heads of their antagonists. The artillerymen lit the fuses of their shells and rolled them down the hill like bowling balls. Before Sherman was totally removed from action, a detachment of Confederates rushed through the tunnel from the back side, catching the Federals from the rear and taking a large number of them prisoner.

The entire Army of Tennessee numbered about 37,000 men at Missionary Ridge. It was facing 80,000 Yankees under General Grant. Faced with overwhelming numbers, and having lost the line of defense upon the ridge, General Bragg ordered the army to retreat as quickly as possible through a break in the Georgia mountains called Ringgold Gap. To Cleburne's fighting division of about 4,000 men was given the task of fortifying this narrow gap and holding off the huge Federal army which was in hot purusit of the retreating Army of Tennessee. On the 27th of November, Cleburne did just that, repulsing every attempt of the sprawling Federal monster, buying precious time for Bragg to get the wagons, artillery, and troops safely down the road. The astounding feat received a resolution of thanks from the Confederate Congress, who recognized that the entire Army of Tennessee might have been annihilated except for Cleburne's action.

After the fall of Atlanta in September, 1864, General Hood (who had replaced General Bragg) ordered the Army of Tennessee to march toward Nashville. Cleburne's Division was a thoroughly trained unit, proud of its fame on many a battlefield, and it was difficult for the warriors of hard fought battles to see the Confederacy going downhill. At Powder Springs, Georgia, his men serenaded him on the evening of October 2. In response, Cleburne made an address in which he encouraged the men to fight on, ending with his famous statement of devotion to the cause: "If this cause that is so dear to my heart is doomed to fail, I pray heaven may let me fall with it, while my face is toward the enemy and my arm battling for that which I know to be right."[23]

On a Saturday afternoon, November 26, General Cleburne stopped to rest at a little red brick church near Columbia, Tennessee. The ivy-covered Gothic church, known as St. John's, rested neath a canopy of tall trees which also sheltered the cool graveyard of the church. Probably reflecting upon the similarities of this place and old St. Mary's where his father was buried, he turned to Captain Hill and said, "It would not be hard to die if one could be buried in such a beautiful spot."[24]

Always a pensive man, the real danger of the battlefield seemed to weigh heavily upon his mind. He often spoke of death, as if he expected it, resolutely prepared to meet the Grim Reaper in defense of his country. In his letter to Robert, on May 7, 1861, he warned, "I may die in this conflict."[25] Two days after pausing at St. John's cemetery, Cleburne addressed his troops, vowing that he would never lay down his arms and that he would rather die than surrender.

At Franklin, General Hood ordered a foolhardy frontal assault against the heavily entrenched Federal army. It was the most foolish advance ever ordered by a Confederate commander, and Hood's generals tried to counsel him against it. Unyielding, the impetuous Hood turned to General Cleburne and told him to fix bayonets and take the breastworks at all hazards, to which Cleburne resignedly replied, "General, I will take the works or fall in the attempt."[26] General Govan, a fellow-soldier from Helena, leaned over and remarked to Cleburne that few of them would ever return to Arkansas to tell the tale. Cleburne responded, "Well, Govan, if we are to die, let us die like men."[27]

The charge was made by 15,000 splendid Confederate soldiers. Bands played *Dixie* and *The Bonnie Blue Flag* while the bravest men on earth marched squarely into the jaws of death. General Cleburne was in the thick of the advance and soon had a horse shot out from under him. A nineteen-year old Mississippi boy named James Brandon offered his bay mare to the general, but it, too, was shot out from under the general as he tried to mount it. General Govan later recalled that Cleburne then moved into the deadly smoke and haze of the battle on foot, holding his sword in one hand while waving his cap in the other. Only seconds later, the sharpshooter found his mark, shooting the gallant Pat Cleburne just below the heart. All night long, his brave soldiers lay in the ditch below the breastworks, waiting for orders that never came. In the morning light, an artilleryman found the body lying about forty yards in front of the breastworks.

The casualties were heavy — 6,252 Confederates killed, wounded, or missing in action. And the figure among general officers was staggering. One general was captured, six were wounded, five were killed, and one was mortally wounded. Never had death claimed as many generals in one battle. The five dead men were Generals Pat Cleburne, S.R. Gist, H.B.

Granbury, John Adams, and O.F. Strahl. General John C. Carter died soon after the battle. Four of the bodies were taken to *Carnton*, the plantation home of John McGavock, located just southeast of the battlefield, where they were laid out on the veranda until arrangements could be made with the families.

Several of the generals and other officers, including Pat Cleburne, were taken to Columbia for funeral and burial in Rose Hill Cemetery, but Chaplain Quintard was greatly bothered by the close proximity of their resting place to graves of Federal soldiers. He immediately arranged for them to be disinterred and buried at St. John's church, in the little cemetery so admired by Pat Cleburne only a week earlier.

The tributes to this great man are impractical to list here. Howell and Elizabeth Purdue's compilation of eulogies and memorials fill an entire chapter in their definitive work, *Pat Cleburne, Confederate General.*

On April 26, 1870, General Cleburne's body was started on its way home. For twenty-four hours it lay in state in Columbia, where all businesses were closed out of respect. Escorted to the depot in a grand procession, the body was placed aboard the train to Memphis. All of the businesses in Memphis were closed, and the largest crowd ever before assembled in the history of that city watched the procession that took the body from the depot to the boat landing. Those involved in the procession and solemn ceremony that day, April 28, were Generals Anderson, Chalmers, Cheatham, Fagan, and Pillow, Bishop Quintard, former Governor Harris, and former President Davis. On April 29, Pat Cleburne was finally laid to rest in his hometown cemetery at Helena. His grave, in the Confederate section of Evergreen Cemetery, is marked by a marble monument, sixteen feet tall, placed there in 1891 by the ladies of The Phillips County Memorial Association. Funds for the monument came from the rich and the poor, including $2.50 from a negro man who remembered how kind Cleburne had been to him as a little slave boy peddling apples in Helena.

On April 28, 1870, the *Memphis Daily Appeal* compared him to Stonewall Jackson:

> Two such men have rarely lived in the same age, and that two such faultless soldiers should have risen in the armies of the same government at the same time, and each should have alike commanded the admiration of mankind, of accomplished soldiers and the undying love of their compatriots, is the chiefest wonder of the late mighty convulsion.

In *A Sketch of Maj. Gen. P.R. Cleburne*, General D.H. Hill wrote, in 1867:

> Patrick R. Cleburne deserves a prominent place among the great heroes, who have illustrated Southern heroism and Southern history. His name brings a thrill of the heart to every true son of the South, just as his presence brought success wherever he moved on the field of battle." Cleburne is here!" meant that "all was well."[28]

ROBERT E. LEE

There has never been — nor will there ever be — a mortal man more admired, more esteemed, or more revered than Robert E. Lee. His enemies were few, his friends legion. By war's end, he was already a legend. He had become the embodiment of the South, and his name synonymous with it. He was the soldier-statesman, and the ultimate hero of the Lost Cause. Today he is, without a doubt, the fundamental southern hero.

Robert Edward Lee was born January 19, 1807, in Westmoreland County, Virginia, at *Stratford Hall*, the ancestral home of the Lees. He was the fifth child of Anne Hill Carter and Henry "Light-Horse Harry" Lee, former governor of Virginia and distinguished cavalry officer of the Revolution. Both the Carters and the Lees were among the foremost families of Virginia.

In 1811, when Robert was four years old, the family was forced to move to Alexandria due to financial troubles. He was educated in the schools of that place, and in 1824 sought appointment to West Point, entering the academy in 1825. The military career of his father, who had died when Robert was only eleven, was an inspiration to him, and it can be said that Robert E. Lee was truly a professional military man. It was the only profession he would know until the last five years of his life, which he spent as president of Washington College.

Lee graduated from West Point in 1829, second in his class and without a demerit against his name. Until the outbreak of the War Between the States, he spent thirty-two years in the routine duty of the military, rising from the rank of lieutenant to colonel. He was stationed at various places around the country, from the east coast to the frontiers of Indian Territory and west Texas.

On June 30, 1831, he married Mary Ann Randolph Custis, great-granddaughter of Martha Washington. The wedding was held at the Custis mansion, *Arlington*, an imposing temple-like structure in the classical Greek tradition which sat high on a Virginia hillside, overlooking the capital city of Washington. In 1857, his father-in-law died, leaving the southern colonial home to Robert E. Lee and his wife, who made it their home until forced to move farther south in 1861. An unfortunate casualty of the War, *Arlington* was sold for "non-payment of taxes" while the Lees were in Richmond. The Yankees, determined that the Lees should not move back into *Arlington*, buried soldiers in the immediate yard so that no one would ever want to live in the house again. Today, it is the focal point of Arlington National Cemetery.

The Mexican War raged from 1846 until 1848, providing almost a dress rehearsal for the War Between the States. Many of the brilliant Confederate generals and statesmen, including Jackson, Lee, Beauregard, and Davis, saw duty in such far away places as Vera Cruz, Buena Vista, and Monterey. At Vera Cruz, Lee's skill was credited for the victory, and he was breveted to the rank of colonel for his services in the storming of Chapultepec.

In 1852, Lee became the superintendent of West Point, making several lasting improvements in the academy, but it wasn't the position most desired by him. With the help of Secretary of War Jefferson Davis, he was transferred to the command of a cavalry regiment on the Texas frontier in 1855.

Mary Lee had developed chronic arthritis, and it was while Lee was on leave at *Arlington* to attend to her that John Brown raided Harper's Ferry. Lee was ordered to Harper's Ferry in October, 1859, quickly disposing of the troubled Brown and his insurrection army.

Though Robert E. Lee was successful throughout his military career, it was the War Between the States that lionized him. He was Abraham Lincoln's first choice to command the Federal army, but Lee was a Virginian first and foremost. "If the Union is to be dissolved and the Government disrupted, I shall return to my native state and share the miseries of my people, and save in defense will draw my sword on none."[29] In early April, 1861, while strolling the grounds of *Arlington* with a northern visitor, he pointed towards the Capitol lying across the Potomac. "That beautiful feature of our landscape," he said, "has ceased to charm me as it once did. I fear the mischief that is brewing there."[30] On April 17, Virginia seceded; on April 20, Lee submitted his resignation from the U.S. Army; on April 23, he accepted the appointment as commander of Virginia forces.

He immediately set about mobilizing the volunteers of the state and fortifying the rivers against enemy movements by water. In May, he was commissioned as full general in the Confederacy and made advisor to President Davis. First dispatched to western Virginia, he stopped a threatened invasion there but was not successful in rallying the pro-Federal citizens to his cause. His next assignment was to make an inspection of the defenses around Charleston, South Carolina, and other defensive positions in the southeast. He was there until March, 1862, bolstering the excellent fortifications that General Beauregard had begun. As a result of their work, Charleston held out against heavy bombardments until the very end of the War.

General Joseph E. Johnston had been wounded, giving President Davis an opportunity to appoint General Lee as commander of the army in Virginia. On June 1, 1862, he assumed command of this congregation of soldiers who would soon become legendary, naming them The Army of Northern Virginia. In the following three years, Lee would at no time have a force comparable to his foes in numbers, artillery, or equipment. The odds against him were always three to two, and many times they were three to one. After the War, while contemplating a history of his campaigns, he wrote to his leading officers, "It will be difficult to get the world to appreciate the odds against which we fought."[31]

General McClellan had 100,000 men who had advanced to within seven miles of Richmond, and another 40,000 were on the Rappahannock, marching to reinforce him. Three other Federal forces were threatening Stonewall Jackson in the Shenandoah Valley to the west. Yankees were swarming into Virginia like bees, and Lee had to devise a plan to confuse them. He ordered General Ewell to join Jackson in the valley, where the forces of those two able officers thrashed the Yankees so soundly at Cross Keys and Port Republic that an attack upon Washington was feared, resulting in the withdrawal of the army on the Rappahannock.

Next, Lee recalled Jackson and took the offensive against the monstrous army of McClellan, pushing him back to Harrison's Landing by July 1, in a series of engagements known as the Seven Days' Battles. Lee had captured a lot of superior small arms for his men, relieved Richmond, and raised the morale and confidence of the army. His stock began to rise with the people of the South. He was their man.

To the north of Richmond, another huge army was advancing under General Pope. Lee marched his army north to attack Pope, crossing the Rapidan in mid-August. Pope withdrew north of the Rappahannock and was backing up ever closer to Washington, screaming for help from McClellan, who was rapidly loading his men onto transport ships. Lee's plan had worked. Before McClellan's men could be unloaded on the Potomac and marched overland to reinforce Pope, Lee had ordered Jackson to swing around to the northwest of Pope and attack his communications and supplies from the rear. On August 22, General Jeb Stuart captured Pope's baggage train, papers and all. On August 29, at the same location of the first Battle of Manassas, Pope discovered Jackson and attacked him. The next day he struck again, wrongly thinking that Jackson was retreating. Lee fell upon Pope while he was engaged with Jackson, and the result was a Federal retreat toward Washington.

Once again, northern Virginia was cleared of the dreaded Yankees by a battle known as Second Manassas.

Lee's obvious desire was to attack the Yankee capital which lay a little over twenty miles to the east, but McClellan's entire force was entrenched there. He then decided to make a strike in the North and headed towards Maryland to destroy the Baltimore and Ohio Railroad. His ultimate goal was Harrisburg, Pennsylvania, where he would have been able to cut the other east-west railroad.

The Army of Northern Virginia advanced to Frederick, Maryland. They were now forty-five miles north of Washington and thirty miles south of Pennsylvania, putting the northern population into a panic. Lee sent five divisions under Jackson southwest to Harper's Ferry, with instructions to capture the Federal force of 12,000 occupying the town. He sent Longstreet northwest to Hagerstown, Maryland. It took Jackson a day longer than anticipated to take Harper's Ferry, but it was a costly day, for McClellan had happened upon a lost copy of Lee's orders for the Maryland campaign and straightway pushed forward for an attack. Lee withdrew to South Mountain and was attacked on September 14 all along his line. Withdrawing to Sharpsburg, Lee set up a defensive line west of Antietam Creek, where McClellan again attacked on September 17. At last, Jackson and his "foot cavalry" arrived, and the Federal advance was halted after what would become known as the bloodiest single day of the War. Lee's dead, wounded, and missing was near 13,000, and he would have to retreat into Virginia to save the rest of his army. For some reason, McClellan did not pursue.

The North changed generals after each failed attempt to ensnare Lee, and it was now Burnside's turn. Advancing down the Potomac, he established headquarters at Aquia Creek and marched a short distance to Fredericksburg. He would have to cross the Rappahannock just east of the town and assault Marye's Heights, a formidable hill west of the town. The town lay between, and on December 11, Burnside began shelling it, causing its inhabitants (mostly women, girls, and children) to leave their homes, trudge through the mud, and bivouac in the open fields with only what assistance the Confederate soldiers could provide against the cold. Lee looked down from his artillery positions on the hill. "Those people delight to destroy the weak and those who can make no defense; it just suits them!"[32] He always referred to the Yankees as "those people."

On December 13, Burnside attacked through the town and, after a terrrible day of battling, was driven back with horrible losses. Lee did not follow up the next day, and Burnside was counselled not to renew the attack. On December 15, Burnside withdrew across the Rappahannock, badly beaten and soon to be relieved of command.

Along came General Joseph Hooker. He had an eleborate plan to cross the Rappahannock above and below Fredericksburg. Lee astonished the world by dividing his army, which was outnumbered by two to one, into three pieces, sending General Jubal Early and 9,000 men south towards Fredericksburg to oppose the Federal left and 26,000 men under Stonewall Jackson north to oppose the Federal right near Chancellorsville. Lee remained in front of the main portion of Hooker's army with only about 13,000 men! From May 1 through May 4, 1863, General Lee's Army of Northern Virginia proceeded to roll up the Union Army. Jackson had outflanked Hooker, and Lee moved forward. On May 5, Lee spent the day preparing to attack the defeated Federals again, but during that day and the following night, Hooker withdrew towards Washington.

Chancellorsville had become the greatest victory for Lee. Students of military warfare still study the strategy and tactics of his brilliant victory and dangerous division of his forces. But, gladness soon turned to gloom. On May 2, Stonewall Jackson had been wounded, living only until the 10th of May. Lee wept bitterly over Jackson's death. Not only had he lost a dear friend, he had lost a partner who could think and act in perfect conjunction with him. Jackson would never be replaced. Lee divided Jackson's corps between A.P. Hill and R.S. Ewell.

The absence of Jackson was evident in Lee's last attempt to carry the War to the North. On July 1, 2, and 3, he engaged an enemy superior in number at Gettysburg, making repeated charges which became disjointed and delayed due to his subordinates. General Ewell was slow to advance, giving the Yankees time to become entrenched at Cemetery Ridge. General Longstreet became obstinate and refused to attack time after time, thinking Lee's plans were bad. When he finally did advance, it was too little too late. On July 4, Lee's army was forced into a rapid retreat from Gettysburg. Once again, the Federal Army — this time under General Meade — did not pursue, and the Army of Northern Virginia crossed back into the South.

There are always those who search for a flaw in the fabric of a great man. Those who look for such things ironically point to Lee's kindness, forbearance, and great capacity for forgiveness, alleging that it caused him to be negligent in discipline. It is true that he was a kind general, attentive to his men. He shunned offers to headquarter in spacious Virginia homes, choosing instead to pitch a tent among his men and eat the fare of his soldiers. A South Carolina private described the affection of his soldiers. "The men hung around him and seemed satisfied to lay their hands on his gray horse or to touch the bridle, or the stirrup, or the old general's leg — anything that Lee had was sacred to us fellows who had just come back. And the General — he could not help from breaking down . . . tears traced down his cheeks."[33] But Lee seldom reprimanded — even for insubordination. After the defeat at Gettysburg, attributable in some measure to the stubbornness of Longstreet, Lee merely looked at him and sorrowfully said, "It's all my fault. I thought my men were invincible."[34]

During the winter of 1863-64, the Army of Northern Virginia had been subsisting on a daily ration of a pint of cornmeal and a quarter pound of bacon — when they could get bacon. The horses were near starvation, hardly able to drag the guns or carry the cavalry, and the army's only equipment consisted of their arms and ammunition. Lee would never be able to take the offensive again. He was reduced to awaiting and countering each move of the superbly outfitted and growing Federal army.

On May 5 and 6, 1864, Lee repulsed Grant, now in command of the Federals, at The Wilderness. On May 7, Grant began to move south, realizing that Lee would have to be beaten by attrition rather than on the field. Through the rest of May and half of June, Grant slashed his way towards Richmond, meeting repulse after repulse, knowing that he could more than replace his lost men, while Lee could not hope to replace one.

On June 18, Grant laid siege to Petersburg. Nine months later, Lee was out of supplies and forced to evacuate Petersburg and Richmond. Heading west, he tried in vain to be resupplied. On April 9, 1865, his small army was surrounded by 200,000 Yankees, and surrender was the only practical course. On February 6, Lee had been designated General-in-Chief of all the Confederate armies, and now he was forced to capitulate. It was a signal to the other armies in the field, and they began to surrender throughout the South.

It was all over. There had been 2,154 military actions of one degree or another in Virginia. General Lee had borne the brunt of many a battle, kept the Yankees out of Richmond, prevented invasion of the lower South via Virginia, and led his famished, rag-tag heroes into the legendry of the South. Lee's successes on the field were attributed to his universal comprehension of the art of war. He possessed the ability to analyze his military intelligence, accurately gauge the strength of offensive and defensive bodies of troops, mentally put himself in the place of his opponent, organize his troops to execute his strategy, and overcome his adversary. And, yet, it was the great sensitivity of Robert E. Lee that caused him to say that he mourned the loss of every soldier in his command. War was a poor way of life to this military genius, who once remarked that it was probably good that war was so terrible, else men would grow too fond of it.

After the War, Lee was exemplary. The eyes of a nation were upon him, and scores of business proposals filled his mail every year. He chose to accept an offer from Washington College in Lexington, Virginia, where he could help shape young minds for future service to his Southland. He served as president until his untimely death on October 12, 1870, and is buried beneath the chapel there. The college was renamed Washington and Lee University in his honor.

Several years after the War, when some were prone to give in to the old *might makes right* adage, wondering if the South had erred in opposing the northern political tide by secession and the resulting hostilities, Lee remarked to General Wade Hampton, "We could have pursued no other course without dishonor. And sad as the result has been, if it had all to be done over again, we should be compelled to act in precisely the same manner."[35]

STONEWALL JACKSON

Among serious students of the War, there is the school of thought that it is not only a good possibility, but a distinct likelihood, that the War could have been won *if only Stonewall Jackson had lived*. It isn't a new idea — just a valid one. Soon after his death, the Army of Northern Virginia suffered a reverse at Gettysburg, and from that time on it was generally perceived throughout the South that things would have been different if only Stonewall could have been spared a couple of more years. In her diary, Mary Boykin Chestnut noted one calamity after another, wishing many times for an Albert Sidney Johnston or a Stonewall Jackson. "And now that they begin to see that a few years more of Stonewall Jackson would have freed them from the yoke of the hateful Yankee, they deify him. They are proud to have been one of the famous Stonewall Brigade, to have been a brick in that wall."[36]

That's the Stonewall Jackson legacy, carved out in less than twenty-five months in the Confederate army. The very brevity of his service only magnifies his monumental achievements. Any survey of the half-dozen greatest American soldiers invariably includes, and usually starts with Robert E. Lee and Stonewall Jackson.

Jackson's beginnings were humble. Like many southerners, he was of Scotch-Irish stock. He was the third child of Julia Beckwith Neale and a lawyer named Jonathan Jackson. His given name was Thomas, but for some reason his parents did not give him a middle name. It was after he was nearly grown that he added the name Jonathan, thus becoming Thomas Jonathan Jackson for the first time. His family had been poor, and his parents died when he was very young, leaving him in the care of a kind bachelor uncle, Cummins E. Jackson. Cummins raised him on a farm in western Virginia, where he could offer him little education.

From this lowly, obscure background emerged a brilliant military strategist. He entered West Point in 1842, handicapped by his meager education, but resolved to dig in and make something of himself. In 1846, he graduated seventeenth in a class of fifty-nine. This was no small accomplishment in a West Point class that would furnish twenty-four generals to the Confederate and Federal armies between 1861 and 1865!

Sent almost immediately to Mexico, he distinguished himself at Cerro Gordo, Vera Cruz, and Chapultepec, for which actions he was brevetted a major. In 1848, he returned to routine duty in the States.In 1851, he accepted a position as professor of artillery and natural philosophy at the Virginia Military Institute in Lexington, Virginia, resigning from the army in 1852.

When Virginia seceded, Jackson took charge of the troops that were collecting at Harper's Ferry. A few weeks later, in May of 1861, he was replaced by Gen. Joseph E. Johnston. Ordered to Richmond, he was made a brigadier general on June 17 and placed in command of a brigade in Johnston's army.

On July 16, Rose O'Neal Greenhow — the intrepid Confederate spy — sent word from Washington that the Federals were advancing towards Centreville and Manassas. President Davis ordered General Johnston, who was covering the Shenandoah Valley, to hurry his troops back over the mountains and reinforce General Beauregard at Manassas. The first brigade to arrive was that of General Thomas Jonathan Jackson. At 4 p.m., the astonished Beauregard looked up to see Jackson walking in to report the early arrival of his 2,500 men. It would be noon the next day before General Johnston and the rest of his men would finally arrive. Jackson had set the precedent for the swift movement of his troops. It would become his trademark, and many an unsuspecting Yankee would turn around to find Jackson suddenly upon him. He moved his infantry around by sudden night marches and over unlikely routes with such lightning speed that his troops became known as "Jackson's foot cavalry."

In the ensuing battle, a Federal column marched around the left flank of the Confederates and began enveloping the left end of the army with heavy fighting. As weakened Confederate troops retreated, they rushed past General Jackson and his troops who were standing steadfastly against the foe. General Barnard Bee rallied the shaken southerners by shouting, "See, there is Jackson standing like a stone wall; rally on the Virginians!"[37] The boys in gray carried the day, and Bee's exclamation gave Jackson his famous sobriquet of "Stonewall," though Jackson always modestly insisted that General Bee, who fell mortally wounded moments after his famous statement, had intended his comment to apply to the entire brigade of Jackson.

In the Valley Campaign of 1862, Jackson made a record for himself and his mighty men by pouncing like a panther upon every force Washington tried to send up the Shenandoah Valley. Jackson, who had been promoted in October, 1861, to the rank of major-general, was in command of the Shenandoah Valley with a force of 17,000. His small command kept four Federal armies at bay, eventually defeating them one by one, ridding the valley of more than 60,000 bluecoats. His activities there kept Washington busy supplying troops to the valley, thus preventing reinforcements to the operations against Richmond.

When Lee needed help, Stonewall would make one of those lightning marches, to the consternation of the enemy who thought he was elsewhere. Mary Chestnut alluded to his pervasive reputation in her diary. "Stonewall cannot be everywhere, though he comes near it."[38]

His command was the most efficient and prestigious in the Army of Northern Virginia. Even though he required much of his men, those who thought they could endure sought a place in his ranks. His brilliant moves and deadly hammer strokes of attack put fear into his opponents, who learned to respect the mere name of Stonewall Jackson. The northern comic writer and lecturer, Artemus Ward, teased his Yankee audiences with

Jackson's preeminance. "One evening, before a solidly pro-Union audience, he said, 'We have among our officers one good general, Stonewall Jackson. . .' At this there was a cry of protest from the audience, which Ward allowed to die down before he concluded his sentence. . . 'but he is among our officers a little too often to be pleasant.' "[39]

Jackson was an absolute master in the art of flanking attacks. A prime example of his prowess in outflanking the enemy occurred at the second Battle of Manassas in August, 1862. Lee's 48,000 men were facing the overwhelming army of General Pope, which numbered 75,000. Stonewall took 20,000 men, marched them up and around the right flank of Pope's army, and, gaining his rear, destroyed his base of operations. He had marched almost half of Lee's army fifty-one miles in two days! Then Stonewall hit Pope from one direction, while Lee struck him from another.

After the death of Jackson, "General Buckner had seen a Yankee cartoon in which angels were sent down from Heaven to bear up Stonewall's soul. They could not find it, and flew back sorrowing, but when they got to the Golden Gate above they found that Stonewall, by a rapid flank movement, had already cut a way in."[40]

Jackson and Lee were perfectly combined, each able to discern the other's intentions perfectly. There was no better coordination in the Confederate Army. Their ultimate victory came in May, 1863, at Chancellorsville, when together they almost annihilated the huge army of General Hooker, an army of 134,000 splendidly equipped Yankees. Though outnumbered by more than two to one, Lee divided his army of 57,000 into three small pieces, sending Jackson with 26,000 men in a circuitous flanking movement around the Federal right. As he wandered through the underbrush of the wilderness, the Federals thought he must be retreating — until he fell upon the rear of the Federal right flank. He routed the entire XI Corps by an attack which started about 6 p.m. Soon, the monstrous Federal army would begin a rapid retreat across the river, once again badly defeated by a flanking movement of Stonewall Jackson.

In the twilight, returning from an inspection of the front, Jackson and his staff were fired upon by some Confederate pickets who mistook them for the enemy. Jackson was wounded in the arm, which soon had to be amputated, and though he insisted upon staying with the army, he was removed to Guiney's Station for his own safety. He had been wounded on May 2 and probably would have recovered had pneumonia not set in. On May 10, he was gone. Lee sorrowfully refused a request from Jackson's men to go to Richmond and march in his funeral procession because the enemy was making movements directly in front of the army.

Stonewall Jackson's strength of character was one of his greatest attributes. He was fundamentally religious, being a strong adherent of Presbyterianism. Both his first wife, who had died shortly after their marriage, and his second wife, Mary Anna Morrison, were daughters of Presbyterian ministers. At VMI, he had a habit of praying for his cadets every day before instructing them, and it was quite well known that he prayed before going into battle. He once said that he never was so ungrateful as to drink a cup of water without thanking God for it.

In some ways, Jackson was eccentric — as are many men of great stature. Upon occasion, he would hold one arm straight up over his head while riding at the head of his troops, and it has been said that there were no chairs in his study at VMI. He supposedly stood for hours memorizing his lectures and studying his Bible.

One thing is sure: He was independent and knew when to take action. At the first Battle of Manassas, he was wounded in the hand and afterwards sought the army surgeon for treatment. The surgeon announced that a finger would have to be amputated, and when he turned to pick up his instruments, Jackson rode away!

NATHAN BEDFORD FORREST

Robert E. Lee often told an amusing anecdote about a negro cook in the army who came into headquarters one day.

"General Lee," he said, "I been wanting to see you a long time. I'm a soldier."

"Ah. To what army do you belong?"

"Oh, General, I belong to your army."

"Well, have you been shot?"

"No, sir. I ain't been shot yet."

"How's that? Nearly all our men get shot."

"Why, General, I ain't been shot 'cause I stays back where the generals stay."[41]

This observant cook was nobody's fool, but he would have been in a heap of trouble had he cooked for the command of Nathan Bedford Forrest out in the *west*, as they called the Tennessee/Alabama/Mississippi arena of the War. Forrest was not a general content to direct actions from the rear. He became so caught up in the charge that he *led* his men into the fray, sustaining the initial impact with his front lines.

While covering the retreat from Shiloh, Forrest launched a smashing charge against enemy cavalry. Well in advance of his men, he penetrated the enemy lines into their reserves, suddenly finding himself surrounded by dozens of blazing rifles. Although he and his horse were severely wounded, he stubbornly grabbed his two Colt revolvers, blasted a hole in the mass of bluecoats, and dashed out to safety. It wouldn't be the last time he would charge wildly into the enemy and have to "cut his way out," nor would it be the last time he was wounded. And, it wouldn't even come close to being the last time he would have a horse shot out from under him. This was the fourth time — there would be twenty-five more!

All of this because Nathan Bedford Forrest stayed at the

front. But, then the army cook had never been in the west, and he had never met this man Forrest. Even General Lee, when asked who was the greatest soldier in his command, replied that he was a man whom he had never met — a man named Forrest.

This extraordinary daredevil, who earned the sobriquet of *The Wizard of the Saddle*, was born July 13, 1821, in Bedford County, Tennessee, to William Forrest and Mariam Beck. In 1834, the family moved into Tippah County, Mississippi. William had given up his blacksmithing in Tennessee to try his hand at farming in the north Mississippi lands of the recently displaced Chickasaws, but before he could get his place carved out, he died, leaving his wife and eleven children in poverty.

It was 1837, and Nathan Bedford — only sixteen years old — had to become the man of the family. In his veins flowed the thrift and pluck of his Scotch-Irish forefathers, and soon it would be evident that the blood was still there. He provided for his mother and his ten younger brothers and sisters by working first as a farm hand, then as an animal trader. Later, he accepted an offer from an uncle to join his mercantile business in Hernando, Mississippi. His partnership in the business enabled him to amply provide for his family, as his earnings steadily increased until he left that enterprise in 1851 to become a real estate broker in Memphis.

In 1845, he had married Mary Ann Montgomery, a well-bred young lady of plantation society. Forrest began to buy up land, and upon moving to Memphis, became a dealer in slaves, an occupation that was frowned upon by southerners. He realized that he was ill-suited for the occupation, never allowing families to be separated and doing his best to find the husband or wife if a slave was brought to sale without his or her mate. In addition, he insisted upon washing and dressing his slaves in clean garments. His treatment was so kind that slaves appealed to him to buy them for his own plantations, and eventually, he did just that. Closing his slave market, he kept those he had on hand and became a planter on a large scale. By the time the guns of war had sounded, he was worth a million and a half dollars.

On June 14, 1861, he enlisted at Memphis as a private in Captain Josiah White's Tennessee Mounted Rifles, but prominent citizens of the community knew he was fitted for much more than the rank of private, and, accordingly, called upon Governor Isham Harris and General Leonidas Polk with a request that he be given a commission. The result was authority for him to raise a battalion of cavalry and appointment as lieutenant colonel in the Confederate army. By October, he had eight companies in his command, having outfitted most of the troops at his own expense. He had paid for over 500 Colt navy pistols, 100 saddles, blankets, and whatever supplies were lacking among the assembled men, who numbered about 650.

Nathan Bedford Forrest was the true swashbuckler of the War — fast-moving, hard-riding, apt to dash directly into the enemy ranks and battle it out one to one (or in some cases, one to a dozen). He did not believe in waiting to be attacked. He had learned as a lad how effectively he could unbalance an opponent by suddenly throwing himself at the would-be attacker. At Parker's Cross Roads, he exhibited his ability to bluff, thereby saving most of his command from what could have been a most conclusive defeat.

They had driven a Yankee force from two positions, and by flanking movements had them nearly surrounded. Forrest and the majority of his command were facing the Yankees, who had thrown up white flags, and were awaiting their official surrender, when all of a sudden a huge Yankee force surprised the Confederates by attacking from the rear. Colonel Carroll, with a great deal of haste, dashed up to Forrest. "General Forrest, a heavy line of infantry is right in our rear, we are between two lines of battle. What shall we do?" Forrest replied, "We'll charge them both ways!"[42] Firing at both sides, they rushed from between the lines, squeezing out just in the nick of time.

346

To cover the retreat, Forrest took his escort and another regiment to the rear while most of his command escaped. The Yankees were in hot pursuit, so Forrest halted every man he could reach, ordering them to get in line and advance upon the enemy. Lieutenant Baxter protested, "General, I am entirely unarmed; have neither gun, pistol, nor sword." Forrest hurriedly shouted, "That doesn't make any difference; get in line and advance on the enemy with the rest; I want to make as big a show as possible."[43] Several men were likewise unarmed, but the sudden dash at the enemy checked their advance, and the Confederates escaped.

In April, 1863, Federal forces under Col. Streight tore out through Alabama, headed towards Rome, Georgia, to destroy the railroad. After several days of running battle with Forrest, Streight was forced to take a stand. Forrest, who was a brigadier general then, captured the entire force of 1700 men by showing Streight, under a flag of truce, that he was facing an overwhelming force. While they were talking, Forrest had prearranged for his artillerymen to circle his two guns around the top of a hill to give the impression that more guns were arriving. After Col. Streight thought he had counted fifteen guns alone, he figured the infantry must be in the thousands, and without too much delay, surrendered his force to Forrest's command of only 400 men!

General Forrest was as independent a man as there was in the army. At the completely unnecessary surrender of Fort Donelson in early 1862, while Forrest was a colonel, he became infuriated with Generals Buckner, Floyd, and Pillow, when he came upon them talking about surrender. The generals feared they were surrounded, but Forrest informed them that he would cut his way out if need be; that he had not come there to surrender; that he had promised his boys' parents to take care of them; that he did not intend to see them die in prison camps that winter; and, that he was going out if only one man followed. Forrest waked his cavalry and led them out unopposed, under

347

cover of darkness. The next day General Buckner surrendered 13,000 Confederates needlessly.

When Forrest, who had never experienced the defeat of his own command, realized the utter folly of trying to win under the inept General Bragg, he lashed out at Bragg and refused to follow him any further. President Davis, knowing full well that he might lose an able cavalry commander under the lackluster Bragg, gave Forrest an independent command and promoted him to the rank of major general.

General Sherman put thousands of men on the trail of "that devil Forrest", as he called him. General Sturgis was sent out twice to find Forrest, writing to Sherman after the first expedition, "My little campaign is over, and I regret to say Forrest is still at large . . . I regret very much that I could not have the pleasure of bringing you his hair."[44]

Sherman ordered Sturgis out again. Leaving Federally-occupied Memphis on June 1, 1864, he caught up with Forrest on June 10, at a little place in Mississippi called Brice's Cross Roads. Sturgis had approximately 8500 men with which he intended to crush only 3500 Rebels. In what has been called the only perfectly executed battle of the War, Forrest leaped at him from the front, charged both of his flanks, and attacked him from the rear. In the ensuing rout, the bridge was blocked by an overturned wagon, and men plunged headlong into the water to flee the screaming Rebels. Forrest pursued vigorously, his men scattering Yankees through the woods and across fields. It had taken Sturgis nine days to march out from Memphis; it took him only sixty-four hours to make the return trip, with a Confederate cavalry close at his heels. Confederate losses were 492 killed and wounded, while the Federals lost 2,240. Forrest had captured the enemy artillery, 176 wagons, supplies, and 1500 prisoners.

Sherman was disgusted. "I cannot understand how he could defeat Sturgis with eight thousand men . . . Forrest is the devil, and I think he has got some of our troops under cower . . .

I will order them to make up a force and go out to follow Forrest to the death, if it costs ten thousand lives and breaks the Treasury. There never will be peace in Tennessee until Forrest is dead!"[45]

No one ever captured General Forrest. His only defeat came at the end of the War. He was a lieutenant general by then, trying to shore up the defenses of Selma, Alabama, against an expected attack from 14,000 Yankee troops. It was April 2, 1865, and the end was very near. Richmond was being evacuated that very day, and men were scarce in the lower South. Forrest could find only 3,000 at Selma, including his cavalry, the militia, old men, and boys. They withstood the onslaught bravely, but were finally forced to cut their way out to avoid capture, heading west towards Marion. On April 15, Forrest concentrated his forces at Gainesville, Alabama, and it was here that he received the tragic news that General Richard Taylor had surrendered the Department of Alabama and Mississippi — including the remnant of Forrest's command — on May 4, 1865. There was talk of going to the Trans-Mississippi Department, or even to Mexico, but Forrest reluctantly accepted the surrender and urged his men to go home and help rebuild the shattered South.

The career of Nathan Bedford Forrest had streaked across the pages of history like a blazing comet in the southern sky. He had deviled the Yankees for four years, captured 31,000 prisoners, come under fire 179 times, and killed thirty Yankees with his own hands. He remarked that the latter feat had made him "one up on them," a reference to their record of having shot twenty-nine horses out from under him. At one time, he had placed artillery batteries on the west bank of the Mississippi, shelling three gunboats, eleven transports, fifteen barges, warehouses, wagon trains, and scores of Federal soldiers, resulting in the destruction of six million dollars worth of enemy supplies and a gunboat fleet.

His reputation as a fierce fighter was universal. "He often brought a smile to the many friends gathered around him in telling of the incident at Cowan's station, when he was being

349

hotly pursued through that village by the Federals, and a fiery Southern dame, not knowing that she was addressing the great General Forrest, shook her fist at him and upbraided him as a coward for not turning about to fight the Yankees. The last words he heard her say as he passed on the roadside were: 'Why don't you turn and fight, you cowardly rascal? If old Forrest were here, he'd make you fight.' "[46]

One of the most famous quotes from the War fell from the lips of Forrest when General John Hunt Morgan once asked him the secret of his many successes on the battlefield. Forrest replied, "To git thar fustest with the mostest!" And, of course, the controversy still rages as to whether Nathan Bedford's grammar and dialect were so colorfully deviant, though it is well known that his spelling was terrible and that he hung on to many of the old expressions of his backwoods upbringing, such as "fetch" and "betwixt" for "bring" and "between," and "thern" for "theirs."

After the War, he successfully redeveloped his plantations, and became president of the Selma, Marion, & Memphis Railroad. He suffered financial reverses several times, but always managed to rebound. When several boys, back from the War, organized the Ku Klux Klan in Pulaski, Tennessee, to while away the dreary hours, it occurred to some astute observers that this game of dress-up and clandestine meetings might be the answer to the carpetbag regime of old Parson Brownlow, governor of Tennessee. Nathan Bedford's curiosity caused him to inquire into the situation. One thing led to another, and before long, he had been named *Grand Wizard of the Invisible Empire*. The Ku Klux Klan spread throughout the South, reclaiming the lost rights of southerners from the despotic rule of carpetbag governments. In 1870, when six states had been redeemed, Forrest ordered it disbanded and withdrew from it, feeling justified that he had gained the ultimate victory over the Yankee North.

On October 29, 1877, Nathan Bedford Forrest died in

Memphis at the age of fifty-six. Thousands followed the funeral cortege to Elmwood Cemetery. Many former Confederate officials and officers, including President Davis, rode in the procession. Few people were aware during Forrest's lifetime that he contributed large amounts of his fortune to the welfare of disabled Confederate soldiers, their widows, and orphans, in an effort to fill the gap left by the U.S. government who steadfastly refused to contribute so much as a dime to alleviate the sufferings of ex-Confederate soldiers, while appropriating millions to Union veterans. After his death, Mrs. Forrest faithfully continued the contributions until she had virtually exhausted the entire estate.

The monuments and memorials to Nathan Bedford Forrest are many. Probably the most impressive single one is the colossal equestrian statue at Forrest Park in Memphis. Though talk of an appropriate memorial began soon after his death, it was 1891 before efforts were organized. The magnificent monument, which was dedicated on May 16, 1905, rests over the graves of General and Mrs. Forrest, whose remains were removed from Elmwood Cemetery.

JOHN HUNT MORGAN

If the knighthood of the Old South could be rolled up into one man as its definition of chivalry, John Hunt Morgan would be the word. He was handsome, perfectly proportioned, worshipped by the women, and idolized by the men of his time. While the South was suffering defeats of their large armies, he was slashing away at the enemy on its own soil, giving new hope to weary southern hearts. Raised in an aristocratic family, he was educated and trained in all the proper graces of the ante-bellum South. At an early age, he acquired that requisite triumvirate of knighthood — the ability to ride, handle a weapon, and physically protect his honor. Like a knight of old, onto the pages of history he rode, avenging the persecuted peasants of Kentucky, rescuing damsels in distress, and, eventually winning the hand of his lady fair in Tennessee.

Born in Alabama on June 1, 1825, to Calvin Morgan and Henrietta Hunt, he was named for his maternal grandfather, John Wesley Hunt, of Lexington, Kentucky, probably the wealthiest man west of the Allegheny Mountains. From the Morgan side of the family, John Hunt Morgan got his dashing, daring, impetuous nature, for the Morgans were highly respected men of their time, esteemed for their valorous deeds. But, it was from the Hunts that John inherited his taste for the finer things of life. His blue blood flowed from the rich Hunt vein.

Depressed economic circumstances, brought on by tumbling cotton prices, necessitated the move from Alabama to Lexington, Kentucky, when John was five years old. In Lexington, Henrietta's father was able to include the family in his successful business empire, insuring to them a comfortable life in upper-class society.

John's education came from home and a neighborhood school, until he was old enough to enter Transylvania University, a prestigious school of higher learning attended by several notables, including the future president of the Confederacy, Jefferson Davis. True to his cavalier instincts and Kentucky custom, John challenged a fellow student to a duel, which, by 1844, had become illegal in that state. Neither of the boys was seriously hurt, but John was expelled.

His education thus ended, he began to search for adventure, a precursor to his daredevil raids during the War Between the States. Never idle for long, he turned to the military for satisfaction of his thirst for excitement, and on June 4, 1846, joined Co. K, a Lexington group of volunteers for the Mexican War. Action at Buena Vista distinguished the entire unit, who were mustered out on June 7 of the following year in New Orleans, where they boarded a train for the tumultuous heroes' welcome in Lexington. Before he could find another unit who would reenlist him, the war ended.

On Nov. 21, 1848, Morgan married Rebecca Bruce, a pretty girl whose father owned interests in several firms, including a hemp factory. In 1853, John and his brother, Calvin, entered into a partnership, manufacturing ropes and bags from hemp. It was a successful enterprise, but it didn't provide the thrill John had found in the military; consequently, he organized the Lexington Rifles in 1857 and was in command of this unit of the state militia. He was already a captain, having attained that rank from a previous artillery outfit he had formed in 1852, a unit that had disintegrated in 1854 when the state militia was disbanded for three years.

When war broke out at Fort Sumter, his wife was deathly ill, and this warrior whose comet was to reach its zenith in the war, made no move to join up. It wasn't because he was vacillating. He knew where he stood — squarely with the South. But, with Becky's illness at hand, and with the state of Kentucky taking a strange stand for nobody, proclaiming itself entirely neutral in the conflict, Morgan was probably in a state of forced limbo.

Two events occurred to shake him from his inactivity. Becky died on July 21, 1861, and the state of Kentucky was taken over by Unionists. The state militia, largely pro-southern, was ordered to turn in its weapons. Morgan went to the armory, hid his guns in hay-filled wagons, and shipped the crates to Frankfort, full of bricks. The real John Hunt Morgan had emerged, ready to do service for the South.

On September 28, he and his Lexington Rifles left town, headed for Bowling Green, where his more than 250 men would join the Confederate army as a unit under command of Morgan. The twenty-seven days of waiting to be mustered in didn't suit an adventurer like Morgan, and he filled the days with raids behind enemy lines in Kentucky. Riding by moonlight, with only ten or twenty hand-picked men, he would prowl around the enemy camps, learning of their strength and how best to use it against them. Morgan's raiders attacked the pickets from the woods, isolated small groups from the main body so that they could be attacked, cut communications lines, and generally harassed the Federal army wherever he could.

On October 27, 1861, the twenty-seven days being up, he and his men were sworn in, Morgan being elected captain of a cavalry company. His brother-in-law, Basil Duke, who would become General Basil Duke, and who would write the history of Morgan's Raiders after the War, became his lieutenant.

John Hunt Morgan, like other cavalry officers, could lead swift attacks upon the flank of an enemy or strike him from the rear like a bolt of lightning while the infantry moved slowly towards a calculated mission. Such was the benefit of the horsemen. Gen. Jeb Stuart, Gen. Jubal Early, and other cavalry-men occasionally made dashes behind enemy lines, striking at communication and supply lines, but Morgan differed in that he spent the entire war raiding behind the enemy. It was an exception to his rule when he stayed close to the main army or participated in a joint attack with the main force. About the time the Yankees thought they had Kentucky muzzled and were moving into Tennessee, Morgan's Raiders suddenly showed up in central and northern Kentucky, spreading terror to pro-Union communities while liberating pro-southern communities from harsh provost marshals. The Yankee advance, more than once, had to be stopped until Morgan could be chased out of Kentucky again. He caused much delay in Yankee movements toward Dixie and thwarted numerous battle plans.

By April, 1862, only five months after joining the Confederate army, his name had become a household word, North and South. To say that he was adored in the South would be too mild. The very mention of his name was exhilarating to an apprehensive South. He inspired southerners with every newspaper account of how he had whipped another bunch of dreaded Yankees. And there were plenty of accounts. The newspapers lauded him at every turn, suggesting that if other officers were as capable as Morgan the War would be carried to the North and won on their soil.

On April 4, Morgan received his commission as colonel. Two days later, his unit was called upon to fight at Shiloh. His cavalry made one major charge in the battle, this with sabers. His mounted men became mixed in with the enemy infantry, and it was nothing but confusion. He never used sabers again, and he never fought in another major battle.

General Bragg's headquarters of the Army of Tennessee had been at Murfreesboro, and it was here that Colonel Morgan met Mattie Ready, one of the most desired belles in Tennessee, and daughter of Charles and Martha Ready. During the rest of the year of 1862 theirs was a celebrated romance that would end in marriage on December 14 in an event that eclipsed any social affair known in that part of the country. There were dances, bonfires, receptions, and serenades by two regimental bands. General Leonidas Polk performed the marriage, while Generals Bragg, Hardee, Cheatham, and Breckinridge looked on. President Davis had been there in the afternoon but had left before the wedding.

Earlier in the year, July to be exact, Morgan and his men, now 900 strong, made their first extensive raid into Kentucky, covering over 1,000 miles in 24 days. They burned railroad trestles, disrupted communications, and destroyed government war supplies. They traveled as far north as Cynthiana, then headed back to Tennessee before any force of Federals could collect the manpower sufficient to subdue them.

His raiding was gaining for him the admiration of southerners who were trapped in a state controlled by Yankees and turncoats. In Lebanon, he perpetuated the Robin Hood image by seizing government warehouses and distributing coffee, meat, flour, and sugar to the citizens of the town. Southern citizens of Kentucky thronged him in the streets, and ladies met him waving handkerchiefs and offering food.

For the first half of his Confederate service, Morgan adhered strictly to the southern code of chivalry, never molesting private property and always paying for the needs of his cavalry in Confederate money; however, an event in Gallatin, Tennessee, coupled with increasing Yankee atrocities, convinced him that retaliation upon the enemy's entire country was not inconsistent with honor, but that it was actually honorable to defend the South in that way. The official consensus in Richmond was that he was not acting in an appropriate manner when he attacked targets other than military, but the southern populace was solidly behind him, and he became the only general of the War who could have gotten away with it.

After destroying the Big South Tunnel above Gallatin and wrecking the train, an action which put the Yankee railroad out of service for more than three months, Morgan left town. The Yankees knew that he had been aided by the citizens of the town, so they plundered the town, arrested every male of twelve years and older, and began marching them to Nashville where they were going to hang them all as spies. A twelve year old boy raced into Morgan's camp, and within five minutes Morgan's Raiders were in hot pursuit. They came upon the

Yankees about halfway to Nashville. The sight of Yankees pushing the Gallatin citizenry at bayonet point was too much. Morgan went after one particular Yankee who prodded an eighty-year old man along with his bayonet. Running him down the embankment at the side of the railroad, Morgan shot him dead in his tracks, a fate that was shared by most of the *brave* Yankees of that command.

Morgan made several large raids into Kentucky. After December 13, 1862, he made the raids as *General* Morgan with larger forces, though his largest force was no more than 3,900 men. His most famous raid was into Indiana and Ohio where he put a righteous fear into Yankee citizens who thought they were safely behind the lines. Streaking across the bottom of both states, he turned northward into east central Ohio and was captured near the Pennsylvania state line at West Point, Ohio. The exultant Yankees threw him and his officers into the Ohio State Penitentiary. Like a caged tiger, he resolved to get out, and by November 27, 1863, he and six of his officers had dug their way out, scaled the outside wall, and scattered through the countryside. The penitentiary had held John Hunt Morgan only four months.

The crowds were waiting in Richmond to see this "Francis Marion" of the Second Revolution. He was honored in a parade on January 9, 1864, and introduced to the Virginia legislature on January 11, where a formal reception was held for him.

On January 1, he had issued a proclamation, calling for the men of his command to reassemble in Decatur, Georgia. Needing about 2,000 recruits, he received over 14,000 responses from men in every branch of the service. The fortunes of the Confederacy being on the decline, he was unable to provide 800 of these new horsemen with horses. On his raid into Kentucky in June, the 800 had to walk until a raid at Lexington brought in enough thoroughbreds for every man, marking the first time Morgan had to move men on foot.

There was another difference in the new raiders. These were

not the *Dixie Cavaliers* he had been used to. Many of his Kentuckian swashbucklers who made the hills of Kentucky ring with their choruses of Morgan's marching song, *Cheer, Boys, Cheer!* were not among the new force. Too many of the new recruits were more interested in high adventure than high ideals, making them hard to control. Private property was ransacked, banks were robbed, and goods were stolen, resulting in an inquiry by the Richmond government into Morgan's command.

Morgan asked for a speedy inquiry to clear his name, but ever so impatient, he went on an attack into eastern Tennessee while awaiting the inquiry. While spending the night in the Williams home in Greeneville, Morgan and some of his staff officers were surprised by a contingent of Union cavalry who raced into town on a little road that had been left unguarded by the main body of Morgan's men, who were deployed around the perimeter of the town. The Yankees swarmed furiously up and down the streets surrounding the large two-story home with its walled gardens and grape vineyard, firing at fleeing guards. Morgan and several officers fled into the gardens and vineyard, where, according to most accounts, Morgan was the only one shot, being the only one who resisted capture.

Mystery still surrounds the death of John Hunt Morgan. Who betrayed him? Did the killer know whom he was shooting? Was he shot while attempting to escape, or was he murdered after he threw his hands up? How did one man escape this hornet's nest while Morgan, the genius of escapes, fell victim to his foes? Did his pledge to Mattie that he would never be taken prisoner again figure into his death?

The body was irreverently thrown across the killer's horse, despite protests that it be carried into the Williams house. Amidst coarse yells and cheers, it was paraded through the streets like some hunter's kill, then taken outside of town to the waiting Union forces under General Gillem, where it was once more displayed from the back of a horse to sadistic cheering.

According to Major Withers, one of Morgan's staff officers

taken prisoner, the body was badly abused, and Withers was forced by the Yankees to dismount and view the bloody, mud-covered body, stripped of its clothing and lying in a ditch. After protest on Withers' part, the body was taken back to the Williams house, where it was washed and dressed.

The most popular folk-hero of the War was gone, and his loss was mourned throughout the Confederacy. John Hunt Morgan was given three funerals. The first one was in Abingdon, Virginia, where Mattie was staying. The date was September 6, two days after Morgan's death. Ten days later, another large funeral was held in Richmond, and the body was laid in a vault in Hollywood Cemetery, where it would rest until after the War. Finally, in April, 1868, Calvin Morgan brought his brother's body back to Lexington for the final funeral, attended by over 2,000 people, still weeping openly for the slain chieftain.

Tributes have been many. Probably the most impressive monument to Morgan's memory is the equestrian statue on the courthouse lawn in Lexington, Kentucky, dedicated at a ceremony in 1911 which drew more than 10,000 faithful admirers.

SAM DAVIS

When you drive up to the rock gates of the lovingly restored home of Sam Davis, you are greeted by these words, written in stone: SAM DAVIS, THE CONFEDERATE HERO.

The Tennessee countryside surrounding the more than 150 acres of the plantation is beautiful, and for those who have not heard the story of Sam Davis, a sort of wondrous anticipation that accompanies any visit to an ante-bellum home begins to take hold. But, this tour will be different, for laughter and gaiety will be left behind as the sad story of a young boy who died for his country begins to unfold in vivid detail. After having read the pitiful letter of farewell to his mother and father, having walked the same floors where his parents waited for days to learn of Sam's fate, and having stood on the same porch where two frantic parents watched the wagon carrying the metal coffin slowly make its way towards them, one will go back through those rock gates with a burdened heart and a hallowed memory which will last as long as sons are sacred to their mothers.

Wars are truly the "times that try men's souls," visiting upon mankind all kinds of cruelty, pestilence, ravage, and death; but, war also has a paradoxical way of demanding the best qualities of an individual, and, in war's tragic arena, some are even called to be heroes. Among these heroic men in every war, there usually arises one single person who stands out above the rest; one who captures the hearts of the people; one who exhibits bravery and chivalry unmatched; one who gives his life. It is rare to find such qualities in a mature man, much less in a youth, but of such stature was our hero, Sam Davis, who, in the tradition of Revolutionary War hero, Nathan Hale, gave his only life in the cause of freedom.

His home, through the stone gates, is not the place where he was born on October 6, 1842, but it is his boyhood home.

"It is the home from which he rode into the service of his beloved Southland" and the home "to which his body was returned as that of an immortal hero."[47] In 1927, the state of Tennessee bought the plantation which has become a shrine to the young boy, who, while facing imminent death, uttered the bravest words of his life — words that have rung down through the years: *If I had a thousand lives, I would give them all rather than betray a friend.*

Sam was one of the most promising boys in Middle Tennessee. He was handsome, friendly, and admired by his friends throughout Rutherford County. In the fall of 1860, when he was eighteen years old, he went away to school. At the Western Military Institute in Nashville, he soon became a favorite with his classmates, many of whom would recall in later years that he was popular and extremely trustworthy. Two of his teachers there had a great influence upon him; they would soon be known to the world as Confederate Generals Bushrod Johnson and E. Kirby Smith.

In April, as Sam was nearing the end of his first year of college, a thunderbolt struck the entire South. Lincoln had provoked a confrontation at Fort Sumter in far-away Charleston Harbor. Shots had been fired, and the first battle of a dreadful war was now history. The enemy would soon be at the door, and Tennessee would have to decide which way to go. There was really little time for deliberation. Tennessee was a southern state and would soon be invaded by hordes of Yankees due to its proximity to the northern states. Kentucky, to the north, would be of only limited help in stopping the murderous onslaught. That poor state was so divided in opinion that its naïve government officials declared it neutral in the coming conflict, rendering it defenseless to Lincoln's army of provost marshals who swarmed into the state and usurped the power of the civil governments.

Like Bushrod Johnson and E. Kirby Smith, Sam was aware that his services would be needed, and everybody would be leaving the Institute, but he had no way of knowing how final his departure would be. One can but imagine the many thoughts that raced through young Sam's mind. He wanted to do so well in college and make his parents proud of him back in Rutherford County. Maybe he could enlist for six months or a year and return to the Institute then. But, if the Yankees came — and come they most surely would — there wouldn't be a college anyway. Or any teachers. Sam, like all of the boys in Tennessee, knew full well what an invasion of Yankees meant. Homes would be burned, schools would be destroyed, and people would be killed — slaughtered. This was war. This was real. And Sam knew it. His father, Charles Davis, was too old to enlist, and Sam, being the eldest son, had to consider the protection of his mother as well as his younger brothers and sisters. The burden was weighing heavily upon his mind, and he was arriving at the only logical conclusion a southern boy could make in 1861.

A boy of only 19, he bravely returned to Rutherford County, joining the Rutherford Rifles, which soon became Co. I, 1st Tennessee Infantry, CSA. A saddened mother and heavy-hearted father bade their son farewell as they watched him ride off with the First Tennessee to Virginia, where he would receive his first war experience under the already legendary Generals Robert E. Lee and Stonewall Jackson in the summer and fall of 1861.

Sure enough, while he was away the Yankees had gotten into western Tennessee easily enough, and the First Tennessee was rushed back to native soil. These tired soldiers were directed to Corinth, Mississippi, just south of the Tennessee state line, where they would immediately muster for the coming fight over in Tennessee, which would become known as the Battle of Shiloh. It was the bloodiest action of the War so far — nearly 11,000 southern casualties in only three days. The northerners also paid a dear price for their unwelcome visit to Tennessee — nearly 14,000 men killed, wounded, or missing. By this time (April, 1862), Sam had served under four of the ablest generals who had ever stepped onto the pages of history: Generals Albert Sidney Johnston (who was killed at Shiloh), P.G.T. Beauregard, Lee, and Jackson.

As fall fell on Middle Tennessee in 1862, General Braxton Bragg, who had been given command of the Army of Tennessee after General Johnston's death, organized a special unit of extraordinary soldiers to be his "eyes and ears." They were commanded by Captain Shaw, who, to protect his identity, was given the alias of *E. Coleman*. Confederate officials and his scouts always referred to him as E. Coleman, and the Yankees did not know that he was the same man who meandered frequently within their lines posing as an itinerant herb doctor.

Yankees were all over Tennessee by late 1862, and the state was in danger of being completely lost to the Federals. Sam Davis, possessing splendid soldierly qualities and a reputation for honesty, was fast making his mark in the military, and many accounts of his excellence had made their way home to his ever watchful and waiting parents. It came, then, as no great surprise to many, that Sam was selected to be a member of the elite, close-knit group of men known as Coleman's Scouts. For about a year, these sleuths operated behind enemy lines, collecting vital information for Bragg's army. Once, when Sam was in Yankee-occupied Nashville, he was seated in the dining room of the St. Cloud Hotel at the same table as General Rosecrans, listening with the ears of a Confederate to the plans of an unsuspecting Yankee general. Many times Sam and his compatriots in Coleman's Scouts boldly wore their proud Confederate gray trousers and their butternut jackets, making their presence behind the lines all the more dangerous. At home, many a prayer rose from the hearts of two anxious parents.

Details of Yankee movements had contributed to the Confederate victory at Chickamauga in September, 1863, and the Yankees were on an all-out alert to round up these men of Coleman's Scouts. Things were getting tense for the Scouts, and yet they were detailed to find out more information as to the plan of action of General Grant's army in Middle Tennessee. Their role was extremely vital to General Bragg.

In November, Sam secretly approached his own home to visit the family. Rutherford County was now deep in Yankee-held territory. He came by night and tapped at the dining room window. His mother let him in and gave him an old Federal overcoat which she had dyed with the only dye available at that time — the hulls of the butternut. This is the coat Sam would be wearing when captured. Worn over gray trousers, it was part of an outfit widely recognized as sort of a homespun Confederate uniform. The general who would soon condemn Sam to death would also claim that he was not in Confederate uniform when captured — that he was, therefore, a spy.

After visiting with his parents and begging a peek at the sleeping children, Sam stole away from his home and family for the last time. Never more would he see his old father's concerned face; nor would he hear his mother's sweet voice as she tenderly guided him through life's trials. He would never see his brothers and sisters again this side of eternity, and even though he did not know this, the dangers he faced may have let it prey upon his mind that night. His father had repaired some boots for him — the boots that would be on his feet as his coffin made its slow, winding way toward home in only a few short weeks.

Sam set out from Smyrna and went northwest to Nashville, a distance of about 18 or 20 miles. He then traveled due south by way of the Franklin pike, and at some point made a rendezvous with Coleman and some of the Scouts. It was here agreed that each man should leave for north Alabama — separately — on Friday night, November 19. Upon reaching north Alabama, they should journey east across that state, perhaps meeting up with each other by chance, finally coming safely within Confederate lines at Chattanooga, Tennessee, where they would give their scouting observations to General Bragg. It was also at this meeting that Coleman (Captain Shaw) gave Sam Davis the papers for General Bragg which were to cost young Davis his life within little more than a week.

Since leaving home, Davis had traveled about 100 miles on horseback, all within enemy lines. Upon reaching Giles County in southern Tennessee, he was captured on November 20 by nervous Yankees at Minor Hill, only seven miles north of the Alabama state line. His Confederate uniform of butternut and gray marked him as a Confederate soldier, entitling him to be confined and treated as a prisoner-of-war, not a spy. He was taken at once to Pulaski, eleven miles north of the point of capture. A large part of the Federal army was located in the area, and this picturesque little county-seat town had been taken over by the Yankees for their headquarters. Davis was jailed and put under the direct charge of General Dodge, the commanding general whose hands would soon be forever stained with the death of a defenseless youth in the prime of manhood, a brave boy whose only offense lay in trying to protect his family and his native soil from the invader.

Sam Davis had one week to live. No one will ever know exactly what papers were found upon Davis, in his haversack, in his saddlebags, or inside the heel of his boots. So many stories have been told by his captors down through the years that nothing but confusion remains; but, perhaps this was the plan, for no details were entered in the Yankee provost marhsal's books when Sam was imprisoned at Pulaski. The whole event was handled so shamefully that it is no surprise pertinent facts were forever buried. Even the northern soldiers were forbidden to discuss it openly.

Davis had been behind enemy lines for ten days, and much of his information had, obviously, been obtained by himself. Together with whatever papers E. Coleman had given him, the evidence was enough to convince the general that Davis knew the true identity of the elusive E. Coleman. Seizing upon the opportunity afforded by the youthfulness of his captive, the general quickly accused Davis of being a spy, threatening him with a Federal court-martial and death by hanging if he didn't tell who gave him the papers. The general was laboring under the delusion that E. Coleman must be, in reality, *someone on his own staff* or very near it, due to the accuracy of the papers, and he was willing to sacrifice a boy's life in order to find that man. In later years, the Yankee general quoted Davis as saying, "I know that I will have to die, but I will not tell where I got the information, and there is no power on earth that can make me tell. You are doing your duty as a soldier, and I am doing mine. If I have to die, I will do so feeling that I am doing my duty to God and my country."[48]

The general held a hasty court-martial in which all of the soldiers in the arresting party testified that Davis was, indeed, dressed as a Confederate soldier — conclusive evidence that he was not a spy. But, in those days of wild emotions and war mania, Union armies were not held so accountable as they are today, and being deep in southern territory helped them to hide some of their black deeds. The general needed a death conviction to hold over young Sam's head, and the military commission gave it to him. The commission sentenced Sam Davis to be hung as a spy, and the date for hanging was to be Friday, November 27, 1863. Thus armed, the general attempted to break Davis down, in hopes of finding the true identity of E. Coleman. He assigned Levi Naron, Chief of Scouts for the Union army in Tennessee, to the task. To the very end, Naron repeatedly offered Davis his freedom in exchange for the information desired, but to no avail. Sam steadfastly informed him that he would never betray the trust placed in him and that if Tennessee could not be restored to the southern Confederacy, he would prefer to die anyway.

This young hero found himself in a tight position, indeed, for on or about November 20, three of the Scouts were rounded up and placed in the same jail as Davis. Joshua Brown and W.L. Moore were two of those placed in the jail, but the most ironic twist of all was that the third person arrested was none other than Captain Henry Shaw — alias E. Coleman! So the man General Dodge was looking for was right under his nose, and the Yankees didn't know it. Oh, how easy it would have been for Sam to point out Coleman and save his own neck! So easy! But, not for Sam Davis. Sam was raised a true southern boy by Christian parents, and no doubt he knew well the Scripture that he was soon to fulfill: "Greater love hath no man than this, that he lay down his life for his friends." Can we imagine the whispered conversations between those three Scouts at night in the jail cells? How breathlessly they must have watched Davis respond to the continual offers of release if only he would name his informants!

Many of the Yankee soldiers, noting Davis's firm resolve, came to have admiration for him. They often visited him in his cell, begging him to save himself from such a useless death. Sam replied that life was, indeed, so sweet and that he did so much want to live, but that he could not betray a friend and would rather die a thousand deaths. Citizens of Giles County visited him, and upon one occasion Sam remarked, "I do not fear for death, but it makes me mad to think I am to die as a spy."[49]

Chaplain James Young, of the 81st Ohio Infantry, was so touched by the plight of this boy — who was some mother's son — that he spent the final day and night with Sam, going even to the gallows with him. He prayed with him to the end. At Sam's request, on the night before the execution, the chaplain sang with him *On Jordan's Stormy Banks I Stand*. He was there when Sam spoke his last words to Levi Naron, who had made a last-minute offer of freedom if only Sam would betray his friend, E. Coleman. Sam sat down on the lid of his coffin and listened to Naron's last offer. Then, looking him steadily in the eye, he replied, "Do you suppose were I your friend that I would betray you? Sir, if you think I am that kind of man, you have missed your mark. You may hang me a thousand times and I would not betray my friends."[50]

What will always remain the mystery in this whole affair is why the commanding general, who was in absolute command, did not, after seeing young Davis's steadfast adherence to his principles, call off the bluff and admit a small failure of strategy, thereby saving the life of a boy who had already won the hearts of many a Union man in that outfit. But, it wasn't to be. Approximately two minutes after Davis refused Naron's last offer, it then being twenty minutes after ten in the morning, the noose was tightened, and Sam Davis was launched into eternity. A soldier named John Randal — one of those who had helped capture Sam — said that never in all his life had he witnessed such a pathetic and heroic scene; that he sat on his horse with tears streaming down his face; that he saw many other Federal soldiers in tears.

L.W. Forgrave, a soldier in the Union army at Pulaski, later recalled the tragic event.

I was a musician at the headquarters of General G.M. Dodge at Pulaski, Tennessee, and helped to play the dead march at the murder of Sam Davis. With four years of service in the Union army . . . I never witnessed such bravery as was portrayed by him at the time of his killing. This boy Davis was offered a reprieve by a chief of scouts named Chickasaw (Naron), at headquarters, if he would tell where his captain was. As I could hear, he told them he would die a thousand deaths first. . .

I can never obliterate the expression of Davis' face, as he was a boy about my own age. He wore at that time a roundabout or pea jacket and a black slouch hat. I have wondered who his folks were very often, and was glad to know that he was not forgotten. Davis is in Heaven, I trust.[51]

After the execution, fellow-prisoners Moore, Brown, and

Shaw were sent north to a Yankee prison, but Shaw jumped from the train in Kentucky and resumed his activities as E. Coleman. Sam Davis's death had saved all three of them.

Before he died, Sam gave the coat that his mother had dyed for him to his new friend, Chaplain Young. The chaplain kept it until he was seventy-three years old; whereupon, he sent it to the editor of the *Confederate Veteran*. On the day before his execution, Sam wrote a heartrending letter to his parents.

Pulaski, Giles County, Tenn.
Nov. 26, 1863

Dear Mother; O how painful it is to write you! I have got to die tomorrow — to be hanged by the Federals. Mother, do not grieve for me. I must bid you good-bye for evermore. Mother, I do not fear to die. Give my love to all.
Your dear son.

Mother: Tell the children all to be good. I wish I could see all of you once more, but I never will any more.

Mother and Father: Do not forget me. Think of me when I am dead, but do not grieve for me; it will not do any good.

Father: you can send after my remains if you want to do so. They will be at Pulaski, Tennessee. I will leave some things, too, with the hotel keeper for you. Pulaski is in Giles County, Tennessee, south of Columbia.[52]

This letter and the things of which Sam wrote were committed to Chaplain Young for delivery to his mother and father.

Pulaski is about seventy-five miles south of Smyrna, but

shortly after the execution, agitation over this heinous crime was so great that word quickly reached Sam's parents about a scout named Davis who had been caught and hanged at Pulaski on November 27. Fearing the very worst, they set about to determine if it was their own Sam. They asked a most trusted and able friend, Mr. John C. Kennedy, to go to Pulaski where he might obtain all of the details possible and, if it were Sam, to bring home the earthly remains of their brave boy. Many years later, Mr. Kennedy recalled that fateful trip.

Mr. and Mrs. Davis were not certain that it was their son who had been executed at Pulaski. They had made diligent efforts through various channels to trace the "grapevine" story that it was their Sam, but were not assured. At last the time was set to start on the search. Mrs. Davis gave me a piece of the plain linsey of that used for his jacket lining, and also described his boots, and told of other things that only a good and loving mother could have thought about. She was interrupted occasionally by suggestions from Mr. Davis.

The start was made with two mules hitched to a very heavy carryall. We had a meal sack containing a boiled ham and about a half bushel of corn pones, on which their son Oscar, a small boy who was to accompany me, and I were to live while gone.

We reached Nashville that evening too late to get a pass, but I procured a metallic case and box and had them put in the conveyance. The next morning I went to General Rousseau, who declined to give me a pass and sent me to General Grant's Adjutant General, who kindly and politely, but positively, refused also, replying to all my pleadings for his mother's sake: "No Sir! No Sir! No Sir!"

I then returned to general Rousseau, whom I had

known in Kentucky in my boyhood days, and again asked for a pass, after some boyhood reminiscences not necessary to repeat, he supplied one for myself, the boy, and team to Columbia, which was as far as his lines extended, telling me that was all he could do. I gladly accepted the pass, which was written on a piece of paper elegantly printed and looked like a large bank note.

We entered the lines at Columbia and drove straight through town, not stopping until we reached the picket on the other side, who after looking over our pass, though he could not read it, and seeing the coffin and small boy, permitted us to go on. The same thing occurred when we reached the picket at Pulaski, who permitted us to enter the town.When near the square, I left Oscar to hold to the mules while I went to the Provost Marshal to get a pass or find out what he would do with us. His office was in the Court House. He asked how I got into Pulaski, and I handed him General Rousseau's pass. He looked up and curtly remarked, "This is no account here. What do you want?" I told him I had come for the body of Sam Davis who had been hanged; that his parents wanted it at home.

His manner at once changed and, extending his hand, he said. "Tell them for me that he died the bravest of the brave, an honor to them, and with the respect of every man in this command." He then asked what more he could do to help me. I requested return passes and a permit to take up the body, which he cheerfully gave. I also asked if he thought I would have any trouble or interference while I was at the graveyard, and he replied, "No sir. If you do, I will give you a company . . . yes, a regiment, if necessary."

Taking advantage of his cordial words, I asked

him how Sam was captured, as Mr. Davis had requested me to spare no pains to find out how and when he was taken. He said he did not know any of the particulars, but showed me two books in which records were kept in his office, and the only entry, after giving his name and description was, as I remember: "Captured on the Lamb's Ferry road by Capt. McKenzie's scouts."

Before leaving home I was referred for assistance, if necessary, while in Pulaski, to a Mr. Richardson, who had been (if not then) the County Court Clerk. We found him willing and ready to aid all in his power. The grave digger agreed to take the body up for $20.00. The next morning, together with his assistants, Mr. Richardson, Oscar and I were busy at the grave when four or five Federal soldiers came up. One of them advanced to me, raising his cap politely and in a subdued tone of voice, proffered for himself and comrades to assist, if desired. I thanked him sincerely, for I had not known what their presence might mean, but declined their services. When the box was raised and lid removed, the cap of white was still over his head down to his neck, tied with long strings, which were wrapped around his neck two or three times. His boots were on, but the legs cut off at the ankles. I took from my pocket the piece of his jacket lining and saw that they were alike. When I removed the cap, I found the face was black, but recognizable. We then transferred the body to the metallic case. During all the time the body was being examined and transferred, the Federal soldiers stood in line with caps off, paying tribute in acts if not words. Upon our return from the cemetery, the Provost Marshal said the Chaplain, who was with Sam at the gallows, had some keepsakes for the father and mother. He gave me a little book, in which was a farewell message to his mother, and the buttons from his coat and vest. . . .

. . . We reached Nashville and drove to where the Adams' Express Company's office now is, which was then where our present townsman, Mr. Cornelius, had his undertaking establishment, and turned the body over to him with specific instructions about the shrouding. Mr. Davis had said to me, "If you think it is best that Jane and I should not see him, do as you think best about the matter."

On the evening of the seventh day after leaving home, we drove in the big gate, some distance from the house. Mr. & Mrs. Davis were watching, and when they saw the casket, Mrs. Davis threw her arms above her head and fell. All was sorrow in that home. I had a boy catch my horse to go home to see my old mother and father, and change clothing, etc., but Mr. Davis prevailed upon me to stay and send for what I needed.

The next morning, while standing out in the yard, Mr. Davis came to me, hesitated, then catching his breath almost between each word, said, "John, don't you think it's hard a father can't see the face of his own child?"

I replied that I thought it best he and Mrs. Davis should remember him as they saw him last. He turned and left me. I drove the carryall that afternoon, with the body, across the creek to the old family graveyard where he was buried.[53]

Memorials of every kind, and in great profusion, were generated by the death of the young hero in Tennessee who would be known forevermore as *Sam Davis, Hero of the Confederacy*. The monuments command the most attention, with the most handsome and impressive one being the granite and marble statue south of the courthouse in Pulaski, Tennessee. In 1950, the state of Tennessee dedicated another shrine to the memory of Davis in the form of a stone building which stands upon the exact spot where once stood the hated gallows. Further south, at Minor Hill, is an inscribed rock where Davis was taken prisoner, and throughout Middle Tennessee bronze markers abound. The Tennessee Division of the United Daughters of the Confederacy raised money for a stained-glass memorial window, which was installed in the Confederate Museum in Richmond in 1912.

Perhaps the most significant monument, though, is a bronze statue standing on the capitol grounds in Nashville.The state legislature passed an act giving the choicest spot for the statue, having allowed only two monuments to that time on the capitol grounds, both of them honoring presidents — Andrew Jackson and James K. Polk. Money for the statue came from every state in the land, and world-renowned sculptor George Julian Zolney was selected to do the likeness. No photographs of Sam were available to the sculptor. The family pictures had been hidden in a hay stack while the Yankees were around, because it was feared that the house would be burned. Ironically, the Yankees set fire to the hay instead. Zolney worked from descriptions and used Sam's younger brother as the model, completing the statue in time for the dedication in 1909.

The Sam Davis Monument Committee presented the statue, and Governor Patterson made the acceptance speech. Having been present, as a school boy, at the dedication of the equestrian statue of Andrew Jackson, he proclaimed, "Little did I think then, even in the day dreams of youth, that one day as Governor I would be called upon to accept in the name of the State another figure in bronze erected on this side of the grounds, not of a man on horseback, but of a young man scarcely more than a boy, who belonged to another and later age of our history, who stands without the marks and accoutrements of rank, without any other sign save that of a soldier ready to fight and ready to die. The name and fame of Andrew Jackson filled the mind with wonder and admiration; the memory of Sam Davis, with infinite love and tenderness."[54] Engraved upon the base of the monument are these words:

"The boys will have to fight the battles without me."

He gave all he had — life;
He gained all he lacked — immortality.

In addition to these lines and other sentences which briefly recall the vital incidents of his short life, there are a few of the inspired lines from the well-known poem of Ella Wheeler Wilcox. The entire poem is so gripping that it would be a mistake not to include it here.

Sam Davis

When the Lord calls up earth's heroes
    To stand before his face,
O, many a name unknown to fame
    Shall ring from that high place!
And out of a grave in the Southland,
    At the just God's call and beck,
Shall one man rise with fearless eyes,
    And a rope about his neck.

The great world lay before him,
    For he was in his youth;
With love of life young hearts are rife,
    But better he loved truth.
He fought for his convictions;
    And when he stood at bay,
He would not flinch or stir one inch,
    From honor's narrow way.

They offered life and freedom
　　If he would speak the word;
In silent pride he gazed aside
　　As one who had not heard.
They argued, pleaded, threatened —
　　It was but wasted breath.
"Let come what must, I keep my trust,"
　　He said, and laughed at death.

He would not sell his manhood
　　To purchase priceless hope;
Where kings drag down a name and crown,
　　He dignified a rope.
Ah, grave! where was your triumph?
　　Ah, death! where was your sting?
He showed you how a man could bow
　　To doom and stay a king.

And God, who loves the loyal
　　Because they are like him,
I doubt not yet that soul shall set
　　Among his cherubim.
O Southland! bring your laurels;
　　And add your wreath, O North!
Let glory claim the hero's name,
　　And tell the world his worth.[55]

Is it any wonder that, when the first Confederate Medal of Honor was bestowed, it went to Sam Davis? Is it, likewise, any wonder that he has always been referred to as the *Hero of the Confederacy*? He gave glory to the Lost Cause and graced his homeland with the ultimate honor — the sacrifice of his own life for the sake of another.

(AUTHOR'S NOTE: The Confederate Medal of Honor was authorized near the end of the War, but the exigencies of day-to-day operations during the last days prohibited the bestowing of the honor upon the South's heroes, though there would have been a multiplicity of candidates of the highest degree. The task eventually fell, quite naturally, upon the Sons of Confederate Veterans, an organization of male descendants who perpetuate the ideals of our Confederate antecedents. One hundred and eleven years after the War Between the States, the first Medal of Honor was finally awarded, and it was my personal privilege to have been a delegate from Oklahoma to that historic convention held in August of 1976 at Memphis, Tennessee. The Sons of Confederate Veterans had before them the name of their first nominee — Sam Davis. It was with great pride that we unanimously bestowed that posthumous award, the Confederacy's highest honor, upon Davis, and it is with ever-increasing humility that I gaze upon that medal each time I visit the Sam Davis Home at Smyrna.)

"There stands Jackson like a stone wall. Rally on the Virginians!"

—GENERAL BARNARD BEE, CSA

VIII

SOUTHERN LORE

Breathes there a southerner without a story to tell? One of the oldest pastimes in the world is the art of storytelling, and yet it has survived every modern invention that vies for our leisure time. Southerners love to hear a good story, but more than that — they love to tell one. Haven't you noticed? When we get together, that's what we do. We begin to tell each other stories. We're good listeners while the other person is telling his story, but in the back of our minds we're racing through our catalogue of good stories, selecting one that ties in with the present line of conversation, and silently rehearsing it while the other half of our brain enjoys the tale being told — and, surprisingly, comprehends what it hears!

What a marvelous thing the brain! For that's where our folklore is stored. Like other cultures of the world, our history is written and stored in archives, but unlike so many, ours is told, and told, and told. Most of our legend and lore will never be written; it simply passes from generation to generation by word of mouth. Everyone wants to tell his story — or stories.

When great-great-grandfather came home from the War, he told about it. It was the same war that historians wrote about, but he wanted to tell it his way. Every succeeding generation passes the story down, each teller rephrasing it in his own style. Thus, the great southern tradition of storytelling is perpetuated, and along with it, our history. I've often wondered why southerners love to listen to stories about the past. Is it because our history is so interesting, or is it because we tell it so well?

The following selections are representative of the vast amount of material that lends itself to a good story. Fortunately, many good stories have found their way onto paper in the form of letters, diaries, and interviews; and, this source was tapped for some of the tales presented here. Others merely came by word of mouth, in the best of tradition, and are finding their way into print for the first time with the publication of this volume. True to the nature of my southern upbringing, I have been both an avid listener and storyteller, and, if my listening took precedence, then it gives me pleasure to balance it by relating some of the following tales that southerners like to tell.

THE BELL WITCH

There are very few people in Middle Tennessee who don't know about the Bell Witch. It's the favorite ghost story in those parts. My connection with the tale came by way of a visit to the home of some friends in Nashville on a hot night in late July, 1987. The thermometer had been hitting 100 degrees for several days, when I dropped in on Charles and Ginger Turner and found everyone huddled under the air conditioner for relief from the heat. A neighbor was there — a young lady by the name of Karen Guy. While introducing us, the Turners mentioned that Karen was the great-great-great-great-great-granddaughter of Andrew Jackson, and it wasn't long before the conversation centered upon stories about the seventh President of the United States. Before the evening was over, Karen gave me an invitation to come out to the old home place at my earliest convenience.

Driving down the old narrow lane with its overhanging trees, back into the woods and occasionally through a pasture, was a relief from the harrowing, everlasting zip of the feverish Nashville traffic. I had been busy, and it was 'way down in the fall now, but I hadn't forgotten about the invitation. Not for a minute. Karen was going to tell me about the Bell Witch, and I had pen and paper in hand when I got out of my pickup in the driveway of a two-story Victorian house surrounded by large English boxwoods and plenty of shade trees. The house belonged to her aunt, Louise Maxwell, a charming elderly lady who graciously seated us in the parlor which was furnished in Victorian heirlooms. The house itself was a piece of history, for it sits upon the old foundation of Jackson's first home, *Hunter's Hill*, which predates the *Hermitage*. In one of his gambling episodes, Jackson lost *Hunter's Hill* and hundreds of acres that surrounded it. The house burned in 1903, and the house in which we were sitting arose upon its foundation.

Before the storytelling began, Karen's sister Judy arrived, and the story of the Bell Witch began to unfold, a story made more intriguing by the fact that Andrew Jackson was involved in an incident with the Witch, plus the revelation, made in that parlor, that Judy is suspicious as to the Witch's possible visitation upon her generation of Jackson's descendants, due to some strange and unexplained happenings.

The Bell Witch is what most of us would call a ghost because, unlike a witch, it was not seen — only heard. But, the slaves of the Bell family called it a witch, and soon it became known far and wide as the Bell Witch. Betsy Bell saw the Witch in the form of a woman strolling about the orchard, and upon a few occasions, her brother and father saw the same apparition, but, except for these instances, the Witch was heard only.

The Bell family was one of the most respected families in Robertson County, Tennessee, having moved to that area in the first decade of the nineteenth century. John Bell bought a thousand acres near what is the present community of Adams, Tennessee, just four miles from the Kentucky line. He and his wife, Lucy, had six children and enjoyed a reputation as one of the most devoutly religious families in the community. Mr. Bell was so kind and honest in his dealings with his friends and business associates that it was all the more puzzling that he should be singled out by the Witch for such suffering as she put him through.

The trouble began about 1817. John Bell saw a strange animal sitting between two corn rows one day. Not being able to identify it, he shot at it, only to see it disappear into thin air. Soon, the children began to see strange creatures in the woods, and before long, the woman appeared in the orchard. Sometime later, there came scratching, knocking sounds at the windows and doors of the house, as if someone was trying to get in; but, upon opening the doors, the Bell family could find no one near their house. Then came the terrifying realization that the thing was in the house. There were sounds of wings flapping against the ceiling and louder sounds as of dogs fighting inside the house. Eventually, the house shook as if in a storm, and the family was not only frightened out of their wits but afraid that someone in the community would find out about the strange things and begin to talk.

The loud noises continued for about a year. Then, John Bell came down with a mysterious illness which affected his tongue and jaw, making chewing and swallowing difficult. The continued annoyance affected his nerves, causing the family to seek advice from friends, advice which necessitated divulging the secret in the Bell home. Whether or not this affliction was caused by the spirit in the house was never known, but the family attributed it to the Witch just the same. What is known is that the Witch soon began to talk and threaten the life of John Bell.

At first, friends came one at a time to witness the bizarre events in the house, but as news of the occurrences spread, people came in great numbers. Those who spent the night with the Bells had the sheets yanked from their bed throughout the night while being subjected to loud, derisive laughter. Frank Miles, a close friend of the family, volunteered to try to get hold of the Witch and crush it in his powerful grip. A large, stout person, and sure of his ability to defeat the Witch, he frequently spent the night with the Bells, awaiting the opportunity to soundly thrash the annoying thing, whatever it was. The bedtick was snatched from under him, his covers were pulled off the bed all night, and finally, the Witch struck him about the head with the most forceful blows he had ever sustained. The spirit then screamed out that he would do well to end his pursuit of her because he could not win a struggle with a spirit.

The Bell Witch began to bother several other people in the community, and there are dozens of tales among the people of that area concerning the Witch and its pranks. It would be easier to dismiss the tales as nonsense or mass hysteria or whatever one might wish to call it if the characters in the story were not of the highest reputation and standing in the community. There were ministers of the gospel and doctors who witnessed the strange goings-on in the Bell home. Yet, none of them could give an explanation as to the cause. In 1849, the *Saturday Evening Post* published a comprehensive sketch of the Bell Witch, and in 1923, *McClure's Magazine* devoted much columnar space to the tale.

The character of the Witch was as mysterious as was her presence. She quoted scripture, preached to various members of the Bell family, and sang hymns; yet, she disliked them very much and inflicted them with much pain. She was very selective, reserving most of her evil for John Bell and his daughter, Betsy. She despised the slaves, and upon several occasions, took great pleasure in whipping them with sticks and rods. Mr. Bell had good slaves who gave no trouble and needed no such discipline. The family had become quite attached to their slaves, yet the Witch had so intimidated them that they were afraid to leave their cabins at night. Her olfactories were so offended by them that she refused to go into their cabins to bother them. One night Mrs. Bell had one of the young girls sleep under her own bed in the house as a method of keeping the Witch out of the room, but the Witch, not to be outfoxed, yelled out that she knew one of the slaves was under the bed. The next thing they heard was a loud, continuous spitting sound. Then the girl was rolled out from under the bed like a log, her head covered in spit. Screaming that the Witch was going to spit her to death, she fled from the house back to her cabin.

The only one that the Witch liked was Mrs. Bell, whom she called "Old Luce." She sang sweet songs to her and comforted her with kind words. When Lucy was ill, the Witch prepared the table for the family meals and dropped big bunches of fruit into their laps. The fruit incident happened when visitors were there as well, further confounding everyone's thoughts.

As the Witch talked more and more freely, she told them that she would stay for four years, go away for seven, then return for a little while. Before the four years were up, experts from Europe visited the Bell home, trying to discover the truth about the entire affair. Each time, they went home baffled.

At one point in this sordid affair, Andrew Jackson, who lived about thirty-five miles from the Bells, decided to try his hand at taming the monster. He started out with several horsemen and a covered wagon laden with tents, supplies, and provisions for about a week. On the road, near the Bell house, one of his burly companions began to speak slightingly about the Witch. At once, the wheels of the heavy wagon locked and wouldn't budge. The driver, in spite of all of his whipping and exhortation, couldn't budge the wagon. The team seemed powerless to move the wheels. Shortly, a sharp voice rang out, "Go on, old General." The wheels moved freely, and Jackson's party went on.

That night, Andrew Jackson's party slept not a wink. Betsy screamed all night from the slapping and pinching she received from the Witch, and Jackson's covers were ripped from his bed as quickly as he could put them back on. The Witch pulled his hair, and slapped the other members of his party around until morning; whereupon, the whole expedition was declared a disaster, and Jackson went home.

Young Betsy Bell was in love with one of the finest boys in the country, and it pleased both families when the engagement was told and a distant wedding date was announced. But, the Witch had other plans. She told Betsy not to marry Joshua Gardner and began to abuse her frequently by pinching her and slapping her face until it was ready to bleed. At night, she pulled Betsy's hair and twisted it into knots so close to the scalp that it took her mother hours to comb it all out. When Betsy and Joshua persisted with their wedding plans, the Witch would yell at them while they were strolling with friends or having parties. Between the embarrassment and the persecution, Betsy was beside herself with apprehension, finally agreeing to call off the engagement. Though asked by Betsy and other family members why the marriage shouldn't occur, the Witch would only say that there were some very good reasons which she didn't intend to divulge.

Near the end of the first four-year visit, the Witch began to bother John Bell with terrible physical pain. His face was contorted, and his body was wrenched in agony. At times, he would get better, but the Witch announced that in time she was going to kill him. Near the end, he tried to walk about his yard, but she would knock his shoes off his feet and throw him to the ground. His son, who wrote about the incident years later, tried to tie his shoes back upon his feet as tight as possible, but the Witch would send them flying through the air over and over. Then, in a fit of rage, she beat him terribly about the head and shoulders, sending him to bed and in need of a physician. The doctor prescribed some potion and left. John began to get violently ill, and in a few days was at the point of death. The doctor called for the medicine bottle that he had left with John Bell. In its place, there was a bottle of odious liquid which defied analysis. The Witch was heard to laugh loudly and to say that she had placed it there. She said old John Bell would soon be dead, and the sooner the better. On December 20, 1820, he was dead.

In 1821, the Bell Witch left, just as it had promised. When it reappeared seven years later, only the two youngest Bell boys were still at home with their mother. The Witch came as it had at the first, with scratching sounds at the window. It stayed only a few weeks this time, bothering no one in the Bell family but telling of its intention to visit others in the neighborhood. The Bell family kept quiet about the second visit and never knew if the neighborhood visits were made or not. A final promise was made by the Bell Witch — a promise to return to the Middle Tennessee area in 107 years.

The year would have been 1935. Did the Witch return? Did it make a visitation upon another family in the area since the Bell homestead is long gone? If so, did the recipient of the unwanted sojourn tell about it or suffer in silence? If it did come back, how long did it stay — or, is it still with us?

Judy Guy isn't sure why the Bell Witch bothers some generations and absents itself from others, or if it is even the Witch at all that is causing some current pranks that seem to be more than coincidence. Several years ago, she and sister Karen were out in the barn when a Mason jar, of its own accord, slid from one end of a level shelf to the other with enough speed to send itself crashing into the wall. One of the girls went to the corner where stood a broom, but upon attempting to remove it from its place, found that it would not budge even though it wasn't attached to anything. What happened next? Karen said, "We hightailed it out of there!"

Recently, Judy was in New Mexico late one night on one of those straight highways in the desert. Her car was full of young children who were restless and tired, so she thought of telling them some ghost stories. Naturally, she told them about the Bell Witch, ending with the comment that there was probably not a real Bell Witch after all. No sooner had she expressed some doubt than her lights went out and the engine went dead. The car she was following came back and tried to start the engine with jumper cables, but to no avail. Nothing worked, and the suggestion was made to leave the car there until morning. The next day, armed with jumper cables, tools, and an extra battery, Judy and her friends went out to the car again. Just for luck, Judy put the key in the ignition and gave it a turn. The car cranked up immediately. No more trouble.

To compound the occurrences of strange events, the doorknobs in Judy's house began to fall off the doors. That wouldn't seem strange for a 107-year old house if it had ever happened before, but it hadn't. As soon as the uncle with whom Judy lives left for a winter in Texas, seven of the thirteen door knobs fell off in only three days.

Was it circumstance, or has the Bell Witch decided to visit itself upon the eighth generation of Jacksons, beginning with harmless but annoying pranks? Who's to say?

My grandmother, Eulalie McRae Burkes, lived to be ninety-one years old. Though I was in my twenties and already hopelessly addicted to resurrecting my family's past as far back as humanly possible, I still hadn't learned to ask the most important questions of my grandmother before she died — and she was my last living grandparent. Tales of danger and intrigue interested me more than the vital statistics of my grandmother's ancestors, and the one story we kids begged her to tell us time and time again was the one about the Indians shooting at the wagon train when my grandparents were moving from Texas to Oklahoma.

Now I knew my grandmother well, and I never suspected that she had ever written anything except letters, postcards, and grocery lists. I was aware that she was a genius at crossword puzzles, and I thought she knew more about the Bible than any living being. And then there was this long, nostalgic poem about Texas that we made her say over and over. But no one, including her seven children, were aware of the little diary she had kept during the move from Texas.

I discovered the diary in Texas while visiting my grandmother's first cousin, Winnie Whited, who still lives on some of the original McRae land near Telephone. This was about two years after my grandmother had passed away, and Winnie was trying to answer questions I should have asked my grandmother. She asked if I had seen a copy of the diary, and finding that none of us had so much as heard of such a diary, she went into her bedroom and brought out a handwritten version that her mother had copied from the original. Winnie said that my grandmother promised the kinfolks in Texas that she would keep a diary of the trip and send it back to them when she arrived at her destination. Evidently, my grandmother didn't even keep a copy of it for herself.

I was delighted to find my favorite story in the diary, though it lost part of its Hollywood glamour when the Indians turned out to be negroes. It just never seemed like an Old West saga again. Of course, Indian Territory never was the Old West in the tradition of New Mexico and Colorado.Muskogee was in the heart of the slaveholding Creek Nation, and after the War, negro slaves gained Creek land and other Indian benefits. Owing to the enormous negro population and my grandmother's alert mind at age twenty-two, I imagine that the passage of time dimmed her recollection, and negroes turned into Indians.

Approximately thirty people, all kinfolks, left Texas on October 27, 1902, in covered wagons and on horseback, driving their cattle before them. They were leaving the Elwood and Telephone communities just south of the Red River in northern Fannin County where the McRaes had lived since 1856. Once they crossed the Red River they would be in Indian Territory, pushing northward towards the brand new community of Broken Arrow, a distance of approximately 225 miles. It took them two weeks to make the journey.

Several years ago, while my Uncle Clyde was still living, I had the presence of mind to ask him why our side of the family got up and left Fannin County. He answered, "Grandpa McRae told me there was too many kinfolks marryin' kinfolks." (This practice was prevalent among the Scotch-Irish clans in the South and was still somewhat acceptable around the turn of the century, though not to Grandpa!)

MONDAY — Oct. 27, 1902. In camps two miles from the river; have just eat supper. Men are dressing squirrels; they killed fifteen this evening. The girls have been gathering pecans. We were about three hours crossing the river. Three cows fell in the river; they got them out. Wes got one by the ear and pulled her across. Uncle George has an Elm pole for a wagon tongue — he broke his wagon tongue out coming through the bottom. We have a big pot of beans on cooking for dinner tomorrow.

TUESDAY — Oct. 28. In camps one mile south

of Blue, twelve or fifteen miles from where we camped last night. The men killed sixteen squirrels this morning; we cooked them for supper tonight. Andrew lost his dog this morning. Edgar has gone back to look for her. If he gets her, Andrew is to pay him five dollars.

WEDNESDAY — Oct. 29. We are now at Caddo Creek, waiting for the rest of the wagons and cows. The sun is about two hours high. One of Uncle George's calves has give out, and he sold it this morning for one dollar. Edgar got back with our dog this morning about ten o'clock. He found her at Telephone. The boys have come with the cows. We will have to go — we want to get to Caddo tonight.

Wednesday night, in camps three miles north of Caddo. We have come about two miles since dark. Have come over some of the roughest road I ever saw. We have been coming downhill and over rocks ever since we left Caddo, and now we are camped down in a hollow. Three or four trains passed us this evening; the mules got scared and tried to run. We were all scared so bad we could hardly sit still.

THURSDAY NIGHT — Oct. 30. In camps eight miles north of Caney. Andrew killed three quails and one rabbit. We put them all in a pot and stewed them and made a big pot of dumplings. They were sure fine! We have had pasture for the cows every night until tonight — just left them out tonight. The grass is about knee high. We crossed a toll bridge at Caney — 25 cents a piece for wagons and buggies, and one cent a piece for the cows. We have been traveling by the railroad. Are camped about one hundred yards from the track now. Five trains have passed since we camped. There comes a train now — I must run or I won't get to see it!

FRIDAY NIGHT — Oct. 31. We are camped tonight

two miles from String Town and five miles from Atoka. Have not had much fun today — has been raining ever since before daylight. We have been traveling by mountains all day. The girls went up on one at noon. They said they were almost give out when they got to the top. They got some huckleberries while they were there; they were the first I ever saw. We crossed another toll bridge today at Boggy. We had cabbage for supper tonight.

SATURDAY NIGHT — Nov. 1. We are camped tonight between Chickie Chockie and Limestone Gap. Have been here all evening. Had to stop and let the cows rest. One of Papa's cows is sick and was almost give out. We women have been washing this evening. The men have been hunting — they killed some birds.

SUNDAY — Nov. 2. In camps three miles from Kiowa. We are camped about half a mile from a place where people have been digging coal. Pearl and Eva Hall went up there and looked in the hole where they have dug out coal and saw a dead horse. Mr. Hall said he read a piece in the paper where a man had been killed, and man, horse, and buggy was all throwed into a pit. We thought that might be the place; we women were scared. One of Papa's cows died today. We crossed another toll bridge today, but did not have to pay for anything but the wagons. It did not seem much like Sunday to us today.

MONDAY NIGHT — Nov. 3. We are camped tonight from McAlester. We are now half way; have been gone one week today. Has been raining all day. The men had to get dinner. We had salmons and hominy for supper; have got a big pot of turnips on cooking for dinner tomorrow.

TUESDAY — Nov. 4. We are camped tonight half mile from Crowder. It is still raining. This is the fifth day it has rained! The men had to get breakfast this morning; it was raining so hard we couldn't get out of the wagons. We have come over the roughest roads today yet. They get a little worse every day — more rocks and bigger ones, more hills and steeper ones. We crossed one branch today and had to double teams to get up the bank. We will get to the South Canadian tomorrow if we have no bad luck. When we get across the river we will be in Creek Nation.

WEDNESDAY — Nov. 5. We are camped tonight in the Creek Nation. We crossed the South Canadian about twelve today. We had to ford it. The river had just begun to rise when we got there. There was a man told us if it rose two inches we could not cross. We had to double teams. We got across all right. We were all scared nearly to death. After we crossed the river we had about two miles of deep sand to pull through. That was one place we didn't have any rocks! I believe the roads are a little worse. Nellie Wyatt has been having the toothache for two or three days; she had it pulled today at Canadian City. It is still raining. This is the sixth day it has been raining, and it looks like it might rain six more. I washed some tonight and had to dry one garment at a time by the fire.

THURSDAY NIGHT — Nov. 6. In camps 8 miles north of Eufaula. Have been here all evening. Stella and me have been washing. We all taken the things out of the wagons and dried them out. The men have been out hunting — killed some rabbits. We are still having some awful bad roads. We crossed the North Canadian this morning. We had to ford it, too. It was almost as bad as the South. The water was deeper, and there was quicksand on this side. We had to stop in the water and wait for Will to get out, and our wagon began to go down, and old Jude lay down in the water. I was scared so bad I could hardly keep from jumping out in the river. Will found out at dinner today that his coupling pole was broke and had to make a new one.

FRIDAY — Nov. 7. We have the nicest camping place we have ever had — plenty of wood and a good spring. We have come about 18 miles today. We camped about two miles from Checota. Today at dinner we had sausage and cucumbers for dinner. I washed the children tonight and combed their heads, and they don't look natural with clean faces and hair platted.

SATURDAY NIGHT — Nov. 8. In camps five miles from Muskogee. Still cloudy and rained some today. We were scared worse this evening than we ever was in our lives. We came through Muskogee about an hour by sun. It is a pretty town about the size of Bonham. We stayed there about an hour or two, and I never saw over two dozen white people. I saw some Indians and more negroes than I ever saw in my life. There was a show in town, and the negroes was so thick we could hardly get through. We had to drive about two hours after dark before we found a place to camp. After we left town there was about two hundred negroes passed us and about half of them drunk. There was a wagon load of negro men passed just before dark, and when they got even with us they began to yell and shoot their pistols. They shot over Aunt Mattie's buggy and over some of the wagons. Edna and Eva were behind in a buggy, and they were nearly scared to death. And so was I! And, after dark, another came from the other way; they shot three or four times. Some of the men said they were white men, but I don't think so. I think it was negroes — it was so dark we could not tell. I don't think there is any white people in this neighborhood. We saw several negro stores and a big fine hotel. The negroes dress fine up here and ride in their fine buggies, and the whites look about like the negroes do in Texas. I forgot to tell you about Will getting lost. He started this morning about daylight to look for his cow. The boys found him about 8 o'clock trying to drive his cow in the opposite direction from camps. When they found him he said he couldn't drive that cow.

SUNDAY NIGHT — Nov. 9. We are camped tonight in the bottom. We crossed the Arkansas River this evening. We got to the river about eleven o'clock, and it was half past two when we got across. We have seen about a dozen white people today. Two white men came out to our camps tonight and stayed a while.We were glad to see them. I tell you, we are glad to see anybody that looks white. Two or three negroes have passed tonight shooting pistols. One passed with a shotgun and shot just as he got in camps. There was two negro men running the ferry boat on the Arkansas River. They put about 50 negroes across while we were there.

MONDAY NIGHT — Nov. 10. We are camped tonight two miles from Coweta. This is a pretty place to camp, but there is no water here except a pool, and it is thick with mud. We haven't seen but a few negroes today.Have seen lots of white people and saw some Indians at Coweta. I like the country I have seen today very well. We had tomatoes and kraut for supper tonight. I guess you know about how we all eat by this time.

TUESDAY NIGHT — Nov. 11. We are at our journey's end, and they say "all is well that ends well." I think I will like this country fine. We are camped on Uncle George's place. Don't know how long we will stay here. Andrew and me will stay until Uncle

George builds us a house. Papa and Will haven't got them any place yet, but I don't think they will have any trouble getting a place. We met several men on the road that wanted to rent to us. Uncle George will get to move into his house tomorrow. There is a sight of cotton here to pick, and it is sure fine, too. We have been offered 80 cents. Everybody we have met since we left the river wanted us to stop and pick cotton. Some said they had a hundred acres that had never been touched.

THE RIOT AT SPRING HILL

There's a story they tell in southeastern Alabama about the incident at Spring Hill. If you're driving southeast on the Jefferson Davis Highway (State Highway 6) out of Montgomery, you'll come upon a historical marker just after you cross the Barbour County line near the intersection of County Road 49. It tells about the clash between the Reconstruction scalawags and the citizens of Barbour County, but of course there is much more to the story than the space on the roadside tablet will allow. My curiosity led me four miles north to the little settlement of Spring Hill where I learned the rest of the story.

Barbour County lies just across the Chattahoochee River from Georgia, with its county seat in Eufaula. The black population has always outnumbered the white by six to one, presenting the carpetbag government with a golden opportunity for establishing Republican rule in a Democratic county. By 1874, the white people had regained the right to vote but were vastly outnumbered by illiterate negroes who were instructed to vote Republican. In addition, the law allowed a man to vote anywhere in the county, a provision that lent itself well to the purposes of the corrupt government in Barbour County. All that was required for the carpetbaggers to win any election was enough transportation or bribery to get a large number of negroes to the desired polling place.

Such was the situation when the general elections of 1874 came around. The election was set for November 3, and two particular places were selected for the Republicans to carry — Spring Hill and Eufaula. Word was sent out to the negroes to gather in those places and vote Republican.

At that time, Spring Hill was a thriving village, and Republicans expected another significant victory. But, the citizens of Barbour County had borne indignities, humiliation, and bankruptcy for nearly ten years. An old lady who lives near Spring Hill looked straight into my eyes, as hers narrowed into grim determination, and, with a serious tone of voice that would almost have convinced you she had been one of the players in the actual drama, said, "We were determined to get rid of those Yankees one way or another!"

For several weeks the men of the community had been meeting and making plans. There were two vacant store buildings which sat side by side, one of them reserved for the polling place. The other vacant building soon became a storeroom for big boxes filled with pint bottles of whiskey. Each man had donated ten dollars for that purpose. Judge Elias M. Keils, a southern white man who had sold out to the carpetbag government, trading his principles for the judgeship, was superintendent of the election. Although he lived in Eufaula, nineteen miles to the southeast, he sensed the brewing storm in Spring Hill and requested General Swayne to send down a company of Yankee soldiers from Montgomery.

The soldiers arrived more than a week ahead of the election and, as usual in such cases, were met by the negroes in old wagons and buggies, ready to carry them to the church and schoolhouse where they were to be quartered. But this time there were others at the depot, waiting in the finest black carriages that could be obtained. These were the white men of the community, who, in their best semblance of hospitality, were accompanied by the ladies of the area. Laden with custards, cakes, and pies, these women of deliberate action greeted the surprised soldiers with smiling faces and well-filled baskets from their southern kitchens. The plan worked well. Ignoring their negro escorts, the Yankee soldiers opted for the transportation provided by the white people and were thus escorted to their quarters. In an effort to neutralize the soldiers, the courtesies (which even included hunting parties for the enjoyment of the soldiers) were kept up until election day.

On the day of the election, the place was a beehive of activity. People came from everywhere, some riding, some walking. Old Keils, the scalawag judge, was one of the first to arrive. Strutting around the polls, he had brought his sixteen year old son, Willie, as protection against violence to himself. Every white man was armed with a pistol or shotgun and a pint bottle from the vacant store on the corner. Spreading out over the town, each man would conspicuously take a drink (or pretend to) from his whiskey bottle, replace the cap, and drop the bottle in plain sight of the negroes. In an instant, the bottle was grabbed and consumed by an overjoyed negro who soon forgot that he was there to vote. They say that even old Dr. Barr, a strict Presbyterian whose deportment confirmed his F.F.V. ancestry, was in the thick of it, raising his arm and exclaiming, "Go it boys. Old Barr is with you."

Before long, most of the "voters" were too drunk to cast their votes, and the scalawag judge began to worry. Already, shots had been fired into the air, causing Judge Keils to summon the soldiers with the old ruse that the white men were killing all of the negroes. Remembering the recent hospitality of the white community and, perhaps, their marksmanship on the hunting trips, the young soldiers rebuffed Keils, sending word that if there weren't enough white men to kill all of the negroes, the soldiers themselves would be down to finish the job. Keils saw his desperate situation and began to beg Dr. Barr to get him out of Spring Hill. Dr. Barr told him that both of them would be killed if they undertook an escape; whereupon, Keils made promises to leave the country and never return, but to no avail.

Brawling and pistol shots punctuated the afternoon hours as the wily old judge became more and more unnerved. Then, night fell. The judge, his scalawag officials, and their guards barricaded themselves inside the old store building and lit the lamps. As they tried to count votes, they could hear threats shouted by the angry mobs milling around the streets. There were several men inside that building who would have given anything they owned that night in exchange for a safe ticket out of there. Several times the door was broken open in spite of the guards, and tension mounted inside and outside of the polling place.

Suddenly, a tremendous burst of gunfire erupted simultaneously with the sound of crashing doors and windows. The lights were shot out, men started screaming, and the building was full of people who shot wildly through the darkness. The main object of the gunfire was judge Keils, and the inside of the building was raining lead. When the gunfire died, a lamp was brought in to reveal Keils down on his knees before J.W. Comer, giving him the Masonic sign of distress. Comer had been shot in the leg by Walter White, who thought he was shooting Keils. A drunk lay under the counter yelling for help, that he had been shot all to pieces, when in reality, not a bullet had touched him. The scalawag Keils was unhurt, but the tragedy of the affair was soon apparent when the body of the innocent

Willie Keils was discovered in front of his wicked father, riddled with bullets. It was impossible to determine who had shot him, but it was believed by everyone involved that the judge had held his son up in front of him, thinking that no one would fire upon the boy. In the darkness, no one knew the boy was being used as a shield.

The dying boy was taken to the home of Grandma Drewry. The judge was also taken there under heavy guard as there were still some who wanted to kill him. In the early morning hours, the boy's mother reached Grandma Drewry's, wild with grief. She cried out to her husband, "I begged you not to bring my child here. You did it to shield yourself." Though there was no pity for Judge Keils when the boy died, there was genuine sympathy for Mrs. Keils, who was a Christian lady and member of one of the prominent families of Barbour County.

The citizens of the county had finally taken charge of their government. The ballot box had been buried in the woods, and not a scalawag dared to show his face in public. Judge Keils had amassed a fortune by embracing the carpetbag government. He had built one of the finest homes in Alabama from money he had taken illegally. But, in so doing, he had wrecked the life of his wife and lost the life of his son, and was eventually run out of the country. It was said that he went to Dakota Territory, then to Washington, D.C., where he could be at home among Republicans.

A Congressional inquisition was held, but the bloody riot at Spring Hill marked the end of Republican domination in Barbour County. One woman, joyous over the abrupt end of the carpetbag regime, exclaimed, "Thank God red blood is still flowing in the veins of our Alabama men!"

The carpetbaggers profited greatly from dissension in Barbour County — or any county, for that matter. If they could keep the black population hostile toward the whites, the radical Republicans were assured of the total black vote in every election. Fomenting unrest was the best way to perpetuate themselves in their corrupt regimes.

There had been other trouble before the riot at Spring Hill. Undoubtedly, the Republicans were drooling over the prospects of spontaneous disturbances that could only serve to augment those of their own careful planning. One such effort was concocted among the negroes, only to be foiled by another negro, a mulatto named Alex Hamilton.

There was a group of eight negroes, four of whom were brothers, who devised a scheme to burn the town of Eufaula. They approached Alex Hamilton, an intelligent negro who proved to be an honest and loyal individual, asking him to help with the proposed plot against the city. Alex had come to Eufaula from Lumpkin, Georgia, as a slave to the prominent and respected Crocker family. After being freed, he had remained in their service for quite some time, while he also sharpened his skills as a contractor and builder.

In sympathy with the white element, who had been good to him, Alex confided in local officials who suggested that he pretend to go along with the negroes and learn the details of the anticipated insurrection. For several weeks, the plotters (with Alex among them) gathered on the steps of the John McNab Bank to discuss their plans. A local citizen, Elliott Thomas, hid in the basement where he could hear what each man said, taking notes of the entire scheme. The plans called for breaking into a large wholesale and retail hardware store called Bray Brothers, which carried a large stock of firearms and ammunition. After arming a large mob of negroes, the ringleaders would set fire to the store. While the men of the community were fighting the fire, the negroes would be free to rob their homes and set them on fire. With the aid of Alex, Thomas was able to discover their signal for a rush upon the store.

On the fateful night, when they yelled their signal of "Keno," they were instantly surrounded by more than fifty men who had been secretly waiting. Armed with shotguns, rifles, and pistols, the citizens arrested every one of the negroes. They were tried, convicted, and sentenced to the penitentiary, where they all served terms.

Alex Hamilton, the loyal negro and hero of the town, was given a gold watch and chain by the citizens. In addition, the city of Eufaula gave him a choice lot for the building of a house. Alex built his house and lived there until some time in the 1880's, while he built some of the finest homes in Barbour County. He later moved to Atlanta where he built one of that city's largest and finest buildings.

A LETTER FROM THE FRONT

Letters from the front tell their own stories. War was a new experience. Life was uncomfortable; death was likely; times were difficult and lonely. And, the soldier wrote home about it. The average soldier in the trench had difficulty with spelling and punctuation, as well as penmanship. The following letter, containing no punctuation, is reproduced here just as the writer penned it, with his words spelled as they sounded to him.

The soldier, Irvin Raglin, was a member of Company H, 44th Regiment, Alabama Infantry.

Ala. Calhoon Coty August the (*date obscured*) 1862. in camps Near alexander Nine Miles from the head of the Rail Road

Dear Beloved Wife

it is again threw the Providence of god that I am Permited this Eavening to seat My Self for the Purpose of Writing you a few line to let you now that I am Not Well at this time My Bowells has Bin Rinnin off for the last month But I am able for Duty yet I am Better than I have Bin Some of the Time but Not Well hoping When these lines come to hand that they Will find you and the children Well and Doing Well I have Nothing of importance to write at this time Onley it is a gloomy looking time now it looks like that the yankees has got us in a narrow Place it look to me that We Was whipped tho I don't now. We have drawn two month Wages 41.40 and Will Draw two month More in a few Days and then if I Dont git to come home I Will Send you Some more Money I reckon I will git afurlow We are Drawing for furlows But if I git one it Will Be But for four Days But I Will come if it was But for two Day Nancy I Want you to Send to the hatter Shop if you can and Git Me a Wool hat for My old hat is Worn out in a Mane and thar is No chance for Me to git a hat for less than 20 dollars I will Send you the Measure of My head it is 22 inches a Round Be surta and git it if you can and send it to me the first Chance for fear I Dont git to come home if I New I wold not git to Coome up here to see Me But you had Better Wain a while I Reckon tho you can do as you Please about cooming if you take a Notion to come Write to me What Day you will come and I Will Meet you at the head of the Rail Road Which is Blue Mountain I wants to see you and the Children away Bad Direct your letters to Blue Mountain Calhoon Coty Ala tell Mathew to Write to me Write Son as you git this letter written

402

July 19 1862 from you and the children But I Want to see a nothen from you very Bad Write often as you can Write as Soon as you git this letters I am glad to hear that the children is Well Satisfied I must come to a close as it is giting Dark Write Soon and often Nancy I Want to see you and the children very Bad But it is uncertain Whether I Even Will or Not But We Must live in hope if We Dont Dispare

I Remain your affection husban till Death Ivin I Raglin to Nancy I Raglin fare well for this time[1]

THE YANKEES CAME A-CALLIN'!

How anyone could take food from a hungry child is beyond comprehension to most of us. *No comprendo*, as the Mexicans say. As far back as I can remember, my dad would always look around at what was offered on our table; then, if very little of a certain dish was waiting to be divided among us, he would say "Now, y'all eat that — I don't want any of it." He was probably hungrier than we were, but we never knew it.

During the War, Yankees were well-fed and provisioned from endless supply lines which stretched behind them to their northern sources; however, they were usually allowed to forage at will. They stole animals, eggs, milk, and any type of food they could find, from already starving families whose menfolk were away at war. It was sort of an outing for the boys in blue and gave them something to do between battles.

But I know of one southern lady who once outfoxed the Yankees and kept her children from starving. The story was told to me by Georgia Grissom Kennemer, my first cousin twice-removed, and is about her Grandmother Grissom (my great-great-grandmother). Georgia, a spry little lady who is now in her 87th year, said that her grandfather, Joseph Grissom, was away in the War, leaving Grandmother alone with five children to care for. The Yankees were steadily moving deeper into the South and were finally into north Alabama. The word got out one day that they were only a few miles away, and Grandmother knew she must act quickly.

Georgia says, "They had their meat already put up — salt cured, you know. Grandmother and the children took all the meat from the smokehouse and put it between the straw mattress and the feather bed to hide it. The straw mattress was just a bedtick stuffed with straw that they used as an under mattress, and they laid it on top of that. Then they put the feather bed on top of the meat and smoothed it out. The Yankees came and searched, but they didn't find it. It was all the meat they had for the winter, and Grandmother's quick thinking saved it."

My great-grandfather was one of those children. He was five years old when the War started and nine when it ended. Abraham Jackson Grissom was his name, but he was "Uncle Abe" to Georgia. In the 1880's he left Alabama after marrying a Mississippi belle, and moved to the Indian Territory by way of Texas, where he spent a few years. Georgia said he would visit her family while she was living in Hollis, Oklahoma, and, being inquisitive by nature, she would get him to talk about the old days while they sat under a big tree in the back yard.

"You know, he wouldn't stay in the house, so I got my

paper and pencil and followed him out to that big tree." According to Georgia, "Uncle Abe told me that he didn't want anything that was made with whole wheat — especially bread. He said that during the War and afterwards they didn't get good white flour; consequently, his mother would make their bread out of something similar to shorts and bran. She would spoon it out, and the only way they could eat it would be out of cupped hands."

The Mississippi belle was only fourteen when my great-grandfather married her in 1874; in fact, someone wrote across the edge of the page in the marriage book at the court house, "Her brother says she is old enough." (My great-grandfather, himself, was only seventeen years old.) Nancy Ann Ferguson was my great-grandmother's name, but they called her Nannie. She had been raised by a negro mammy on the plantation near Hernando. Her mother had died during the War when Nannie was only five years old. When she was thirteen, her father, Joseph Ferguson, died, leaving her orphaned during the troublesome days of Reconstruction.

The Fergusons lived in DeSoto County, Mississippi, several miles southeast of Hernando, and not too far from the Mississippi River. This is delta country, running south out of Memphis, Tennessee, and like Gen. Nathan Bedford Forrest, who was a planter in DeSoto County, the Fergusons raised lots of cotton. As is too often the case among southern families, ours might have been a wealthy lot had war not come to the inhabitants of the rich delta land, for it was here that cotton was king in the fullest sense of the word. Nowhere in the world did cotton grow better than in the South; and, nowhere in the South did it grow better than in the delta. Before the War, Mississippi had more millionaires, per capita, than any state in the Union.

Joseph had 500 bales of cotton ready for shipping when the Yankees came. Each bale was worth about $500, and it was hard, indeed, to watch the Yankees burn it. And, if it wasn't enough to burn a man out, they stole his horses, some of the finest in the county. Joseph had some expensive thoroughbreds which he had hidden down in a thicket, but the Yankees had become so adept at their "profession," very little escaped their attention. With little more than a trinket, they often bribed a weak slave who pointed them in the right direction. One of Joseph's servants thus obliged these invaders, and the horses were confiscated. With his fortune gone, my great-great-grandfather became one of thousands who lived the rest of their days in a broken, debt-ridden South, where once they had been blessed by all of the comforts that day and age could afford.

In 1975, I found the old homestead in DeSoto County, and to my delight, the house that Joseph had built in the 1840's was still there, due largely to the practice in the South of roofing buildings with that everlasting tin. The home was not grand, but a rather comfortable-looking, four-room house with a large breezeway, called a *dog-trot*, running through the center and connecting the front porch with the back. Though the tombstones had been destroyed, the graves of my great-great-grandparents remain under a large water oak west of the house, according to some of the old-timers in the area.

The land has long since been out of the family, and the old house is being used for a barn. As I stood in the dog-trot, I couldn't help but ponder the consequences of a reversal in the events of history. What if, instead of a northern invasion of our idyllic Old South, we southerners had been of a more aggressive breed than what we are and had launched an invasion of the north? Where among the magnates of Wall Street might be the names of Vanderbilt, Morgan, Rockefeller, and Ford?

Would these names, synonymous with wealth and riches, even be known to history? Indeed, where might Wall Street itself be? Itta Bena, Mississippi, perhaps?

Walter Tripp told me about the time the Yankees came to his grandmother's home in North Carolina while his grandfather, Johnathan Wylie Tripp, was away with the 44th North Carolina Infantry.

The threat of a visit by the Yankees hung constantly over southerners' heads. When they appeared at his grandmother's house, Mrs. Tripp and the youngsters were huddled in the yard, terrified at the very sight of these blue-clad devils whose reputation for monstrous deeds had long ago preceded them.

The Yankees must have been rather playful that day. They asked the children if they had ever seen snow. The children, trembling with fright, answered, "No." In the South, many a southerner had for a mattress what was called a feather bed, a canvas bedtick filled with heaps of chicken feathers. Into the house dashed the Yankees, emerging only minutes later, laughing like ghouls from the depths of Hades while dragging all of the feather beds out into the yard. There, before the little mother and her brood, they ripped open the ticking and scattered feathers everywhere. Then, as the last remnants of the family beds were drifting off on the wind, the Yankees gleefully announced to the horrified children, "There! Now you've seen snow!"

Sometimes even the most Christian among us have to wonder if all mankind truly sprang from the same Adam.

Alabama suffered heavy destruction during the War, not so much from battle as from the unnecessary and wilful wreckage by vindictive northern troops as they passed through the state time after time. Magnificent homes, schools, and business buildings were torched in pure mischief, and at Tuscaloosa, the beautiful Greek Revival structures of the University of Alabama went up in smoke at the hands of General Croxton.

To human life they assigned little more significance than the property they destroyed. Southerners were open to insult by virtue of little protection against the bands of vicious invaders. Unduly antagonized, they were struck down whenever bold enough to protest against their indignities.

In far northeast Alabama, near the Georgia state line, is the small community of Mentone, perched upon the northern stretch of the long ridge known as Lookout Mountain. The able-bodied men were off in the War, leaving the town virtually unprotected from the Yankee herds traversing the unfortunate state. There were a few older men who had formed an armed unit called the Home Guard, but, of course, they were no match for any well-equipped unit of U.S. regulars.

One day, the unwelcome northern soldiers were searching for food in the community, which was already hard-pressed to feed itself. One Yankee vulture was caught stealing peaches from a peach tree in the yard of Eldridge Jones, but he wouldn't write home about it. The Home Guard shot and killed him on the spot.

The following day, while Eldridge Jones was innocently repairing his front gate, a U.S. officer rode up and accosted him about the shooting. An argument ensued, with the officer accusing Jones of having threatened to kill the first Yankee that set foot upon the premises — as if Jones had no right to be outraged at the trolls who were devouring civilization in Alabama. The angry officer picked up a piece of lumber and struck Jones a blow which laid him up in bed.

That night, Union soldiers returned. They broke into the

house and dragged Jones from his bed and out into the darkness, while his frantic family screamed and pleaded with the Yankees. The next morning he was found dead about three miles from home, his body riddled by sixteen bullets.

Malcolm Alexander McRae, was born in South Carolina to Scottish parents, Hugh Bain McRae and Nancy McDuffey. Following the natural westward migration in America, he eventually settled permanently in Texas. It has been said that he walked into the general store in Elwood, Texas, a gun over his shoulder and $20,000 worth of gold in his knapsack. In 1880, he retired at the age of seventy, giving each of his children 100 acres of land. On April 2, 1896, he wrote to a Bonham, Texas, newspaper and told his own story. Eight months later he died at the age of eighty-six and was buried in the cemetery he had given to the community of Elwood.

Elwood, Fannin Co., Texas
April 2, 1896

Editor Journal:
It is said multiply and replenish the earth. I was born on the 15th day of May, 1810. I was at one dance at about 17 years of age — my first and last. I have never gambled in my life. I commenced farming in the year 1830 and quit when I was three score and ten. I am now living a retired life, except working my

garden.

I was married on the 22nd day of February, 1832. I have raised four sons and five daughters, all living to the age of maturity, and all learning to read and write. No free schools then. I have 44 grandchildren, 75 great grandchildren and one great-great-grandchild. In the time of raising my family I made three long moves, first from Georgia to Southern Missouri. I made one crop and after gathering it I started to Texas on the 18th day of November, 1843. I came on foot and was gone 70 days with my gun and knapsack. I was in Dallas during my first trip to Texas. There was but one house between Bonham and Dallas.

When I got back to Missouri, I rested two weeks, and found that I weighed 212 pounds. While I stayed in Newton County, Mo., I found 25 bee trees, killed 60 deer and 69 turkeys, made rails and fenced 40 acres of land and made two crops. On Nov. 12, 1844, I started back to Georgia, arriving at my old home on the 8th of January, 1845, having been gone three years and one month.

It is strange to say, the number of years I have been a farmer, and the long moves that I have made, I have never put gears and harness on a pair of horses or mules and hitched them to a wagon and drove them this fashion.

On the 4th of October, 1849, I started to Texas from Georgia in company with 97 persons, but on account of sickness was compelled to stop in Pike County, Arkansas. In 1851 I bought a farm on the main road leading from Little Rock, Ark., to Texas, after remaining until 1856 I resumed my trip to Texas and stopped in Fannin County, Tex., where I have made my home until the present.

In my travel since coming to Texas, I have visited

Ft. Smith, Ark., Ft. Towsend, near Red River in Choctaw
Nation, Ft. Graham on the Brazos River, within a few
miles of Ft. Arbuckle in Chickasaw Nation, Ft. Riley
in the north part of Kansas, Ft. McCullough, Ft.
Washita, Ft. McDonald in Kansas. I have crossed the
northwest plains in two places; one at the mouth of
the A. and R. Ry. tunnel at the timber line on the
Rocky Mountains in a snow storm. I was in St. Louis
on the 18th of December and found snow about six
inches deep. After returning home I traveled but little.
I will be glad to hear from anyone who can beat my
record.

M.A. McRae

THE HANGIN' AT ADA

There are few people around eastern Oklahoma who are
old enough to remember the days when hangings settled the
question of what to do with a murderer, but there are a lot
of people who grew up in the shadow of the most sensational
hanging — and maybe the last — in the southwest. This outright
lynching, which occurred in 1909, is the one the oldtimers like
to tell about.

Ada, Oklahoma, is a community quite representative of what

411

you might call the rural South. It is the county seat; it has a small state college; its permanent population numbers about 16,000. It is surrounded by very small towns scattered throughout Pontotoc County, and is situated eighty miles from the nearest metropolitan area. Ada is located in an area of Oklahoma comprising roughly the southeastern one-third of the state known quite proudly as "Little Dixie." After the War, this section of Indian Territory was settled nearly exclusively by people from the old Confederate states. In 1954, the local newspaper ran a survey of the 205 people who had lived in Ada since 1903, asking them to list the states from which they had emigrated. Various towns within Indian Territory were listed by the native-born residents, with others giving their home states as Tennessee, Texas, Arkansas, Alabama, Mississippi, and Missouri. One lone soul admitted that he was from Kansas!

Today, Ada's street names reflect those Old South roots — names like Forrest, Johnston, Stonewall, Texas, Mississippi, Arlington. A typically rural southern town, you'll see magnolias, oaks, dogwoods; and, in mid-May, the whole town is delightfully perfumed with the heavenly smell of honeysuckle. And, of course, every mother's boy in town can be found on a baseball diamond at least every summer night — all of them, that is, except those who are fishing in someone's farm pond out in the country. Ada is a nice town.

But it hasn't always been that way. You see, Indian Territory not only presented a good opportunity for ruined southerners to start over; it soon became a haven for criminals who could get away with literal murder, due to the laxity of the territorial law. The whole territory was becoming a refuge for people "running from the law." An elderly neighbor of mine once told me that when he was growing up around there, you never asked a man where he was from — he might have come here to get out of trouble.

By the turn of the century, Ada — now only seven years

old — had gained the reputation of being one of the roughest places in the southwest. If you disliked someone intensely and had a little money to invest in his discomfort, you could hire a killer with near impunity from the law.

When statehood arrived in 1907, things didn't get appreciably better. In 1908 alone, there were thirty-six murders in the Ada vicinity. Over in Pauls Valley, a criminal lawyer named Moman Pruiett was notorious for getting desperadoes off the hook. Of the 343 persons he defended against murder charges, he won 303 acquittals. Only one of his clients was ever sentenced to death, and even this one was saved by presidential clemency.

Ada was being ridiculed in state newspapers as a lawless, dangerous place to be — a reputation not wholly deserved by this young town of 5,000. There were fine Christian families, law-abiding citizens, and businessmen who were trying to establish some semblance of law and order in the community. But, even their own lawmen were ineffective when the state courts were so lax that men were permitted to murder for a price. Long-suffering Ada was getting fed up.

Ada's particular problem was rooted in an ongoing war between two factions. A.A. Bobbitt owned a large spread of cattle in Pontotoc County. He was always at odds with the owners of another large ranch — Joe Allen and Jesse West. Both sides had the largest bunch of gunfighters they could hire, and Ada was holding its breath, waiting to be the scene of an all-out war between them. The anticipated gunfight never did explode on the streets, and quite unexpectedly, A.A. Bobbitt began to court the law-abiding element in the town. He had a few things in his favor as he began to improve his image. He had been a U.S. marshal at one time; he was a Mason; and, he had a family which included a handsome, twenty-year old son who was the fancy of all the young ladies.

When Ada's society responded, hoping its acceptance of Bobbitt would defuse the situation, Joe Allen and Jesse West threw in the towel and moved their ranching and gunslinging operations to Canadian, Texas. One of Ada's most notorious gunmen went over to the side of the now somewhat respectable Bobbitt, and the community breathed a sigh of relief. Bobbitt had more foresight than the city fathers, though, and he fully expected more trouble from the recently departed Allen and West. Bobbitt was especially hated by West, who had always believed that he had had a lot to do with the killing of West's son; consequently, Bobbitt lost no time in drawing up a will, in which he left a $1,000 reward for the capture of the guilty party in the event that he was killed.

As if in fulfillment of a prophecy, the will soon had to be executed. It was an afternoon in February, 1909. Bobbitt was headed back out to his ranch southwest of Ada. When he got within a half-mile of the house, a shotgun blast ripped open his left side. With deadly accuracy, the killer quickly fired the second barrel of his gun, which rested in the fork of a tree, and soon Bobbitt was laid out dead at his own house. His hired hand, Bob Ferguson, was driving a second wagon just behind Bobbitt, and he got a good description of the fleeing killer.

When word of this violent, cowardly ambush reached Ada, the community saw red. Livid with anger and having no faith in its peace officers or the law, a large crowd met and resolved to take action. A reward fund was set up, and citizens left the meeting in search of the killer.

Soon — very soon — the killer's horse turned up at John Williamson's farm. Jailed at Ada, Williamson talked, and Ada learned the name of the killer. I don't think the community was prepared for what it uncovered. They were now on the lookout for one of the deadliest and most feared outlaws in the country — Jim Miller. He had killed over thirty men in Texas and New Mexico Territory and had arranged the killing of Pat Garrett, the famous peace officer who shot Billy the Kid.

But, Ada had a new weapon in its arsenal. It was a man named Robert Wimbish, who just happened to be the county attorney, Ada's first since statehood. And, he was just new

414

enough to dare to do right. Wimbish sought Jim Miller with a vengeance, and before long the surprised Miller was caught near Fort Worth by Ada's police chief, George Culver. Miller had influential friends in Texas who could get him out of trouble about as easily as he could get into it, and he probably expected to ease out of this killing in Oklahoma. He just didn't know that Ada was mad, and this was the last straw with them. They would have justice, and they weren't afraid of Jim Miller, even if the rest of the southwest was!

During the meantime, the details of this sordid affair came to light. Oscar Peeler had made some arrangements ahead of Jim Miller's arrival in Ada — like renting him a house to stay in. When Peeler was thrown into jail; he talked. Ada's vigilantes now knew who they were really after: Joe Allen and Jesse West. Those two hoodlums had hired Miller to kill Bobbitt, and a professional bondsman named B.B. Burwell had acted as go-between. Soon, both Allen and West were in Ada's jailhouse, and when Burwell showed up to make bail for them, he was thrown in, too. All five were in the jail together — Allen, West, Miller, Burwell, and Peeler. Ada wasn't joking around.

To make matters worse, or as we might say, to add insult to injury, Jim Miller behaved like an exiled prince. He threw his money around even while in his cell, and Ada took note of everything. He wouldn't eat the regular fare, but ordered porterhouse steaks from the Elite Cafe for himself and the other prisoners. He shaved every day, and he wore stiff-bosomed shirts which he sent out to the laundry, along with a $5 tip to the jailer each time. He had fresh linen sent up for the beds, and the jail smelled of incense. He even had rugs brought in for the floors of his cell. He seemed to be laughing at Ada, and Ada grew quiet — mysteriously quiet.

Letters and telegrams poured in, praising him and vouching for his sterling character. These came from judges and prominent people, including Texas Rangers. Jim Miller was awaiting another quick, "ho-hum" trial in a state known to go easy on murder by contract, and with all of his Texas character references, he would be out in no time and back to his nefarious deeds. Or, so he thought.

On a Sunday night in April — a misty night, characteristic of Oklahoma in the spring — things were especially quiet. By midnight the town was deep in slumber. By some coincidence (or was it?) county officials had made themselves scarce that night. The sheriff found urgent business over in Arkansas, and several deputies were "out of town." An unsuspecting jailer and one innocent deputy blew out the lights about midnight and went to sleep on cots in the hall of the jailhouse.

About 2:30 in the morning, the jailer and deputy awakened to a command of "Git up and dress" and found themselves surrounded by about fifteen masked men, who tied the two up with baling wire. Finding the keys to the cell block, the men entered the cells holding Allen, West, Burwell, and Miller, telling them to get dressed. Peeler was left alone because he had turned state's evidence against the killers at the preliminary hearing three weeks earlier. Jim Miller, arrogant even in the face of death, took all the time he wanted in dressing, putting on a stiff-bosomed shirt and tie, complete with diamond stickpin. While he combed his hair slowly and deliberately, the crowd was growing, numbering about forty by now. It was also growing impatient. Finally, Miller stepped out of his cell and made some wisecrack, although he did go along peacefully. Burwell and Allen, realizing the jig was up, gave no trouble. Jesse West was a different story. He came out fighting, trying to slug his way through the mob. He was pistol-whipped until he fell unconscious, then dragged along behind the other three to an old livery stable next door to the jail.

It wasn't far, and it didn't take long. Inside the barn, the suspects' hands were tied behind their backs with baling wire. Then their feet were tied. The mob tried to make them talk about the murder, but none of them would cooperate. Ropes were put around their necks and tightened. Then, the other

416

end of each rope was thrown across a rafter. One by one, the doomed suspects were hauled up into the air and left hanging. Jim Miller was the first to go up. After his body stopped wiggling, someone picked up his hat and put it on his head. Allen was second, and Burwell was third. West was last.

Their job done, the mob, numbering nearly fifty, disappeared into the misty night. The gray light of dawn brought curious men and boys to the barn for a peep through the slatted doors and cracks between wall boards. Some of the braver and more agile climbed up into the loft for a bird's-eye view, while the town photographer waited for enough light to snap an early morning picture of the bizarre scene. It's been said that he made a small fortune from his picture and the penny postcards that followed.

The news spread like wildfire across the nation's telegraph wires, each story growing a little larger than the one before; and, a couple of days later, newspapers in other parts of the country castigated Ada for its "frontier justice." They didn't understand the lawlessness that had preceded the hanging, nor were they aware of Ada's patience, worn thin. But it didn't matter to Ada what these editors half-way across America thought. On that April night in 1909, Ada had begun to gain control over the killers and outlaws that stalked its citizens. That one determined community may well have rung down the final curtain on killers in many a frightened town throughout the southwest, for it seemed that the courts tightened up almost overnight in Oklahoma; and, many were the telegrams of congratulations from individual citizens and whole communities throughout Texas, New Mexico, and Arizona, who had suffered at the hands of Jim Miller and his gang for years. Ada itself disposed of three more of its notorious hoodlums, one being sent to prison, one being sentenced to hang, and the other being shot in a pool hall by Ada's police chief.

Forty-two years later, Oklahoma City's newspaper giant, the *Daily Oklahoman*, left no doubt as to how it felt about the

Ada hanging. On March 4, 1951, it wrote, "So many were the fruits of this hanging that it can be written down as one mob action in America entirely justified in the eyes of God and man. . . . Echoes of the hanging still resound throughout Oklahoma, and those who took part in it have no reason today to be ashamed or conscience-stricken. . . . Those four men hanging in the gray light of dawn symbolized the end of America's old west in the sense of men murdering and being murdered without full justice thereafter."[1]

The direct effects upon Ada's citizens were more than symbolic, however, and when one of the local oldtimers is asked for his reaction to the celebrated lynching, he usually answers quite simply, "Well, it sure straightened up Ada."

Recent interviews with several Ada citizens, including A.A. Bobbitt's granddaughter, have revealed some interesting reflections upon that event of seventy-nine years ago. To this day, no one knows the name of any of the participants in the hanging. It is not sure that anyone outside the circle ever knew who participated, and as they wore hoods, the participants themselves might not have been fully known to each other, although Bobbitt's granddaughter believes that her dad knew who some of them were.

The most widely-held belief among the citizenry of Ada is that the Masons did the hanging. In support of this opinion, they point to the story that the men, whoever they were, met at the Masonic Hall prior to the hanging. As the story goes, the men came down the steps two by two, each group having a special duty to perform. One group went to the city's electric plant and forced the engineer to turn off Ada's lights between

418

2 and 3 a.m. Others cleared the streets of anyone who might happen to be out at that dark hour. One thing is for sure: It was a well-organized group, and one that surely could keep a secret.

A LETTER FROM THE FRONT

Fort Washita, Indian Territory, was located about fifteen miles east of the present town of Madill, Oklahoma, and is today being restored to the way it looked when it was a Confederate supply depot. Major J.W. Mayrant was stationed there with the 3d Regiment of the Texas Cavalry in 1861, when he wrote this letter to his wife back in Grayson County, Texas.

In the third paragraph, there is a discrepancy in the excited report of the results of the Battle of Manassas, which occurred on July 21, 1861. Either the letter was dated wrong or the account refers to the victory at Blackburn's Ford which preceded the Battle of Manassas. Either way, the encouraging news received at Fort Washita was grossly exaggerated. At Blackburn's Ford, there were only fifteen casualties for the Confederates and nineteen for the Federals. Even at Manassas the battlefield fatalities were far, far less than what Major Mayrant reports, and even though the report of a great victory was accurate, the Confederates made a tragic mistake in not going on to take Washington. The opportunity for a follow-up into the Yankee capital was so obvious that its anticipation was probably reported as fact even though it never happened.

Fort Washita
July 19, 1861

My Dear Wife

Your kind letter came to hand yesterday evening. I am sorry to hear that our children are sick but I hope they will not be very sick. We may expect a good deal of chills and fevers this fall caused by having so much rain. I have been very well except for a bad cold and cough.

We will look for you all next Monday and I am anxious for the day to come because it brings you. We cannot promise to treat you all very fine when you come but will give you a hearty welcome and give you the best we have to eat.

Lieut. Hendricks is preparing himself to receive the Flag and I expect he will make a good speech on the occasion. I wish you had told me who would present the Flag. Monday is not far off but it will appear long to me. I will probably go home with you when you go back. We have news here that Washington City has been taken by Genls. Davis & Beauregard with a loss of 9000 on our side and 27000 on the other. We have Lincoln's message; he calls for four hundred thousand men and four hundred millions dollars and says the south must be subdued.

We also learn that Governor Jackson & Genl. Lyon has had a fight in Missouri and that Jackson whipped him, Killing sixty or eighty & only loosing two or three men they were two to our one. Genl. McCulloch got to the battle ground two hours after the battle: I have no more news: Kiss the children give my respects to all. Your affect. husband

J.W. Mayrant

P.S.

Sorphlett Smith is here a soldier in the Bowie County Company. he has moved and lives in Bowie County.

Your husband
J.W.M.[3]

A TRIBUTE TO TEXAS

In the last half of the nineteenth century, someone had a story to tell about Texas, a story which found expression in the form of a poem and life in the heart of my grandmother. The author remains unknown to me, but he or she had to be someone who loved Texas as much as my grandmother did.

My grandmother left Texas with this poem of her youth firmly etched in her mind. She was twenty-two when she bade farewell to her native state. For the next seventy years she kept us all entertained with her recitation, which at times came more readily to mind than at others. We grandchildren used to coax her into saying it for us often, while we sat on the floor in a great semi-circle at her feet, hanging on to every word. If she thought she had left out a line or two, we would jump on that as an excuse to urge her to try it again.

We were never able to find a copy of the poem, and as she got way on up into her upper eighties, we were afraid it would slip from her mind and be gone forever. Finally, Aunt Hazel began to sit down with pencil and paper every time my grandmother said the poem. Eventually, what we believe to be the entire poem was on paper, just as my grandmother remembered it down through the years. Like the author, the title remains a mystery as well.

> Missouri is a grand old state
> In history we are told;
> She is one among the many,
> Her sons among the bold.
> She was foremost in the struggle
> We have often heard it said,
> And many of her patriots
> Are numbered with the dead.
> But now that time is passed away
> And she's at peace again
> While St. Louis and Kansas City
> Spread abroad her righteous fame.
> Oh yes, she's rich and powerful,
> Her people grand and free,
> But with all of her pomp and glory
> She is not the home for me.
>
> Illinois, too, does well to boast
> And be exceeding glad,
> For a brighter prospect to her size
> No other state has had.
> Calmly and serenely,
> Chicago, her crowning star,

SOUTHERN BY THE GRACE OF GOD

Stands upon Lake Michigan
And spreads her fame afar.
But what is grandeur and splendor
Where the heart cannot be free?
With all of her magnificence,
She is not the home for me!

But Texas is a model state;
Her sons are statesmen too.
No people half so free as hers,
No hearts are half so true.
She has no St. Louis of which to boast,
Or no Chicago grand,
But, among the pretty cities are hers;
She's the most promising in the land.
She's the home of fruits and flowers,
Likewise of meadows green;
And all that's pleasing to the eye
In Texas can be seen.
Her soil is rich and fertile —
Her prairies broad and fair,
Bedecked with natural ornaments
With which none can compare.

Yes, Texas is a grand old state,
And grander yet she'll be.
For all the days that I may live
Texas is the home for me.
Texas bright and fair!
Grant me this wish, I trust:
That when my body turns to clay
It shall mingle with her dust.

THE BLOOD-STAINED FLOOR

I guess everyone has a favorite story. Mine is the one they tell at *Carnton*, a stately old mansion in Franklin, Tennessee.

Carnton was one of the most elegant homes in Williamson County when it was completed in 1826 by Randal McGavock, just one year after he finished a term as mayor of Nashville, some twenty miles to the north. The large, two-story home of red brick was surrounded by more than a thousand acres of the estate, and it was host to many notables, among whom were James K. Polk, Andrew Jackson, and Sam Houston.

Today, *Carnton* is being restored by the Carnton Association, an incorporated group of preservationists who acquired the historic old place when the descendants of Randal McGavock deeded it over to them as a gift to posterity. Unlike many groups who sit and wait for Federal or state funds, which sometimes arrive after the property has rotted down while bureaucrats were dragging their feet in the best tradition of the government's ability to create chaos out of order, the *Carnton* bunch flew in and opened the house to the public — as is! They've had the home for only a few years, and it is nowhere near being fully restored, but you can tour the house and grounds and see the steady progress being made. Although this wonderful old home, situated in a large field that slopes down to a clear-water spring in the woods at the southeast edge of Franklin, is in its infancy as a tourist attraction, 10,000 visitors passed through its doors last year.

The furnishings, which are being gathered from various sources, are required to be of the 1865 period or earlier. There are several exquisite pieces, including the rosewood piano and the bedroom suites on the second floor. The unusual windows on the first floor, featuring twenty-eight panes each, still contain some of the glass from 1826. And, the newly restored slave quarters give a good indication of how Randal McGavock adequately provided for his good servants.

But the most memorable thing about *Carnton* is the appearance of large patches of blood on the wide boards of the hardwood floors. Near the front door is a dark streak of reddish-brown color that looks as if someone had tried to remove it from the grain with only a measure of success. The hostess points to the blood stain and begins to tell the story behind it.

The Battle of Franklin was one of the major engagements of the War. The Yankees had entrenched within the town itself, awaiting a reckless, head-on charge from the impetuous General John Bell Hood and his Army of Tennessee. Not given to strategy and careful execution of separate movements, General Hood obliged his waiting hosts and rammed his army up against formidable fortifications. It was like feeding them into a sausage grinder. The exposed southern army was mowed down in waves. Five Confederate generals were killed outright, and one was mortally wounded. Never had so many general officers been lost in one battle. Even though Hood was trying desperately to retrieve the waning fortunes of the Confederacy, which in late 1864 were on a precipitous decline, the senseless blood bath was a poor remedy for the situation.

The rear lines of Stewart's Corps were fighting along the lane by the railroad track west of *Carnton* on that cold November day. A steady stream of dying and wounded soldiers wandered across the lawn and into a grove of trees just south of the house. By the early evening hours, the slaughter now over, there were two hundred pitifully wounded men lying under the barren trees south of the house. Their agonizing cries of pain were heart-wrenching to John McGavock and his wife.

Before long, it began to sleet, and the lot of the bleeding heroes became miserable indeed. Mrs. McGavock called in the servants and ordered them to move all of the furniture back against the wall. Next, she had them roll up all of the carpets and bring every one of the soldiers inside the house. She turned the back parlor and the upstairs nursery into operating rooms, while they laid horribly injured men all over the floors in the splendid mansion.

With the help of her servants and several others, Mrs. McGavock turned her home into a make-shift hospital. All through the night they tended to the wounded soldiers. There were no bandages to stop the bleeding, so Mrs. McGavock began tearing up her old linens. The need was always for more, and her extra linens were soon used up. Finally, everything was torn into bandages — her towels, sheets, pillow cases, table cloths, anything that might save a life.

By morning, Mrs. McGavock was exhausted. Her skirts were stiff with dried blood from working among the injured men. Then, someone stepped up to her and said, "Mrs. McGavock, the bodies of four of our generals have been laid out on the back veranda."

The bodies of Generals Adams, Cleburne, Granbury, and Strahl were left at *Carnton* until arrangements for their proper burial could be made. The wounded soldiers remained in the house for several days until a field hospital could be set up in the yard. General Quarles and other wounded officers stayed in the house until February, when a Yankee officer came for them. The officer named Stilwell marched them out the front door, put them on a wagon, took them to the train depot, and sent them north to prison.

After the Battle of Franklin, Mr. & Mrs. McGavock donated two acres adjoining the family graveyard as a cemetery for the Confederate dead who were resting in temporary graves on the battlefield. In April, 1866, this tranquil cemetery became the final resting place for nearly 1,500 Confederate soldiers from the terrible Battle of Franklin. Through the efforts of Miss M.A.H. Gay, of Macon, Georgia, a handsome wrought iron fence was placed around the hallowed ground, and other Confederate soldiers were buried there later.

Over the years, several attempts were made to remove the

blood stains from the floors of *Carnton*, but the blood had soaked in almost immediately. The floors were then painted, covering some of the stains. Some of the floors were stripped during restoration, revealing the dark red patterns once again. Upstairs, in the southwest bedroom, one can see big drops and smears of dark red blood as clearly defined as the tragic night it was spilled. The directors of *Carnton* have resolved to leave it as a vivid, lucid reminder of our blood-bought heritage, lest we become forgetful of the sacrifices of those who paid so dearly for our matchless southern legacy.

A LETTER FROM THE FRONT

Isaac W. Crabtree was a member of Company B, 6th Regiment, Texas Cavalry, under the celebrated command of General Nathan Bedford Forrest. In April, 1863, they were camped near Spring Hill, Tennessee, and Crabtree took the time to write his brother back in Greenville, Texas, telling him about his life in the military. Two and a half months later, Isaac Crabtree's short life came to an end at the age of twenty. On July 6, 1863, he was killed in fighting east of Vicksburg, although his body was never recovered. He was reported as "lost in action," and his sister saved this, his last letter.

His spelling, punctuation, and capitalization appear here as they do in the original letter. I have added one word (in parenthesis) that I believe he inadvertently left out. *Rozencraze* is his spelling of *Rozencrans*, the name that southerners called Yankee General W.H. Rosecrans.

April the 18/1863

Dear Brother

I take my pen in hand to let you know that I am Well and hope this may fine you all enjoying the Same blessing I received yours of the 15th of Feb. which gives me grate pleasure to know that you was among the living and in good health for I never Expected to hear of you living again I was Sorry to hear of the deaths of So many in that neighborhod but glad to hear of the fall of M.D. Hart and his accomplices I have got no news of very grate importance Our Brigade is not Exactly on out front Service at this time we are for the presant wresting our horses We are camped 2 miles from Spring hill William Co Tenn We are for the presant doing Well we get plenty of Bacon & Beef cornmeal & flour to eat and tolerable plenty of Forage. General Forest is in front next to Franklin picketting the Several Tenn Pikes it is not believed that a general Battle will come off Soon beetwein Bragg vs Rozencraze though it may be tomorrow that the guns may Roar and the work of Desolation go on.

From the last letter I got or rather the first you Seem to be some what dishartened in Consequence of reverse of the army West of the River but you need not be alarmed at all for we now occupy a good portion of country that they occupied this time last Spring We are now getting So we can Support our army from our own products and one more year of the war has passed consequently every hour brings the war nearer a close. and as regards Confederate money I would

GENERAL ROBERT E. LEE

Photograph made in April, 1865, shortly after the end of the War. Lee reluctantly posed for Matthew Brady on the back porch of his Richmond home.

GENERAL PIERRE GUSTAVE TOUTANT BEAUREGARD

This photograph of the wealthy Creole general from south Louisiana was taken toward the end of the War.

BELLE BOYD

The celebrated Confederate spy, photographed here about the time of the War, was only 17 in 1862 when she endangered her life to advise Stonewall Jackson about Yankee strength at Front Royal — information which allowed him to destroy the command of General Banks two days later at Winchester.

JEFFERSON DAVIS

This handsome photo was made in 1853, while Jefferson Davis was Secretary of War under President Franklin Pierce. Davis was forty-five years old at the time.

PRESIDENT DAVIS AT THE BEGINNING OF THE WAR.

GENERAL PAT CLEBURNE

This Irish-born general was one of the leading citizens of Helena, Arkansas, before marching off to a war that would claim his life. This photo is the only known photograph of Cleburne taken during the War. It was made in Mobile, Alabama, in January, 1864.

GENERAL JOSEPH R. KERSHAW

of
South Carolina

ROSE O'NEAL GREENHOW

The famous Confederate spy, Mrs. Greenhow, and her daughter, "Little Rose," were photographed here at Old Capitol Prison in Washington, D.C., possibly on the day they were released with explicit instructions never to reenter the United States. After five months in the northern prison, she was released in June, 1862, and made her way to Richmond. On October 1, 1864, she drowned off the coast of Wilmington, North Carolina, while bearing dispatches from England for the Confederacy. She was weighted down in the stormy surf by $2,000 in gold, some of it sewn into her clothing and some of it hanging from her neck in a large reticule. She is buried in Oakdale Cemetery at Wilmington.

GENERAL NATHAN BEDFORD FORREST

SAM DAVIS

For more than 120 years, it was generally believed that no photograph of Sam Davis existed. This amazing picture surfaced only a few years ago in the old family album of Capt. John W. Morton, Chief of Artillery under Gen. Nathan Bedford Forrest. Morton and Davis were the same age and attended the Nashville Military Academy together. (Courtesy Mike Miner)

Sam Davis, before his accusers, who threaten the young boy's life. Faced with certain death, he bravely tells them, "If I had a thousand lives to live, I would give them all rather than betray a friend." This picture is from the old painting (below) by Harold Von Schmidt, who, like the sculptor, Zolney, had to work from descriptions and portraits of other family members to create a likeness of Sam Davis. All photographs of Sam were lost when the Yankees set fire to a haystack at the Davis home. Mrs. Davis had hidden the family pictures in the haystack, thinking the Yankees would burn her home. (Courtesy Sam Davis Memorial Association)

"Dear Mother,
    Oh how painful it is to write to you. I have got to die to-morrow morning . . ."

MAJOR JOHN PELHAM

"The Gallant Pelham" was what they called him, this young Alabama boy who was a member of Jeb Stuart's Horse Artillery. Known for his bravery and daring deeds, he was already a hero when death took him at Kelly's Ford, Virginia, on March 17, 1863.

GENERAL STONEWALL JACKSON

This photograph was made a few days before Jackson was shot at Chancellorsville on May 2, 1863. His wife, Anna, visiting him at the front with their infant daughter, Julia, encouraged him to have his picture made. He died on May 10, 1863 from his wounds.

COLONEL JOHN S. MOSBY

This picture of the "Gray Ghost" was made shortly after the War. There was not a man in the Confederacy who was as fierce as this small man. He soon became the most feared and best-known guerilla fighter in the War.

GENERAL JOHN HUNT MORGAN

GENERAL ALBERT SIDNEY JOHNSTON

At the outset of the War, President Davis made him the highest ranking general in the Confederacy. His reputation was unmatched. Davis said, "If Sidney Johnston is not a general, we have no general." In the midst of a victorious attack at Shiloh on April 6, 1862, General Johnston was severely wounded. He unselfishly sent his own doctor to tend his poor wounded soldiers and died on the battlefield shortly afterwards in the arms of Gov. Isham Harris. The brightest light in the South had gone out.

not care if it was out of Existence perhaps the very grate many Speculators (should) Shoulder muskets and Serve there country a might I can inform you that I am not home Sick yet though I would be the gladest in the world to see all of you. and I hope and pray that I soon may See home in Peace. If John's Regt is ordered to Port Hudson I had a thought of Sending my horse home and getting a transfer to that Company I want you to write often and tell all the girls God Bless all thir Sweet little Souls and may He keep them under the Shadow of his Wing till peace is made and we all Return.

I will give you Some of the prices of Produce paper is worth $4.00 per chorir corn $1.00 $2.00 goods of all kinds an live Stock also

I want you to give me aletter immediately tell liz & kate to write. you must Excuse my bad hand and worse composition I must close for the Butcher has Shot a beef and I must go and draw as I am acting Orderly Sergent for the company

Give my best Respects to all and Receive the Same I Remain your affectionate Brother till Death Fare Well for a Season

I W Crabtree to W B Crabtree

Remember me thoug far away I be

PAPA AND THE KKK

No one can doubt the effectiveness of the original Ku Klux Klan. Without it we might never have shaken off the curse of the carpetbag/scalawag governments which bound us hand and foot after the War. But, there arose another Klan sometime before World War I, and southerners have viewed it with both admiration and disgust ever since. The Klan's own ambiguity did more to confuse people than anything else. And, it wasn't only southerners who were involved with the 20th century Ku Klux Klan. It spread into parts of the north, where it found strongholds in places like Indiana and Illinois.

The period surrounding World War I brought the "red scare" to America. Europe was in political turmoil, and the communists took Russia in 1917. The labor movement in America was turning violent and looking more like socialism than anything since the days of Reconstruction. As a result, the average American was suspicious and uneasy about liberal movements and social issues. The times were just right for the appearance of a militant, patriotic response, and the Ku Klux Klan stepped forward. Most southerners could agree with the stand against communism which was taken by the Klan. In addition, the Klan did a tremendous amount of benevolent work among the poor. By the 1920's, it was even fashionable to avow membership in the Klan, and many a politician, from governor on down, was elected by the powerful clout of the Ku Klux Klan. The negative perception of the Klan came from the sudden bursts of violence which began to emanate from the hooded society, especially when directed at southern Catholics and Jews, many of whose recent ancestors had been as loyal to the Confederacy as those of the white-robed Klansmen.

The secrecy of the Klan membership, protected by the hoods and robes, was a factor in its rise to power and prestige, but, it likewise provided the same measure of anonymity to thugs and criminals who eventually destroyed the effectivenss of the Klan. If someone had a personal score to settle, he could perpetrate his act under a hood, and the Ku Klux Klan would get the blame. The Klan was powerless to control the criminals utilizing its famous costume, and, as its reputation began to suffer, its prominent citizens withdrew from the circle.

My grandfather lived in Hughes County, in the east central portion of Oklahoma, on an eighty-acre farm. Across the road was the schoolhouse where he sent his four children to school and drove one of the school buses. He was also on the school board and was known far and wide as a man of high integrity — one who couldn't be moved when he knew he was right.

Six miles to the north is the county seat of Wetumka, in the heart of the Creek Nation and named for an old Creek town in Alabama. As in most of the South, the Ku Klux Klan was quite active in the area. During the first World War, it vigorously enforced the rationing that was necessary to the war effort. Aunt Norma told me about the man who went into Wetumka in a wagon and started back out to Pleasant Ridge with several more bags of sugar than he was allotted. She was about twelve years old at the time, and it made a lasting impression upon her when the Ku Klux Klan stopped the man and gave him a good beating. They poured his sugar out all over the road, and he never tried to cheat on the rationing again.

Then there were the IWW's. Aunt Norma said it stood for "I Won't Work." In reality, it stood for Industrial Workers of the World, but the people of Hughes County had the right idea. The IWW's were part of a national labor organization who were radical, violent, socialistic, and opposed to the war effort. Several years after the war, their organization dissolved, with many of their members joining the communist party. Aunt Norma used to tell how they threatened to poison Wetumka's water supply during World War I. She told how the Ku Klux Klan came to the rescue and placed guards around the lake twenty-four hours a day.

One night the Ku Klux Klan came for Papa. There were three of them dressed in white robes and hoods, standing in the front yard near the porch. Mama heard them hollering for Papa to come outside and talk to them. My dad was about ten years old then, and he knew by my grandmother's voice that something was wrong. Papa stepped out on the front porch, and the men raised their voices in anger, telling him that he was going to go with them. My dad watched through the open door as Mama grew white with fear. As quick as a flash, Papa jumped back inside and grabbed a great big pistol. Then he leaped back out onto the porch, leveled the gun at their heads, and told them to disrobe or they'd be dead men. That's when Mama fainted.

The men threw their hands above their heads but were a little hesitant about removing their cowardly hoods. Papa jumped off the porch and waded into them, jabbing the pistol into their ribs a few times as he walked among them. He told them to get those hoods off pronto or he would kill all three of them. As my dad watched from the safety of the house, he saw Papa making them show their guilty faces. Papa found just what he expected. There stood three of the sorriest humans in the community. One of them had threatened him because he didn't stop the school bus in the right place; one was trying to get back at him for refusing to hire a woman of loose morals to teach at the school; the other was a constant complainer about all of his school board decisions.

None of them were members of the Ku Klux Klan, but had Papa not disrobed them, the Klan would surely have caught the blame. Papa had no more trouble out of them, and Mama was revived. But the Klan began to disintegrate from incidents such as this.

DESERTED SURRENCY

Every community has a story concerning its beginning. Some villages were settled near an old spring to avail themselves of a supply of fresh water. Others were first established as forts along the ever-changing frontier. Still others were extensions of old Indian villages. The circumstances surrounding the choosing óf a townsite are about as varied as the individual characteristics of the communities themselves; but, it is probably safe to say that few of them had their locations chosen by a ghost. In fact, Surrency, Georgia, may be the only place in the South to hold that distinction.

Surrency is located on Highway 341 about sixty miles from the coast in southeast Georgia. It's been there since 1870, when it was relocated from a spot just a short distance down the railroad. The original Surrency was a large plantation owned by the Surrency family, which later grew into a small village of scattered houses. In 1870, mysterious things began to happen at the Surrency home which eventually caused the town to be deserted.

The strange stories coming out of southeast Georgia persisted for years. In 1905, Mrs. I.K. Reno, a talented writer from Nashville, Tennessee, traveled to Deserted Surrency to investigate for herself. She reported that the town had been deserted for about thirty-five years when she came upon the son of old Mr. Surrency, who took her to the scene of the ghostly affairs of 1870.

I was accompanied to the old homestead by Mr. Samuel D. Surrency, a gentleman of pleasant address and seemingly 50 or 55 years of age. He was the presiding magistrate in his neighborhood, and a citizen of high standing. The house was a double frame structure, two stories high, with a wing in the rear.

The gates and outside doors were nailed together with boards, the shutters hung loosely from their hinges, the windows were broken, and the wind swept through the old house with a mournful sound as if lamenting its ruin and desolation.

The special interest of the strange and mysterious drama which was enacted there thirty-five years ago, centered in the old house before which we stood. And there at my side stood Esq. Samuel Surrency ready to relate what had been a terrible reality to him and the entire family.[5]

The old house had never been occupied since the family left it in 1870, and the entire area was considered to be under the influence of a bad spirit. Despite a flood of bad memories, Mr. Surrency began his story.

My father, A.P. Surrency, built the old house you see standing there, away back in the forties. His large family spent many happy years there, before the trouble came that drove us away.

One summer afternoon, 1870, my mother was sewing in that first room to the left of the entrance to the old, old house there. She was unusually happy at that date. The older children were at home to spend their summer vacation, her household was well ordered, and father was in prosperous circumstances.

Mother was of a calm, placid disposition, and not easily aroused by trifles. On this same afternoon that I mention, her attention was attracted by a strange noise from a wash stand in the room. She looked in the direction and saw a pitcher in the bowl on the washstand rocking back and forth.

She went to see if a string or wire were attached to it, thinking it perhaps a boyish prank; finding none, she resumed her sewing, when she was amazed to see the pitcher lift itself several inches from the bowl, then settle down into it again, with a loud noise.

Then the pitcher was lifted entirely out of the bowl and placed with deliberate care, beside it on the washstand.

Immediately after this the bowl was flung from the washstand, and fell in fragments at mother's feet, and in quick succession the smaller pieces of the entire toilet set followed, adding their several little heaps to the debris on the floor. From that day the peace and quiet of the happy old homestead was destroyed.

The next day, the family was eating dinner, when a door opening on the front gallery, and which was standing open, began to move slowly, and was shut with calm deliberation.

"That was done," said mother, quietly, "by the wind."

But she had scarcely spoken when the door opened, and was flung back against the wall with great violence. At the same time two windows in the room were raised and lowered many times, breaking the panes into tiny bits.

These were only small beginnings. Frequently during the meal hour, milk, tea, coffee and soup were flung into the faces of those at the table, several times inflicting painful scalds and burns. Spoons were broken, or suddenly twisted out of shape in their hands.

At first the demonstrations were confined to the dining room and mother's bedroom, but after a few days they spread until there was not a room in the house free from the frightful phenomenon.

At all hours of the day and night, the heavy old fashioned furniture would creak and groan, then as if moved by unseen giants, it would rush from its place in a mad dance about the room, and would either move quietly back to its accustomed place or would be dashed to splinters on the floor, with noise like a thunderbolt.

One of the most singular phases of the phenomenon was the affect that the presence of the young daughter of the house, Miss Clementine Surrency, had upon the strange demonstrations. From the very beginning of the trouble it was noticed that when she was present, the manifestations were more potent and varied.

Anything she chanced to lay her hands upon seemed drawn to her by some strange law of magnetism, and would follow her movements through the house, floating slowly through the air behind her, several feet from the floor, as if supported by invisible hands.

Her mere entrance into a room would frequently be cause sufficient to send all the furniture in it spinning around in a mad whirl, lasting several minutes, and would either end suddenly in profound quiet, or in a loud crash, wrecking some favorite heirloom.

Father and mother were thoroughly mystified and unhappy. They were constantly alarmed for their own and their children's safety, and having become unnerved, they were earnestly discussing the advisability of moving away, when something occurred that brought them to a sudden and definite decision.

. . . It occurred in there. That was our sitting room, and one afternoon in February, as I entered the hall, I glanced into the sitting room and saw my elder brother, Robert, sitting at a table reading.

A low fire was flickering in the open fireplace,

and several logs which had burned through, had fallen apart and rolled from the andirons to the hearth.

... Just as I entered the room I noticed a commotion on the hearth, when to my surprise, I saw one of the huge andirons lift itself from the fire and began to move across the room. It gathered momentum as it went, and rose swiftly in the air till it reached the level of my brother's head when it dealt him a heavy blow on the temple.

He sprang to his feet, stunned and bleeding, while I grasped the andiron in my hands, trying thus to shield my brother; but I may as well have essayed to hold a thunderbolt, for it wrenched itself free from my grasp and struck my brother again on the head.

"Run," I called to my brother, "run for your life!" If you stay here you will be killed, and I cannot help you." The poor boy did run out of the room and the andiron followed, striking him heavy blows till the poor victim, covered with blood, fell unconscious at our mother's feet.[6]

The next day, his father moved the whole family to another farm, taking nothing with them except their clothes. The other house was furnished, and it was thought best to leave as much undisturbed as possible. A long illness followed the brother who had been beaten with the andiron, but he eventually recovered.

After about ten days, the ghost began to haunt their new abode, and Mr. Surrency had a small cottage built a short distance away. While the new house was under construction, Miss Clementine's parents determined it best to send her away on a vist to calm her nerves. Samuel Surrency continued his story.

So father and I drove her over here one day for

her to pack a trunk of clothes she had left here. . . .
She ran up to her old room, and father and I waited
there on the porch.

She closed the outside shutters of the room and
came below, saying the trunk was ready for us to bring
down. At that moment we heard a noise, as if some
heavy object was being dragged over the floor, then
the crash of wood and glass, and the next moment
my sister's trunk was lying on the lawn there. . . .

We made a thorough search through the house,
but found it all locked and barred as we had left it
a few months before, and it had remained untenanted.
Yet my sister's trunk had been dragged across the floor
and hurled through the closed sash and shutters by
the same unseen agency which had, for nearly a year,
destroyed the happiness of our home.[7]

The news spread throughout Georgia, bringing all kinds
of curious people to the place which would become known as
Deserted Surrency. Even the editor of the *Macon Telegraph* came
for a big story. Foster, the clairvoyant and medium of the day,
came and spent a week in the house. He was accompanied
by other mediums who were assisting him in detecting the cause
of the trouble. At the end of the week, he emerged and made
a statement.

I saw no materializations, but I asked the spirits
why they had driven you from your home, and through
certain raps on the table, I received this reply:
"The entire Surrency family is strongly medium-
istic, especially Miss Clementine Surrency; therefore
we have sought to make them recognize our power,
for we have need of them to deliver our message to
the world."[8]

Medium or no medium, the citizens of the little village were not taking any chances with the spirits that obviously haunted the place. Deserting old Surrency rapidly, they began to cluster around the new house built by Mr. Surrency, and it was there that the present town of Surrency arose. The two homes deserted by the Surrency family were left empty by surviving owners who would not occupy them nor till the land around them.

So it was that the present location of the town of Surrency, Georgia, was decided by a ghost.

THE MYSTERY OF JOHN HUNT COLE

About twelve years ago, I stumbled onto one of the most bizarre stories I have ever heard in my life. It stuck with me partially because of its bold claim, but mostly because of the incredible aggregation of evidence with which the teller proceeded to validate his claim.

The story took its flight on November 8, 1899, upon the death of one John Hunt Cole near Vian, Indian Territory. Only a few people in the world have ever heard this tale, and I relate it here just as it came to me, followed by uncanny revelations produced by further inquiry.

First, the story.

While teaching school in Wynnewood, Oklahoma, I had the good fortune to be associated with a congenial football coach named Darvis Cole. Attempting to organize a local chapter of

Sons of Confederate Veterans, of which membership requires proof of a Confederate military ancestor, I made mention of my efforts to Coach Cole. At once interested, he said, "I have a good Confederate ancestor; in fact, he's a general, and he's my great-grandfather."

Realizing immediately the amount of prestige that would accrue to my local chapter (or *camp*, as it is called in SCV) by virtue of enrolling a direct descendant of a Confederate general, not to mention the pleasure I would take in personally fraternizing with such "royal blood", I quickly responded, "Who is it?"

"Have you ever heard of General John Hunt Morgan?" His question-answer dropped my mouth wide open. Had I ever heard of John Hunt Morgan? This was no obscure general among the 425 men who served the South in the capacity of that rank. This was *the* John Hunt Morgan — Dixie Cavalier — Kentucky's favorite son — dashing, daring John Hunt Morgan! Oh yes, I had heard of General Morgan and his famous Raiders whose exploits were indelibly written in the heroes' section of my heart, and nothing would do but to enroll Darvis Cole in my SCV camp immediately, if not sooner!

"There is a problem, though," he interrupted. "I can't prove it." The great-grandson of John Hunt Morgan, and he couldn't prove his lineage only three generations back? I guess the question must have asked itself through the expression on my face, for he continued, "History books tell us that John Hunt Morgan was killed near the end of the War, leaving only one child who died before she could have children, so there are supposedly no descendants. But, he did not die in 1864 as supposed. He escaped, changed his name to Cole, and came to Oklahoma."

There are a lot of people, including myself, who would like to claim descent from a Confederate hero, and to be quite honest, I became a little skeptical at that point in the story, fearing that someone had invented the tale and had passed it off to

Coach Cole as truth. Evidently skeptics had frowned before, and he was next suggesting, "You might want to talk to my brother's wife. She has all of the details."

I lost very little time in contacting brother Darrel and his wife, June. She was well-versed in her husband's genealogy, and the story began to unfold.

It seems that the surprise attack upon the house where Morgan and his men were sleeping on September 4, 1864, and the resulting confusion (which is well-documented) afforded General Morgan a chance to escape (which is not documented). According to the story, he changed coats with an aide in an effort to confuse his foes in the event of his capture or death. During the melee, shots rang out from every direction, and Morgan caught one in the side. Managing to effect his escape, he received help from a negro family in the area and spent some time recuperating before riding north to find a woman named Maggie Critzer, whom he had met on a business trip into Illinois, presumably before the War when he was exporting woolen goods and hemp products.

Changing his all-too-familiar name to John Hunt Cole, he married Maggie, and the couple lived with her parents who were running a grist mill at the time. The name *John Hunt Morgan* was notorious in the North, and it was commonly known that many Yankees were sworn never to take him alive. Even after the change in surname, five men showed up one day, saying that they had discovered his true identity. A fight ensued and several men were killed.

Having been found after only five months, John Hunt Cole recognized the necessity of an immediate move. With his wife and the Critzers, he made a drastic dash to the wide open plains of Kansas, settling in Marion County, between Florence and Marion, on the Cottonwood River, where Mr. Critzer again operated a grist mill. Early in 1879, Cole and his wife moved to a rural area near South West City, Missouri, a small community that sits virtually astraddle the border with Indian Territory.

The move was made in response to Maggie's failing health, though she passed away soon after arriving there.

Cole now had five children who needed a mother. On May 8, 1879, he remarried, this time to Carolyn Reardion. She would bear him four sons, none of whom would live past childhood.

Having more education than most of the men in the remote area of southwestern Missouri and Indian Territory, Cole practiced medicine and became known thereabouts as Dr. Cole. He was also distinguished by his marksmanship with a pistol and his love for horses, being always in possession of at least one good horse.

One of Cole's younger boys, Charles Alexander, married while living near South West City. The court records show that, on March 3, 1892, John Hunt Cole gave his written permission for the marriage, his permission being required because Charles was not of age.

Shortly thereafter, the family moved to the area around Vian, Indian Territory, deep in the heart of the old pro-Confederate Cherokee Nation. Still, Cole kept his secret and continued to practice medicine as Dr. Cole. Sometimes, a man would come from a long way off, always arriving after dark. Neighbors could see the lamps burning in the Cole house all night long, and before daylight the visitor would depart. In relating this part of the story, June Cole told me that one of John Hunt Morgan's brothers knew about the escape, and most of the family believe the visitor was that brother.

In the autumn of 1899, the wife of Cole's oldest son became ill. Though Cole himself was sick also, he saddled a horse and rode to care for her. It was a fateful ride, for she died, and Cole contracted pneumonia from the trip.

Realistically suspecting that he would not survive the pneumonia, John Hunt Cole decided to divulge the long-held secret of his identity and suggested that the family be summoned quickly. Probably fearing that he would become irrational or unconscious before the entire family arrived, he had only his oldest son, John Morgan Cole, and his wife, Carolyn, at his bedside when he took pen and paper and signed *John Hunt Morgan*. Some friends may have been present, but the other family members did not arrive in time. Handing the signature to the person closest to his bed, he said, "This is who I really am." On November 8, 1899, the *real* John Hunt Morgan died.

Why he chose to *write* his true identity rather than verbalizing it to the bystanders will never be known. He may have intended to leave a sample signature for comparison with earlier signatures of John Hunt Morgan, or perhaps he merely wished to heighten the drama. Whatever the reason, he actually did leave the family with a perfect tool for substantiating his claim. His wife kept the paper for a while, but it disappeared before comparisons could be made.

Long before he died, he had confided in his wife and his oldest son, thus the deathbed revelation was no surprise to those two trustworthy confidants. And, there was a Mr. McKee, who lived near Stilwell, Indian Territory, who claimed to have known the secret, though no one ever knew just how he came by his knowledge.

So ends the story.

Well, at least part of the story ends there, for in reality, the story will never end until it is proven beyond the reasonable shadow of a doubt, or until the descendants of John Hunt Cole can find some antecedents for him. The recurring dead end with the person of John Hunt Cole only serves to strengthen the Cole family genealogists' theory that Cole actually was John Hunt Morgan.

So, what kind of evidence do they have other than the apparent end of the Cole line? For starters, they have the testimony of Cole's oldest son, John Morgan Cole, who passed the information to his son. John Morgan Cole once asked his father why he kept holding the secret after the fear of imprisonment or assassination had passed, to which Cole answered that it would bring much dishonor to the proud Hunt and Morgan names in Kentucky as he was legally married to Mattie Ready of Murfreesboro, Tennessee. Matters were further complicated when Mattie married Judge James Williamson of Lebanon, Tennessee.

Then, too, there is the testimony of Cole's daughter-in-law, who was the wife of Cole's fourth child, Charles Alexander, and the grandmother of my source, Darrel Cole. One thing that struck me as more than coincidence is that Darrel learned to plait ropes from his grandmother, who was taught to plait by John Hunt Cole himself. The Coles are quick to point out that John Hunt Morgan's primary business before the War was plaiting ropes from hemp. Darrel's grandmother stated that while Dr. Cole was teaching her to plait ropes he told her that he had been in the hemp business. And, was it mere coincidence that Morgan and six of his officers scaled the penitentiary wall in their escape by making a strong rope, according to Morgan biographer James Ramage, out of the bedticking?

When I requested more evidence, they mentioned the interesting similarity between Morgan, Hunt, and Cole family names. The most obvious repetition was found in the name of Cole's first son, John Morgan Cole. His second child, a daughter, was named Margaret Charlotte Cole. John Hunt Morgan had an aunt named Margaret and a brother named Charlton. Cole's fourth child was named Charles Alexander. Could this child have been named after John Hunt Morgan's Uncle Alexander and his brother Charlton, whom his father called "Charly"?

The question of Morgan's choice of Cole as his pseudonym came up. Grandson, Wiley Cole, said that his grandfather had selected the name because one of his aides was named Cole. Indeed, the Adjutant General's Report shows a John Cole assigned to Morgan's Kentucky Cavalry. In addition, Pollard's *Southern History of the War* refers to a Captain Coles, on page 212 of Volume II, as an officer in Morgan's command.

The plausibility of Morgan's escape also required some

rationale before I could be considered a prospective convert. I must admit here that the Cole family had certainly done its homework. It was recalled that Morgan had made a solemn vow to his wife, Mattie, that he would never be taken prisoner again, a pledge alluded to several times by biographer Ramage, who points out Morgan's affirmation of that oath in the last letter he would ever write to Mattie the day before his supposed death.

The contention that Morgan made good his escape by changing roles with an aide is supported, at least in logic, by several illustrations. Morgan's biographers, of whom there are several, have given ample indication of his proclivity toward masquerading as someone else, at times for military advantage while at others seemingly for the mere satisfaction he derived from deceiving someone, especially when it called for posing in the guise of a Yankee — a ruse he frequently used.

Although Morgan's fame was known far and wide, he was living in an age devoid of television and mass media, a factor that worked to his advantage in that his physical likeness was not in wide circulation. He managed to avoid capture more than once due to the inability of his enemies to identify him by face. Again, Ramage portrays a classic example of Morgan's subterfuge on page 155 in his biography, *Rebel Raider*. A Federal cavalry dashed into McMinnville, Tennessee, surprising Morgan and a small force of forty men. Morgan and most of his men escaped due to the deceptive action of Major Dick McCann, who surrendered to the Yankee force, proclaiming that he was the unfortunate General Morgan, a story swallowed hook, line, and sinker by the unsuspecting Federals. A singular characteristic of Morgan's men is that their undying allegiance belonged to him, and they were ready at any given moment to divert danger their way in order to save his neck.

June Cole provided me with a description of John Hunt Cole, the information having come to her from Darrel's grandmother. Cole was described as six feet tall, weighing 180 pounds, and having grayish-blue eyes. Ramage again corroborates the account on page one of his 1986 biography of Morgan, where the description matches that of Cole except for Morgan's weight, listed at 185 pounds.

Similarities between even the facial features of Morgan and Cole continue to fuel the belief that the men are one and the same. A photograph of Cole in his sixties and one of Morgan in his thirties was provided to me upon request, both of which are reproduced herein for the reader's comparison.

The mystery of the man named McKee tends to thicken the plot when it is remembered that Morgan's commander in the Mexican War was Col. William R. McKee, from Lexington, Kentucky.

And what about the Critzer family from Illinois? Was it only coincidence that Cole's second child, Margaret Charlotte, was born in 1867 in East St.Louis, Illinois? Is it only circumstance that Darrel and June Cole visited the Kansas home site and found local residents referring to an area called Critzer's Ford? It may even be pure happenstance that two unmarked graves were identified by area inhabitants as those of Mr. & Mrs. Critzer who did not make the move to South West City, Missouri in 1879.

It seems also worth mentioning here that the strange story of John Hunt Cole caused enough controversy early in the century as to draw a response from Richard Morgan, brother of John Hunt Morgan, and to command mention by the popular Morgan biographer, Cecil Fletcher Holland. Disclaiming the story, he writes, "Even more fanciful was a story current some years after Morgan's death that he was not killed at all but escaped and went to Kansas where it was said he lived under the name of Dr. J.W. Cole until his death in 1899. At a Confederate reunion in Oklahoma in 1915 a Mrs. L.F. LaRue was reported to have made a speech in which she claimed to be the daughter of General Morgan by a wife he married in Kansas."[9] Holland says that Richard Morgan accused the woman of laboring under a hallucination. The Cole family verified the speech as having been made by Cole's third child, Lizzie.

Was the coffin opened at the funeral on September 6? If so, was it not clearly Morgan's body? Or, was even his burial service a well-planned subterfuge to quell the relentless pursuit of John Hunt Morgan? Was the casket opened in Richmond ten days later? Morgan's brother, Calvin, attended to all of the arrangements for the body, accompanying it everywhere it went, including the final stops between Covington and Lexington, Kentucky, in 1868; but, the casket was closed, and a guard sat up with the body at night. The guard was composed of several members of Morgan's former staff, including Major Withers, who had helped wash and dress the body shortly after the killing. Could a cover-up for Morgan's escape have been this elaborate? Was Calvin the brother who visited John Hunt Cole in later years? And, is it not significant that Major Withers, in sworn testimony that is recognized by all to be the most authentic account of the killing, has stated that Morgan, rather than make a dash to the Williams house for safety, shook hands with Withers and parted company with him there in the garden, saying, "You will never see me again"?[10]

Admittedly, much of the evidence seems to be circumstantial, yet there is the haunting suspicion that the abundance of coincidental material lends a certain credibility to the whole story. It would have been easier to dismiss the case from my mind as something of a coincidence had I not looked upon the actual tombstone of John Hunt Cole at Vian, Oklahoma. There was just something cold and convincing about that gray granite birth date: *June 1, 1825*. The exact date of the birth of John Hunt Morgan!

THE PALMYRA MASSACRE

During the War Between the States, emotions ran high both North and South, but they rode at fever pitch continually in the border states — Missouri, Kentucky and those western counties of Virginia which would be railroaded by the Lincoln government into seceding from Virginia in 1863 to form a new state within the U.S. government, an operation which was full of hypocrisy, considering Lincoln's vociferous rhetoric that secession upon the part of the southern states was causing him to perpetuate a bloody conflict.

Perhaps one of the prime reasons for the bitter tension that pervaded the atmosphere in those border states was their awkward juxtaposition between North and South. Unlike the lower South, which was united in its opposition to the Federal government, there was great division between people of the same community in almost every hamlet, especially those of northern Kentucky and Missouri.

Nowhere was this discord more graphically and grotesquely illustrated than in the small northeastern Missouri town of Palmyra in 1862. The story first came to me in 1980, but I am indebted to Bob Ravenscraft, County Clerk of Marion County, and Corbyn Jacobs, local historian, for the details of this incredible story of horror which has been indelibly imprinted upon the minds of Missourians and has become forever known as *The Palmyra Massacre.*

The little country town of Palmyra is located a few miles southwest of Quincy, Illinois. On the Missouri side of the Mississippi River, it lies fifteen miles northeast of the river city of Hannibal and is the county seat of Marion County. On September 12, 1862, Col. Joe Porter and his Confederate command made a raid on Palmyra, endeavoring to free it from its Yankee occupation. They captured and made prisoner a man by the name of Andrew Allsman, a sixty-year old citizen of

Palmyra who had been the cause of much disturbance in the area.

Allsman had enlisted in the Union army when war broke out in 1861, but he was soon discharged due to his age and the idea that he could better be used as an informant in the local area. An ardent, outspoken, and stubborn old man of Union sentiment, he had lived in this divided community for over thirty years, having moved from Kentucky when he was younger. He knew something about every man's politics in the area and was well-acquainted with the entire county. Many a time, he had led forces to the home of a person with southern sentiment, and many a time a home had been ransacked upon his pointing of the finger.

Quite frequently, Allsman was called upon to testify as to the disloyalty of certain individuals, and, if he said a man was a Rebel, the authorities believed him without question. These accused Rebels were thrown into jail upon the slightest provocation, while their families were robbed at home by the Federal soldiers. Understandably, there was a deep resentment of this old spy among the southern citizens of the area. In fact, some of the ladies of Palmyra had said to Colonel Porter, "Don't let old Allsman come back."

So stood the situation upon the third day of Allsman's detainment. It was the 15th of September, and Colonel Porter was forced to make a change in plans and begin a retreat southward. He informed Allsman that his original plan of carrying the old tattletale off into another state had been thwarted and that Allsman was now at liberty to go wherever he desired. This was not altogether good news for Allsman. The Confederates were camped on Troublesome Creek in Lewis County, some twenty-five miles northwest of Palmyra, and Allsman was afraid to leave their camp alone. Fearing that his enemies along the way would kill him, he requested to remain a prisoner under guard.

Colonel Porter was unwilling to drag him along, suggesting,

instead, that he choose six of Porter's men as an escort to the home of some Union sympathizer. Allsman chose three or four men whom he had known, making no objection to the remainder. They started off in the evening toward Marion County but were soon overtaken by others who had followed them from camp. The guard was changed, and Allsman became worried. Before long, the party stopped in the woods, and Allsman was told that he was going to pay for his deeds. He was shot by three men, and his body was covered with brush and leaves in the dense underbrush of the thicket. To this day, his body has never been found, nor were his executioners ever identified.

Even the fact that he had been killed was not known until long thereafter. It was only assumed that he was still in the custody of Colonel Porter, although the whereabouts of that body of Confederate soldiers was unknown at the time. After more than two weeks had passed with no word of Allsman, the talk began, and the Union newspaper in Palmyra, the *Courier*, fanned the flames into a raging fire by assuming a murder had occurred. The newspaper called for avenging the murder, and the Union citizens took up the cry.

In reality, they were right in believing that Allsman had met with foul play, but no one could say for sure. On October 8, there was published in the *Palmyra Courier* a notice to Colonel Porter that he must produce Mr. Allsman, unharmed, within ten days, or rest assured that ten Confederate prisoners in Marion County jails would be shot in retaliation. A supplementary notice was sent to Porter's wife.

Palmyra citizens of Confederate proclivities were shocked at the terrible stipulations of the order and, disbelieving that such an atrocity would actually be carried out, made virtually no move to intercede upon the part of the ten endangered soldiers. But, in the jail at Palmyra, there were some mighty worried men who remembered the murder of Colonel McCullough and fifteen of their comrades in August at the direction of Union authorities in Kirksville, only seventy miles to the northwest. Some thought that Yankee General Merrill would intervene from his headquarters at Macon, but the waiting prisoners remembered how he had executed ten "oathbreakers" on September 25 in Macon for simply not swearing allegiance to a government in which they had no faith.

In addition to these hard facts, the Palmyra prisoners knew the unsavory characters who held their lives in the balance. That fact alone was enough to strike mortal fear into the heart of all of the men imprisoned, none of whom yet knew for sure if he was to be among the ill-fated ten who would have to die if Allsman were not produced pretty quickly. The death threat had been issued by the provost marshal of northeast Missouri, William R. Strachan, the true villain of the story. When approached by someone who pled for revocation of the order, the red-faced Strachan, who was more often than not intoxicated, blustered that the ten men would be shot according to the notice. With him there was no appeal. His authority came through another black bart, the brigadier general commanding the state militia in that area, Gen. John McNeil. With a wave of the hand, General McNeil could have averted the calamity but rather chose to rebuff even citizens of northern sympathies, who pleaded with him to stop this exercise in the macabre, by merely saying, "My will shall be done."

On the ninth day of the order, when it became apparent that ten days would elapse without the appearance of Andrew Allsman, the hideous certainty of it all dawned upon Palmyra. Entreaties were made by local citizens, but they fell on deaf ears. Neither General McNeil nor Provost Marshal Strachan had the slightest compunction about slaying ten innocent men in cold blood. Their government had given them the right, and they were willing actors in the tradegy. The local citizens were helpless, and no one could produce Allsman. Colonel Porter had been making his way southward since before the threat was issued, and it is doubtful that he had seen or ever heard of General McNeil's warning.

It was Friday evening, October 17. General McNeil ordered Strachan to go to the jail and select ten men, notifying them to prepare for death the following day. He knew most of the men, and Strachan knew them all, for they were all from neighboring counties and had families in the area. McNeil was probably satisfying a grudge when he instructed Strachan to select the "worst rebels," his definition being those who could read and write, were educated above the others, and were of higher military rank. He further directed that those who could not read or write were to be left alone, taking instead those "of the highest social position and influence."

Strachan walked into the jail where twelve trembling souls awaited the verdict. They had no way of knowing that only five would be selected from among them, while at the same time five others were being called to their grave from out of the Hannibal jailhouse and started on a late night journey to Palmyra for the execution. There was an exceptionally mean undercurrent in the occupation of northern Missouri, and most of the men and boys in the jails were being held there for nothing more than being southern sympathizers — something we would call political views today. Others were soldiers of the South who had been taken in battle — all native residents of the area.

With eyes as cold as steel, his mouth turned up at the corners in a wicked little smile of satisfaction, Strachan called all of the prisoners to attention, reading off the names of all ten men who were selected to die. "You and each of you will be shot tomorrow at 10 o'clock in the forenoon as a punishment for your crimes and in retaliation for the murder of Andrew Allsman." It was an awful moment. The condemned men and their fellow prisoners stood for a space of time as if suspended between heaven and earth. Silence. Deathly silence! Then when the horror of the thing burst upon them like a cannon blast from the depths of Hell, men broke down and wept as if their very hearts would break inside their manly chests. Some prayed, their faces buried deep in their hands, remembering their scenes of childhood, their families, their boyhood chums, and their sweethearts. In less than twenty-four hours, those minds, now wild with despair, would never think another thought. So much had to crowd into such little space now.

Soon the five prisoners from Hannibal arrived, and by and by came a Baptist preacher. Next morning would come a minister of the Christian Church, doing what he could to console and prepare them for eternity. Together, these men of the cloth persuaded the unfortunate souls to forgive their executioners, and were convinced that all of the doomed prisoners had repented and forgiven the authors of their death. All, that is, except old Willis Baker.

Willis Baker, a sixty-year-old man, was not even remotely suspected of being religious. He stormed and swore that he had done nothing to deserve being shot like an animal, and that he would see "old McNeil and Strachan miles in Hell" before he would forgive them. Baker was a resident of nearby Lewis County and had never been in the Confederate service, but he had two sons who fought the Federals like tigers. Mr. Baker was charged with harboring them and their companions, and, when a Union man turned up murdered in the area, he was charged with complicity in that crime. He was known to be loud and profane in his denunciation of the Yankees, and the death sentence did little to quieten him down. He would denounce them to the very end.

The names of the other nine men selected that night were:

Capt. Thomas A. Sidenor, from Monroe County
Thomas Humston, from Lewis County
Morgan Bixler, from Lewis County
John Y. McPheeters, from Lewis County
Herbert Hudson, from Ralls County
John M. Wade, from Ralls County
Marion Lair, from Ralls County
Eleazar Lake, from Scotland County
William T. Humphrey, from Lewis County

They were all soldiers in the regular service of the Confederacy. All were church members and small farmers, men of limited means but upright citizens in their communities. Thomas Humston presented a particularly pathetic scene. He was only nineteen years old. Though the youngest of the lot, and just approaching the prime of manhood, this single boy, whose life might have lay full ahead of him, tried to be the bravest of them all. He simply said, "A man has to die sometime, and I suppose one time is as good as another." Contrary to General McNeil's arbitrary stipulations, Humston could neither read nor write, yet Strachan got away with choosing him for the slaughter. The poor boy was in jail only because he had been picked up by a scouting party on routine duty.

Captain Sidenor had been in the service under General Sterling Price, but had seen his command decimated at Whaley's Mill; whereupon, he disbanded the rest of his command and decided he had seen enough of war. To elude the Yankees, he disguised himself as a woman and headed for Illinois and civilian life. At Shelbyville, he was discovered and sent to the Palmyra jail. Like the others, he sat down and wrote messages of farewell, one to his sweetheart who was waiting for him in Monroe County.

The very first name Strachan had put on the death list was that of William T. Humphrey. He had been captured, then paroled, promising to stay in the vicinity. When Colonel Porter's raid occurred, culminating in the disappearance of old Allsman, Strachan unjustly accused him of joining Porter and engaging in bushwhacking. Humphrey was thrown back into jail.

Up in her little cabin home in Lewis County, Mary Humphrey got the tragic news of her husband's impending execution. She was only twenty years old, unlearned in many ways, but she determined to beg for her husband's life and sought out her brother-in-law to drive her to Palmyra. With her two little step-children and her two-weeks-old baby, she fled to the office of the provost marshal, only to hear Strachan

470

tell her to go to McNeil. With only hours remaining, she raced to General McNeil and found him grimly determined to kill her husband. At length, however, she succeeded in convincing him that her husband, though invited by Porter's men, refused to rejoin them, fearing that his parole would be revoked. Once assured of the veracity of her statement, McNeil sent word to Strachan to choose another man to replace Humphrey.

It was about 8 o'clock on Saturday morning that the decision was made to reprieve Humphrey. The execution was rescheduled for 1 o'clock. Back at the jail, old Willis Baker was somewhat more calm than before, only occasionally calling down an imprecation upon the Yankees. He was seated in one corner of the jail, telling a young boy named Hiram Smith what to tell his family after he was gone. Tears streamed down young Hiram's face as he listened to the old man speaking in low, sad tones. How he dreaded relating all this to the tortured faces of Willis Baker's wife and sons.

From the hallway came the jailer, who stepped near the cells and called in a loud voice, "Hiram T. Smith!" Brushing the tears from his eyes, young Smith walked to the cell door and looked through the bars. At that moment, Provost Marshal Strachan appeared, asking "Is your name Hiram Smith?" "Yes, sir," was the polite reply. "Well, then, you will prepare yourself to be shot with the other men today at 1 o'clock."

Silence fell like a rock. Then, as Smith's fellow prisoners tried to comfort him, William Humphrey, reprieved but saddened at Strachan's diabolical choice of another youth who could neither read nor write, offered to write a letter to his family. His parents were dead, so young Hiram Smith dictated a letter to his sister, written in detail by the man whose place he would take before the firing squad.

Shortly after 12 o'clock, three wagons pulled up in front of the jail. There were three rough, pine coffins in each of the wagons, with the exception of one wagon which held four. The condemned men bade farewell to their companions and shook hands with their kind jailer, Captain Reed, who cried like a child. Like Marie Antoinette in her tumbrel, each man was made to sit upon his coffin and ride to his fate in the back of an open wagon.

Down the streets of old Palmyra went this mournful cavalcade. Few persons witnessed it at all. A sickening horror gripped the citizens of this community as they closed their shutters against a barbaric deed reminiscent of the dark ages, an act committed by full authority of the United States government which was, incredibly, demanding their fidelity and devotion daily. Now and then, a woman's voice could be heard, wailing as one laments the dead; and faint crying behind draped windows told of the mourning in Palmyra as that death train slowly wound its way to the fairgrounds.

East to Main Street, then south as far as the livery stable. East again, the creaking old wagon wheels adding their own part to the dirge that all nature was singing for these brave hearts that would soon beat no more. Shortly, the slow-moving cortège entered the Hannibal road as the beauty of the countryside appeared. Rural Marion County. How could she be the scene of such gore?

Only half a mile east of town stood the center of Palmyra's recreation, the pretty fairgrounds, where most of its important events were held. The citizens of Palmyra found it hard to accept that their fairgrounds were to be used for this crime against humanity; but their civil government had been usurped, and they were without voice in the military government now ruling over them.

The fences were thrown down when the wagons reached the fairgrounds, and the last leg of the fateful journey was completed when the small band of martyrs were halted within the circular ring of the amphitheater. Only about a hundred people watched in ghastly horror, but it was enough to remind one of the days of Rome and the slaughter of Christians as mere entertainment for heathen rulers.

The prisoners huddled together as their coffins were removed from the wagons and placed in a row about six feet apart, just to the east of the bandstand in the center of the ring. What a spectacle was being made of this madness! Next, the helpless men were made to sit upon the ends of their respective coffins. They were offered blindfolds, but only two accepted. A minister came forward, and the doomed men knelt upon the grass between their coffins and their executioners, while one last prayer was offered up to their Heavenly Father, who must have stood at the Gate in surpassing compassion, ready to welcome them Home.

At the conclusion of the prayer, they all resumed their seats upon their humble coffins. The minister shook hands all around, and Strachan followed suit. When Strachan reached Willis Baker, who was still defiant, Baker looked him straight in the eye and, refusing his hand, said, "Every dog shake his own paw!"

The scene that followed is difficult to describe in mere words. Seventy-five men were drawn up in dread array with weapons at their sides, as they stood only thirty feet back from those ten defenseless men who were being forced to pay for a deed in which they had no part. There were thirty soldiers in the front line, forty-five behind them as reserves! It was as if Goliath had come to do battle with little David.

There, in the fairgrounds arena, the awful spectacle was about to be played out. Ten pitiful human beings looked straight at their killers, who were waiting for the order to shoot. Captain Sidenor, a handsome man who was engaged to be married, was attired in his best suit of broadcloth with a shining white vest. He placed his hand over his heart and called out to his executioners, "Aim here, please." The other men, simply dressed in plain clothing, swallowed hard — or tried to, their mouths and throats dry with exhaustive fear. Wild thoughts raced through their minds. Would they be killed with one shot? Would they only be wounded and have to go through another volley at their vital organs? Would they be conscious and suffer great pain? Would someone fire into their brains? What a cruel, cruel thing is man's inhumanity to man!

"Ready!" The rattle of musket-locks almost stopped the heartbeat of every soul there. "Aim!" The thirty gun barrels were raised and aimed at the gently sobbing men who tried to think of mother and home and still appear as brave men in the service of their beloved South. The next word must have echoed around the whole Christian world. "Fire!"

What an irregular crashing and discharge of bullets there was. Thirty men, and so many of their shots went wild. Some believed there was poor understanding among the soldiers as to when to fire. It was evident that many of them were extremely nervous and had never murdered in cold blood before. War is one thing, but this was another, and they didn't relish their task. Some probably fired astray purposely, in hopes of standing faultless upon the Judgment Day.

Whatever the reasons, only three men were killed outright. Captain Sidenor's request had been met only too well. He fell forward with his hands clasped upon his bosom, his left leg drawn up and his muscular chest torn all to pieces. He did not move again. Two of the others fell backward upon their coffins, dead. All of the remaining prisoners fell forward upon the ground. Morgan Bixler had not been hit at all, but, in the despair of the moment, fell forward with the rest. It must have been a gruesome thing, indeed, for him to watch as the reserves moved in to finish the job.

With revolvers, they moved up to the wounded "rebels," as they called them, and fired at close range into the bodies that lay writhing and groaning in agony. The sight of their struggling and the sound of their moaning was sickening. Like wounded horses, they were "put out of their misery." Old Willis Baker died the hardest, gazing upon his assassins as they shot him seven times. The *Palmyra Courier*, which had sounded the constant drumbeat for this occasion, smugly reported, "The other seven were not killed outright; so the reserves were called in who dispatched them with their revolvers."[11]

At last, when all of the lifeless bodies were pronounced dead, their mangled corpses were gathered up from the blood-soaked arena, dumped into their coffins, and returned to town where friends and relatives claimed the precious remains.

Sometime after the War, when the troops were gone, the managers of the fair association refused to hold any more fairs on the old grounds. The place had become an Aceldama, and the citizens would not attend functions there. By 1883, all that was to be seen was a wheat field. A new fairgrounds was built in the northern part of town.

The news of the Palmyra Massacre sent shock waves around the entire world. The leading journals of the North reported it, with comment, in New York, Philadelphia, Boston, and elsewhere. The newspapers of London, The *Times*, the *Star*, and the *Herald*, published accounts and wrote editorials on the affair. It was a topic of discussion at two of Lincoln's cabinet meetings, and the South was ablaze with indignation and revulsion at the grisly killings. President Davis made a written demand upon the United States authorities to deliver General McNeil into his hands, with the warning that ten Union officers would be executed if McNeil were not surrendered forthwith. The demand was refused, but the Confederate government could not bring itself to emulate the dastardly deed and, consequently, did not follow through with the executions.

General McNeil was generally censured for his authorship and perpetration of the crime. He was denounced from the pulpit, in the papers, and from the hustings. On the other side, the occupying forces rallied to his support. General Merrill, his superior, stationed at Macon, fully approved and congratulated him. The Union newspapers of northeast Missouri applauded him, while hard-bitten Union sympathizers signed petitions to retain him as commander of their local troops. Lincoln rewarded him with a fat promotion to Brigadier General of U.S. Volunteers.

In 1880, President Hayes nominated him for U.S. Marshal, but bitter opposition quickly developed over his part in the Palmyra Massacre, and his confirmation by the U.S. Senate was defeated.

As to the profligate Strachan, his subsequent actions proved him to be totally depraved. On Sunday, less than twenty-four hours after the execution, the young Mrs. Humphrey called upon him in an effort to secure the release of her husband. Although he had been reprieved the day before, there were the wildest of rumors circulating throughout northeast Missouri. One was to the effect that McNeil was going to shoot ten men *every* Saturday until old Allsman showed up unharmed. Nearly beside herself after the event at the fairgrounds, she was grasping at every straw to save her husband from a like fate.

Strachan seized upon the weakness of the terrified young wife, who was there all alone with her small children. He reminded her that he could either have Mr. Humphrey released or shot, as he well pleased. There was nothing she wouldn't do to save the father of these little children, and Strachan knew it. The perverted price he demanded became known almost simultaneously with the act. Some passing soldiers observed the little step-daughter crying outside Strachan's building. They investigated at once and learned enough to know that Strachan had forced her to submit to him. Word spread among the soldiery, where there was scathing denunciation of him.

Even after such display of his base character, politics under military rule in wartime Missouri were so absurd that he was elected to the House of Representatives in that state — and often considered for the speakership of that strange body. A New Yorker by birth, he had lived in Missouri most of his forty-four years. In addition to his other sins, he had a lust for money and had been in the business of extracting money from prisoners in return for their release and other favors.

Finally, a Union officer brought charges against him in 1863, during his term in the House of Representatives. Other officers, having the utmost distaste for him, began to aid in the collection of evidence against him, shunning him socially and professionally at every chance. At the trial, he was charged with multiple offenses, including *embezzling, demanding large sums of money from prisoners, drunkenness, gross immorality,* and *placing levies upon the citizenry for release of certain prisoners..*

He was found guilty on two counts: *embezzlement,* and *prostituting his position as an officer for base and immoral purposes.* He was sentenced to imprisonment for one year and fined $680, but General Rosecrans, then his commander, said that he was the victim of persecution and ordered him released. It was January, 1864, fifteen months after the Palmyra Massacre, and Strachan set out for New Orleans.

Fortunately, for the good of humanity, Strachan wouldn't live long. He rambled around between New Orleans and Old Mexico for a while, before dying of consumption in a hotel in New Orleans on February 10, 1866, friendless and alone.

In 1901, the noble citizens of Palmyra formed themselves into an association known as The Palmyra Confederate Monument Association and began raising funds to memorialize the ten heroes who were so viciously murdered there forty years earlier by McNeil and Strachan. In 1907, they unveiled a stately monument of granite, topped by a marble statue of a Confederate soldier. On the south side of the sacred shrine is the date of the awful event, *October 18, 1862.* The north side contains two crossed swords and two olive branches. On the west face are the words: *Erected by the Confederate Monument Association and its Friends, Feb. 25, 1907.* But, most importantly, are the names graven upon the front of the granite block:

Capt THOMAS A. SIDENOR
WILLIS T. BAKER
THOMAS HUMSTON
MORGAN BIXLER
JOHN Y. McPHEETERS
HIRAM T. SMITH

SOUTHERN BY THE GRACE OF GOD

HERBERT HUDSON
JOHN M. WADE
FRANCIS W. LEAR
ELEAZER LAKE

Words by
Earnest Halphin.

Music by
Chas. W. A. Ellerbrock.

PUBLISHED BY MILLER & BEACHAM, BALTIMORE.
REPUBLISHED BY BLACKMAR & BRO. AUGUSTA, GA.

Richmond, VA
J W RANDOLPH
P H TAYLOR

Macon Ga   Mobile Al.
J. W. BURKE Agt H C CLARKE.

Savannah Ga
E KNAPP & CO

Montgomery Al
W. S. BARTON

Charleston S C
JOHN SIEGLING

B DUNCAN & CO. Lith COLUMBIA S C

BEAUVOIR

IX

RESEARCHING YOUR CONFEDERATE ANCESTORS

Before reading this chapter, please read the following caution label very carefully.

**WARNING: GENEALOGICOL RESEARCH MAY
BECOME ADDICTIVE!
THERE IS NO KNOWN CURE FOR THIS DISEASE.**

The following symptoms may occur: burning, itching eyes; tired feet; lack of sleep; confusion; temporary loss of memory; hallucinations; writer's cramp; rapid heartbeat; uncontrollable urge to visit courthouses; inordinate desire to walk through cemeteries; longing to speak with the dead; tendency to live in the past; habitual inclination towards excessive questioning; unnatural desire to take long trips; frustration; exhaustion; manic-depression; and telephonitis.

If symptoms persist, contact a professional genealogist.

How well we know it! Once bitten by the genealogy bug, you're hooked for good, and those of us who once equated libraries with absolute drudgery will sit for hours, yea days, reading microfilmed census reports, marriage records, and ships' passenger lists. Sometimes the results are immediately gratifying — sometimes it takes weeks to find a tidbit or two; but, the satisfaction of seeing the pieces of the puzzle fall into place, no matter how long it takes, is enough to keep you going onto the next clue.

Southerners love a good story, especially if it's about someone they know, or better yet, if it's about some of their kinfolks. And, kinfolks might be someone living now or someone who lived a hundred and fifty years ago. It makes no difference to a southerner — they're all kinfolks. And, those stories are the important aspect of genealogy to a southerner. The birth and death dates, names of children, and places of residence are what we write down; but, the uppermost questions in the mind are: What was he like? Was he good-natured? Did he ever kill anybody? Did he go to church every Sunday? Was he a horse thief? Was he brave? The answers to those questions are the ultimate goals in our pursuit of genealogy (or as we say down South, "lookin' up your family tree"), for therein lie the stories.

Most of us have a sort of haunting curiosity about our past. Even if it never causes us to start looking up our family tree, nearly all of us wonder where we came from and what kind of blood flows in our veins. If we happen to be lucky, some great-aunt or third cousin might have done all of the hard work for us, and all we have to do is ask for xerox copies. But, if we aren't so fortunate, as most of us aren't, we have to depend upon ourselves to make the long, diligent search which may or may not end with satisfactory results.

So, how does a novice begin — from scratch? Having been there, I can give you a few guidelines. The very first place to start is right at home. Ask your mother and father what they know about their family tree — names, dates, stories. Write down the facts. Record the stories on a tape recorder (or write them down if you have the patience). You will find varying types of information, depending upon the memory of your parents. My dad remembered all of the stories told by his parents and the two grandparents who were living when he was a child, but he didn't ask questions. So, there were lots of stories, but few names to go with them. My mother knew only one set of grandparents, and her own father died when she was only three, so very few names were available from that side. And, what was worse, she grew tired of hearing those old folks talk; consequently, she didn't remember a story!

The next step is to backtrack until you have talked to your oldest living relative. Obviously, that relative is going to remember further back than anyone else (unless he too was bored with hearing the old folks talk!). I waited until all of my grandparents were gone before learning the right questions to ask. It was then that I had to turn to *collateral* kinfolks (aunts, uncles, cousins) for further information. Even though your main interest centers on your *lineal* ancestors (parents, grandparents, great-grandparents, etc.) don't overlook queries to your aunts and uncles, for they have the same parents as your mother or father.

If any family member, no matter how distant the relation, is in possession of an old family Bible, find it and look for the records that so often were kept there (births, baptisms, marriages, and deaths). One of my lucky breaks came when I searched the old family Bible belonging to my grandmother's first cousin who lived in north Texas. It contained information which took me back five generations to the year of 1810.

After gathering as many names, dates, and places as you can, it is time to visit a genealogical library where you will find sundry lists of people of the past, among which you will probably find some of your ancestors. The census roles usually produce the richest initial yield. By utilizing them, you can begin to

483

narrow the location to state, then county, and eventually, to precinct.

Based upon the foregoing information, a trip to the appropriate county courthouse can produce good results. Some counties provide photo copies at a minimal charge in answer to requests by mail. Courthouses are rich in public records (marriages, deaths, court actions, wills, probates, etc.). Some courthouses contain cemetery records for the county, though the public library in the county seat is a better bet for those compilations. Bound copies of county and community histories are usually to be found in libraries and can sometimes offer a biographical sketch of the ancestor in question. And, finally, tombstones themselves can sometimes reveal a wealth of information that can lead you to another generation back.

The preceding outline for research is admittedly a brief treatment of a complex procedure, but it is understood that the family sleuth will certainly devise many ways of his own once he begins the journey backwards into his own personal past. At least it provides a basic method by which we can approach the main topic of this chapter: *how to find a Confederate ancestor.*

One of the primary objectives of a southerner's investigation of his pedigree (Yes, humans have pedigrees, too.) is to confirm that he has an ancestor who served in the Confederate military (or as we say, "fought in the War"). Not only does the discovery and authentication of such an ancestor add a measure of prestige, it qualifies the descendant for membership in one of the two national societies of Confederate descendants — the *United Daughters of the Confederacy* and the *Sons of Confederate Veterans.*

The procedure is much the same as searching for any ancestor. Find out what you can from your primary sources until you have the name of a man who would have been of age for military duty between 1861 and 1865. A point to remember: Before the War ended, the shortage of manpower in the South led to the enlistment of able-bodied males in every conceivable age group, as long as they could shoulder a gun. Though the average fighting man was in his thirties, there were soldiers as young as eleven and twelve and soldiers who were in their seventies. I've seen many a Confederate tombstone with a birthdate of 1846 or 1847, making that soldier a mere fifteen in the first or second year of the War.

The next step is to determine, from your information at hand, the state in which he was living at the time of the War. (Most men initially joined units within their own states, though there were some exceptions.) Using the addresses provided in the following pages, write to the appropriate agency in the state of his probable enlistment, requesting his military unit designation. (I found a great-great-grandfather named Hugh James McRae in the 1860 census of Fannin County, Texas. I wrote to the Texas State Library in Austin, who, in turn, wrote back with his unit designation: Co. C, 31st Regiment, Texas Cavalry, CSA). If, in the case of the border states of Kentucky, Missouri, and Maryland, you do not find your ancestor in a Confederate unit there, write to the surrounding southern states. Though each of those states, especially Missouri and Kentucky, furnished many soldiers to the Confederacy, some of the volunteers crossed into the Confederacy to enlist. For example, most of the secessionists from Maryland joined Virginia and North Carolina units upon Lincoln's rapid invasion of Maryland and subsequent suppression of civil government in that state.

Another approach you might take involves the Confederate pensions granted to needy Confederate veterans after the War. The individual southern states provided for the pensions, in the wake of refusals upon the part of the national government to aid our ailing, destitute veterans, and you will need to determine where the veteran was living *after the War*. Detailed affidavits were required of the applying veteran, and these documents reveal various types of information about the individual — including, of course, the unit or units in which he served. Write the appropriate state depository and request a search of its pension records.

When you have acquired the military unit designation of your ancestor, you have the information which qualifies you for membership in the SCV or the UDC; however, you will probably have been bitten so severly by the genealogy bug by this time that you will crave more information. It is then that you begin an in-depth research which could lead in several directions.

There are two primary sources which deserve mention here. One is the National Archives, whose holdings are described in the ensuing pages. (From this source, I learned several interesting things about my great-great-grandfather: color of eyes, complexion, height, weight, enlistment date, rank, date of rank, when present for duty and on leave, military pay, illnesses, etc.) The second source is the *unit history*, a researched story of the battles and assignments of a given Confederate military company, regiment, or battalion. If a unit history has been written, it can usually be found in book form in a public library or genealogical library. To my knowledge, the best source of unit histories *for sale* are to be found in the extensive catalogue of Morningside Bookshop, whose address appears at the end of the resource list in this chapter. Your ancestor just might be mentioned by name in one of these annals, but if not, you will at least be able to determine the battles in which he participated by tracing the record of the unit itself.

A reminder: Don't forget about those collateral antecedents. If you cannot authenticate a Confederate record for some lineal ancestor, pursue the records of your uncles who would be in the appropriate generation for Confederate military service. If they are blood-kin, as opposed to kin by marriage, their records will qualify you for membership in UDC or SCV.

The following list contains the addresses of the main depositories of material concerning Confederate soldiers. There are many smaller collections to be found throughout the South in city libraries, county and city historical societies, genealogical libraries, county courthouses, and museums; however, it is virtually impossible to list all of them and their holdings. The larger research centers in this guide will be more likely to contain the information you seek and can more readily direct you to some of the smaller depositories in their areas.

Each listing in this guide attempts to give a general description of items held by that particular agency. Keep in mind that all of these places have hundreds of additional items (i.e., manuscripts, books, diaries, occasional cemetery lists, and other offerings too numerous to mention here). The holdings described herein are those which are indexed and can be obtained in most cases by mail. In addition, most of these agencies will provide one or two items per letter of request at a modest charge or no charge at all.

For several reasons, difficulties may be encountered in your search for Confederate records. Many courthouses and city halls were fired by Yankee torches during the War, and many valuable records went up in smoke. Subsequent fires, though purely accidental, destroyed more records. In addition, official records from commanders in the field are incomplete, due partially to the neglect in writing reports and to the nature of the desperate movements towards the end. Following the War, the vengeful Radical Republican Congress placed such blame upon Confederate military leaders as to cause many Confederate generals to destroy or hide their military records. Some were only recently discovered under the floor of a Georgia bank.

SOUTHERN BY THE GRACE OF GOD

State of Alabama
Department of Archives & History
Montgomery, Alabama 36130

HOLDINGS:
Muster rolls; Record rolls; Lists of soldiers buried in various cemeteries throughout the country; Veteran and widow's pension applications; Newspaper items; Lists of condition of claims; Governor's correspondence; Individual letters; Regimental histories; 1907 Census of Confederate Soldiers Living in Alabama.

Auburn University
Auburn,
Alabama 36830

HOLDINGS:
Microfilmed Service Records from the National Archives.

Birmingham Public Library
Birmingham,
Alabama 35203

HOLDINGS:
Microfilmed Service Records from the National Archives.

SOUTHERN BY THE GRACE OF GOD

Public Library of Anniston and Calhoun County
Anniston,
Alabama 36201

HOLDINGS:
Complete Index to Alabama Confederate Military Service Records.

Huntsville Public Library
Huntsville,
Alabama 35901

HOLDINGS:
Complete Index to Alabama Confederate Military Service Records.

University of Alabama
University,
Alabama 35486

HOLDINGS:
Complete Index to Confederate Military Service Records for Alabama, Florida, Georgia, Mississippi, North Carolina, and South Carolina.

Arkansas History Commission
300 West Markham Street
Little Rock, Arkansas 72201

HOLDINGS:
Consolidated index to Confederate soldiers of all states;
Confederate service records, Arkansas; Index to Confederate
service records, Arkansas; Confederate pension records,
Arkansas; Confederate muster rolls and card index, Arkansas;
Confederate Veterans' Reunion of 1911, registration lists;
Confederate veterans' census of 1911, Arkansas; Official Records,
Confederate armies and navies, 1861-1865.

Arizona State College
Flagstaff,
Arizona 86001

HOLDINGS:
Microfilmed Service Records for Arizona Territory from the
National Archives; Complete Index to Arizona Territory
Confederate Military Service Records.

Arizona Historical Foundation
Tempe,
Arizona 85282

HOLDINGS:
Microfilmed Service Records for Arizona Territory from the National Archives; Complete Index to Arizona Territory Confederate Military Service Records.

University of Arizona
Tucson,
Arizona 85721

HOLDINGS:
Microfilmed Service Records for Arizona Territory from the National Archives; Complete Index to Arizona Territory Confederate Military Service Records.

Florida State Archives
Department of State
The Capitol
Tallahassee, Florida 32304

HOLDINGS:
Compiled Service Records of Confederate soldiers who served in organizations from Florida; Consolidated Index to Compiled Service Records of all Confederate soldiers; Florida Confederate Pension Application Files.

SOUTHERN BY THE GRACE OF GOD

University of South Florida
4202 East Fowler
Tampa, Florida 33620

HOLDINGS:
Complete Index to Florida Confederate Military Service Records.

University of Florida
13th & West University
Gainesville, Florida 32611

HOLDINGS:
Microfilmed Service Records for Florida from the National Archives; Complete Index to Florida Confederate Military Service Records.

Florida State Genealogical Commission
Jacksonville,
Florida 32203

HOLDINGS:
Complete Index to Florida Confederate Military Service Records.

SOUTHERN BY THE GRACE OF GOD

Hillsborough County Historical Commission
Tampa,
Florida 33602

HOLDINGS:

Microfilmed Service Records for Florida from the National
Archives; Complete Index to Florida Confederate Military
Service Records.

Georgia Department of Archives & History
330 Capitol Avenue, SE
Atlanta, Georgia 30334

HOLDINGS:

Compiled Service Records of Confederate soldiers who
served in organizations from the state of Georgia; Compiled
Service Records of Confederate soldiers who served in
organizations raised directly by the Confederate Government;
Confederate pension records, 1879-1960; Records of the
Governor's office and the office of the Georgia Adjutant and
Inspector General for the war years; Georgia Soldier Roster
Commission; Official Records of the Confederate Soldier's Home
of Georgia, 1901-1941.

Archives & Records Service
Commonwealth of Kentucky
Frankfort, Kentucky 40601

HOLDINGS:

Compiled Service Records of Confederate soldiers who served in organizations from Kentucky; Travels-in-Confederate-States Series.

Librarian
Kentucky Historical Society
Old State House Annex
Frankfort, Kentucky 40601

HOLDINGS:

Index to Kentucky Adjutant General's reports; Index to Kentucky Confederate pensions.

Department of Military Affairs
War Records Office
Daniel Boone Guard Center
Frankfort, Kentucky 40601

HOLDINGS:

Records of the Adjutant General's report.

Murray State University
Murray,
Kentucky 42071

HOLDINGS:
Complete Index to Kentucky Confederate Military Service Records; Microfilmed Service Records for Kentucky from the National Archives.

Western Kentucky University
Bowling Green,
Kentucky 42101

HOLDINGS:
Complete Index to Mississippi Confederate Military Service Records.

Louisiana State Archives & Records Service
Post Office Box 44222, Capitol Station
Baton Rouge, Louisiana 70804

HOLDINGS:
Records of Louisiana Confederate soldiers and commands; Complete Index to Louisiana Confederate Military Service Records; Microfilmed Service Records for Louisiana; Applications for Confederate pensions in Louisiana.

Louisiana State University
Highland Road
Baton Rouge, Louisiana 70803

HOLDINGS:

Microfilmed Service Records for Louisiana from the National Archives; Microfilmed Service Records for Mississippi from the National Archives; Complete Index to Louisiana Confederate Military Service Records.

Louisiana State University
Alexandria,
Louisiana 71301

HOLDINGS:

Complete Index to Confederate Military Service Records for Louisiana and Mississipppi.

New Orleans Public Library
New Orleans,
Louisiana 70112

HOLDINGS:
Complete Index to Louisiana Confederate Military Service Records; Microfilmed Service Records for Louisiana from the National Archives.

Maryland State Archives
350 Rowe Boulevard
Annapolis, Maryland 21401

HOLDINGS:
Miscellaneous collection of books which contain several histories of Confederate military units.

Mississippi Department of Archives & History
War Memorial Building
Box 57
Jackson, Mississippi 32905

HOLDINGS:
Official Confederate Military Records of Mississippi soldiers; Some original muster rolls of Mississippi organizations in the Confederacy; Pension applications of Confederate veterans and widows; Microfilmed Service Records for Mississippi from the National Archives.

University of Southern Mississippi
Hattiesburg,
Mississippi 39401

HOLDINGS:

Microfilmed Service Records for Mississippi from the National Archives; Complete Index to Mississippi Military Service Records.

General William D. McCain
Adjutant-in-Chief
Sons of Confederate Veterans
Southern Station, Box 5164
Hattiesburg, Mississippi 39401

HOLDINGS:

This is the general headquarters of SCV, which holds all of the official records of that organization. Much genealogical information is contained in the application forms for membership alone. It is not known what other information is held by this organization, nor to what extent they offer services. (This address will be good for a few more years. The organization has acquired land for a new headquarters south of Franklin, Tennessee. When the permanent headquarters are opened, the address will be Highway 31 South, Franklin, Tennessee 37064.)

SOUTHERN BY THE GRACE OF GOD

Adjutant General's Office
Industrial Drive
Jefferson City, Missouri 65101

HOLDINGS:
Records of approximately one-half of the 40,000 Missourians
who served in the Confederacy with Missouri units; Confederate
pensions, 1913-1924; Applications for Confederate Home;
Cemetery records for the Confederate Home Cemetery.

North Carolina Department of Archives & History
Post Office Box 1881
Raleigh, North Carolina 27602

HOLDINGS:
Roster of North Carolina troops in the War; Adjutant
General's *Roll of Honor* of North Carolina Confederate troops;
Pension Records of Confederate veterans and their widows;
Microfilmed Service Records for North Carolina soldiers from
the National Archives.

The Genealogical Research Library
Wiley Post Memorial Building
State Capitol Complex
Oklahoma City, Oklahoma 73105

HOLDINGS:

Pension applications for Oklahoma Confederate veterans and their widows; List of Confederate soldiers buried in Oaklawn Cemetery, Wynnewood, Oklahoma; Rosters of Confederate soldiers from various southern states, including Indian Territory; Records from Confederate Home; UCV listings of Confederate veterans living in Oklahoma.

South Carolina Department of Archives & History
1430 Senate Street
Columbia, South Carolina 29211

HOLDINGS:

Compiled Service Records of South Carolina Confederate soldiers, with Index; Pension records; Confederate General & Staff Officers & Nonregimental Enlisted Men.

Tennessee State Library and Archives
403 Seventh Avenue North
Nashville, Tennessee 37219

HOLDINGS:

Service Records of Tennessee Confederate soldiers; Consolidated Index to Confederate veterans from all states; Register of appointment of officers in the Confederate service from Tennessee; Tennessee Confederate pension records for soldiers beginning in 1891 and their wives beginning in 1905;

Rosters of officers of regiments and battalions; Confederate election returns for Tennessee officers; Records of the arrival and departure of Tennessee Confederate troops at Richmond; Strength reports; Clothing and ordnance account books; Records relating to Confederate naval personnel; Letters to and from Generals Hood, Longstreet, Polk, and Pillow; Benton County claims against the Confederates; Confederate Pension Board minutes, files, and investigation reports; Records of the Confederate Soldiers Home at *The Hermitage.*

Cossitt-Goodwyn Libraries
33 South Front Street
Memphis, Tennessee 38103

HOLDINGS:
Microfilmed Service Records of Tennessee Confederates from the National Archives.

Tennessee Polytechnic Institute
Cookeville,
Tennessee 38501

HOLDINGS:
Complete Index to Tennessee Confederate Military Service Records.

Knoxville Public Library
Knoxville,
Tennessee 37902

HOLDINGS:

Complete Index to Tennessee Confederate Military Service Records.

Confederate Research Center
Hillsboro Junior College
Hillsboro, Texas 76645

HOLDINGS:

Records of Hood's Texas Brigade (1st, 4th, & 5th Texas Infantry Regiments, 18th Georgia Infantry Regiment, 3d Arkansas Infantry Regiment, and the Infantry companies of Hampton's Legion); Microfilms of Texas newspapers published during the War; Numerous letters, diaries, and manuscripts.

Archives Division
Texas State Library
1201 Brazos Street
Austin, Texas 78711

HOLDINGS:

Muster roll abstract records for Texas soldiers serving the Confederacy; Confederate audited military claims; Confederate pension applications from veterans and their widows.

Rice University
6100 Main Street
Houston, Texas 77005

HOLDINGS:
Complete Index to Texas Confederate Military Service Records.

Houston Public Library
Houston,
Texas 77002

HOLDINGS:
Complete Index to Confederate Military Service Records for Alabama, Arkansas, Kentucky, Maryland, Mississippi, Missouri, and South Carolina.

Archives Division
Virginia State Library
Richmond, Virginia 23219

HOLDINGS:

Confederate military records for soldiers who served in Virginia units; Compiled manuscript rosters for Virginia Confederate soldiers; Pensions to Confederate veterans, their widows, and "maiden or widowed daughters"; Complete Index to Virginia Military Service Records from the National Archives.

Business Office
United Daughters of the Confederacy
Memorial Building to the Women of the South
328 North Boulevard
Richmond, Virginia 23220

HOLDINGS:

This is the general headquarters of the UDC, which holds all of the official records of that organization. Much valuable genealogical material is contained in the applications and worksheets submitted by each member. In addition, many records concerning Confederate soldiers throughout the Confederacy are located here. It is not known to what extent the UDC provides genealogical research assistance.

Military Service Records (NNCC)
National Archives (GSA)
Washington, D.C. 20408

SOUTHERN BY THE GRACE OF GOD

HOLDINGS:

I. COMPILED MILITARY SERVICE RECORDS

A jacket-envelope shows the name of the soldier, the name of the state from which he served, the name of his company and regiment, and his rank. The cards and papers in the envelope show other information, such as the dates of changes in the soldier's rank, the date and place of his enlistment and discharge, his occupation, and his personal description. If the soldier was captured, they may show the date of his death if it occurred in camp, or the date of his release and parole. References to the original records are included on the cards.

II. RECORDS RELATING TO NAVAL AND MARINE PERSONNEL

A. *Compiled Hospital and Prison Records*

The cards and papers show the name of the person and his ship or station and such other information as the date and place of capture, release, or parole, and place of confinement; and the date, place, and cause of admission to a hospital and the date of discharge. References to the original records are included on the cards.

B. *Reference Cards and Papers*

The records show the name and rank of the sailor or marine and are a possible means of finding other information about his service.

C. *Shipping Articles*

An entry on the shipping articles shows the name of the enlisted man, his rating, his signature, and the date of his enlistment.

D. *Muster Rolls and Payrolls*

An entry in the rolls shows the name and rank of the naval serviceman or marine.

III. CITIZENS FILES
   A. *Confederate Citizens File*
   A document shows such information as the name of a citizen, the place of his residence, and the date of his transaction with the Confederate Government.
   B. *Union Provost Marshal Citizens File*
   The records show such information as the name and place of residence of a person, together with a varying amount of information depending upon the circumstances in the case.

IV. AMNESTY AND PARDON RECORDS
   A. *Amnesty Oaths*
   An oath shows the name of the person, the place the oath was taken (which was often the place of his residence), the date the oath was taken, and usually the signature of the person taking the oath. Some oaths give the ages and personal descriptions of persons taking the oaths and, in appropriate instances, the identifications of their Confederate military organizations.
   B. *Amnesty Papers*
   An application file gives the name, age, occupation, and place of residence of the applicant, together with autobiographical data.

V. COTTON SALE RECORDS
   Each entry shows the name of the cotton seller, the name of the county or parish in the state where the sale occurred, the number of bales of cotton sold, the value in Confederate currency or bonds, and the date of sale.

Broadfoot Publishing Co.   Morningside Bookshop
Route #4, Box 508-C   258-260 Oak Street
Wilmington, N.C. 28405   Dayton, Ohio 45410

HOLDINGS:
To my knowledge these are the largest retail distributors of books about the War Between the States. Especially pertinent are the extensive lists of histories of various military units available for sale. In addition, both companies reprint many old titles which have been out of print and unavailable for many years. Write and request their catalogues.

UNITED DAUGHTERS OF THE CONFEDERACY

The noble women of the South are the true unsung heroes of the late War. Jefferson Davis, in 1889, dedicated his monumental work to "the women of the Confederacy, whose pious ministrations to our wounded soldiers soothed the last hours of those who died far from the objects of their tenderest love; whose domestic labors contributed much to supply the wants of our defenders in the field; whose zealous faith in our cause shone a guiding star undimmed by the darkest clouds of war; whose fortitude sustained them under all the privations to which they were subjected; whose annual tribute expresses their enduring grief, love, and reverence for our sacred dead; and whose patriotism will teach their children to emulate the deeds of our revolutionary sires."[1]

Phoebe Yates Pember, matron of Chimborazo Hospital in Richmond during the War, remembered their wartime role as nothing less than monumental.

> The women of the South had been openly and violently rebellious from the moment they thought their states' rights touched. They incited the men to struggle in support of their views, and whether right or wrong, sustained them nobly to the end. They were the first to rebel — the last to succumb. Taking an active part in all that came within their sphere, and often compelled to go beyond this when the field demanded as many soldiers as could be raised; feeling a passion of interest in every man in the gray uniform of the Confederate service; they were doubly anxious to give comfort and assistance to the sick and wounded. In the course of a long and harassing war, with ports blockaded and harvests burnt, rail tracks constantly torn up, so that supplies of food were cut off, and sold always at exorbitant prices, no appeal was ever made to the women of the South, individually or collectively, that did not meet with a ready response. There was no parade of generosity; no published lists of donations, inspected by public eyes. What was contributed was given unostentatiously, whether a barrel of coffee or the only half bottle of wine in the giver's possession.[2]

On September 10, 1894, the UDC was organized in Nashville, Tennessee, as the result of two southern ladies, Mrs. Anna Davenport Raines of Savannah, Georgia, and Mrs. Caroline Meriwether Goodlett, of Nashville. In fact, the organization is the second oldest patriotic association in the country, second only to the DAR who were organized in 1890; but, in practice, the UDC is the oldest, for it officially grouped itself together in 1894 from many local and statewide ladies' aid societies, who, since the late 1860's, had been working independent of each other all across the South.

The name was inspired by an incident at West Point, Georgia, on April 30, 1886. Former Confederate General John B. Gordon, standing on the rear platform of a train, introduced President Davis's daughter, Varina Anne (Winnie) Davis, to an applauding throng as "The Daughter of the Confederacy." The next day, at the unveiling of the monument to Benjamin H. Hill in Atlanta, the Honorable Henry W. Grady introduced her again as "The Daughter of the Confederacy," and the name was indelibly imprinted upon the hearts of the southern people.

In every southern state, women were collecting themselves into groups, raising money for hospitals, Confederate Homes for aging soldiers, monuments, and relief in general for widows and orphans of Confederate soldiers. By 1890, the women in Texas, Missouri, and Georgia were calling themselves *Daughters of the Confederacy*. In 1892, the Ladies Auxiliary of the Confederate Soldiers Home in Tennessee adopted the same name. In 1894, Mrs. Raines suggested to Mrs. Goodlett that "we should have one name and one badge all over the South."[3] The organizational meeting grew out of that suggestion, and Mrs. Goodlett became the first President of the National Association of the Daughters of the Confederacy on September 10, 1894. A year later, the name would be changed to the *United Daughters of the Confederacy*.

The objectives of the UDC are described as *historical, educational, benevolent, memorial* and *patriotic*. They are a non-political, non-sectarian group of ladies who endeavor to see that southern heroism is remembered, that a truthful history of the War is preserved, and that the priceless southern heritage is passed from generation to generation. Throughout the years they have provided relief, scholarships, and support to those in need. Their motto is: *Love, Live, Pray, Think, Dare*. The official flag of the UDC is the Stars and Bars, the first flag adopted by the Confederate Congress in 1861.

The United Daughters of the Confederacy have appropriately been called "the monument builders." Dixie's beautiful landscape is literally studded with sparkling monuments to the glory of the South, and it can be truthfully said to the credit of those invincible ladies of the UDC that the vast majority of the memorials have been placed by the UDC alone; morever, it would be difficult to find a Confederate monument anywhere, whether sponsored by any other organization or state agency, that wasn't built by major contributions from the UDC.

Membership in the organization is available to ladies over sixteen years of age who are lineal or collateral descendants of men and women who served honorably in the Army, Navy, or Civil Service of the Confederate States of America or who gave material aid to the Cause, provided that authentic proof can be furnished. The UDC places a special emphasis upon honor and honorable service; therefore, it is explicit in their tradition of high standards that no applicant whose ancestor took the oath of allegiance prior to April 9, 1865, shall be considered eligible. Membership is accomplished at the local level through a chapter. The national headquarters, whose address appears in the preceding list, can help a prospective applicant locate the nearest chapter.

There is an auxiliary association for boys and girls under twenty-one called the Children of the Confederacy. It has similar goals and is sponsored by the UDC.

SONS OF CONFEDERATE VETERANS

After the War it was only natural that the former soldiers of the Confederacy should desire to meet together and reminisce about the late conflict. Meetings began to spring up throughout the South, though large gatherings were made more difficult by the ever-present overseers of Reconstruction rule. As the carpetbag governments were systematically overthrown and the wearing of the gray, as well as the display of the Confederate flag, became legal once again, the soldiers increased their activities and associations. On June 10, 1889, the venerable southern veterans organized themselves into a national association called the *United Confederate Veterans*. On December 11, 1889, an impromptu mass meeting was held at 8 o'clock in the evening in the hall of the Washington Artillery, New Orleans' largest assembly hall. Taking advantage of the presence of eight southern governors, many former generals, and thousands of former soldiers and officers who were in town for the funeral of President Davis, the newly organized UCV, under the leadership of former General John B. Gordon, called for the meeting, which was the largest gathering of former Confederates since the end of the War. Probably the most awesome and sentimental reunion ever held in North America, it ushered in the era of the great Confederate reunions which were held every year in a chosen southern city.

One of the most celebrated reunions was held June 3-7, 1917, a reunion made conspicuous by its location in the unlikely place of Washington, D.C. By tradition, the veterans always marched in a magnificent parade. This time, they would have the honor of passing in review before the first southern President of the United States since the War — Woodrow Wilson. A noble Virginian, proud of his Confederate past, President Wilson attended the memorial service at the Confederate Monument in Arlington Cemetery on June 3, birthday of

511

Jefferson Davis. On June 7, he received the review of the troops in gray in the most magnificent such spectacle since the grand review of Federal troops at the end of the War fifty-two years earlier. The *Philadelphia Press* was somewhat overcome with the splendid march of the aged gray veterans.

> No inauguration procession within the memory of Washington brought forth enthusiasm that compared at all with that which swept over the hundreds of thousands who saw the thin gray line today. It had no shimmer of gold lace, no rich investiture to view with the hundreds of parades that this city of gorgeous spectacles has known. But it did have more poignant humanity, more direct appeal to the American heart, than all the processions that have preceded it. Every rank had its distinctive note. Every little gray group held a cheer compelling or a tear compelling motive.
>
> Never can I forget that last rank of the Arkansas Division. We were waiting opposite the President's stand fronting the White House. There was the usual flutter of flags, the usual applause as the fine old commanders of the division on their sedate livery stable horses paced by. Then came the ranks on foot. Clad in the peculiar death gray of the backwoods, they came with the slow, silent movement of oncreeping age. Almost involuntarily my eyelids narrowed to get the full effect of the drifting gray haze. As it crept up to the stand the fog resolved itself into its human elements. Faces made noble by wartime sacrifice and by hardships nobly endured stood out softly in the mist, each like a Moses carved from cloud by a Michelangelo. Never have I seen such fitting of leonine mane and beard to the human countenance as in the ranks of those Arkansas Veterans that came last. Never have I seen such majesty of Americanism as in the

slow, loving salute with which they turned their faded eyes and withered hands towards the President. It was an expression of eternity, of the unquenched and unquenchable spirit that, please God, will hold America together while life lasts.[4]

Like the daughters of these declining veterans, the sons had been active in assisting their fathers after the War. The realization of the need for a national effort resulted in the formation of the United Sons of Confederate Veterans on July 1, 1896, at a meeting of the United Confederate Veterans. Former Confederate General Stephen D. Lee gave them a commission. "To you, Sons of Confederate Veterans, we submit the vindication of the Cause for which we fought; to your strength will be given the defense of the Confederate soldier's good name, the guardianship of his history, the emulation of his virtues, the perpetuation of those principles he loved and which made him glorious and which you also cherish. Remember it is your duty to see that the true history of the South is presented to future generations."[5]

The organization adopted the Confederate battle flag as its official emblem and elected J.E.B. Stuart, Jr., as its first leader. In 1912, the name was shortened to *Sons of Confederate Veterans*. As long as there were national reunions of the UCV, the SCV held its national meetings at the same time and place.

Until the last veterans were gone, the SCV remained faithfully committed to the aid and assistance of the old soldiers and their wives, continuing afterwards to care for their widows and orphans. In keeping with the admonition of General Stephen D. Lee, the SCV upholds essentially the same ideals embraced by the UDC. They are committed to historical, benevolent, patriotic, and educational pursuits and are unalterably opposed to general encroachments by the Federal government upon states' rights. The constitution of the organization expressly forbids endorsement of a particular political party, candidate, or religious denomination. SCV strives to maintain the immutable values of honor, justice, and Christian virtue and to pass on to subsequent generations the southern culture.

Many grand monuments across the South have been erected by the men of the SCV. They have helped maintain the Confederate Memorial Hall in Washington, purchased the property encompassing the Manassas Battlefield, and acquired and maintained *Beauvoir*, the Shrine of the South, at Biloxi. One of their main goals has always been the collection and preservation of relics of the War, coupled with the preservation of the truth surrounding that conflict and its relics. Pursuant to that aim, they publicize local southern history, celebrate Confederate anniversaries, display the flag, commemorate the Confederate dead, and try to reply to the many false and slanderous statements against the Confederacy, which, in today's hypnotized society, is a full-time labor. The association has fallen heir to bestowing the Confederate Medal of Honor — posthumously, of course — upon the outstanding heroes of the War, the first such presentation having been made in 1976.

Other activities include the publishing of a national magazine, the *Confederate Veteran,* and the sponsorship of auxiliary reenactment groups. The reenactment units are composed of authentically outfitted men who participate in mock battles, parades, and historical exhibitions. The most important charge given to each local chapter (called a *camp*) is that it observe a memorial day in honor of Confederate soldiers on the appropriate day each year.

The highlight of the year is the general convention, held in a selected southern city in August. During the four-day event, there are business meetings, receptions, evening dinners and lectures, a memorial service honoring departed members, sight-seeing tours, a memorial service at a Confederate monument, and renewing of old acquaintance. The crowning event is the cotillion ball on Saturday night, an affair complete with live orchestra and hoop-skirted debutantes escorted by men in Confederate uniforms.

The Sons of Confederate Veterans describes itself as "an association of male descendants of those who served the Confederate States of America."[6] Membership is available to lineal or collateral descendants of those who served in the Confederate military until the end of the War, who died in prison, who were killed in service, or who were honorably discharged. An applicant must be twelve years of age and able to provide proof of Confederate lineage. If there is no camp near the prospective member, membership may be held in the general headquarters camp. For further information, it is suggested that an applicant write to the headquarters address given in the preceding list of Confederate research centers.

THE CONFEDERATE MEMORIAL ASSOCIATION

A couple of years ago, while reading through the *letters to the editor* column in one of my favorite southern magazines, I ran across one that seemed to stay with me. The writer was dismayed over his inability to locate an ancestor who had been in the Confederate military. The consequent impossibility of attaining membership in SCV was disappointing to him, and he protested that his failure to produce a bona fide Confederate ancestor cast no reflection upon his allegiance to the Cause, that he was just as southern as those who hold documented proof, and that there should be formed a group of southern partisans who only require loyalty to the South as a prerequisite for membership.

It was a point well-made. For years I was one of those who didn't even know how to begin the search, and I consider myself fortunate to have been rewarded at the end of that quest with some documented proof. But, we have to face the facts. There are those who will never find a Confederate ancestor for any of a multiplicity of reasons, but who, nevertheless, have a burning desire to join kindred hearts in perpetuating the splendid Confederate legacy.

It was the next issue of the magazine that introduced many of us to the *Confederate Memorial Association*. It is precisely the organization that fills the bill. Any friend of the South may join upon paying a membership fee which is currently only $20.

The Confederate Memorial Association administers the Confederate Memorial Hall in the heart of Washington, D.C. The only southern shrine in the nation's capital, the Hall has miraculously survived debts, burdensome local taxes, and an onslaught from the IRS.

The building itself has a colorful history. Standing among a group of Victorian mansions in the Logan Circle district, the circle having been designed as a part of the original L'Enfant plan for the city, the four-story building in the second Empire style is listed on the National Register of Historic Places. What makes it especially dear to southern hearts is that it was purchased to house and care for aged Confederate veterans many years ago. As the number of Veterans dwindled, the association turned to other philanthropies which included donations to Walter Reed Hospital, the Salvation Army, the Red Cross, and two French orphans who were adopted during World

War I.

In 1919, the first floor of the mansion was converted into a convention hall, library, and museum. Since then, the Confederate Memorial Hall has been the scene of patriotic, historical, and benevolent activity. A few years ago, the association was infused with new life and began a renovation of the hall in conjunction with a vigorous membership drive.

Today, the Hall serves as the Confederate Embassy, firmly establishing the southern presence in Washington. Members of the Confederate Memorial Association will receive a quarterly newsletter called the *Embassy News*, a catalogue of available gift items, and invitations to southern balls and Congressional receptions. The embassy is available to members upon visiting the nation's capital.

The present Ambassador is John Edward Hurley. For passport and membership information, write to:

The Confederate Embassy
1322 Vermont Avenue, N.W.
Washington, D.C. 20005

OFFICIAL PROGRAMME

ALABAMA DIVISION
UNITED CONFEDERATE VETERANS

TWENTY-FIFTH ANNUAL REUNION

TUSCALOOSA, ALABAMA
OCTOBER TWENTY-FIRST, TWENTY-SECOND

1925

X

RECOMMENDED READING

Since the War Between The States, a regrettable effort has been made to grind out histories of that period which simplify that complex era into a struggle between good and evil, the North representing the good and you-know-who cast as the eternal evil. Southerners could see it happening immediately after the War. Alarmed at the prospect of history books which would teach their own children a lie, several capable southerners set about writing their own accounts of the War. Jefferson Davis finished his scholarly work, *The Rise and Fall of the Confederate Government*, in 1881. Edward Pollard was quick to publish his *Southern History of the War* in 1866 and *The Lost Cause* in 1867. Many of the Confederate generals and lesser officers wrote their memoirs, in which invaluable information pertaining to the battlefield was faithfully recorded for posterity. Some enlisted men wrote what they saw, one of the best-known works being Pvt. Sam Watkin's *"Co. Aytch"*.

With the passing of time, it is disconcerting to note that the situation has not improved and, if anything, has worsened.

Many factors enter into the foggy picture that we now receive as our view of the War, besides the overriding premise that the victors write the histories — and in the way they please, regardless of veracity. One hindrance to truth nowadays is the lack of time spent in reading, the vast majority of us opting for the television set where we can be as lazy as the Caesars of old Rome, while our information is fed to us like Pablum. The problem in that method is that TV is not an intellectual medium; therefore, we get the trite, narrow views that are currently in vogue. One of the other elements, among many that serve to cloud the facts, is the pseudo-intellectual notion that history must be constantly reinterpreted in light of the trend of the day. For about twenty years, it has been fashionable to dwell deeply upon social issues; consequently, the actions of history's players have been revised to reflect the War as a great social movement.

History should stand upon its own record. We are misdirected to play tricks upon the dead. It is especially unfair to educate our southern school children upon modern, *northern-produced*, trendy textbooks which portray the South as an evil force which has always been a little out of step with democracy, and which, if not for the strong power of the Union in the 1860's, would have destroyed the American dream. It may sound like hogwash when synopsized like that, but a glance through any current school history text will bear it out. In fact, most any "patriotic" television special that alludes to the period paints us as the belligerent, often ending with a P.T. Barnum style rendition of the South-hating "hymn", *The Battle Hymn of the Republic*.

Unless southerners are quite willing to take on the media, the education system, and the weather vane politicians, about the best thing we can do is to read and become educated ourselves. Then, individually, we can pass on bits of truth when the need arises. At least, we will be armed with truth if there be enough "secesh" left among us to tackle one of the aforementioned and formidable Goliaths who tread upon our priceless heritage so carelessly. Oh, for the right rock!

Nevertheless, the fringe benefit of reading southern history is the element of pure pleasure. I cannot recall reading a single southern account of the War that wasn't intriguing, and ninety-five percent of them have been absolutely delightful. When one can get away from this modern critical pessimism and become absorbed in the comfortable reading of a southern author who happens to be on our side for a change, the satisfaction of being southern takes on a broader and more gratifying perspective.

Southern history includes much, much more than the War Between the States and related issues, and southern literature is a vast and varied field; however, most of the following recommendations are pertinent to the War era for all of the reasons discussed in this book. In some instances, I have found it desirable to include remarks about the selection, in hopes of helping the reader to make a better choice. I have not read all of the books listed here but have included them in this section upon the recommendation of southern scholars and historians who have expertise in that field.

There are thousands of other books by southern authors, books which space alone will not permit me to include. This offering is intended to assist the beginner in locating a substantial amount of knowledge about his Confederate heritage. Hopefully, he or she will become addicted to the point that an insatiable appetite will result in a relentless search for further volumes and, in the long run, an unending loyalty to our heritage of the Lost Cause.

A Diary from Dixie, Mary Boykin Chestnut, edited by Isabella D. Martin and Myrta Lockett Avary, D. Appleton & Co., New York, 1905. (This is the first version of the most popular diary of the War to be printed. Mrs. Chestnut was dead, and the editors, for various reasons, elided many of her remarks — in fact, more than half of them. Still, it is a rich source of history and is quoted as much or more than any eye-witness account of the period.)

A Diary from Dixie, Mary Boykin Chestnut, edited by Ben Ames Williams, Harvard University Press, Cambridge, Mass., 1980. (This is the expanded edition of Mrs. Chestnut's diary, nearly twice as long as the original publication. Her wit, charm, intelligence, sarcasm, and southern loyalty combine to make this book one of the most fascinating books in the English language.)

A History of Morgan's Cavalry, Basil W. Duke, Indiana University Press, Bloomington, Indiana, 1960. (General Duke was a brother-in-law to General Morgan and took over the command after the death of General Morgan.)

A Lieutenant of Cavalry in Lee's Army, G.W. Beale, Boston, 1918.

An Aide-de-Camp of Lee, Charles Marshall, Boston, 1927.

A Rebel Private, Front and Rear, W.A. Fletcher, Austin, Texas, 1954. (A realistic account of soldier life in Hood's Texas Brigade.)

A Rebel's Recollections, George Cary Eggleston, New York, 1875.

A Southern Woman's Story, Phoebe Pember Yates, edited by Bell I. Wiley, Mockingbird Books, St. Simons Island, Ga. (This is a 1959 version of the 1879 original, providing an interesting look at the world's largest hospital, Chimborazo, at

Richmond, through the eyes of a thirty-seven-year-old Jewish lady who became matron there during the War. An intensely southern lady, she writes with humor and great pathos.)

Autobiographical Sketch and Narrative of the War Between the States, Jubal A. Early, Philadelphia, 1912. (This work is largely a compilation of General Early's articles in the Southern Historical Society Papers.)

Autobiography, Eppa Hunton, Richmond, 1933. (Colonel Hunton's history of Garnett's brigade includes a discussion of Longstreet's responsibility for the failure at Gettysburg.)

Caddo: 1,000, Viola Carruth, Shreveport Magazine Publishing, Shreveport, La., 1970. (The history of Shreveport and Caddo Parish, this book contains two excellent chapters on the War and Reconstruction in north Louisiana.)

"Co. Aytch", Sam Watkins, Morningside Press, Dayton, Ohio. (This is the 1982 reprint of the 1882 edition. Watkins, an enlisted man, wrote his own history of the War as he saw it from the ranks of Company H, 1st Tennessee Infantry.)

Confederate Echoes, Albert T. Goodloe, Zenger Publishing Co., Washington, D.C. (This is a 1983 reprint of the 1893 original by a Confederate lieutenant who became a Methodist minister after the War. Concerned by the northern distortion of facts that have continued to this day to find their way onto the pages of history, Goodloe wrote his account in an effort to give southerners the straight of it.)

Confederate Military History, twelve volumes, edited by Gen. Clement A. Evans, Confederate Publishing Co., Atlanta, 1899. (Now available from Broadfoot Press, Wilmington, N.C.)

Confederate War Poems, edited by Walter Burgwyn Jones, Bill Coates Ltd., Nashville, 1984. (An excellent collection of poetry from the War era. Includes the Magnolia Cemetery Ode, considered to be the most perfect ode ever written. Its author, Henry Timrod, was acclaimed by Alfred Lord Tennyson, who said that Timrod deserved to be called the "laureate of the South.")

Dixie After the War, Myrta Lockett Avary, Houghton-Mifflin Co., Boston, 1937. (Originally published in 1906. This work has long been recognized as one of the best accounts of the horrors of Reconstruction, though Mrs. Avary, herself, admits that even she hadn't seen the worst of it. Virginia was spared some of the atrocities of the lower South. Her book is flawed by an unrealistic portrayal of Lincoln as the kind, fatherly overseer of the human race, who had very little to do with the War. If it sounds out of context for a southern woman, it can be recalled that Reconstruction was so very cruel that southerners were forced to dwell upon the "what if" to the extent that a belief was conjured up that Lincoln would have been beneficent after the War. His assassination aroused sympathy, and some southerners were almost hypnotized into perceiving him as a kind old country philosopher who couldn't possibly have prosecuted such a bloody war.

It should also be noted that Mrs. Avary moved north for a while where she worked as a journalist. Living in the land of Lincoln, she was undoubtedly caught up in the fanatic effort to canonize the man. Wishing to get along with her associates, and, out of a sincere desire to foster good relations between North and South, she probably glorified the war president under a barrage of social pressure. Mrs. Avary, in editing Mary Chestnut's diary in 1905, removed many of the derogatory references to Lincoln, which were restored in the 1980 version.

Still, this look at Reconstruction by Mrs. Avary fills a void in that field and is heartily recommended to modern readers. It is impossible to read this gripping account without drawing a parallel between the persecution of the white South during that period and similar events of the past twenty years, a parallel Mrs. Avary could not have foreseen in 1906.

Dixie After the War has been widely quoted by historians and has been called the literary forerunner of *Gone With the Wind*.)

Detailed Minutiae of Soldier Life in the Army of Northern Virginia, Carlton A. McCarthy, Richmond, Va., 1882.

Embattled Confederates: An Illustrated History of Southerners at War, Bell Irvin Wiley and Hirst D. Milhollen, Bonanza Books, New York, 1964. (An interesting collection of southern photographs pertaining to the War.)

Facts the Historians Leave Out, John S. Tilley, The Paragon Press, Montgomery, Ala., 1951. (A small book of refutations of northern myths in history textbooks.)

Father Ryan's Poems, Abram J. Ryan, John B. Piet Pub., Baltimore, 1880. (The wonderful collection of the poems of Ryan, the "Poet-Priest of the Confederacy.")

Five Tragic Hours, James Lee McDonough and Thomas L. Connelly, University of Tennessee Press, Knoxville, 1983. (The story of the disastrous Battle of Franklin.)

Four Years in the Stonewall Brigade, John Overton Casler, Morningside Press, Dayton, Ohio, 1982.

Four Years With General Lee, Walter H. Taylor, New York, 1877.

Full Many a Name, Mabel Goode Frantz, McCowat-Mercer Press, Jackson, Tenn., 1961. (The story of Sam Davis.)

Generals in Gray, Ezra J. Warner, Louisiana State University Press, Baton Rouge, 1959. (An easy to use reference, providing a thumbnail sketch of each of the 425 Confederate generals. Warner is no southern admirer, and the book should be used only as a starting place. He also did a work called *Generals in Blue.*)

Gray Fox, Burke Davis, Fairfax Press, New York, 1981. (This is a reprint of the 1956 edition. *Gray Fox* is a must for the student of Lee and the fighting in Virginia. It is concise, easy to read, and riveting. Once the reader begins, it is hard to put this book down.)

Gray Ghosts and Rebel Raiders, Virgil Carrington Jones, Mockingbird Books, Atlanta, 1956. (For those who have wondered about the activities of Col John S. Mosby, the "Gray Ghost," this book outlines vividly his daring career behind the enemy lines. In addition, other raiders and partisan rangers are studied. Northern troops are shown to be the devils they were in the Virginia theater of war. Jones paints a vivid picture of Yankee Gen. Phil Sheridan as he laid waste the Shenandoah Valley. It is unfortunate that the author was not more judicious in the use of cursing throughout the narrative.)

History of Marion County, Missouri, R.I.Holcombe, E.F. Perkins Pub., St. Louis, 1884. (An old, hard-to-find, local history, it is nevertheless valuable for its story of the wicked Palmyra Massacre, the cold-blooded slaying of ten southern soldiers by official Yankee decree.)

History of the Coles-Cooke Brigade, Henry W. Thomas, Atlanta, 1903.

History of the Twentieth Tennessee Regiment, William J. McMurray, Elder's Bookstore, Nashville. (This is the 1976 reprint of the 1904 version.)

Hood's Texas Brigade, J.B. Polley, New York, 1908. (A history of General John Bell Hood's Brigade, with the most detailed and informative material on the Gettysburg action at Devil's Den and Little Round Top.)

I'll Take My Stand, Harper & Row Pub., New York. (The 1962 edition of the famous 1930 essays by twelve southern writers, whose association centered around Vanderbilt University at Nashville. Five of them were poets, two were novelists, one was an English professor, two were historians, one was a journalist, and one was a psychologist. The scholarly essays have one thing in common: They articulately advocate the old southern way of life and warn of the urban, industrial, melting-pot psychosis that was already at work in 1930.)

I Rode With Stonewall, Henry Kyd Douglas, Chapel Hill, 1940. (A personal first-hand account by one of Jackson's staff officers.)

Jeb Stuart, John W Thomason, Jr., New York, 1930. (A marine colonel looks at his hero, the flamboyant and inspiring "Cavalier of Dixie.")

Jefferson Davis, Clement Eaton, The Free Press, New York, 1977.

Jefferson Davis, Herman S. Frey, Frey Enterprises, Nashville, 1978. (A good, short book on the life of the great president. This is the version usually found at souvenir shops near historic attractions throughout the South. It contains the seldom seen photograph of the funeral procession in New Orleans that astounded the smug north, who thought they had "reconstructed" southerners to the point that they had rejected the memory of President Davis.)

Jefferson Davis: American Patriot, Hudson Strode, Harcourt, Brace, and Co., New York, 1955.

Jefferson Davis, Constitutionalist: His Letters, Papers, and Speeches, edited by Dunbar Rowland, Mississippi Dept. of Archives & History, 1923.

Jefferson Davis: Private Letters, 1823-1889, edited by Hudson Strode, Harcourt, Brace, & World Pub., 1966. (The letters selected by Strode present an opportunity to look into the mind of Davis. One can't help but be impressed with the intelligence, compassion, and sincerity of the Confederate president after reading the words he penned to his wife, his children, and friends. Despite two years of cruel imprisonment, there are no words of bitterness to be found in his correspondence.)

Jefferson Davis: Tragic Hero, Hudson Strode, Harcourt, Brace, & World Pub., New York, 1964.

John Bell Hood and the War for Southern Independence, Richard M. McMurry, University Press of Kentucky, Lexington, 1982.

Kentucky Cavaliers in Dixie, George Dallas Mosgrove, McCowat-Mercer Press, Jackson, Tenn., 1957.

Kirby Smith's Confederacy — The Trans-Mississippi South, 1863-1865, Robert L. Kerby, Columbia University Press, New York, 1972.

Lee's Last Campaign, Clifford Dowdey, Little, Brown & Co., Boston, Mass., 1960.

Life and Campaigns of Major-General J.E.B. Stuart, H.B. McClellan, Richmond, 1885.

Life and Labor in the Old South, Ulrich B. Phillips, Little, Brown & Co., Boston, 1963. (Phillips is *the* authority on slavery. A much-neglected book in today's craving for the sensational and the prurient, it nevertheless presents the facts as they were. The history of the cotton industry and its work force are examined in scholarly fashion. The title is apt for the book.)

Life of General Nathan Bedford Forrest, John Allan Wyeth, Morningside Press, Dayton, Ohio. (This is the 1975 reprint of the well-known biography of 1899.)

Memoirs of the Civil War, William W. Chamberlaine, Washington, 1912. (Chamberlaine was a soldier in Gen. A.P. Hill's corps, Army of Northern Virginia.)

Memoirs of the Confederate War for Independence, Heros von Borcke, New York, 1938. (The Prussian baron volunteered for Confederate service and rode with Jeb Stuart.)

Military Memoirs of a Confederate, E.P. Alexander, Morningside Press, Dayton, Ohio. (1974 reprint of the 1907 edition.)

Morgan and His Raiders, Cecil Fletcher Holland, The MacMillan Co., New York, 1942.

Old Baldhead: General R.S. Ewell, Percy Gatling Hamlin, Strasburg, Va., 1940.

Old Jube: A Biography of General Jubal A. Early, Millard Kessler Bushong, Boyce, Va., 1955.

Pat Cleburne, Confederate General, Howell and Elizabeth Purdue, Hill Junior College Press, Hillsboro, Texas, 1973. (The definitive work on Pat Cleburne, the Irish-born Confederate general who earned the sobriquet, "The Stonewall Jackson of the West.")

Personal Reminiscences of General Robert E. Lee, J. William Jones, New York, 1875. (Written by the same man who wrote the first biography of Jefferson Davis. Jones was a close friend of Lee's, serving as chaplain at Washington College while Lee was its president. The work is valuable for its first-hand view of the legendary southern knight and the attitudes of his contemporaries toward him.)

Rebel Boast, Manly Wade Wellman, New York, 1956.

Rebel Rose, Ishbel Ross, Mockingbird Books, St. Simons Island, Ga., 1954. (One of the inspiring books about an almost forgotten heroine of the War, Rose O'Neal Greenhow. This book is highly recommended. It is one of those books that holds one's attention through suspense and intrigue, for it is about a southern woman who chose to stay in Washington after secession of the southern states, acting as a spy for the new Confederacy. It was a dangerous life, and she moved in the highest of Washington's social and political circles. The dignified Mrs. Greenhow was imprisoned, threatened, followed, and banished to the Confederacy in due course. Her untimely end came off the coast of North Carolina while in the service of her beloved Confederacy. She drowned trying to make her way ashore with enough gold to weight her body down in the rough seas. A true heroine of the South.)

R.E. Lee, Douglas Southall Freeman, Charles Scribner's Sons, New York, 1934. (Recognized as the major work on Lee, it is in four volumes and is considered the ultimate biography of Lee.)

Recollections and Letters of General Robert E. Lee, Robert E. Lee, Jr., New York, 1905.

Recollections of a Confederate Staff Officer, Moxley G. Sorrell, New York, 1917.

Reminiscences of the Civil War, John B. Gordon, Morningside Press, Dayton, Ohio. (This is a 1985 reprint of General Gordon's 1903 work. An interesting book. Gordon was with General Lee's army at the end.)

Robert E. Lee, John Esten Cooke, New York, 1871. (Though the book may be hard to find, it is worth the effort. Cooke was an ante-bellum writer by profession and the cousin of Jeb Stuart's wife.)

Sam Davis, Hero of the Confederacy, Edythe Johns Rucker Whitley, Blue & Gray Press, Nashville, 1971. (Though the first part of this book gets bogged down in genealogy, the story of Sam Davis is there — all of it. Drawing from rich sources, Mrs. Whitley spins the pitiful tale and includes many touching tributes in the last chapter. This book needs to be read.)

Southern History of the War, Edward A. Pollard, Fairfax Press, New York, 1977. (Originally published as a two-volume work in 1866, it now is available in a handsome one-volume edition of 1,255 pages. If you want a feel for the times, this is the book to read. Pollard was the editor of the *Richmond Examiner*, and he wrote the book while the war was happening. At war's end, then, he was ready to publish quickly, and we soon had a southern version to offset the barrage of cover-ups that emanated from the north. We are indebted to Pollard for sharing the great wealth of information he had at his command as editor of a newspaper in the Confederate capital. He is sharp with his criticism of Yankee barbarity but too sharp in his constant disagreement with President Davis over government policy in nearly every area. A stricken South could have better been served after the War by kind words for a president who was imprisoned in Fortress Monroe during the time that Pollard was producing his history. Allowing for his personality conflict with the president, *Southern History of the War* is an absolute must for the modern reader.)

Southern Horizons: The Autobiography of Thomas Dixon, IWV Pub., Alexandria, Va., 1984. (Dixon wrote the enormous success, *The Clansman*, which was based upon his bitter memories of Reconstruction. He spent his youth growing up in the hard days of that era in North Carolina. Although I have not read this book, it is included here with a recommendation by *Southern Partisan Magazine*, along with a caution. The reader should be warned that revisionist editors have tampered with Dixon's forthrightness by adding footnotes here and there in an effort to explain away the author's intent.)

Southern Side; or, Andersonville Prison, R. Randolph Stevenson, Turnbull Brothers, Baltimore, 1876. (A good answer to those who would perpetuate the myth of southern cruelty at the Confederate prison in Georgia.)

Stonewall Jackson and the American Civil War, George F.R. Henderson, New York, 1936. (A standard work, it is valued for its discussion of the inability of Lee to return to the successful and daring tactics he used with Jackson. A thorough study of the warfare waged during Stonewall's brief span of life in the conflict.)

Story of the Confederate States, Joseph D. Terry, Arno Press. (A 1979 reprint of the 1895 edition which was published in Richmond by B.F. Johnson.)

The Army of Tennessee, Stanley F. Horn, University of Oklahoma Press, Norman, 1952. (High on the recommendation list, Horn's work is the definitive work on the major Confederate army otuside the Richmond theater. Horn was the recognized authority on the Army of Tennessee.)

The Battle of New Market, William C. Davis, Doubleday & Co., Garden City, N.Y., 1975.

The Clansman, Thomas Dixon, Jr., University of Kentucky Press, Lexington, 1970. (Reprinted from the 1905 original, this book is a revelation to most modern Americans who are never exposed to the truth about times in the South after the War. Dixon wrote this story as, in his description, a "historical romance" of the era. The characters are fictional, but the story is based on the happenings of his childhood. His characters are mirror images of people he knew. The book was so controversial that it was reportedly "banned in Boston" and, conversely, clamored for in the South. It became so popular that it inspired the epic silent film of 1915, *The Birth of a Nation*. The fly in the ointment is Dixon's strange affinity for Lincoln. He labors through a good part of the first half of the book to convince his southern readers of the "goodness" of the man who brought them the horrors of war and the resultant afflictions of an occupying army and freedmen so despised by Dixon. For all of its puzzling, drifting beginning, though, it is an essential book for understanding the plight of the white South after the War. Dixon is a master at developing a story.)

The Confederate States of America, E. Merton Coulter, Louisiana State University Press, Baton Rouge, 1950.

The Civl War Day by Day, An Almanac, 1861-1865, E.B. and Barbara Long, Doubleday & Co., Garden City, N.Y., 1971. (This book is as essential to the avid reader of the history of the War as is a dictionary to a writer. The major events of the war years are chronicled day by day. In addition, there are several special studies at the end of the book, making the entire work an excellent reference that will be used over and over. The only drawback is that the authors are not southern, and the bias, though subtle, shows. Confederate successes are downplayed, while Yankee routs are merely orderly retreats. Southerners, who are used to reading around the bias, will find a handy tool in this volume.)

The Death of a Nation, Clifford Dowdey, Alfred A. Knopf Pub., New York, 1958. (Hooray for Clifford Dowdey! He writes for us. You don't have to wonder who's side he's on. After reading this book, you'll agonize over the defeat at Gettysburg and realize how close we came to victory. Well worth the reading, even if it does have an unpleasant end.)

The Flags of the Confederacy: An Illustrated History, Devereaux D. Cannon, Jr., St. Luke's Press, Memphis, and Broadfoot Publishing, Wilmington, N.C., 1988. (This is the latest, most inclusive, and informative work on the subject.)

The History of a Brigade of South Carolinians, J.F. Caldwell, Marietta, Ga., 1951.

The History of the United Daughters of the Confederacy, by a committee of their membership, Garrett and Massie Pub., Richmond, 1938. (A very readable and informative book about the UDC — its origin, goals, rules, and impressive accomplishments through 1938.)

The Last of the Confederate Privateers, David and Joan Hay, Crescent Books, Great Britain, 1977. (An interesting tale of Captain John Clibbon Brain, of the Confederate States Navy.)

The Leopard's Spots, Thomas Dixon, Jr., Irvington Publishers, New York. (A 1979 reprint of the 1902 edition by the same author who wrote *The Clansman*.)

The Long Surrender, Burke Davis, Random House, New York, 1985.

The Lost Cause, Edward A. Pollard, E.B. Treat & Co., New York, 1867. (This version of the War appeared one year after Pollard's *Southern History of the War* and is not as lengthy.)

The Memorial Volume of Jefferson Davis, J. William Jones, W.M. Cornett & Co., Dallas, 1890. (This 672-page book is now a rarity. I have been able to find two copies. Information written on the flyleaf of each book indicates that one was purchased in Beef Creek, Indian Territory, in 1890, while the other was bought at an auction in Hillsboro, Texas, on September 22, 1891, for 65 cents. It is not known how many of these were published, but Jones was the first to get out a biography after the death of President Davis, which occurred on December 6, 1889. The biography, with the blessing of Mrs. Davis, was out in 1890, and, due to the extreme popularity of the deceased President of the Confederacy, it must have sold in record numbers. A most valuable work, done by a man who knew Davis well, it contains minute details concerning the funeral and burial of the president. Letters of condolences, dispatches from notables, and records of who attended and where they rode or marched in the procession are here preserved for posterity.)

The Orphan Brigade: The Kentucky Confederates Who Couldn't Go Home, William C. Davis, Doubleday & Co., Garden City, N.Y.,1980.

The Private Mary Chestnut, C. Vann Woodward and Elizabeth Muhlenfeld, Oxford University Press, New York, 1984.

The Rise and Fall of the Confederate Government, Jefferson Davis, D. Appleton & Co., New York, 1881. (The monumental and celebrated work that Davis wrote at *Beauvoir,* his seaside home. Be careful to look for the two-volume work. There is an abridged version of only one volume on library shelves now.)

The Seven Days, Clifford Dowdey, Little, Brown, & Co., Boston, 1964.

The Story of a Cannoneer Under Stonewall Jackson, Edward A. Moore, New York, 1907.

The Story of a Confederate Boy in the Civil War, David E. Johnston, Portland, Ore., 1914.

The Story of the Confederacy, Robert Selph Henry, Peter Smith Pub., Gloucester, Mass. (A 1970 reprint of the 1931 original edition.)

The Story of the Great March, George W. Nichols, Corner House, Williamstown, Mass., 1972. (This is not a southern book. It is pure Yankee through and through. Written by Brevet Major Nichols, aide-de-camp to the infamous General Sherman, it was published in 1865, as soon as Nichols could get to a printer. Its value to us, as southerners, is in the revelation of the northern attitude towards the southern race. Nichols had utter disdain for southerners, considering them an inferior order of life. He uses words like "extermination" and "annihilation" and revels in the fun of burning and destroying southern property. The "judgment of the Christian world," writes Nichols, has justified Sherman in his barbarity. "This rebel horde should be swept from the earth." Those who doubt that our ancestors contended with arbitrary death at the hands of the invaders need to read this book. Nichols, and others like him, saw themselves as the instruments of God in bringing the "terrible swift sword" of justice to the South. If that meant genocide, then so be it. Nichols was a product of the anti-South rhetoric that had permeated the north for years, a rhetoric which became a war frenzy. Such frenzied, fanatic passion pushes many over the brink, directly into the arms of a waiting Sherman or Hitler.)

The Women of the South in War Times, Matthew Page Andrews, 1920.

This Band of Heroes, James McCaffrey, Eakin Press, Austin, Texas, 1985.

War Years With Jeb Stuart, William Willis Blackford, New York, 1945.

When the World Ended: The Diary of Emma LeConte, edited by Earl Schenck Miers, Oxford University Press, New York, 1957.

In addition to the foregoing list of ninety-three books, intended to get the new reader started upon a good, solid, southern footing, I feel compelled to mention two periodicals. Both magazines are doing an admirable work in the area of southern pride and heritage, and I couldn't be more privileged than to call my readers' attention to these two publications with a hearty recommendation for a subscription to each one.

SOUTHERN BY THE GRACE OF GOD

Southern Living, edited by Gary McCalla, is published monthly in Birmingham, Alabama. Current subscription price is $21.95 per year in the southern states, although specials are to be had from time to time. All new subscriptions should be sent to P.O. Box C-119, Birmingham, Alabama 35283. (*Southern Living* probably needs no introduction to most readers. If you are not receiving it, your next door neighbor probably is. And, it can be found on most news-stands throughout the South. The magazine has become very popular, due primarily to its guiding principle of presenting the South in a most positive light, which, by the way, was no easy task when the magazine began. Northern writers, and some southerners who tried to curry favor with the press for lucrative positions, had been having a heyday ripping the South apart. Muck writers could be had a dime a dozen. Then, there appeared upon the scene *Southern Living,* a magazine devoted to the beautiful South, its wonderful people, its matchless heritage — the *true* South.

I can remember hearing, at the outset, that it would not survive. Northerners scoffed. Why did the South need a magazine — as if to say, "Can they read down there?" Well, not only did it survive, but it is one of the success stories that we all like to tell about. So, if you want to learn to cook like a southerner, make quilts, plant a garden, landscape your property, build a southern home, learn about southern history, build a gazebo, travel across Dixie, or do anything else that makes southern life enjoyable, you'll find it here. There's nothing negative in this high-class magazine.

Incidentally, they're buying it up north, too, but it costs them more up there. Maybe they laughed too loud!)

Southern Partisan, edited by Richard M. Quinn, is published quarterly in Columbia, South Carolina. Current subscription rates are $12.00 per year. All new subscriptions should be sent to P.O. Box 11708, Columbia, South Carolina 29211. (This is the conservative literary voice of the South that is heard too dimly nowadays. In a day and age when writers are the most liberal segment of society, it is refreshing to open *Southern Partisan* magazine and find a collection of southern authors engaging in intellectual combat with the liberals who have burdened us down with busing, pornography, rampant crime, hamstrung police forces, and no control of our local society.

This is a publication for the serious reader. It deals with politics and politicians, usually calling a spade a spade. For those southern politicians who embrace northern liberalism from time to time, there is the Scalawag Award, and the hammer comes down hard.

Southern Partisan keeps abreast of the times and reports them like our hometown newspapers ought to but don't. Their conservative editorials sound like the ones we used to read in our southern newspapers before Gannett bought them up. The Confederate flag comes in for a lot of criticism by the liberals nowadays, and this magazine races to the rescue like all of us would like to do if we had a way to go. There's also a lot of Confederate history included in the issues, and they're not afraid to say that we were right and the Yankees were wrong!

There are six editors and several contributing writers on the staff, and even though total agreement cannot be expected on every issue, you can bet that most of the editorializing will come down on the conservative side. It's a delightful magazine; really, it ought to be in every high school library in the South.)

A third periodical is making its debut in May, 1988, under the name of the *Journal of Confederate History*. It is described as "a quarterly devoted to the publication of scholarly articles on the War Between the States." As an alternative to the 1880's treatment of the War by the Federal Government, called the *Official Records of the War of the Rebellion*, this new publication advertises itself as "an Official Record created by those who rebelled." It is published four times a year at the price of $12 per issue. Each issue is in the form of a paperback book of approximately 200 pages. Subscriptions should be addressed to The Guild Bindery Press, Box 2071, Lakeway Station, Paris, Tennessee 38242.

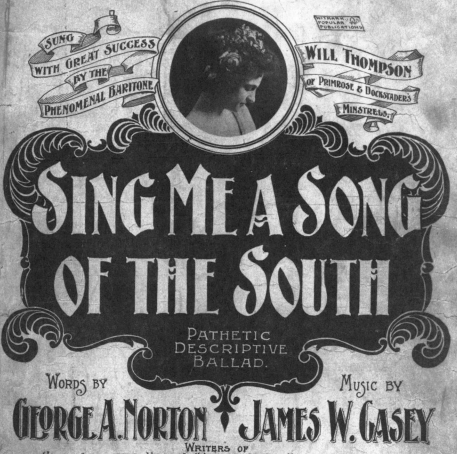

Also sung with Immense Success by ADA GREENHALGH.

SUNG WITH GREAT SUCCESS BY THE PHENOMENAL BARITONE

WITMARK POPULAR PUBLICATIONS

WILL THOMPSON OF PRIMROSE & DOCKSTADER'S MINSTRELS

SING ME A SONG OF THE SOUTH

PATHETIC
DESCRIPTIVE
BALLAD.

WORDS BY

MUSIC BY

GEORGE A. NORTON  JAMES W. CASEY

WRITERS OF
"IN THE SHENANDOAH VALLEY," "WHERE IS MY BOY TO-NIGHT," ETC. ETC.

5 BAND. ORCHESTRA. BANJO. MANDOLIN. GUITAR.

NEW YORK
WITMARK BUILDING

M. WITMARK & SONS

CHICAGO
SCHILLER BUILDING.

LONDON   TORONTO   HAVANA

MINNIE HINES,
SHEET MUSIC.
18 KENNEDY ST.
BRADFORD, PA

Acknowledgement

I once read that no one writes a book all by himself, and, while I can't vouch for everyone, I can say that it is certainly true in my case. In addition to my mother and father, Elba and Alma Grissom, who suffered through this whole thing with me, and my brother, Pat, who supplied me with several necessary things, including a home xerox machine, I wish to thank the following institutions and individuals for their contributions, no matter how great or small, to this work now completed:

The governors of all of the southern states, with a special thanks to Governor Hunt of Alabama, and former Governor Edwards of Louisiana.

The librarians and staff of the many libraries I visited during the preparation of this volume, including especially the Nashville Metropolitan Libraries; the Public Library, Wynnewood, Oklahoma; the Metropolitan Libraries of Oklahoma City; the Bizzell Memorial Library, University of Oklahoma; the County Bookmobile, Garvin County, Oklahoma; the Carnegie Library, Eufaula, Alabama; the Public Library, Norman, Oklahoma; the Pontotoc County Historical & Genealogical Society Library, Ada, Oklahoma; the Public Library, Ada, Oklahoma; Linscheid Library, East Central State University, Ada, Oklahoma; Linebaugh Library, Murfreesboro, Tennessee; and the Tennessee State Library and Archives.

The Board of Directors of the Sam Davis Association; the Oklahoma Division, United Daughters of the Confederacy; and, the Gen. Joseph E. Johnston Camp, Sons of Confederate Veterans, Nashville, Tennessee.

Norman Burns (Manager, Sam Davis Home), Mary Vaughan Gallagher (President, Oklahoma Division, UDC), Bernice Seiberling (Director of Carnton), Delores Kestner (Curator, Carter House), James Hoobler (Executive Director, Tennessee Historical Society), Ralph Green (Commander-in-Chief, Sons of Confederate Veterans), Roberta Robertson (President, Tennessee Division, UDC), Dr. James Edwards (Chief of Protocol, Military Order of the Stars and Bars), Mrs. Donald Perkey (President-General, UDC), Mildred Logan (Assistant Editor, OU Press), Dr. William D. McCain (President Emeritus, University of Southern Mississippi), and Charles Smith (Lt.Commander-in-Chief, Military Order of the Stars and Bars).

Also, Jamie Walton, Sharon Burkes, Cheryl Smith, Joyce Jordan, Curtiss Baker, Troy Tipton, Ruth Hamernik, Betty Bobbit Poe, Jessie Glover, Leonora Beverly, Verna Dell Tolson, Velma Zinn, Mr. & Mrs. Dean Isaac, Mamie Farnham, Richard Shacklett, Dr. & Mrs. William F. King, Mr. & Mrs. Paul Mott, Marilyn Geiger, Mr. & Mrs. Roger Risenhoover, Delphia McNeill, Ouida Elliott Jones, Maynita Warren, James Cochran, Sharon Schantz, Beverly Cady, Devereaux Cannon, Mr. & Mrs. Lanier Merritt, Mr. & Mrs. Darrel Cole, Ginger Turner, Joann Schnorrenberg, David Holland, Ron Johns, Kemper Kimberlin, Carolyn Pruett, Jody Baltz, Darvis Cole, Karen Guy, Judy Guy, Louise Maxwell, Mrs. John Farringer, Jr., Corbyn Jacobs, Bob Ravenscraft, Rob Hager, Mr. & Mrs. Ed Joe Mitchell, Elizabeth Baker, Leta Ferguson, Georgia Kennemer, Sharon Calhoun, Howard Kelley, Leta Rae McClain, Carolyn Fox, Hazel Dunn, Steve Rogers, Jackie Purdy, Marthalie Johns, Albert Baxendale, Betty Earl, Cam Cox, Annie Meek, Jesse Wayne, Mr. & Mrs. Cletues Dixon, Mr. & Mrs. Conley Shirley, Al Thomas, and Dr. James L. Jackson.

A special word of gratitude goes to my friend, Leona Holland, formerly my high school English teacher, who constantly encouraged and urged me to write this book.

Notes

PREFACE

1. *Gone With the Wind*, MGM, from the introduction to the movie.
2. Pollard, Edward A., *The Lost Cause*, p. 752.

CHAPTER I

1. *My Mammy*, Joe Young, Sam Lewis, and Walter Donaldson, © 1920, Irving Berlin Music, New York.
2. *Detroit City*, Danny Dill & Mel Tillis, © 1963, Cedarwood Publishing Co., Nashville.
3. Purdue, Howell and Elizabeth, *Pat Cleburne, Confederate General*, p. 108.
4. *You Ain't Just Whistling Dixie*, David Bellamy, © 1979, Famous Music Corporation and Bellamy Brothers Music, New York.
5. Davis, Burke, *The Civil War: Strange and Fascinating Facts*, p. 13.
6. Ryan, Abram J., *Father Ryan's Poems*, pp. 53-54.

CHAPTER II

1. *My Home's in Alabama*, Teddy Gentry and Randy Owen, © 1980, Maypop Music, Nashville.
2. *Southern Style*, Knoxville, Tenn., July/August, 1987.
3. *Southern Partisan*, Volume III, No. 3, 1986, p. 7.
4. Mitchell, Steve, and Rawls, Sam, *How to Speak Southern*, p. 43.

CHAPTER III

1. Chestnut, Mary Boykin, *A Diary from Dixie*, p. 19.
2. *Ibid.*, p. 235.
3. *Ibid.*, p. 268.
4. Pollard, Edward A., *Southern History of the War*, p. 40.

CHAPTER IV

1. Chestnut, Mary Boykin, *A Diary from Dixie*, pp. 113-114.
2. Altman, James David, *Mr. Lincoln's War on the South*, p. 9.
3. *Ibid.*, p. 5.
4. Ross, Ishbel, *Rebel Rose*, p. 90.
5. *The War of the Rebellion: Official Records of the Union and Confederate Armies*, Volume I, Part 1, p. 294. The letter from Maj. Robert Anderson, USA, to Col. Lorenzo Thomas, Adjutant-General, US Army, is dated April 8, 1861.
6. Nichols, George W., *The Story of the Great March*, pp. 68, 81, 119, 139, 268, 277.
7. Tilley, John S., *Facts the Historians Leave Out*, p. 39.
8. *Ibid.*, p. 50.

9. *Ibid.*, p. 50.

10. Pollard, Edward A., *Southern History of the War*, p. 59.

11. Tilley, John S., *Facts the Historians Leave Out*, p. 51.

12. Dowdey, Clifford, *The Death of a Nation*, pp. 41-42.

13. *Ibid.*, p. 42.

14. Davis, Burke, *Gray Fox*, p. 131.

15. Alexander, E.P., *Military Memoirs of a Confederate*, p. 223.

16. Dowdey, Clifford, *The Death of a Nation*, p. 45.

17. *Histories of the Several Regiments & Battalions from North Carolina in the Great War, 1861-1865.*, Vol. 5, p. 264.

18. Chestnut, Mary Boykin, *A Diary from Dixie*, p. 495.

19. Jones, Virgil Carrington, *Gray Ghosts and Rebel Raiders*, p. 104.

20. Pollard, Edward A., *Southern History of the War*, p. 20.

21. Davis, Burke, *The Civil War: Strange and Fascinating Facts*, p. 34.

22. Pollard, Edward A., *Southern History of the War*, pp. 208-210.

23. *The War of the Rebellion: Official Records of the Union and Confederate Armies*, Volume XXVII, Part 3, p. 943.

24. Dowdey, Clifford, *The Death of a Nation*, p. 8.

25. Pollard, Edward A., *Southern History of the War*, pp. 628-629.

26. *The Lanyard*, Volume XIII, No. 5, p. 5.

27. Chestnut, Mary Boykin, *A Diary from Dixie*, p. 534.

28. *Ibid.*, pp. 92-93.

29. Dowdey, Clifford,*The Death of a Nation*, p.46.

30. Chestnut, Mary Boykin, *A Diary from Dixie*, p. 122.

31. Davis, Burke, *Gray Fox*, p. 110.

32. Pollard, Edward A., *Southern History of the War*, p. 105.

33. *Ibid.*, pp. 105-106.

34. *Appleton's Cyclopaedia of American Biography*, p. 391.

35. Pollard, Edward A., *Southern History of the War*, p. 119.

36. *The Lanyard*, Volume XIII, No. 5, p. 5.

37. Chamberlain, Joshua, *The Passing of the Armies*, pp. 258-

265.

38. Cooke, John Esten, *Life of Gen. Robert E. Lee*, p. 461.

CHAPTER V

1. McCain, William D., President Emeritus of the University of Southern Mississippi. I first heard Dr. McCain use this quote at the annual Confederate Memorial Day Service in Little Rock in April, 1976. After a diligent search of several months, we have not been able to locate the source of the quote. In searching his papers at the Mississippi Department of Archives and History, Dr. McCain was able to determine that he has been using the quotation for over forty years.

2. Pollard, Edward A., *Southern History of the War*, p. 656.

3. *Southern Partisan*, Volume V, No. 2, 1985, p. 36.

4. Pollard, Edward A., *Southern History of the War*, Vol. II, p. 142.

5. *Ibid.*, p. 365.

6. *Ibid.*, p. 365.

7. *Ibid.*, pp. 365-366.

8. Current, Friedel, and Williams, *A History of the United States Since 1865*, p. 10.

9. Carruth, Viola, *Caddo: 1,000*, p. 72.

10. *The Lanyard*, Volume XIV, No. 5, p. 2.

11. Current, Friedel, and Williams, *A History of the United States Since 1865*, p. 8.

12. Carruth, Viola, *Caddo: 1,000*, p. 73.

13. Adams, James Truslow, *The March of Democracy*, Vol. III, p. 204.

14. Carruth, Viola, *Caddo: 1,000*, p. 70.

15. *Ibid.*, p. 80.

16. *Ibid.*, p. 83.

17. *Southern Partisan*, Volume IV, No. 4, 1984, p. 56.

18. *Red Shirt Shrine*, p. 4.

19. *Southern Partisan*, Volume IV, No. 4, 1984, p. 55.

20. Current, Friedel, and Williams, *A History of the United States Since 1865*, p. 29.

21. Watkins, Sam, *"Co. Aytch"*, p. 49.

CHAPTER VII

1. Jones, J. William, *The Memorial Volume of Jefferson Davis*, pp. 27-28.

2. *Ibid.*, p. 52.

3. *Ibid.*, p. 54.

4. *Ibid.*, p. 55.

5. *Ibid.*, p. 61.

6. *Ibid.*, p. 28.

7. *Ibid.*, p. 110.

8. *Ibid.*, p. 212.

9. *Ibid.*, p. 301.

10. *Ibid.*, p. 340.

11. Strode, Hudson, *Jefferson Davis: Private Letters, 1823-1889*, p. 123. Part of the letter from Jefferson Davis to Varina Davis, written from Montgomery Alabama, on Feb. 20, 1861.

12. Jones, J. Williams, *The Memorial Volume of Jefferson Davis*, p. 317.

13. Watkins, Sam, *"Co. Aytch"*, p. 228.

14. Jones, J. William, *The Memorial Volume of Jefferson Davis*, p. 352.

15. *Ibid.*, p. 340.

16. *Ibid.*, p. 653.

17. *Ibid.*, p. 493.

18. *Ibid.*, p. 536.

19. Purdue, Howell and Elizabeth, *Pat Cleburne, Confederate General*, p. 39.

20. *Ibid.*, p. 69.

21. *Ibid.*, pp. 74-75.

22. *The War of the Rebellion: Official Records of the Union and Confederate Armies*, Volume X, Part 1, p. 584.

23. McKinnon, John L., *History of Walton County*, pp. 299-300.

24. Purdue, Howell and Elizabeth, *Pat Cleburne, Confederate General*, p. 392.

25. *Ibid.*, p. 75.

26. *Ibid.*, p. 419.

27. *Ibid.*, p. 420.

28. *The Land We Love*, Vol. II, p. 460.

29. Davis, Burke, *Gray Fox*, p. 9.

30. *Ibid.*, p. 5.

31. Jones, J. William, *The Memorial Volume of Jefferson Davis*, p. 310.

32. Davis, Burke, *Gray Fox*, p. 164.

33. *Ibid.*, p. 280.

34. *Ibid.*, p. 250.

35. Jones, J. William, *The Memorial Volume of Jefferson Davis*, p. 309.

36. Chestnut, Mary Boykin, *A Diary from Dixie*, pp. 330-331.

37. *Appleton's Cyclopaedia of American Biography*, p. 391.

38. Chestnut, Mary Boykin, *A Diary from Dixie*, p. 261.

39. Morningside Bookshop Catalogue, No. 16, p. 42.

40. Chestnut, Mary Boykin, *A Diary from Dixie*, p. 341.

41. Davis, Burke, *Gray Fox*, p. 353.

42. Wyeth, John Allan, *Life of General Nathan Bedford Forrest*, p. 128.

43. *Ibid.*, p. 135.

44. *Ibid.*, p. 393.

45. *Ibid.*, p. 425.

46. *Ibid.*, p. 628.

47. Whitley, Edythe Johns Rucker, *Sam Davis, Hero of the Confederacy*, p. 217.

48. *Confederate Veteran*, Nashville, Vol. III, p. 182.

49. Whitley, Edythe Johns Rucker, *Sam Davis, Hero of the*

Confederacy, p. 136.

50. *Ibid.*, p. 158.

51. *Ibid.*, p. 139.

52. Letter from Sam Davis to Charles and Jane Davis, Nov. 19, 1863. This heartbreaking letter can be seen at the small museum located behind the Sam Davis House near Smyrna, Tennessee.

53. *Confederate Veteran*, Nashville, Vol. IV, pp. 35-36.

54. *Ibid.*, Vol. XVII, p. 280.

55. *Ibid.*, Vol. XVI, cover of the December, 1908 issue.

CHAPTER VIII

1. *The Sparrow Hawk*, Vol. III, No. 3, pp. 43-44.

2. *The Daily Oklahoman*, March 4, 1951. The article was written by Welborn Hope.

3. Letter from J.W. Mayrant to Mrs. J.W. Mayrant, July 19, 1861, in possession of Wynnewood Historical Society, Wynnewood, Oklahoma.

4. Letter from Isaac W. Crabtree to W.B. Crabtree, April 18, 1863, in possession of Sandy Mott, of Wynnewood, Oklahoma.

5. *The Nashville Banner*, May 13, 1905. The article was written by Mrs. I.K. Reno, of Nashville, Tennessee.

6. *Ibid.*

7. *Ibid.*

8. *Ibid.*

9. Holland, Cecil Fletcher, *Morgan and His Raiders*, p. 347.

10. Thoma, Edison H., *John Hunt Morgan and His Raiders*, p. 109.

11. Pollard, Edward A., *Southern History of the War*, pp. 525-526.

CHAPTER IX

1. Davis, Jefferson, *The Rise and Fall of the Confederate Government*, dedication page.

2. Pember, Phoebe Yates, *A Southern Woman's Story*, p. 16.

3. Poppenheim, Merchant, McKinney, White, Wright, Hyde, Campbell, Woodbury, and Lawton, *The History of the United Daughters of the Confederacy*, p. 15.

4. *The Philadelphia Press*, June 7, 1917.

5. *What is the Sons of Confederate Veterans?* March 25, 1979.

6. *Ibid.*.

Bibliography

PUBLISHED BOOKS

Adams, James Truslow, *The March of Democracy*, Charles Scribner's Sons, New York, 1933.

Alexander, E.P., *Military Memoirs of a Confederate*, New York, 1907.

Augspurger, McLemore, and Shafer, *United States History for High Schools*, Laidlaw Brothers, River Forest, Ill., 1961.

Avary, Myrta Lockett, *Dixie After the War*, Houghton-Mifflin Co., Boston, 1937.

Botkin, B.A., *A Civil War Treasury of Tales, Legends, and Folklore*, Promontory Press, New York, 1960.

Carruth, Viola, *Caddo: 1,000*, Shreveport Magazine Publishing, Shreveport, La., 1970.

Chamberlain, Joshua, *The Passing of the Armies*, New York, 1915.

Chestnut, Mary Boykin, *A Diary from Dixie,* edited by Isabella D. Martin and Myrta Lockett Avary, D. Appleton & Co., New York, 1905.

Chestnut, Mary Boykin, *A Diary from Dixie*, edited by Ben Ames Williams, Harvard Univerity Press, Cambridge, Mass., 1980.

Cooke, John Esten, *Life of Gen. Robert E. Lee*, D. Appleton & Co., New York, 1871.

Current, Friedel, and Williams, *A History of the United States Since 1865*, Alfred A. Knopf, New York, 1967.

Davis, Burke, *The Civil War: Strange and Fascinating Facts*, The Fairfax Press, New York, 1960.

Davis, Burke, *Gray Fox*, The Fairfax Press, New York, 1956.

Davis, Jefferson, *The Rise and Fall of the Confederate Government*, D. Appleton & Co., New York, 1881.

Dowdey, Clifford, *The Death of a Nation*, Alfred A. Knopf, New York, 1958.

Duke, Basil W., *A History of Morgan's Cavalry*, Indiana University Press, Bloomington, Ind., 1960.

Freeman, Douglas Southall, *R.E. Lee*, Charles Scribner's Sons, New York, 1934.

Gibson, Arrell M., *Oklahoma, A History of Five Centuries*, Harlow Publishing Co., Norman, Okla., 1965.

Hay, David and Joan, *The Last of the Confederate Privateers*, Crescent Books, Great Britain, 1977.

Holcombe, R.I., *History of Marion County, Missouri*, E.F. Perkins, St. Louis, 1884.

Holland, Cecil Fletcher, *Morgan and His Raiders*, The MacMillan Co., New York, 1942.

Horn, Stanley, *The Army of Tennessee*, University of Oklahoma Press, Norman, Okla., 1952.

Jones, J. William, *The Memorial Volume of Jefferson Davis*, W.M. Cornett & Co., Dallas, 1890.

Jones, Virgil Carrington, *Gray Ghosts and Rebel Raiders*, Mockingbird Books, Atlanta, 1956.

Jordan, Robert Paul, *The Civil War*, National Geographic Society, 1969.

Kantor, MacKinlay, *If the South Had Won the Civil War*, Bantam Books, New York, 1960.

Kirwan, Albert D., *The Confederacy*, Meridian Books, Inc., New York, 1959.

Long, E.B. and Barbara, *The Civil War Day by Day, An Almanac, 1861-1865*, Doubleday & Co., Garden City, N.Y., 1971.

Lytle, Andrew Nelson, *Bedford Forrest and His Critter Company*, G.P. Putnam's Sons, New York, 1931.

McKinnon, John L., *History of Walton County*, Atlanta, 1911.

Miers, Earl Schenck, *The Golden Book History of the Civil War*, Golden Press, New York, 1963.

Nichols, George W., *The Story of the Great March*, Corner House Publishers, Williamstown, Mass., 1972.

Pember, Phoebe Yates, *A Southern Woman's Story*, edited by Bell I. Wiley, Mockingbird Books, St. Simons Island, Ga., 1959.

Phillips, Ulrich B., *Life and Labor in the Old South*, Little, Brown & Co., Boston, 1963.

Pollard, Edward A., *Southern History of the War*, Fairfax Press, New York, 1977.

Pollard, Edward A., *The Lost Cause*, E.B. Treat & Co., New York, 1867.

Poppenheim, Merchant, McKinney, White, Wright, Hyde, Campbell, Woodbury, and Lawton, *The History of the United Daughters of the Confederacy*, Garrett and Massie, Inc., Richmond, 1938.

Pratt, Fletcher, *Civil War in Pictures*, Garden City Books, Garden City, N.Y., 1955.

Purdue, Howell and Elizabeth, *Pat Cleburne, Confederate General*, Hill Junior College Press, Hillsboro, Texas, 1973.

Ramage, James A., *Rebel Raider*, University Press of Kentucky, Lexington, 1986.

Ross, Ishbel, *Rebel Rose*, Mockingbird Books, St. Simons Island, Ga., 1954.

Ryan, Abram J., *Father Ryan's Poems*, John B. Piet, Baltimore, 1880.

Strode, Hudson *Jefferson Davis: Private Letters, 1823-1889*, Harcourt, Brace, & World, Inc., 1966.

Thomas, Edison H., *John Hunt Morgan and His Raiders*, University Press of Kentucky, Lexington, 1975.

Tilley, John Shipley, *Lincoln Takes Command*, University of North Carolina Press, Chapel Hill, 1941.

Tilley, John S., *Facts the Historians Leave Out*, The Paragon Press, Montgomery, Ala., 1951.

Warner, Ezra J., *Generals in Gray*, Louisiana State University Press, Baton Rouge, 1959.

Watkins, Sam, *"Co. Aytch,"* Cumberland Presbyterian Publishing House, Nashville, 1882.

Whitley, Edythe Johns Rucker, *Sam Davis, Hero of the Confederacy*, Blue & Gray Press, Nashville, 1971.

Williams, T. Harry, *P.G.T. Beauregard: Napoleon in Gray*, Louisiana State University Press, Baton Rouge, 1954.

Wyeth, John Allan, *Life of General Nathan Bedford Forrest*, 1899.

DIARIES AND LETTERS

Diary of Eulalie McRae Burkes, Oct. 27 — Nov. 11, 1902, in possession of Winnie Whited.

Letter from Isaac W. Crabtree to W.B. Crabtree, April 18, 1863, in possession of Sandy Mott.

Letter from J.W. Mayrant to Mrs. J.W. Mayrant, July 19, 1861, in possession of Wynnewood Historical Society.

Letter from Sam Davis to Charles and Jane Davis, Nov. 19, 1863, in possession of Sam Davis Association.

BOOKLETS, PAMPHLETS, ESSAYS, NEWSLETTERS, ETC.

Altman, James Davis, *Mr. Lincoln's War on the South*, Charleston, S.C., 1987.

Confederate Veteran, Hattiesburg, Miss., Volumes XXIX and XXX.

Gone With the Wind, MGM, 1939.

McCain, William D., Confederate Memorial Day Address at Little Rock, Ark., April, 1976.

Mitchell, Steve, and Rawls, Sam, *How to Speak Southern*, Bantam Books, New York, 1976.

Napier, Cameron Freeman, *The First White House of the Confederacy*, The First White House Association, Montgomery, Ala., 1986.

Red Shirt Shrine, UDC, Edgefield, S.C., 1945.

The Lanyard, Memphis, Tenn., Volumes XIII, XIV, XV, and XVI.

The Palmyra Massacre, The Palmyra Confederate Monument Association, Palmyra, Mo., 1903.

The Rebel Yell, Oklahoma City, Okla., Volumes V, XI, and XII.

What is the Sons of Confederate Veterans? SCV, Hattiesburg, Miss., March 25, 1979.

MAGAZINES, NEWSPAPERS, PERIODICALS

Blue and Gray, Columbus, Ohio, Vol. IV, No. 2, 1986.

Confederate Veteran, Nashville, Tenn., Volumes III, IV, XVI, and XVII.

Morningside Bookshop Catalogue, No. 16, Dayton, Ohio, Jan. 2, 1985.

Southern Partisan, Columbia, S.C., Volumes IV, V, VI, and VII.

Southern Style, Knoxville, Tenn., July/Aug., 1987.

The Bonham Journal, Bonham, Texas, April 2, 1896.

The Daily Oklahoman, Oklahoma City, Okla., March 4, 1951.

The Land We Love, Vol. II, 1867.

The Memphis Daily Appeal, Memphis, Tenn., April 28, 1870.

The Nashville Banner, Nashville, Tenn., May 13, 1905.

The Philadelphia Press, Philadelphia, Pa., June 7, 1917.

The Sparrow Hawk, Centreville, Ala., Vol. III, No. 3, 1978.

The Sunday Oklahoman, Oklahoma City, Okla., Jan. 11, 1987.

GENERAL REFERENCE WORKS

Appleton's Cyclopaedia of American Biography, James Grant Wilson and John Fiske, Appleton & Co., New York, 1888.

Confederate War Poems, edited by Walter Burgwyn Jones, Bill Coates Ltd., Nashville, 1984.

Dictionary of American Biography, edited by Allen Johnson, Charles Scribner's Sons, New York, 1957.

Histories of the Several Regiments & Battalions from North Carolina in the Great War, 1861-1865, edited by Walter Clark, Raleigh, N.C., 1901.

The War of the Rebellion: Official Records of the Union and Confederate Armies, Washington, 1884.

N° 3 First Series.

THE DIXIE QUEEN CAKE WALK

BY

CLAUDE S. MINTER,

5

Published by

C. S. MINTER,

Little Rock, Ark.

MUDDY WATER

(A MISSISSIPPI MOAN)

NORA BAYES

WORDS by
"JO" TRENT

MUSIC by
PETER DE ROSE
HARRY RICHMAN

BROADWAY MUSIC CORPORATION
WILL VON-TILZER PRESIDENT
723-7TH AVE. NEW YORK

WITH UKULELE
ACCOMPANIMENT

MADE IN U.S.A.

If You Want To Miss A Heaven On Earth
Stay Out Of The South
With
UKULELE
Arrangemt
by
HAROLD DIXON
ADA RIVES
JACK MILLS INC.
Music Publishers